The Two Eyes of Spinoza
& Other Essays on Philosophers

©POLAND

The translation of *The Two Eyes of Spinoza and Other Essays on Philosophers* has been supported by the Adam Mickiewicz Institute – © Poland Translation Program.

Books by Leszek Kolakowski

My Correct Views on Everything (St. Augustine's Press)

Religion: If There Is No God . . . On God, the Devil, Sin, and Other Worries of the So-Called Philosophy of Religion (St. Augustine's Press)

Husserl and the Search for Certitude (St. Augustine's Press)

Bergson (St. Augustine's Press)

Main Currents of Marxism, 3 vol. (Oxford University Press)

The Presence of Myth (The University of Chicago Press)

Modernity on Endless Trial (The University of Chicago Press)

God Owes Us Nothing: On Pascal's Religion and the Spirit of Jansenism (The University of Chicago Press)

On Freedom, Fame, Lying and Betrayal (Westview Press)

Other Titles from St. Augustine's Press

Rémi Brague, *Eccentric Culture: A Theory of Western Civilization*

Francisco Suarez, *On Creation, Conservation, & Concurrence: Metaphysical Disputations 20–22*

William of Ockham, *Ockham's Theory of Terms: Part I of the Summa Logicae*

William of Ockham, *Ockham's Theory of Terms: Part II of the Summa Logicae*

Roger Bacon, *Roger Bacon's Philosophy of Nature*. Translation of *De multiplicatione specierum and De speculis comburentibus*

Thomas Aquinas, *Disputed Questions on Virtue*

Roger Scruton, *An Intelligent Person's Guide to Modern Culture*

Roger Scruton, *On Hunting*

Roger Scruton, *Art and Imagination: A Study in the Philosophy of Mind*

Roger Scruton, *Aesthetic Understanding*

Josef Pieper, *Leisure, the Basis of Culture*

Josef Pieper, *Scholasticism: Personalities and Problems*

Josef Pieper, *The Silence of St. Thomas*

Jerome J. Langford, *Galileo, Science and the Church*

Mario Enrique Sacchi, *The Apocalypse of Being: The Esoteric Gnosis of Martin Heidegger*

Zbigniew Janowski, *Augustinian-Cartesian Index*

The Two Eyes of Spinoza
& Other Essays on Philosophers

Leszek Kolakowski

Translated by Agnieszka Kolakowska and others

Edited by Zbigniew Janowski

ST. AUGUSTINE'S PRESS

South Bend, Indiana

2004

Manufactured in the United States of America.

1 2 3 4 5 6   10 09 08 07 06 05 04

Library of Congress Cataloging in Publication Data
Kolakowski, Leszek.
    [Essays. English. Selections]
    The two eyes of Spinoza and other essays on philosophers / Leszek Kolakowski ; edited by Zbigniew Janowski ; translation by Agnieszka Kolakowska and Frederic Fransen.
      p. cm.
    Includes bibliographical references (p.   ) and index.
    ISBN 1-58731-875-X
    1. Philosophy. I. Janowski, Zbigniew. II. Title.
B4691.K5862 E5 2003
190 – dc21   2002151643

∞ *The paper used in this publication meets the minimum requirements of the American National Standard for Information Sciences – Permanence of Paper for Printed Materials, ANSI Z39.48-1984.*

St. Augustine's Press
www.staugustine.net

Contents

Foreword

There are two persons who made this book and are responsible for it. One is my friend Zbigniew Janowski; he came up with the idea of this collection, he chose and found the texts (written in the late 1950s, in the 1960s and early 1970s, scattered over many places, written in various languages; some were lost, or beyond my reach); he contacted the publisher; and he forced me to read some texts, essays, or articles which I had forgotten. The only reason for this ungrateful labor was - incredibly - our friendship.

The other worker who made this book and without whom it would have never existed is my daughter Agnieszka; she translated all the texts written in Polish or French (only two, if I remember, were written in German) and corrected whatever was originally in English. She is a merciless translator. Some of the texts (not all, thank God) were constructed in long, uselessly complicated sentences which she had to shorten, to cut, and to make it clearer. That is what she did, apart from the translation.

I cannot entirely evade my part of responsibility for the book, though. There is no common theme in it, although most of these texts deal with seventeenth-century philosophy and theology. They were written independently of each other. The only, albeit shrewdly concealed, message can be (perhaps) summed up in the title of a sixteenth-century treatise by Francisco Sanchez: Quod nihil scitur, That Nothing Can Be Known. But even this might be exaggerated.

L. K. September 4, 2001

The Two Eyes of Spinoza

Monist doctrines always have trouble with the idea of negative freedom. It is only with great effort, and at enormous cost, that they succeed in salvaging it within their constructions; indeed it is doubtful whether this has ever been achieved without sacrificing coherence. Perfect solipsism aside (never seriously proposed and existing only in the realm of the imaginable), the monist project – to interpret all the qualities of existence as relative to one primordial being – inevitably ends up abolishing the entire realm of the subjective (understood as an irreducible realm). In this relativized monist world, subjectivity is always a particular state, arrangement, manifestation or phenomenon of something else – something that is not subjective – and can thus be defined entirely in terms of the object.

Belief in freedom as a negative quality of the subject is the belief that some if not all actions of the self-knowing subject have an unconditioned beginning: a perfect, ultimate source and spontaneous origin. It presupposes that when we ask about the reasons for our freely-made decisions, we will always reach an impassable barrier, a point where our question can go no further: the ultimate reason of our wanting something is, in the end, simply our wanting it – just that and no more. I can always ask why I want one thing rather than another, and sometimes I will be able to find an answer, but each new answer will be another "because I want . . ." After a number of such answers, going further and further back, the chain of explanations comes to an end, and I am left only with "I want this just because this is what I want."

A subject to which we attribute this ability to evade determination, to refuse the question concerning the reasons for its own choices, is one whose every action must be considered as an unconditioned beginning: a new and unpredictable act of self-creation; a crack, or rather a kind of self-formed whirlpool, in the great mass of existence. Thus there are as many absolutes as there are self-conscious subjects capable of choice: at every point of subjectivity in the universe, the unity of the divine absolute, or of the absolute of nature, breaks down. When we consider this, we can appreciate the difficulties with which the scholastics had to grapple in their search a non-contradictory formula that would reconcile God's definition as the absolute and only beginning with freedom of choice – a freedom that determines *ex nihilo* but is not itself predetermined. The search is ultimately pointless, the solutions proposed fragile as porcelain, and the results paltry; but the huge efforts expended by Christianity, in all its varieties, to avoid the either/or – the disjunctive choice between divine omnipotence and human freedom – also have their roots in the monist temptation, present in the doctrine of creation.

Cartesianism disentangled itself from this predicament through the epistemological decision expressed in the *cogito*. The *cogito* allows us, in fact compels us, to salvage our own existence – existence as it is experienced by us; it is the uniquely compelling starting-point of thinking about existence. As a result, we can more easily endow this epistemological primacy with ontic meaning. Indeed we cannot avoid doing so: if we tried – if we considered that what is "given" in the most primary sense is merely an appearance – then we could not legitimately pass from the appearance to the reality. But the cognitive absoluteness of a self-directed act of thinking endows that act with the right to claim absoluteness in the ontic order for itself as well. Consequently, freedom is not hopelessly entangled in the shackles of divine Grace as soon as we begin to think about it; its foundations can be built long before we are even aware of such a thing as divine Grace. We do not need to rescue it with excuses and evasions. Cartesian freedom, being negative, knows no restrictions; it is, from the start, simply our inalienable ability to add our own *fiat* to that of God. This is something we do with each act of subjective consciousness, and through each such act we become equal with our creator. It is a freedom that lies in the power of our self-defined creativity to choose.

But the Cartesian construction suffers from a fundamental lack of continuity, for which there is no cure. How are we to go about reconstructing the world if the only absolute, unconditioned starting-point is the self-intentional act of consciousness – an act in which experience acquires just enough distance towards itself to glimpse itself for a fleeting moment in the act of reflection which splits it in two? Descartes' famous appeal to God as the guarantor of truth, the savior of our belief in the reality of heaven and earth, was almost immediately revealed by his critics to be riddled with holes so gaping that the majority of Cartesians preferred to renounce it; and the very first critics found that the Cartesian construction, for all its monumental sweep, was organically incapable of reconstructing physical existence from its initial principles. Freedom – the negativity which defines the particularity of human existence – remained a reward promised to those willing to suspend judgment about the reality of the world.

Thus Cartesianism split philosophies into two distinct groups: those that start from the experience of the subject and try to return to the objective world from there – a feat they can accomplish only through invalid proofs; and those that start from existence itself, establishing it without anyone's cognitive assistance – which bars the road to subjectivity, so that they are forced to treat human existence as part of objective reality, endowing it with the same status as objects, unless they endow it with a different status by arbitrary decree.

Spinoza's metaphysics suffers from exactly the opposite problem. Whereas Descartes wanted to build up the external world from the raw data of our mental experience, the *cogito*, Spinoza's starting-point (at least in the *Ethics*) was the unique, absolute, primary being; divine substance, definitively established by ontological proof, was the material of thought. This metaphysical picture leaves no room for self-consciousness, and Spinoza's doctrine struggles in vain to find a way of accommodating it. For what does it mean to say that to be human is to have not only a body but also a soul, a soul not existentially identical with that body, if we, like all other things in the world, are modifications of infinite substance, and like them partake of that ideal or "mental" quality in which each individual existence shares? We are "soul" only to the extent that everything is. One thing only makes us specifically human: the fact that, in addition to the idea, we also have the idea of that idea – self-consciousness, which is not given to other things. But why is it not? The sole metaphysical justification for endowing us with it is the fact that the idea of everything, and therefore also the idea of the idea, is in God. But if so, one is tempted to ask why the idea of other things should not be similarly duplicated: why should perfect being – the participation of all things in the logical order of being – be deprived of this double endowment by virtue of which it becomes self-knowing, so that it not only knows, but also knows that it knows?

Spinoza refused to recognize the absurd consequences of his metaphysics. The restriction whereby he distinguished human existence was utterly arbitrary, with no foundation whatsoever in his metaphysical doctrine. His critics had good reason to accuse him of haziness on this point, and good reason to remark on his fundamental inability to take any kind of theoretical step that might confer legitimacy on the subjective realm. They had good reason, too, for saying that human existence cannot be reconstructed in a way that would be consistent with the basic principles of his metaphysics; it can be distinguished only by purely objective, empirical qualities.

Spinoza's version of the freedom and immanent necessity of the Absolute is not, in fact, very different from the kind of freedom that Platonist scholastics attributed to the Creator. For Spinoza, the nature of divine existence is such that the Absolute being cannot be said to be "free" in the sense in which human action is commonly said to be free, i.e., non-determined, because the Absolute does not exist in time. As a perfect being, the Absolute is by definition extra-temporal: it cannot be bound by temporal succession or subject to temporal change. A being for which there is a distinction between past and future could not have the Absolute's direct cognitive link to the world; it would need mediation, in the form of memory and foresight. But if its relation to events were indirect, mediated through recollection of the past or projection into the future, its knowledge of the world would not be that direct cognitive participation which defines the Absolute's relation to all that exists and takes place; it would entail a distinction between the possible and the actual. And since it is inconceivable that for God there should be a distinction between the possible and the actual, it is also inconceivable that He should exist within the framework of temporal succession.

By the same token, it is inconceivable that God should enjoy freedom from determination in the sense of being free at any given moment to choose how He will act. God cannot choose, for choosing entails choosing between possibilities, and He is by definition perfectly actualized; it is inconceivable that He could be confronted with an event to which His relation was not already determined. For God there can be no "already" and no "given moment" in time, for there is no distinction between past and future, actuality and potentiality. His relation to events can be said neither to be determined nor to be pre-determined; the distinction between what is necessary and what is free and undetermined makes no sense when applied to God. Thus God is "free" only in the sense that He cannot be constrained or influenced by any external circumstance – a freedom that follows logically from His definition as the absolute Creator. This is all Spinoza means when he calls God free and His actions necessary and inevitable: He is free because He is not constrained by anything outside Himself, and His actions are inevitable because, being perfectly actualized, He is bound by His own necessity. Always fully actualized in His immobile and immutable self-identity, God is temporal only for us; the framework of individual events, causally linked and succeeding each other in time, exists only in our perception. But in fact past and future are both actualized, for they are actualized in God-Nature. He is the only reality, the only independent being;

apart from Him there is nothing, and nothing else merits the name of being in the true sense.

In this absolute unity of being there is no crack that could shatter God's primordial self-identity, no imaginable opening through which something as yet undetermined could in the course of time become determined. Nor can we imagine this God engaged in any purposive activity, for God can have no purpose that is not yet fulfilled: purposive action is evidence of imperfection; it implies something not achieved, some need unsatisfied. But the Absolute being is completely fulfilled; it would be blasphemy to say that God acts towards a goal. Everything that will ever happen in the world has already happened; it is already a fact. There can be no hope of any spontaneous, freely self-determined irruption into the inevitable succession of events, no possible break of their continuity. Such a break would be a break in the chain of logical consequence: it would mean that something that follows logically from a given proposition or state of affairs could be made not to follow from it by an arbitrary decision, a whim. For the course of physical events proceeds with the same inevitability as that with which conclusions follow from premises in Euclid's *Elements*. Thus the very nature of the Absolute is such that there can be neither contingency nor purposiveness in the world – unless we decide to consider as contingent everything whose causes are unknown to us. But that contingency would be related to our own ignorance, not to any property of being itself.

Given these principles, the absurdity of attributing what we commonly call free will to the human individual is so glaring that it would scarcely be worth pointing out but for the fact that we do so attribute it, and for the singular role played in our lives by the persistent illusion of free will, maintained by theologians in the face of all common sense. Spinoza believes the illusion to be so childishly easy to shatter that the task seems almost beneath his dignity; the ample space he devotes to the problem is owing only to its social importance, not to its philosophical complexity. For since everything is in God and nothing apart from God can be conceived, and since, further, God exists necessarily, it follows that every manifestation of His indifferent (i.e., non-purposive) creative power is also necessary; and in particular that "reason and will are [proper] to God's nature [in the same way] as movement and rest." Thus human behavior is just like the behavior of all other things: no less dependent, no freer, no more self-determined, no more purposive. Our power of choice is illusory. Whatever happens happens because it must; whatever does not happen does not happen because it cannot. In reality there is no middle ground between impossibility and necessity: what we think of as the realm of the contingent exists only in our imagination, and reflects our defective understanding of the world.

Divested of the peculiarly Spinozean vocabulary in which it is couched, this metaphysics may be summed up as follows. The world is indifferent to the fact that we are part of it. It has no intentions towards us, either hostile or friendly. In its perfection it has actualized everything than can exist. It has no aim, and does not intend to change anything in view of human suffering; indeed, is inconceivable that it would or could. There is no providence in the world; nothing protects us or watches over our lives. There is neither punishment nor reward, neither good nor evil, neither justice nor injustice. Good and evil, justice and injustice, exist in the world only through and for us, called into existence by our needs. Nature is not interested in our constructs.

But here is the paradox: the thing that makes us uniquely human, that inalienable feature of our existence which is its ability to experience itself, is metaphysically quite groundless; and yet it is the source not only of our specificity as human beings but also of our erroneous ideas about that specificity. In other words, the very thing that makes us human also gives rise to our misconceptions about what it is to be human; and that thing has no logical connection whatsoever with the rest of Spinoza's metaphysical doctrine. The world according to Spinoza knows everything, but does not know that it knows. We know pitifully little, but know that we know, and what we don't know, we know that we don't know. Our physical behavior is subject to the same necessity as the movement of waves on the surface of the sea or the movement of a rock falling from a cliff-face. If a rock had our capacity of self-knowledge and could understand its movements, it would imagine, just as we do, that it controls them; it would think it was falling downwards rather than flying upwards as a result of its own free choice. But its movements are determined in exactly the same way as our actions; we have no more freedom than the rock. Our observation of ourselves is just that and no more – powerless observation; and it is this very capacity of self-observation that deludes us into thinking, with pathetic arrogance, that it is we who are the creative force behind our physical movements, which in fact are all purely mechanical. There is no efficient causal connection between our thought and our movement: we observe our own bodies as through a pane of glass, imagining that we control them, like boys who play at pretending to control thunder by ordering a thunderclap just at the moment when it comes.

Are we, then, not responsible even for our own bodies, buffeted about independently of our will, at the mercy of forces exerted by the motion of material particles? Spinoza would reply that here, again, the question is wrongly put; it is like asking why, in that case, we should lock away criminals, if we think they are not responsible for their actions. When we lock away criminals, we do so in order to protect society from harm, not because the criminal determines himself "freely" in his criminality; we act from the instinct of self-preservation, exactly as we would in killing a poisonous snake or removing a rock that blocks our path. We do not remove the rock or kill the snake because we consider them to be free, and similarly with the criminal: he is no freer than they. Nor can responsibility be identified with the absence of determination: there is no such thing as a non-determined human decision, nor any action that is not the result of a necessary causality. Responsibility in this sense does not exist in the world; it is the product of our deluded imagination.

A bad doctrine, said Spinoza's critics; a dismal, hopeless philosophy.

I don't know whether it is good or bad, Spinoza replied; all I know is that it is true.

But how wretched, they said, how tragic, to live in such a world!

Knowledge of the truth can never be tragic and wretched, he replied; and a life based on illusion cannot be happy. And anyway, why tragic and wretched? To understand the true nature of the universe, to grasp its infinite perfection, its total self-sufficiency, is to love it for what it really is. This love is not the kind of love we would feel for another person; it comes from reason, and is arrived at by mental effort. It cannot be returned, nor do we expect its return, for it knows, being rooted in our understanding, that the Absolute is not subject to emotions. But it is a happy love, for it can never disappoint us, and through it we can free ourselves from the vain hope that the world might be different from what it is. Our only freedom is the freedom of the Stoics – the understanding of necessity; and it is freedom insofar as all independence of spirit in a situation which we are powerless to control can be called freedom. If we recognize this, we can attain the position of disinterested observers, untouched by human passions, indifferent to quarrels, despair, suffering or injury, able to contemplate them with the same dispassionate equanimity that characterizes the chains of our logical reasoning about abstract geometry. The effort required to achieve this state will have been well worth it: no more absurd regrets, grudges against the world, railings against fate that it has not treated us as we think we deserve; no more bitterness at failure and thwarted ambition; no more outrage at human wickedness or horror at the sight of evil; no more vain and fruitless pity. All this we shall rise above, to enjoy the happy certainty that we are part of an infinite whole, with whose timeless, eternal existence we can to some extent identify, since we have grasped it. We shall no longer be afraid of death, oblivion or damnation, for in a world whose necessity we truly love we shall see death as an inevitable part of a perfectly coherent whole.

A masochist's philosophy, commented the historian Lewis Samuel Feuer. Who else could find joy in the boundless indifference of the absolute world, a source of happiness in loving it with an unreciprocated love, a cause for rejoicing in an order of things that destroys us as inevitably as the wind shakes the leaves off trees, eternally imposing its irresistible force on our frail powers?

A resigned mystic's, let us say, rather than a masochist's: the philosophy of a mystic who has clothed his personal mysticism in Cartesian concepts and categories. An escapist philosophy; a theory of freedom attained through the spiritual denial of the finite order of the world.

But we know this is only one aspect of Spinoza's world. The philosopher who would have us bow down in admiration before an immutably determined chain of events, would have us worship a perfectly indifferent divinity and seek freedom in understanding and accepting a world in which everything that can ever happen has already happened – this same philosopher was also a militant theorist of the liberal party in the Netherlands, a defender of toleration and political freedom, a writer of partisan articles in support of the republican movement, the author of the *Tractatus Theologico-politicus*, and a vicious critic of theologians and the Church.

Chronology may explain some of these contradictions, but it cannot explain them all. Spinoza's metaphysics alone already contains a general outline of that duality which characterizes both his life and his moral philosophy. It may be that a vision of the world in which individual things have no autonomous existence, but are entirely swallowed up in the divine Absolute, cannot be reconciled with that other in which everything is guided by an instinct of self-preservation and is destroyed only by violence or by death. But both visions find expression in Spinoza's advice to us, which is on the one hand to flee our own finiteness and seek freedom through an intuition about being that will unite us with the Absolute, and on the other to look after our own interests and preserve our bodies and souls, to which end we may, if necessary, resort to equivocation, evasion and half-truths.

No doubt this double perspective is in part explicable by Spinoza's view that the supreme values of life, attainable only through persistent intellectual effort, will in any case be accessible to only a few. Those few who do not allow the passions and concerns of everyday life to blind them to the true order of values (not a transcendental order, established by nature in normative form, but one where a value is simply a quality that is in harmony with human nature, and thus strengthens our bodies or souls) cannot disagree about them, for what they all equally enjoy – knowledge of eternal reality and an understanding adapted to it – and can enjoy without diminishing its enjoyment by anyone else, they will all equally value. But one cannot restrict one's thinking about the world of human affairs to things which are of interest only to that tiny elite: life in a community requires rules, and these rules must take into account our most common natural inclinations. Human nature cannot be denied; we may praise or condemn it, but we must recognize that it exists. It would be absurd to delude ourselves that the world of human interaction can be sensibly ordered on the basis of the assumption that we can all be free in the sense in which to be free is to participate in the cosmic indifference of perfect being.

Let us consider freedom in its humbler sense – not the freedom that comes from an understanding of reality but freedom in the sense in which Hobbes was able to use the word consistently with his absolute belief in universal causality. Freedom in this sense is not a human attribute, innate or acquired, but describes a situation where nothing prevents us from doing what we want to do (which does not, of course, imply that our wanting it is spontaneous and undetermined by the conditions in which we find ourselves). In other words, it is the absence of constraint. The main question Spinoza asks about freedom in this sense is the following: since there is no supreme law that could *a priori* restrict or regulate our actions, the extent of our freedom to act being commensurate with the extent of our powers, how best should a human community be ordered so as to minimize constraints on the freedom of the individual while preventing the general war which would inevitably break out if there were no laws to restrict individual actions?

His answer – at least in its general theoretical formulation – is simple: abolish the tyranny of the Church and end its competition with secular government; reject the demands of the clergy, who in the name of the infallibility of their dogmas would bind the whole world in the shackles of their catechisms; establish religious tolerance and freedom of speech for all; maintain free trade and freedom of conscience; combat fanaticism, superstition and claims to a monopoly on truth. But here, too, restrictions are needed: freedom of religion, for instance, cannot be understood as extending to anything we decide, on a whim, to define as religious; such a law would be worthless and absurd, for it would be a license to do anything we please by calling it religion. Freedom of religion must therefore be defined. Hence some form of established state religion is needed – a conclusion many people in Spinoza's time concurred with, tired and disenchanted after a century and a half of religious wars. A religion subject to the authority of the state could not transform itself into a clerical despotism. Moreover, its content would be extremely limited, comprising only those beliefs which everyone – even Spinoza – could accept, although each could interpret them in his own way. Even Spinoza would be willing to agree, for example, that God exists and rewards or punishes human deeds, although he believes neither in God in the ordinary sense nor, *a fortiori*, in His legislative or executive powers. But what we believe isn't the important thing; to each his own interpretation of the truths of faith. What matters is that we do our duty towards our fellow men: support them in our joint undertakings, loyally do our share, inflict no suffering and do no harm. In its content, then, a state religion would not go beyond our basic moral precepts and rules of behavior, and would not threaten the body politic of tolerant state. In such a religion the Bible plays a role not because it contains any truths about the world, for it contains none, but because it contains those most basic teachings about how we should live and behave towards one another – teachings which simple folk will more easily absorb through anecdotes than through laborious philosophical inquiry. We may assume that the masses will, in great majority, cling to their superstitious beliefs: to their belief in God the Father, Protector and Ruler of the world; in life after death; in heaven and hell. This is perfectly all right as long as their faith contains no elements of fanaticism or hatred for unbelievers, and if it can accomplish what philosophical reflection cannot, at least not on a mass scale, namely rein in harmful passions and subdue the natural human tendency to greed, selfishness and lust for power.

This is what Spinoza's advice comes down to if we see it as a series of strictly philosophical precepts within the framework of his moral theory. It seems, when viewed in this way, quite useless: too vague, too general, almost banal. But when we look at it in a practical rather than a purely philosophical light, and consider it within the context of the political conflicts in which Spinoza was embroiled as a writer, it reveals itself as rather more substantial, and much more interesting.

From quite early on in his life, even before his excommunication from the Jewish community, Spinoza had moved in an atmosphere of republican freethinking. This was owing mostly to the influence of his friend Francis van der Ende – ex-Jesuit, political radical, mocker of men and enemy of the Church and the monarchy. Van der Ende believed in the absolute sovereignty of the people, and he was true to his beliefs: when he became embroiled in an anti-monarchist conspiracy in France, he demonstrated his constancy by paying for them with his head. It is quite possible that Spinoza's religious views were only a pretext for his excommunication, and that the real reason lay in his republican sentiments and allegiances: if they had somehow come to light, they would have been considered dangerous for the Jewish community, allied by tradition to the House of Orange. In any event, the young Spinoza, having absorbed this atmosphere of cosmopolitan freethinking, soon came into contact with republican politicians and activists. The Netherlands was a republic at the time, but a frail and shaky one, swaying under the weight of constant conflict with the aspirations of the Calvinist clergy on the one hand and the monarchist claims of the House of Orange on the other.

Spinoza's *Tractatus Theologico-politicus* was directed both at Jewish claims to be the chosen people, with a special place in history, and at Christian claims of infallibility; it was an attack on churches as breeding-grounds of superstition and obscurantism; and it was a defense of toleration, democracy and republicanism in politics. In its essentials it resembled the doctrine expounded by the de la Court brothers – a tandem of republican theorists – in their political and economic writings. Thus its main thesis was not revolutionary; on the contrary, its aim was to strengthen the party in power – a party that was weak and disorganized, and had its support base in the interests of the liberal, peace-loving and tolerantly inclined merchant class in the most developed cities of the United Provinces.

Most of the rest of the population was ill disposed towards government by an enlightened elite, and from time to time made it abundantly clear that its sympathies (fostered and stoked by the Calvinist clergy by every means at their disposal) lay with the princes of the House of Orange. The Protestant ethos which Spinoza so hated was well suited to organizing and channeling the resentments of the less privileged; moments of particular instability were deftly exploited to rally mass support for a conservative coup – which did indeed finally take place, in 1672, at a time of military defeat. At the moment of crisis, the freethinking patrician elite, the tolerant republicans, the sympathizers of Arminianism in theology all found themselves without popular support. The leaders of the republican oligarchy, the de Witt brothers, were lynched: torn limb from limb on the streets of the Hague by a vicious mob whipped up to a frenzy of fanaticism.

The question of democracy had to be reconsidered. If democracy meant lawless mob violence directed by demagogues, what arguments could Spinoza find in its favor – he, a philosopher whose sympathies lay with liberal and freethinking but comfortably prosperous regents? He did defend democracy, in his 1670 *Treatise*; but he never defended revolution in the name of democracy. He valued not only freedom but also stability of government, and therefore believed that it is better to submit to a tyranny than to overthrow it by violence. Besides, democracy as he conceived it, the democracy he defended, had always been more a political system of reason than a system of government by the majority; and then, he had always mistrusted the rabble. His mistrust, indeed his contempt, is far too evident in his writings for him to have been a credible spokesman of revolutionary tribunals. He was more concerned to inculcate the feeling of freedom than to propagate freedom itself: to establish a rational government which, acting on the recommendations of the Florentine master of the political art, could through careful steering make its subjects believe that they ruled themselves. He never achieved the synthesis he wanted: he found no way of satisfactorily reconciling the values of freedom with those of reason and common sense, just as he failed to reconcile the need for tolerance with the need for stability of government.

When all the things he had condemned and opposed – the regular army as an independent political force, the theocratic aspirations of the clergy, the fanaticism of the mob – came into their own and became fact, Spinoza decided it was time to revise his theory of freedom. This he attempted to do in his unfinished *Tractatus Politicus*. Here the emphasis – the way in which he formulates the issues – has shifted somewhat by comparison with his famous earlier treatise, written in support of the republican government then in power. True to his conviction that active political disobedience does more harm than good, he now concentrates less on the general question of the ideal form of government than on the problem of ensuring the stability of various particular forms of government, monarchies included, while preserving as much political freedom as is conceivable in the given circumstances. But even the best laid plans will fail if we do not keep in mind that people's blind, thoughtless passions will always prevail over considered analysis and rational calculation; we must never assume that human behavior will be guided by reason. We should rather seek to harness people's untamed passions and exploit them for the public good.

Let us sum up.

Freedom, in Spinoza's conception of it, is not an attribute of human nature. In particular, it is not what we commonly call free will – the possibility of undetermined, spontaneous, self-willed action. The will is an abstract thing, which exists only in theory. In reality there are only individual instances of wanting, and these are inevitably conditioned by the circumstances in which they occur.

Nor is freedom a natural human right, a capacity we should exploit in the name of higher values. There are no rights except that of power and force – the power which we are able to exercise to impose our desires on a particular situation.

If freedom is possible at all, it is our freely given assent to the eternal and immutable order of nature; our understanding and acceptance of nature's indifference and lack of purpose. The freedom that comes from this understanding is freedom from dependence on our passions: freedom from superstition, from anger, from despair and pointless regrets, from fear of death and of the terrors of hell. In this sense it is a negative freedom. But it is also a positive freedom: it is the joy of knowing that one is part of the eternal essence of the supreme being, united with it through an effort of ultimate intuition; the happiness of intellectual love for the cosmic order. This freedom, however, requires a certain sacrifice on our part; it can be attained only at the cost of giving up certain things. Not just external goods (which we will be giving up in the sense that they will have ceased to have value for us), but also our individual identity: our self-affirmation as separate beings. And while in theory this freedom is accessible to everyone, in practice it can be enjoyed only by a select few. It is the supreme reward of intellectual effort, and can be enjoyed in full by those who attain it, regardless of their circumstances, for it is infinitely resistant to the pressure of events and entirely insensible to the blows of fate.

This, however, is not what Spinoza means by freedom in those passages of his writings where the word crops up most often – passages where he is concerned to define what it means for a thing to be free in any given circumstance. There, when he says that a thing is free, he means simply that its behavior is not determined by external conditions. This freedom, too, characterizes situations rather than human beings; but our understanding alone is not enough to ensure that any given situation will be characterized by it, and it is unclear whether it is possible at all. God is free in this way, but can this kind of freedom also characterize human existence? Spinoza says that it can, apparently unaware of the contradiction between this view and his own insistence on human powerlessness and dependence on external causality. It is hard to see how the view that our capacity of self-consciousness is no more than passive observation, and cannot be the efficient cause of our physical actions, could be reconciled with the view that our behavior is not, or need not be, externally determined. And indeed, between the fully internalized freedom of the Cartesian-style mystic and the positive freedom which affirms human individuality through the instinct of self-preservation there can be no true reconciliation.

These are the two faces of Spinoza – the two eyes of his thought, one directing its escapist gaze towards the all-encompassing power of the Absolute, the other concentrating it on the world of finite things, observed with the dispassionate rationalism of the scientist. One eye belongs to the apostle of deductive reasoning, the follower of Euclid, the rationalist who attempted, and failed, to construct his metaphysics on Euclidean principles; the other belongs to the mystic. This dual vision can perhaps be explained by the dual aspect of Spinoza's life: his contacts with the petit-bourgeois mysticism of sectarian freethinkers and his involvement with the republican bourgeoisie are certainly responsible for that other, mystical strand of his thought, at least in its principal ideas.

Spinoza's political doctrine, where he considers the freedom of the individual in relation to social institutions, is similarly marked by the uncomfortable coexistence of two conflicting tendencies, each pulling him in a different direction. The strain produced by their conflict is expressed in an endless indecisiveness: he is torn between his natural sympathy towards the disinherited of the earth and his hatred of the rabble – primitive, irrational and unpredictable; between the value of toleration and the need for stability of government; between democracy and the need for an oligarchy of men of reason, unsusceptible to the temptations of fanaticism and dogmatism.

His deluded and quite fantastic hope that reason alone can enable us, always and everywhere, to act in accordance with our better instincts is at least restricted to a select few, which slightly mitigates its absurdity: Spinoza does not attempt to base his assessment of political systems on it. But one suspects that there is no overlap whatsoever between the freedoms he reserves for his select few aristocrats of the spirit and those he defends for simple folk. For the former, the act of freely identifying with the cosmic order and freely adoring its infinite perfection is the supreme value, next to which all other values pale into insignificance; the select few need no more. The wise man can lack nothing, and it is hard to see what form of coercion or physical constraint could diminish his uniquely authentic freedom. For the latter, on the other hand, concrete political freedoms are important values, since that highest and most perfect form of liberation which makes all other freedoms unnecessary is in all likelihood beyond their grasp. And such freedoms must be secured for them, since they cannot secure them for themselves.

It is clear, when we look at Spinoza's doctrine stripped down to its core of fundamental ideas, that there is no way of reconciling its inconsistencies. Its duality and internal incoherence were to bear abundant fruit in the following century. These, roughly speaking, were as follows. Its "German reception," which one might qualify, very generally, as pantheistic, singled out an idea elaborated in one part of the doctrine and present as a motif throughout in the whole: the hope of an ultimate reconciliation with the Absolute through the mystical abandonment of individual identity. The "French reception" stressed the republican freethinking aspects, generalized the slogans calling for freedom and concentrated with satisfaction on highlighting the anti-clerical and anti-ecclesiastical sentiments. These two perspectives, that of the political radical and that of the metaphysician engaged in an attempt to encompass infinite being, are so different that it seems churlish to complain of inconsistency and lack of synthesis, as if others had succeeded where Spinoza miserably failed: it is not as if anyone else had ever managed to unite these two ways of looking at the world – one directed at being and one at the subject – into a coherent whole.

And Spinoza was aware of the incoherence. He was fond of saying, or rather of repeating after Epictetus, that human happiness and misery depend only on the nature of the things we love; but at the same time he admitted that he himself had been unable to free himself completely of his attachment to those worthless goods which reason dictates that we should reject as insignificant. So he knew that his metaphysical eye and his scientific eye were at odds. He looked at the world through both and saw differently through each. Thus he saw freedom alternately as mystical liberation – the proud relinquishment of all that the world of objects has to offer – and as free choice – that situation in which reason and intellectual effort allows us to choose freely within the world of objects. He knew that, whether he wanted it or not, he was part of the human world, and as such embroiled willy-nilly in worldly concerns, conflicts and responsibilities; but as Spinoza the mystic, the Spinoza who had rejected God and belief in immortality, he wanted to deny his finiteness and touch being itself with his reason. He even thought he had achieved his aim, until the disturbing questions of his more penetrating friends undermined his certainty. Whether he died feeling satisfied or defeated we shall never know.

Translated by Agnieszka Kolakowska

Spinoza
A Metaphysics of Suicide
or of Survival?

My main thesis is contained in the title of this lecture. I believe that Spinoza's moral philosophy is built upon two reciprocally limiting principles: the moral affirmation of the individual – or the principle of self-preservation – and a tendency that aims at the individual's destruction or his metaphysical and moral derealization. In Spinoza's conception of the world, this contradiction, I believe, is not accidental. It is rooted in the two conflicting tendencies of his ontology. It can also be interpreted as a conflict between ontology and physics. As far as the historical sources of Spinoza's philosophy are concerned, this contradiction leads back to the impossibility of reconciling the neo-Platonic theory of the Absolute and the Cartesian philosophy of nature. Although I cannot justify this interpretation by way of a detailed textual analysis within the confines of a lecture, my position, I hope, will be understandable for all those who are familiar with this philosophy.

Spinoza's metaphysics can be seen as the continuation of a stream of thought that received its first impetus in European philosophy from Parmenides. And if we accept Mircea Eliade's philosophy of religion, according to which each religious act ultimately can be reduced to making time stand still or to grasping timeless being, then Spinoza's metaphysics can also be seen as a continuation of that which stands in the center of religious experience. It attempts in abstract concepts to express something that at one time used to be expressed in mythological narratives and visible symbols. It could not do this, however, without falling into contradiction.

The fundamental intuition of metaphysics that goes back to Parmenides is the belief that we not only can meaningfully speak about timelessness (as differentiated from everlastingness) but that "to be" in the actual sense means "to be timeless"; or, inversely, "to be in time" is the same as "not to be." That Absolute Being remains timeless (and not everlasting) is true by definition. Its perfect actuality necessarily belongs to its absoluteness. Consequently, there is in it no difference between *potentia* and *actus*. By contrast, a time-bound being – were it even eternal (in the sense of everlastingness) – must mediate its relation to itself with the help of memory or anticipation, and as a consequence it cannot be a *"totum simul,"* a pure actuality.

Here lies the difficulty: if the timeless being really *is*, is it at all possible that it isn't the *only* being? Is it not the case that, in the assumption of its existence, all particular beings (i.e., all finite time-bound beings in time) are unreal or an illusion in a nebulous sense? This naturally gives rise to the question: whose illusion? That of the Absolute Itself? It cannot succumb to any illusion. Are particular beings therefore their own illusion? They must be, so it seems, to fall victim to the illusion. And so we return to the apparently absurd, ridiculous, and dizzying question of the poor doctor in Anton Chekhov's *Three Sisters*: "Perhaps we don't exist at all; perhaps it only appears to us that we exist?"– a question to which we are in no position to give a clear answer within a normal logical framework, but which psychologically, or empathetically, is understandable.

The same ambiguity also arises on the ground of Christian philosophy, if one wants fully to draw out its consequences. The idea that *Deus est quodammodo omnia* – that is, God is, in a certain sense, everything – comes from Aquinas. However, when we push the matter further, and when we ask *"quo modo?"* (in what way?), we naturally come to the conclusion formulated by Meister Eckhart: God and being are the same. Consequently, all creatures are nothing – i.e., they are not quite something – or rather: pure nothingness, *purum nihil* (This formula was judged by Pope John XXII in 1329 to be heretical, impudent, and ugly-sounding[1]). Moreover, because the total active energy in the world is of divine origin, it follows that evil also originates from God, or that the difference between good and evil has no grounding in being.

This philosophical act of destruction of contingent being – that is, of the entire creation – leads to the destruction of human subjectivity. With

---

1   "Omnes creaturae sunt unum purum nihil: non dico, quod sint quid modicum vel aliquid, sed quod sint unum purum nihil" (526). ". . . Nos . . . quindecim primos articulos et duos alios ultimos tanquam *haereticos*, dictos vero alios undecim tanquam *male sonantes, temerarios, et suspectos de haeresi*, ac nihilominus libros quoslibet seu opuscula eiusdem Ekardi, praefatos articulos seu eorum aliquem continentes, damnamus et reprobamus expresse" (529) "Errores Ekardi (de Filio Dei etc)," in *Enchiridion Symbolorum*, ed. by Henricus Denzinger. Editor's note.

this, the entire multiplicity of the world of created things cannot even be described as an illusion, and thus it becomes completely incomprehensible. There is no solution here unless we accept this contradiction, that is, unless we recognize that our logic in treating of infinite being is not applicable in this case, because our language in this field cannot attain any precision and thus unavoidably falls into contradictions. Rarely, however, does it happen that philosophers dare expressly to accept this last conclusion (although Causanus is one who did).

The key question of neo-Platonism is: what kind of ontological status can one ascribe to the world of finite things (subjectivity included), assuming that *to be* means to be *infinite,* and that we are allowed to use the concept of *actual,* fulfilled infinitude? That is also Spinoza's question *par excellence* – a question that he never solved, and that he was aware not to have solved. He did not need, of course, to answer the hopeless question of what an infinite subjectivity would be, because for him there was no such thing. Instead of this he posed another question, which seems equally hopeless: what is the attribute of thought, which is not a subjectivity, and that is attributed to Absolute Being?

In Spinoza this tendency to make the created world unreal, which Hegel called Spinoza's "acosmism,"[2] is especially strong. In Spinoza's *Ethics,* we feel an unavoidable consequence, which takes us, however, in the opposite direction: to say that the world is God, as Thomas Hobbes observed, amounts to the same thing as saying that there is no God. Yet one might also turn this sentence around and say: if there is no God, there is no world. What, however, can this mean?

In the architectonics of Spinoza's metaphysics, the lack of a logical transition from substance to the world of *modi* (infinite *modi* included), appears to be the consequence of the method of his proof of God's existence, or to put it more precisely, of the *ontological* proof of God's exis-

2   "Spinozism might really just as well or even better have been termed Acosmism, since according to its teaching it is not to the world, finite existence, the universe, that reality and permanency are to be ascribed, but rather to God alone as the substantial. Spinoza maintains that there is no such thing as what is known as the world; it is merely a form of God, and in and for itself it is nothing. The world has no true reality, and all this that we know as the world has been cast into the abyss of the one identity. There is therefore no such thing as finite reality, it has no truth whatever; according to Spinoza what is, is God, and God alone . . . nature and the individual disappear in this same identity: and [those who accuse him of atheism] cannot forgive Spinoza for thus annihilating them." Georg Wilhelm Friedrich Hegel, *Lectures on the History of Philosophy,* translated by E.S. Haldane and Frances H. Simson (Lincoln & London: University of Nebraska Press, 1995), vol. 3, pp. 281–82. Editor's note.

tence. This comes out of Spinoza's proposition that existence can be analytically established and thus raised to truth (only in the case, however, of Absolute Being). The ontological proof is nothing less than a statement that is at once existential and analytical. (Such a connection for Kant as well as the whole of empirical philosophy is logically impossible). Now, for Spinoza this proof is grounds not only for a logically compelled necessity of the being of substance, but also for the fact that there can only be one substance. The grounds for this is that "being by oneself," *per se esse*, is equivalent to "being able to be conceived by oneself," *per se concipi posse*. (This equivalence follows from the characteristically Spinozistic identification of the ontological and the logical order.) On the other hand, "only conceivable through itself," *per se solum concipi posse*, means as much as "to be determined through no other concepts." It appears that this presupposition implies that God is defined as that which cannot be defined (which is an antinomy, analogous to Poincaré's antinomy: the antinomy of the smallest number that is impossible to define with less than a hundred words).

In order to be valid, Spinoza's proof for God's existence must presuppose the traditional nominalist idea, according to which the attribute is identical with the substance (and, moreover, every property with the thing to which it belongs). In short, it has no special ontological status. At the same time, however, it implies that the difference between attributes is not a *distinctio rationis*, i.e., a distinction made by reason. If it were, each attribute, in order to be real, would require the existence of human reason, that is, a modus. Yet this supposition is impossible. (For this reason it appears to me that Spinoza's reading of Maimonides in this respect is untenable.) This denial of the ontic difference between substance and attributes allows Spinoza to claim that there can only be a single being endowed with an infinite number of attributes; otherwise there would have to be several beings that share the same attributes. But these beings, by virtue of the same identification, must also be identical. On the other hand, from the concept of the most perfect being, we know that there must be an infinite number of attributes; that we can only know two of them should follow (as Spinoza explained in a letter to Schuler) from the fact that our ability to think extends only to that which is contained in the idea of the body, and this idea grasps only two attributes. This explanation, however, appears to run counter to the opinion expressed elsewhere that the cause of all things is God, i.e., Nature composed out of infinitely many attributes.

Once we know that each finite thing participates in both attributes – that is, that everything that is is at once both body and idea, without ceasing to be one and the same thing – and that at the same time these two aspects of each thing remain completely independent of each other, we know neither in what this participation consists, nor in what way it is possible that finite things can have an independent ontic status. We know that each act of knowing which brings certainty – the only one that deserves to be held – proceeds *from God* to the things and not the other way around. Therefore, God can in no way be known through His effects, or, inversely, that things cannot be known without God. Spinoza accepts the principle that Descartes had formulated earlier in responding to Gassendi's objections, namely, that infinite being is not a negative concept, in the sense of a lack of limits (as, for example, Hobbes claimed, when he declared this concept to be essentially incomprehensible on this basis). Rather, for Spinoza infinity is a positivum whereas each limitation is the negation of the infinite, not the other way around. This is how things stand in their relation to God in Spinoza. (This principle might not be of great significance in Descartes' thought, but it was known in the pantheist tradition, e.g., in Eriugena.)

At first glance it is not at all clear what it means to say that things are modifications of the only substance, that is, that they are its limitations (*determinationes* for Spinoza or *limitationes* for Descartes). The concept of limitation, like other categories in Spinoza's metaphysics, has both a spatial and logical sense. But even the spatial sense is difficult to apply here. It is not clear what it means that things are not simply limited, but rather should be defined as the limitations of infinite substance. Substance, for Spinoza, is not a collection of things, since it is indivisible; things are not parts of the substance but of the infinite modus, and the latter, as we know, belongs to the *natura naturata*; the extended or bodily substance is not composed of parts, as a line is not composed of extensionless points. Nor is substance *materia prima,* because no potentiality exists in it; it is rather pure actuality. Substance is an indivisible and timeless whole – an individual. To differentiate parts in it – that is, to grasp particular things in the cognitive process – is the task of the empirical approach, which is precisely the result of abstraction. Abstract knowledge that consists in the ability to examine things as limited and separate may be indispensable for practical purposes, but it is a distorted way of getting to know.

Spinoza's doctrine of substance was especially attacked by the rationalists as absurd. Starting with Pierre Bayle, the rationalist critique of Spinoza's doctrine concentrated on this point.[3] It follows from Spinoza's doctrine, Bayle writes, that all things are essentially the same, that the same substance is a substratum of other contradictory and incompatible properties, and indeed in both its attributes. In other words, the same thing could be at the same time round and square; God as executioner

3   See "Pierre Bayle and the Critique of Spinoza's Metaphysics of Substance" included in this volume. Editor's note.

would kill Himself as victim, and the same God, modified in the German army, would massacre itself in the form of the Turkish army[4]; the variety and difference among things would be lifted, the principle of contradiction would be declared invalid, and thus the whole construction would reveal itself as an empty fantasy.

Fantasy or not, this idea belongs to a genuine body of thought within the neo-Platonic tradition and also to the tradition of Dutch mysticism.[5] It is older than philosophy; it can be found in the classical religious literature of India, even if it is expressed in Spinoza in a partly Scholastic, and partly Cartesian language. It implies that there is only a single concrete entity which has no parts; what appears to us to be parts appears as such only as the result of empirical, that is abstract knowledge (a crippled, *mutilata*, knowledge) which artificially partitions reality into separate fragments.

Each thing is essentially the whole modified in the act of cognition; just as in a line no points *in actu* exist – they are cross sections (Durchschnitte), not parts – so the concrete things thought of within empirical knowledge are actually useful fictions. According to Spinoza, mass, i.e., quantity, is only a way of thinking, a subjective operation. Quantity, that is a limitation, is ascribed to things as a result of our cognitive interventions. They are no more anchored in reality than are any sense qualities.

Is there at all in Spinoza something like a *principium individuationis* within extended substance? It appears as if Spinoza has such a principle in mind when he, following the Cartesian method, makes movement and rest into the only nameable attributes that mark specific bodies. Otherwise, however, this way out appears irreconcilable with the observation that parts in nature can only be subjectively differentiated, because nature in and of itself knows no parts.

There is no solution for this inconsistency, no way out that would bring Spinoza's thought into inner harmony without destroying what is the most genuine in it. In his letters to Spinoza, Walter von Tschirnhaus (perhaps the most astute of the critics of the time) asked three times how one can derive out of a single substance the multiplicity of things. The philosopher was finally forced to confess that he did not know how to

---

4 *Dictionnaire historique et critique*, 1740 ed., vol. IV, article "Spinoza," p. 261. Editor's note.

5 See "The Mystical Heresy and the Rationalist Heresy in Dutch Calvinism at the End of the Seventeenth Century" included in this volume. Cf. the author's discussion in his *Chrétiens sans église. La conscience religieuse et le lien confessionel au xvii siècle*. Translated from the Polish by Anna Posner. Éditions Gallimard: Paris, 1987. Editor's note.

explain this point – which is of a key significance for his doctrine – sufficiently.

A few commentators have pointed in this context to the concept of the *modi infiniti,* the intermediate members between the substance and individual natures. This intermediate member does not suffice to remove this contradiction, however. As little as we know of the *modi infiniti,* we know that they are created and should operate within the two attributes – as the infinite collection of all individual things. The transition from the timeless and indivisible God to the *modus infinitus* – the divisible and in time (eternal, however, in the sense of lasting forever) – is and remains just as puzzling as the transition to particular things. This category illuminates the question of the relations between God and the world just as little as – to use a clumsy example – the way in which Descartes tried to solve the puzzle of the interaction between the body and the soul by means of introducing the *glandula pinealis.* Wherever the soul has its place in Cartesian metaphysics, its intercourse with the body remains incomprehensible. From the point of view of substance – and that is the only point from which truth is revealed – the distinction between things for Spinoza is obfuscated; things must be observed as illusion, or in any case as something that is only subjectively valid. If it is an empirical knowledge, however imperative for life, it is an infirm kind of knowledge, *mutilata cognitio.* On the other hand, there is also a *conatus ad suum esse conservandum,* a generally acting drive, that resides in each individual thing which also appears as a law, just as unshakeable as the law of the indivisibility of substance. These two cannot be reconciled and are mutually exclusive, though they form the backbone of Spinoza's philosophy. This contradiction cannot be set aside within the world of Spinoza's thought. It repeatedly reappears in all the pieces of his philosophical edifice.

This contradiction was probably also responsible for the fact that the spread of Spinoza's philosophy was so ambiguous. One sees this when one places the bare outlines of its two main streams in the reception of Spinoza next to one another: the stream of German pantheism and the stream of French Free Thought.

The *principium individuationis* becomes even more puzzling when one considers it within the attributes of thought - although here each thing does indeed participate. Despite the interpretations of the Enlightenment, which the 19th century critics also shared (Kuno Fischer, Tönnies, Empiriocritics), the all-encompassing attribute *cogitatio* is not a universal "psyche"; nor does it depend on human thinking about things. It is an omnipresent intelligibility of the world, its existence as an object of knowledge. It is not a relative, but rather an absolute property of the world, and it continues to exist, independent of whether or not someone thinks about it. Such an interpretation would presuppose something possible, a potentiality, in God, which obviously stands opposed to the concept of God as pure actuality. Perhaps one could explain this by no means simple side of Spinoza's system by bringing it into relation with Heidegger's concept of being. Being is constructed by Heidegger as that which "opens us up." That it "opens itself up," however, is part of its own constitution and does not depend upon us. That for Spinoza each body is also an idea means neither that each body is endowed with consciousness, nor that its existence depends upon our knowledge; it has to do with the participation of the objective logic of being, with something that we can describe as a knowledge without a knowing subject.

This is perhaps a way for Spinoza to avoid the aporia of Cartesianism: how is it possible to explain the influence of bodily things upon the soul through sensations, and the opposite influence of the human will upon the body in free actions, when we otherwise know that there is no mutual effect between the two substances? The solution offered by Geulinx, Malebranche, and other Occasionalists presupposes that, without such influence, God alone can be the direct author of all changes in the soul, and that in any case He brings into harmony the states of the soul with that of the bodily world. In this way the Cartesian theory of substance was saved, but at the price of a picture of the world in which God forms the human soul's only environment, so that there is no natural intercourse between the soul and the physical universe. Spinoza's teaching on general intelligibility avoids the same difficulty in exactly the opposite way: it makes all things into participants of the same attribute that makes up the human soul.

At the same time, however, this solution, in place of the difficulty just set aside, brings about a new and no less embarrassing problem. Not only does the previously mentioned question of the *principium individuationis* within the *cogitatio* become unanswerable, but so does another question: how can one ontologically identify the specific idea of the human body – that is the soul - which by definition is identical with this body? In this case "the idea" is, indeed, not only the "objective knowledge" of the bodily thing, of whose idea it is, but also that of conscious experience – a subjectivity. We know that in *this* sense not all things are "ideas"; but how, then, is the exceptionalism of the human soul supposed to be understood?

It has been repeatedly demonstrated by many critics – among them Mendelssohn, Hegel, and Maine de Biran – that one cannot construct the notion of subjectivity within Spinoza's philosophy. Indeed, the soul can only be differentiated from the idea of other bodies through the fact that its object, its *ideatum*, is the human body. It is therefore knowledge of the body (there are no other grounds to assume that it is "knowledge" in another sense), such as a rock's knowledge of itself, and that means that it is the objective participation on the same subjectless logic of nature. It does not help us to call to mind in this context the other category, the "idea of an idea," because this category extends itself just as much to all things. And therefore with Spinoza we have only the free-floating axiom: "Man thinks," without knowing, however, what exactly this means. Finally, one cannot anticipate how the specific human form of the "animatio" (subjectivity directed toward itself) can be saved on the grounds of this metaphysics.

When there is no *principium individuationis* in the attribute of thinking (and what such a principle could be is something we can imagine even less in the case of extension), we find no conceptual tools to take up the objectivity of the subjective world in harmony with Spinoza's doctrine. We may only assume that the perception and cognitive processes do not consist in the fact that in them things are robbed of their materiality, but rather in the fact that we ourselves, as it were, come in contact with the intelligent side of reality.

The world of ideas, as is known, cannot be brought into causal relations with that of bodies, even if the same thing happens in both, because the order of ideas presents objective knowledge of that which happens with the body. Through this perception, it appears clear, however, that human subjectivity cannot be anything other than the consciousness of that which happens to the human body. Therefore Spinoza's man, as Jacobi has correctly observed, is only an observer of his own motion, but not its author (since the human as a thinking being is not the author of anything that happens in the bodily world). This place of observer, however, is not justified within Spinoza's metaphysics, because subjectivity itself remains completely inexplicable.

Spinoza's difficulty is, as I pointed out earlier, the flip side of that which we find in Descartes. Descartes' difficulty has to do with how the reality of the world can be constructed under the assumption that in perception only the perceiver himself can be directly perceived. With Spinoza, it is the question of how, when one takes as the point of departure the order of intelligible nature, the path to subjectivity can be found. In both cases this connection is an artificial concoction. One is tempted to conclude that perhaps a philosophical language that simultaneously encompasses these two areas is simply impossible.

Immortality or eternity, which the soul also places into view, for Spinoza is certainly not the eternal life of a personal self-consciousness. It has to do much more with each idea's perpetuity outside of time. Because each idea participates in the same eternal attribute of thinking, it would also be as little foreseeable as if it were without contradiction to be able to speak of its individual existence. Independent of the question of how far Spinoza proceeded in this point from the transmission of Arabian Neo-Platonism with its belief in the immortality of a single universal reason (not an individual soul), unification with God through intellectual love was certainly for him the highest goal for which the human can and should strive. Reason, whose use is our main value, appears, so to speak, as a receiver that is tuned to the signal of eternity: it lies in the nature of reason that it recognizes things *sub specie aeternitatis*.

This unification with God presupposes, however, a dispensing with personality. At the same time, it is an affirmation, a preservation of the individuality of the body and of the soul, its recognition as a value in and of itself, a natural drive that belongs to all things (and indeed, therefore, because the nature of the thing is the same as its definition, and the definition establishes existence). Reason accepts this drive as a necessary component of nature, just as it otherwise accepts everything in nature. Suicide is against nature, Spinoza expressly establishes. But insofar as reason moves us to become one with God, spiritual suicide also appears to be given in nature, or is in accordance with nature. How a particular modus – the human individual – can at once crave his self-preservation and his dissolution in timeless Being, we cannot comprehend. Obviously it often happens that humans can harbor contradictory desires. Spinoza, however, never pointed out that there is a contradiction here, let alone that it is anchored in the fundamental contradiction of his metaphysics. In fact, the roots of these two tendencies – to overcome the world in the act of mystical union and to affirm oneself in the world – lie in Spinoza's inability to bring two world-views into agreement. On the one hand, the world appears as an indivisible, timeless substance, in which each difference is abolished; on the other hand, it is conceived of as *modus infinitus*, as the infinite mass of living-in-time, finite and destructible individuals. There is no synthesis of these worlds, and no transition from one to the other. For this reason there is no synthesis between the ethic that has its pinnacle in mystical self-destruction, and the ethic of self-preservation; there is no harmony between the point of view of a mystic and that of a free-thinker.

In this sense, Spinoza's philosophy demonstrates a failure, but a highly meaningful failure; not a trivial confusion. It is the failure of a man who had believed that the absolute truth could be expressed in discursive language, or that the Absolute, so to speak, could be intellectually tamed, using the same terms as those in which the empirical world can be expressed. This contradiction in Spinoza is a philosophical contradiction *par excellence*, and, hence, only failures are important in philosophy. Whatever is completely coherent is either trivial or uninteresting or simply not philosophy in the legitimate sense.

*   *   *

One hundred years ago, two hundred years after Spinoza's death, Ernest Renan gave an anniversary dedication lecture in the Hague. At that time he proposed to conceive of this philosophy as a model of secular, rationalistic religion, a religion without the supernatural. It could, Renan says, play a meaningful social role, because it is acceptable to the educated classes and would strengthen their authority, an authority that has been undermined through the fact that these classes continue to bring the Volk (common people) closer to a traditional religion in which they themselves no longer believe.

I do not believe that Renan was right. A rationalistic religion is neither desirable nor possible; actually, it is a contradiction in terms. The fate of Spinoza's philosophy offers one of many proofs – and not the least of them – that the idea of a religion of reason is hopeless, that it is not in our power to master the absolute and the empirical, the infinite and the finite, within the same language. We cannot simultaneously possess both in the same sense as our intellectual property. Put briefly, we cannot acquire both God and the world in the same act.

Translated from the German by Frederic J. Fransen

Pierre Bayle and the Critique of Spinoza's Metaphysics of Substance

Bayle's role in the posthumous life of Spinoza's thought has been much studied.[1] Indeed it is thanks to Bayle that Spinoza came to be seen as the ideal example (often invoked in struggles for toleration and freedom of conscience) of the "honest atheist": his life was proof that the supposedly necessary connection between religious faith and human morality was nothing but the fabrication of theologians. It is also thanks to him that the popular stereotype of the absent-minded but respectable philosopher – a very popular image of Spinoza – was formed and took root in the philosophical tradition. And it was he who started what was to establish itself as a strong current in the critique of Spinozism: an approach that was empiricist, skeptical, anti-metaphysical and *positivist* – in the sense of being an intellectual attitude characterized on the one hand by the denial of a distinction between essences and phenomena, and on the other by a scientism which questions the value of philosophy in general, in the traditional meaning of that word.

The sketch of Spinoza in Bayle's *Dictionary* had a strong and enduring influence on the more enlightened thinkers of Western Europe; Lucas's biography being little known, Bayle's article, despite all its deficiencies, was the richest and often the only source of information about the author of the *Tractatus theologico-politicus* and his thought. In Bayle,

1 Most recently by Paul Vernière, who in the first volume of his remarkable book (*Spinoza et la pensée française avant la révolution*, Paris, 1954) analyzes Bayle's attitude to Spinoza. Vernière shows that Spinoza's influence was instrumental in shaping Bayle's belief about liberty and Providence (that they do not exist), natural laws (that they are immutable) and creation (that it is impossible), and his conviction that only this view of the matter accords with reason.

Spinozism – a protean system, immensely fertile in its interpretative possibilities, its many incarnations and its later influences – found a lay critic who attacked it not from the point of view of a scandalized and threatened orthodoxy but from an attitude of rationalist common sense: the objection was not to the temerity of its open disbelief, but rather to a surfeit of vague metaphysical speculation, excessive in its pretensions and riddled with logical errors. In the Age of Enlightenment the heritage of Spinoza was an abundant source of ideas: his critique of religion, his anticlericalism and his republican spirit, but also his metaphysics (above all the universal mechanicism), his strict determinism, his denial of individual immortality – all these things were much drawn upon. But it was Bayle who first pointed out that certain aspects of Spinozism were incompatible (at least ostensibly) with the spirit of the age and with the empiricism of later generations. And these were the aspects which, uninspiring though they were to a Holbach or a Helvetius (both confirmed Spinozists in other respects), determined the fate and influence of Spinozism in German philosophy.

These generalities, widely accepted, would not by themselves be worth repeating. But there is one point in Bayle's critique which deserves more detailed analysis, for it seems more important than the opponents of the analogous trend in the eighteenth century believed – those who, like Condillac, accused Spinoza of mental confusion and verbal scholasticism, and considered him unworthy of the attention of independent and liberated minds.

Bayle's critique in the *Dictionary* was essentially aimed at Spinoza's metaphysics of substance. It is the idea of substance as indivisible, and the way it is related to Spinoza's *modi*, that awakens Boyle's logical suspicions and gives rise to his most serious objections; it is here that he finds what he considers to be the fundamental flaw in Spinoza's thought. He points out the contradiction inherent in asserting both the unity of substance and its indivisibility – a contradiction which destroys the idea of substance in both its aspects, extension and thought. He rejects as unsustainable the distinction between a "modification" or "modality" (terms supposed to designate particular things in their relationship to substance) and a "part" (a word to be understood in its usual sense), dismissing it as purely verbal and utterly lacking in any intelligible content, and concludes that Spinoza's unified substance must possess all the possible accidents and properties (often mutually contradictory) to be found in the world. He lists the absurd logical consequences which follow from Spinoza's misleading distinction: all things are essentially one; the same extended substance finds itself possessing contradictory physical qualities; the same thinking substance possesses contradictory thoughts, emotions and moral properties; the same thing can be both rounded and square; God as a young Jew is also the young Spinoza, who wants to kill himself; the German army is also the Turkish army, and massacres itself. The diversity of things disappears; the principle of contradiction no longer obtains. The whole system, says Bayle, is an impossible fantasy, a chimera. Incompatible properties cannot coexist in the same thing at the same time; to say that they can is to abandon reason. We must attribute them to different things, and accept that a substance modified by one property cannot be identical with a substance modified by another that is incompatible with it. Nor can contradictory thoughts coexist simultaneously in one human mind; we must attribute them to different subjects. Spinoza, however, considers that they all emanate simultaneously from a single intellect; he wants to abolish the diversity and individuality of minds as well as bodies.[2]

In the abundant literature on Spinoza Bayle's critique is much cited, and has often been condemned for its frivolity, its superficiality and its errors of interpretation. But considered closely, it emerges as doubly significant, for it is not only a confrontation between two eras and two entirely different ways of thinking, but also an attack on a sensitive spot in a great current in philosophical thought – and a particular weak spot for Spinoza.

Bayle takes us to the heart of Spinoza's metaphysics. It is on the points raised by Bayle that the enigmatic world of the *Ethics* has always engaged the philosophical imagination of both his adversaries and his apologists. What is the relation of the world of *modi*, infinite in number, to the world of substance, unique and infinite? Is Spinoza's God, considered *sub attributo extensionis*, identical to the sum of particular bodies? And is his other aspect, the thinking God, identical to the sum of finite ideas? If He is not, how is the diversity of things to be explained, and where are we to seek the principle of individuation, as necessary for the material world as it is for the world of ideas?

We know that Spinoza condemned as false the popular image of God as visible in the way that things are visible.[3] God, he says, is inaccessible to the senses; substance can be seen only with the eyes of reason.[4] Visibility is contrary to divine nature; the passages in Scripture which seem to suggest otherwise may be easily explained by the limited

2   Pierre Bayle, *Spinoza*, in *Dictionnaire historique et critique*, 4th edition, vol. IV, pp. 253–71, Amsterdam-Leiden, 1730. See especially pp. 259–61.
3   *Ethica* II, 47 schol.
4   *Epist.* XII, in Gebhardt, *Opera*, 4 vols., Heidelberg, 1924 (henceforth G); vol. IV, p. 56.

understanding of the prophets, who were incapable of grasping the idea of an incorporeal being.[5] If nature is defined as matter, it cannot be identical with God.[6] But nor can matter be defined solely by the attribute of extension,[7] otherwise it would be indistinguishable from substance, which is defined as something extended.

It is the infinite *modi* which are supposed, but fail, to bridge the gap between substance and things. Spinoza is not lavish with the details he provides about them,[8] but everything seems to indicate that, far from being indistinguishable from substance, they are, in fact, the sum of particular things, which also belongs to "*natura naturata*".[9] It is with respect to the *modus infinitus extensionis*, the infinite mode of extension, that a body may be called a "part" in the ordinary sense of the word; it cannot be so called with respect to that other kind of infinity which is substance itself. The obscure relationship between these two kinds of infinity, described in the famous letter to Meyer, has always been the greatest difficulty plaguing interpreters of Spinoza; as they struggle with it, they often betray a tendency to make Spinoza's doctrine clearer than it was to

5 *Tract. Theol.-Pol.* II, G3, p. 40 (para.43 in Bruder). In a sense, this explanation may be seen as a continuation of the struggle waged by Maimonides against the theological anthropomorphism of the orthodox rabbis. (see the *Guide for the Perplexed*, vol. I, esp. chapters 1–28). Materialist, or rather realist, interpretations of the divine being were fairly common from the time of the Sadduceans; Jewish mythology, at least in the Torah, was based on everyday imagination and far removed from any kind of spiritualism. This was not, of course, the consequence of any philosophical doctrine, but simply the result of the naive, realist imagination of a pastoral people. God's corporeal nature is easily derived from the Old Testament. We cannot assess the reliability of Lucas's account of discussions during which the young Spinoza allegedly demonstrated, for the benefit of his later detractors, the mortality of the soul and the corporeal nature of God, but certain observations in the *Tractatus Theologico-Politicus* (G III, pp 19 and 25) on the corporeal nature of the God of the Scriptures suggest – although philosophy has rejected this interpretation – that Spinoza may have had some materialist leanings in his period of Bible study; and most historians, Dunin-Borkowski included, concede that the young Spinoza went through at least one materialist period.

6 *Epist.* LXXIII, GIV, p. 307. But nature is not *only* matter; it is also an infinite variety of other things. (*Tract. Theo.-Pol.*, ch. VI, p. 83, para. 10.)

7 *Korte Verhand.* I, ch.2, GI, pp. 23–24 and 29.

8 *Ethica*, I.12; 15 schol.; *Epist.* XII, pp. 55 and nn.

9 *Epist.* LXXIII, p. 334: "*Nam huc usque nihil de his ordine disponere mihi licuit.*" This is concerned with the possibility of deducing the diversity of bodies from the fact of extension alone. Carl Gebhardt, for whom Spinoza's agnosticism was a favorite topic, considered this difficulty as one of the tragedies of Spinoza's life (*Einleitung z. Spinozas Briefwechsel*, in *Sämtliche Werke*, 1914, v.III, pp. XIV–XV).

its author – who, when responding to Walter Tschirnhaus's incisive comments, himself confessed to a certain perplexity on the issue.[10] The importance of the question has not escaped any of Spinoza's interpreters, and there is nothing that can usefully be said about it here, except that its solution would have to explain exactly what Spinoza meant by divine immanence and the sense in which God is independent of the existence of the created world.

What Spinoza says on the subject in the *Ethics* is as follows: God is the immanent cause of things.[11] He is that which is common to all things,[12] and as such is both in a part and in the whole, but is not the essence of any particular thing, and cannot be conceived except adequately.[13] Corporeal substance is no more composed of parts than a line is composed of points, or a solid of planes; its divisibility and composedness are only products of abstraction, that is to say [!] of empirical knowledge, which is more accessible to us [than other kinds]. The changes which seem to us to occur in substance are merely apparent, not real: water comes into being and perishes as water, i.e., as a particular *modus*, never as substance.[14] Corporeal substance is an individual, i.e., the sum of all bodies; these are so tightly bound that they communicate their movements to one another with a determined regularity, and can undergo changes in their movements without altering the nature of the whole:[15] "*totam naturam unum esse individuum.*"

There have been countless interpretations of what Spinoza meant by this; his definitions, inspired as they are by Aristotelian categories, are obdurately resistant to exegesis: substance (perceived by us only in its extended aspect) can be interpreted neither as an aggregate of bodies,[16] nor as a metaphysical substratum of its perceptible properties,[17] nor as

10 Walter Tschirnhaus, who in his attitude towards Spinoza can in a sense be said to have been a precursor of Bayle, thrice asked for an explanation on this point (*Epist.* LIX, p. 268; LXXX, p. 331; LXXXII, p. 333).

11 *Ethica* I. 18, cf. I.15.

12 *Ethica* V. 20 schol. ("*ad rerum communes proprietates vel ad Deum*")

13 *Ethica* II. 37, 38 (lemma 2. ibid., demonstrates sufficiently clearly that it is the attribute of extension that is "common" to all these things.

14 Ibid., 15 schol.

15 Ibid., lemma VII.

16 P. Vernière found a similar interpretation in Malebranche (*op. cit.*, vol.I, p. 267) and in Poiret (p. 53); German Spinoza scholars, among them Lau and Stosch, also accepted it, as did many other German critics of that time, who repeated Bayle's objections (cf. L. Bäck, *Spinozas Erste Einwirkungen auf Deutschland*, 1895, pp. 15, 50 and 61). More recently, it often appears in Marxist literature on Spinoza (Plekhanov, Deborin, Tymianski and others).

17 Kuno Fischer (*Spinoza*, p. 377) thought that Spinoza's *modi* were relative to substance: that they were properties of things.

an externally actualized *materia prima*, nor as "Gestalt" – i.e., as something distinct from its elements by virtue of certain specific properties,
although it possesses those properties by virtue of the particular compo-
sition of those elements[18] – nor as a universal which is reproduced in its
instances.[19]

We could, however, try to reconstruct Spinoza's corporeal world in
terms of our modern categories. It might look as follows: each material
object, being a participant in the universal and incessant interaction of
the sum of all things in the universe, fills up, so to speak, all of nature.
To conceive of an object as a separate (and therefore limited) thing,
ignoring its connections with other things and its infinite influences on
them, is to perform an act of abstraction. "In reality" there are no separate and limited objects; there are no parts in the world. To know an
object fully and completely can only mean to know all of nature fully
and completely, for that object influences all of nature, and at the same
time is itself affected by the constant influence of all nature's other elements or so-called "parts". There is only one real concrete thing, and that
is the totality of nature; a particular *modus*, excised from the universal
aggregate of things, is only a product of abstraction – of our cognition.
And our cognition, determined as it is by our practical needs, artificially
picks out certain properties from the totality of the individual; to know
a thing without cutting up the total unity of the world in this artificial
way would have to mean knowing the world in its entirety. Abstraction,
then, is knowledge not only of species and genera (which have no real

18 This is more or less how the main participants of "Pantheismusstreit" saw
   the question. Mendelssohn thought that the relation between Spinoza's substance and the sum of all things was one of "totality" and "agglomeration,"
   but that the difference between them existed only in the mind: "*Aber dieses
   Totale, dieses Zusammennehmen, vieles in einem, dieser Inbegriff setzt . . . ein denk-
   endes Subjekt voraus, das in seiner Vorstellung umfasst, sammelt und verbindet.
   Ohne dieses vereinigenden Subjekt bleiben die Theile isoliert und unverbunden . . .*"
   (An unsustainable interpretation, given that the objectivity of substance and
   its properties – in the modern, non-Spinozean sense of the word "objectivity"– is a subject Spinoza returns to so often that there can be no doubt as to
   his opinion on the matter.) Jacobi thought that this transition from the limited to the unlimited was the principal difficulty of Spinozism, threatening the
   whole doctrine by its unintelligibility. Herder opposes the interpretation of
   Spinoza's view of God as the sum of all things, and leans towards a theist
   interpretation: as an attribute of Thought, God is not the sum of all thoughts
   but their independent self-consciousness (cf texts on Pantheismusstreit in: F.
   Mauthner, ed., *Spinoza-Büchlein*, München, 1913).
19 This is precisely Bayle's interpretation; he mentions it in his article on
   Abelard in the *Dictionnaire* (vol. I, p. 19).

existence) or (as Aristotelian nominalism would have it) of relations and properties,[20] but also of parts; for parts have no more autonomous existence than relations and properties, and insofar as they do exist they do not differ from the whole in which they inhere. On this view, all empirical knowledge is abstraction, precisely *because* of its empirical nature: for coming to know something is an activity which consists in artificially dividing up material reality into isolated fragments, mutilated and deformed by this cutting up. The world-composed-of-parts which presents itself to our senses is only the phenomenal world; metaphysically, every one of these parts is *literally* identical with the Whole.[21] The limit-

---

20 As we know, Porphyrus's *Isagoge* and Boethius's *Commentary* played a crucial role in the medieval development of conceptual categories. Nominalism was to attempt a further reduction of Aristotle's ten categories. By the fourteenth century, Occam had reduced them to two: substance and quality. John of Mirecourt admitted only one – substance. The reduction was completed by Nicholas d'Autrecourt, who abandoned even that. Cf. K. Michalski, *Wpływ Oxfordu na filozofie Jana z Mirecourt* (*The Influence of Oxford on the Philosophy of Jean de Mirecourt*), Krakow, 1921; and *Odrodzenie nominalizmu w XIV wieku* (*TheNominalist Revival in the Fourteenth Century*), Kwartalnik Filozoficzny, 1926.

21 This way of thinking seems strange to anyone schooled in the analytic, and thus to some degree mechanistic, tradition. Paradoxically, the current in contemporary philosophical thought that is closest to Spinozism understood in this sense is represented by Bergson – who is consciously hostile to Spinoza, considering his doctrine to be radically mechanistic. Bergson's nominalism is of the sort where the totality of the world is the only thing that is genuinely concrete, its parts being merely the products of analytic operations, which underlie practical activity but do not lead to true knowledge: *"Le tout réel pourrait bien être . . . une continuité indivisible: les systèmes que nous y découpons n'en seraient point alors,à proprement parler, des parties; ce seraient des vues partielles prises sur le tout. Et, avec les vues partielles mises bout à bout, vous n'obtiendrez même pas un commencement de recomposition de l'ensemble. . . . La matérialité d'un corps ne s'arrête pas au point où nous le touchons. Il est présent partout où son influence se fait sentir. Or, sa force attractive, pour ne parler que d'elle, s'exerce sur le soleil, sur les planètes, peut-être sur l'univers entier. Plus la physique avance, plus elle efface d'ailleurs l'individualité des corps et même des particules en lesquelles l'imagination scientifique commençait par les décomposer; corps et corpuscules tendent à se fondre dans une interaction universelle . . . la spatialité parfaite consisterait en une parfaite exteriorité des parties par rapport aux autres, c'est-à-dire en une indépendance réciproque complète. . . . Si l'on remarque qu'une chose est véritablement là où elle agit, on sera conduit à dire . . . que tous les atomes s'entrepénètrent et que chacun d'eux remplit le monde. Dans une pareille hypothèse, l'atome ou plus généralement le point matériel devient une simple vue de l'esprit."* (*L'Evolution créatrice*, 1923, pp. 33, 205 and 221) The above passages (Bergson's theory of evolution apart, of course) may be seen as one possible

ed capacity of our imagination can never reveal this identity to us; our empirical contact with reality does not allow us to conceive of infinity, even of spatial infinity.

The mutual connections between things could be reduced to a purely mechanical activity, which would have the advantage of allowing us to dispense with the concept of "totality", in its modern meaning, to characterize Spinozism. But even on such a reductionist interpretation, finite objects could not be ontologically real entities; they would remain the products of practical reason.

This identification of the Whole with its parts – an idea instinctively abhorrent to any rationalist mind and certainly repellent to the critical intelligence of a Pierre Bayle, who attacked it for its absurd consequences – is in fact as essentially and authentically Spinozist as it is possible to get. The difference between a "modification" and a "part" which Bayle found so unintelligible was not mere artifice, a purely verbal bit of juggling on Spinoza's part: he really did believe that every object was a modification of substance, in other words that it was nature seen in a certain aspect and distorted by our cognition. It is indeed God modified-as-the-Germans who massacres God-modified-as-the-Turks; everything indicates that Spinoza would have accepted this proposition, despite its apparent absurdity. But its absurdity seems glaring only if we retain in our minds the common image of objects – our perceptual image of them as distinct things – and identify them as such; it disappears if we are able, by an effort of intuition, to go beyond our everyday habits of perception and perceive two things as identical – not as distinct parts of nature but as essentially identical to the whole of substance, by virtue of the universal interaction of all things. For in this interaction, this interpenetration of everything, the imaginary individuality of objects is dissolved. The *modus* is to substance as a point is to a line: not a part of it but rather an abstract slice of it, cut out of it, as it were, by the operations of our reason and without any real existence of its own. Infinite substance is the only real, concrete thing, and therefore (on the nominalist view, which Spinoza unhesitatingly adopts) the only thing to which we may attribute real existence. The objects of sensory perception are pseudo-objects, which only appear concrete; in fact they are entirely abstract and illusory, their existence no more real than that of Platonic ideas. Thus Spinoza's nominalism is safe: only concrete things have an independent

way of summing up that part of Spinoza's metaphysics with which we are now concerned. In them, Bergson has not yet gone beyond a mechanistic view of the world, if by a "mechanistic" view we mean one that allows for an interpretation of all phenomena in the world by the laws of classical mechanics alone.

existence, but there is only one concrete thing, and that is the infinite universe.[22] All determination, for Spinoza, is negation: the finite is only the negation of the infinite, or its lack. Only the infinite is pure affirmation. (This idea can be found, in a general form, not only in pantheist texts – in the writings of Erigenes,[23] Eckhart, and Campanella[24] – but also in the Cartesian tradition.[25]) Consequently, the act of negation might be seen not as ontological but as epistemic: as a relation between things which has its source in the operations of human reason alone and does not exist beyond them.[26] The conclusion seems logical, but there is no

22 Hegel used the word *"Totalität"* to refer to what Spinoza meant by substance, and it seems more appropriate than any other. Feuerbach seems to have entertained a similar interpretation; he sums up Spinoza's idea of substance as follows: *"Alle Dinge zusammen und zugleich, nämlich alle Wesen nicht nacheinander und folglich nicht aussereinander, sondern in Wesenheit zusammengefasst, als Eines, als ein Untheilbares, d. i. alle Wesen zusammen, inwiefern sie als nicht von einander unterschieden, nur Ein Wesen, Eine Sache, Ein Ganzes ausmachen, constituiren daher Gott selbst. Deswegen ist aber Gott nicht etwa zusammengesetzt aus den Wesen oder Dingen als seinen Theilen, sondern ist er das absolute Prius, die Substanz ist früher als ihre Affectionen, ist das absolut Eine, das einzig Selbständige."* (Feuerbach, *Geschichte d. neuern Philosophie*, 1833, p. 361).

23 *De divis. Nat.* I.4.

24 The Solarians had a similar metaphysics, which admitted two metaphysical elements: essence, or God, and its absence or negation. All finite beings were composed of essence and its absence.

25 Descartes expresses this idea in his Response to the Fifth Set of Objections to the *Meditations*, saying that infinity is not the negation of limitation, but that, on the contrary, all limitation is the negation of infinity. Hobbes (*Leviathan*, I.3; *De Cive* XV, 14) thought the opposite, considering infinity to be pure negation. He also thought it was an idea without any cognitive value, used only as a symbol in the religion established by the State.

26 This principle has its roots in negative Christian Platonism (mainly in Denis the Pseudo-Areopagite), but as it evolved it became radically opposed to the Christian dualism between God and the world. In particular, it wanted to *replace* the idea of creation by that of limitation. According to this principle, when we define a thing we distinguish it from other things; consequently, in establishing what it is, we also establish what it is not. To exist in a certain relation to things is not to exist in other relations; to be defined in one way is not to be defined in another. All determination, and thus every determined and finite instance of being, can also be defined in terms of non-being – in terms of what it is not. Being and non-being are linked: every finite being is also, because it is finite, definable in terms of its non-being. In some spiritual pantheists this way of thinking led to a monist view of the world: the God-absolute, since he is not determined, has no essence; strictly speaking, he is not a being, since, not being a determined thing, he cannot be distinguished

evidence that Spinoza drew it: he does not formulate it explicitly any-where in his writings. It is, in a sense, the logical conclusion towards which his thought seemed to be advancing but which it failed for some

from any other thing or defined by his relation to other things. Absolute real-ity is an infinity which contains no negation, and therefore cannot be defined by its relationship with other things or distinguished from them by its char-acteristics. Individual things, or beings, must therefore be modifications of a single substance. A particular thing can only be considered as relative to the absolute – as a limitation or immanent determination of it. In a sense, every-thing is composed of affirmation and negation, being and nothingness. This theory ought to lead to the conclusion that pure being and pure non-being are the same thing, but it was a conclusion only Hegel drew. For Spinoza, whose famous principle *"omnis determinatio est negatio"* (cf. *Ethica* I, 8 schol., *Epist.* XXXVI, p. 184, and L, p. 240) clearly entails the possibility of eliminat-ing creation as a category in the traditional sense, negation remains a con-ceptual tool within the structure of a Parmenidean rather than a Heraclitean metaphysics, to use the conventional terms. This means that it has no histor-ical sense, only a metaphysical one. It does not refer to a process of sup-planting certain situations by others, nor to the principle by which all things can in a sense be said to contain within themselves the seeds of their future destruction. It refers, rather, to certain immutable relations that exist between the world of perception and the absolute (setting aside the subjective nature of determination, which is a consequence of Spinoza's doctrine that Spinoza did not formulate). It is in this context that Hegel complained of the imper-fection of Spinoza's doctrine and accused it of immaturity.

The principle whereby all determination is a form of negation reveals itself as crucial to the subject under discussion when we consider how pro-foundly it alters the Aristotelian idea of substance. Bayle is only partly justi-fied in accusing Spinoza of having smuggled in an idea of substance that is different from its traditional idea as simple extension – *ens per se subsistens*, as opposed to accident, *ens in alio* – without explicitly rejecting the latter and without any awareness of the inevitable contradictions of such a position; for the idea of *"per se subsistere"* or *"per se esse"* acquires a different meaning in light of the above-mentioned principle. *"Per se esse"* now means to be free of all external determination – in other words, to be infinite. The only inde-pendent being, being *par excellence*, is that infinite being which exists because by its very nature it must exist, and which is therefore *causa sui*. Bayle's objec-tions, and the whole controversy surrounding his and Spinoza's view of the world, center on this principle: the principle that determination is negation. The Aristotelian, empiricist tradition takes as its starting point, as the only datum on which a valid philosophy can be constructed, the concrete, finite, perceptible object; the Platonist, or rather Neo-Platonist, tradition considers that infinity is the *"primum in cognoscendo"* from which the world of individ-ual things must be built.

reason to reach: the natural culmination of a doctrine which, though clearly tending in a certain direction, was perhaps never followed through to the end.

That direction itself, however – the natural intellectual tendency of Spinoza's thought – is vigorous and strongly defined. It becomes clearer still if we consider the idea (familiar in other contexts) that measure is a purely subjective phenomenon, a way of thinking we impose upon the world: we think in terms of measure because this is how we define and determine quantity. Insofar as things are quantitatively measured, and perceived as measurable, they are no more than subjective images; applying this idea more broadly, we can say that things are merely subjective images insofar as they are finite, perceptual, isolated and differentiated.[27] And if dividing up corporeal space into separate fragments is an artificial procedure, and the resulting distinctions without any basis in reality, then dividing up time into finite segments is equally artificial.

The principal difficulty of such a view is how to formulate a principle of individuation whereby particular things might be distinguished from their substantial totality. All non-atomist physical theories which attribute continuity and homogeneity to matter are faced with this problem, and they all deal with it in the same way: in such theories it is always movement which intervenes to multiply particular bodies and provides a basis for distinguishing them. The answer is the same even in the case of theories which, like Descartes', reject qualitative differentiation between things. Here, however, the difficulty is somewhat different. Spinoza cannot take this way out[28] (although he made efforts to do so[29])

27 Cf. *Epist*. XII, pp. 56–57: "*. . . ex eo, quod Durationem, et Quantitatem pro libitu determinare possumus, ubi scilicet hanc a Substantia abstractam concipimus, et illam a modo, quo a rebus externis fluit, separamus, oritur Tempus et Mensura . . . Mensura ad Quantitatem tali modo determinandam, ut, quod fieri potest, eas facile imagineremur. Deinde* ex eo, quod Affectiones Substantiae ab ipsa Substantia separamus, et ad classes ut eas . . . facile imagineremur, redigimus, oritur Numerus . . . Mensura, Tempus, et Numerum nihil esse praeter cogitandi, seu potius imaginandi Modos.*" It is clear from this passage that Spinoza considered all representations of individual things to be the work of our imagination, and the result of our deficient knowledge. The idea of a thing as measurable and finite is (given that "*. . . nec Numerum, nec Mensuram, nec Tempus . . . posse esse infinitos*", ibid., p. 58) purely subjective; there is nothing finite in real being.

28 As Couchoud believed (*Benoit de Spinoza*, 1902, pp. 178–83).

29 Spinoza wants to reconstruct corporeal individuality by means of the ideas of motion, speed and rest – the only properties of bodies that can individualize them (*Korte Verhand.* II, Voor Reeden, G I, p. 52; *Ethica* II, lemma 1) – and

without self-contradiction: if he denies, absolutely and unequivocally, that substance has parts, he cannot at the same time claim that such parts are constantly being created in nature "in itself" by virtue of the objective properties of movement and rest. If we permit ourselves the impertinence of explaining a philosopher's own philosophy to him (a discourtesy which is an essential part of the intellectual historian's profession), we ought to point out that, since substance itself remains indivisible (indivisibility being, of course, not our inability to divide up extended things, but the essential property of nature "in itself"), the property of being divisible or composed of parts belongs to the thing called the infinite *modus* of extension – defined precisely as the sum of all particular perceptual things. But this does not solve the difficulty, for the relationship between the two kinds of infinity remains inexplicable; and if the doctrine is carried through to its logical conclusion, particularity cannot be saved: every particular thing by itself, as well as the sum of all particular things (and this includes the infinite *modus* of extension), can only be the product of *experientia vaga*. The indivisible totality of substance must remain the only true reality – the only reality in the metaphysical sense. But if this is so, then there is no way to express our knowledge of this ultimate and only reality by means of language, for language is intended precisely to distinguish things, to designate them by virtue of their being qualitatively and quantitatively distinct. And if the Spinozist intuition is the only instrument capable of wresting from infinity the secret of its hidden essence, it must transcend human discourse; in other words, it must be ineffable.

Spinoza's intuition is two-sided. The Cartesian, rationalist side is apparent above all in the *Tractatus de Intellectus Emendatione*: here intuition is no more than the faculty of forming analytical judgments, true by virtue of the meaning of their terms alone and requiring only an understanding of that meaning to be recognized as such. The other side reveals an intuition of a different kind: a sort of inarticulable feeling of man's unity, indeed his identity, with all of nature.[30]

define individuality in terms of them (*Ethica* II, def. post ax. 2, post lemma 3; cf. *Epist.* XXXIII, GIV, pp. 170–71). Like Descartes (*Princ. Phil.* II, 4), like Hobbes (*Leviathan*, I.3.34), and in accordance with all mechanistic systems of physics, whether atomist or not, he considers perceptual qualities to be subjective (*Epist.* VI, GIV, p. 28).

30 Intuition as described in the *Tract. de Intell. Emend.* (G II, p. 10, para 19) is certainly knowledge mediated through language. It is knowledge of things by their nature or essence, and according to the *Ethics* (II, 47 schol.) is equivalent to definition (essence in the order of being is definition in the order of intelligibility, the two orders being ontologically identical). According to the *Short*

Because of the isomorphism and ontological identity of the two attributes of mind and body, this essential flaw of Spinozism – the inability to formulate a principle of individuation for the material world which would not be in contradiction with the rest of the doctrine – extends to the intelligible world as well. The individual mind fares no better than the body in the search for a metaphysical justification of its existence: both remain illegitimate from the point of view of the supreme law of substance, products of an alienation of nature that is difficult to conceive.

Yet there are many signs that Spinoza's thought revolted against such a conclusion. His revolt was expressed chiefly through another principle, as firm and absolute as the principle of the indivisibility of substance – the principle of the instinct of self-preservation that is com-

Treatise, however, intuition is also knowledge through feeling and enjoyment (*Korte Verhand.* II, 2, G I, p. 55). But it seems impossible to prove on the basis of the texts alone that Spinoza himself considered intuition to be direct knowledge of things, unmediated through language. It is also unlikely that his statements about the unity with nature which we can achieve through intuitive knowledge, and the intellectual love of God which is the consequence of that knowledge, etc., apply only to the activity described in the *Treatise on Reform* when it is understood literally, i.e., to the knowledge of definitions, which necessarily impose themselves as true through the meaning of their terms alone. Here, as elsewhere, the fundamental theses of Spinoza's metaphysics seem to lack a definitive interpretation imposed by the logic of the whole system. Spinoza's friend Pieter Balling, on the affinity of whose thought with Spinoza's Carl Gebhardt remarks (*Die Religion Spinozas, Archiv für Geschichte der Philosophie*, vol. 41, 1931), explicitly describes supreme knowledge as something that comes about outside language, directly, mystically, by an immediate connection to truth that we discover within ourselves: "*Alle uyterlijk teken, deze kennisse nootwendich moet voor onderstellen; zoo moetze onmiddelijk zonder enich uiterlijk teken wezen. Dat de tekenen en zodanigen kennisse moeten voor onderstellen, is onwedersprekelijk, want deze tekenen zouden, of woorden of uit werkingen moeten zijn. Zoo het woorden zouden zijn, met ziet voor eerst een onmogelijkheit, in de zak zelve: want woorden zijn geschapen, en bepaalt; Ghodt die zich hier door te kennen zoud geven, is ongeschapen en onbepaalt: en derhalven is hier een oneindich verschil; alzo dat'r geheel geen overeenkominge, noch iets is in de woorden, waar doorze daartoe bequaam zouden konnen zijn.*" (*Het Licht opden Kandelaar*, 1662, pp. 8–9). It is just possible that this idea of direct knowledge, in its irrationalist form, was indeed what Spinoza meant by intuition; for it is precisely the idea of the incommensurability of the finite and the infinite which prevents us from expressing our intuitive knowledge of substance through language – also a product of the cutting-up of the world into bits that have no correspondence in reality, and which must be overcome.

mon to all things: "*conatus ad suum esse conservandum.*" And this appetite for existence is attributed to particular things – the very things which Spinoza's metaphysics consigns to non-being, denying them autonomous existence by definition. These two radically opposed, incompatible principles – indivisibility on the one hand and the instinct of self-preservation on the other – are both essential to Spinoza's thought; their continual opposition embodies the incurable internal contradictions of the doctrine. The flaw, in other words, cannot be repaired; it can only be explained. The contradiction between the world of substance and the world of *modi*, the universe-as-God and the universe-as-infinite-*modus*, infects every aspect of Spinoza's doctrine. It is there in his metaphysics, as the contradiction between the part and the Whole; and in his methodology, as the contradiction between intuition and deduction. In his ethics it is embodied in the contradiction between the principle of self-contemplation and that of self-preservation. In his politics it manifests itself in the conflict between liberalism and authoritarianism; in his literary style, as the tension between the tragic spirit and realism; in his life, as the opposition of Stoicism and Machiavellianism.

This internal contradiction of Spinoza's doctrine in turn reveals the heterogeneity at the root of his thought, hinting at its two conflicting and essentially incompatible sources: Cartesianism and mysticism. The first is the spirit of an individualist and scientist rationalism, characteristic of the thought of an upwardly mobile bourgeoisie; the second is the spirit of a plebeian mysticism to which the idea of scientific progress is foreign. Spinoza's failure to achieve a synthesis of his thought was owing to the irreconcilability of these two sources; it was, in other words, a logical and necessary failure, not a historical and contingent one.

It is mysticism, the second source of Spinoza's thought, that inspired the (centuries old and still vigorous) tendency to see all individuality as a kind of pathology, and to seek the cure for man's alienation not in his individual life, private or social, nor in the petrified orthodoxy of established religion, but rather in communion with the absolute: in the mystical tradition it is here, and only here, that the promised land was thought to lie.[31] Spinoza's theory of indivisible substance which overrides and destroys all individuality – eradicating not only things, but

31 It is in the German mysticism of the time that this nostalgia for the suppression of individuality found its most distinct expression: "*Mensch, hüte dich von dir, wirst du mit dir beladen, Du wirst dir selber mehr als tausend Teufel schaden,*" exhorts John Scheffler (*Cherubinischer Wandersmann,* V, 144), certain that through the essence of his being he is identical with the absolute: "*Ich bin so breit als Gott, nichts ist in aller Welt, Das mich (o Wunderding!) in sich umschlossen halt.*" (ibid., I, 86).

also man as an individual – can be seen as a philosophical transposition of this: it is the expression of a mind discouraged by petty-bourgeois life. His principle of self-preservation represents the opposing, rationalist tendency: it is the confident and optimistic face of the scholarly life of his age, flourishing along with economic progress.

The fruits of Spinoza's work were equally heterogeneous: his rationalism nourished Europe's libertine minds for over two centuries, while his integrating vision of the world strongly influenced the development of dialectical thought, especially in Germany. It seems reasonable to say that the logical failure of his doctrine was counterbalanced by its historical success.

It is also in this light that Bayle's critique of Spinoza's bipolar philosophy should be viewed. Bayle concentrates with an insistence that seems akin to obsession on the problem of the unity of substance. He returns to the topic several times,[32] each time repeating the same formulas and betraying by his tone an almost personal engagement and an unconcealed irritation: "*On ne peut assez admirer qu'une idée si extravagante, et remplie de contradictions absurdes, ait pu se fourrer dans l'âme de tant de gens si éloignez les uns des autres et si différens entre eux en humeur, en coutumes, et en génie,*" he remarks of a Japanese philosophical school which he considers essentially Spinozist. But at the same time he reveals, more explicitly than in his analysis of Spinoza's doctrine, the reasons for his irritation at human stupidity. The chief of these is the fear that the repugnant idea of the metaphysical unity of the world might exert a harmful influence on people, causing them to engage in futile contemplation, to reject the external world and to scorn ordinary language – a necessary condition for all scientific activity. He condemns the adherents of the school in question because "*ils négligent l'exterieur, ils s'appliquent uniquement à méditer, ils renvoient au loin toute discipline qui consiste en paroles, ils ne s'attachent qu'à l'exercise qu'ils appellent SOQUXIN SOQUBUT, c'est-à-dire le coeur.*" And he stresses that Possevin's remarks, which he quotes in his article, also apply to Spinoza: "*Omnia unico verbo putant se dissolvere dicentes hominum non interesse hujus principii vim, et naturam perscutari inquirendo aut disputando quod totum manifeste constat, ex ignoratione profectum et natum.*"[33]

There are, in fact, several issues on which Bayle's interpretation of Spinoza is just plain wrong. When he compares Spinoza's ideas with those of the Scotists, Guillaume de Champeaux, etc., he sees them as a

32 In the articles on Spinoza in the *Dictionnaire*, and also those on Abelard, Averroes, Abumuslimus, Cesalpin, Critias, Democritus, Japan, Jupiter, Leucippus and Origenes.

33 In *Japan*, vol. II, pp. 831–32.

form of Platonic realism, assuming that Spinoza's substance is multiplied in particular things as a *universal*. But of the hundreds of doubtful aspects of this allegedly deductive doctrine, Spinoza's nominalism is the least questionable. It is not the relation between a universal object and particular concrete objects that links Spinoza's God to His finite modifications or affections; on the contrary, it is substance, the only concrete thing, that is subject to determination and modifications, which are produced by the human faculty for abstract thought. Spinoza's rejection of universals remains firm throughout, from the *Short Treatise*[34] to the *Ethics*.[35] For the same reason it is difficult (to put it mildly) to find justification for another of Bayle's feats of misinterpretation, which consists in attributing to Spinozism the Averroist theory of the unity of the intellect (although it must be said that this is a misconception under which quite a few modern historians of ideas have labored). Bayle's interpretation of Spinoza's determinism is also questionable. Nevertheless, setting these infelicities aside, the main emphasis of Bayle's critique is on attacking Spinoza's weakest and at the same time most important spot: the impossibility of coaxing from his metaphysics a coherent principle of individuation, and consequently the impossibility of justifying – except by man's practical needs – the use of human language as an instrument in acquiring adequate knowledge of the real. This is Bayle's essential objection; it is the revolt of the encyclopaedic spirit against a vision of the world where human reason, with its supreme and unique faculties of apprehending the real, is deprived of all analytical instruments, its only resource being an obscure contemplation through which, in a way that is unfathomable and inarticulable, it is identified with the absolute. In spite of his frequent errors of interpretation, Bayle brought out and identified the deepest current in Spinozism – the opposition to rationalism. Compared to Voltaire's "plats écoliers" which passed as critiques of Spinozism, Pierre Bayle proved the most penetrating (if unilateral) critic of his age.

Translated by Agnieszka Kolakowska

---

34 *Korte Verhand.* X, 6, G I, pp. 42–43: ". . . *eerst die byzondere alle alleen hebben oorzaak en niet de algemeene, dewyle die niets zyn.*" Cf ibid., II.16, p. 82 and *Epist.* II, G IV, p. 9, on the way in which man creates general things, such as "man" in general or "will" in general.

35 Cf. *Ethics* II.49 schol.; *Epist.*XIX, p. 91; *Epist.* L, p. 239. Is the same nominalist tendency discernible in Spinoza's Hebrew Grammar, where every part of speech except particles and conjunctions is reduced to a substantive? (*Compendium Gramm. Linguae Hebraeae*, c. V, G I, p. 303).

Dutch Seventeenth-Century Non-Denominationalism and *Religio Rationalis*
Mennonites, Collegiants and the Spinoza Connection

The following essay is taken from Chapter III of Kolakowski's *"Swiadomosc religijna i wiez koscielna; studia nad chrzescijanstwem bezwyznaniowym XVII wieku"* (*"Religious Consciousness and Church Allegiance; Studies in Seventeenth-Century Non-Denominational Christianity"*), PWN, Warsaw, 1965, 1997. Preceding it, by way of introduction, is a summary of the salient points of the chapter's previous sections. The essay on Mystical and Rationalist Heresies, in this volume, will also provide helpful background.

Introduction: Galenus and Boreel

Adam Boreel[1] was twenty years older than Galenus,[2] but the "rationalizing" tendency in his religious writings is much clearer and stronger. It is not yet evident in his main work, *Ad Legem et Testimonium*, an anti-denominationalist and "biblicist" text which goes much further than

---

1   Adam Boreel (1602–1655) studied theology and philosophy in Leiden. In the 1630s he went to England, where he made some contacts among the Cambridge Platonists and was imprisoned (probably for his non-denominational opinions) and ordered to leave the country. On his return he took up Hebrew studies (he published an edition of the Mishna in 1646, but no copy of it survives), and in 1645 published his most important work, the treatise *Ad Legem et Testimonium*. In 1646 he moved to Amsterdam and there, together with Daniel de Breen, established a Collegium, in which Galenus later became involved. He is considered an activist in the Collegiant movement. The most detailed biography of Boreel is Walter Schneider's *Adam Boreel. Sein*

Galenus in its conclusions about the absolute inadmissibility, in religious worship, of any interpretation of religion that goes beyond the Biblical text. (Galenus merely says that no "human" interpretation can lay claim to infallibility or be considered as binding on anyone.) From this in turn Boreel concludes that all catechisms and creeds ought to be abolished (while Galenus confines himself to saying that they merely represent the opinions of those who wrote them) and that a true Christian should leave the church and worship in private if his church refuses to return to purely "biblical" principles of worship.

Boreel's rejection of existing forms of religious organization and of the ministry is not only more radical than Galenus's but also based on different assumptions: his insistence on pure "Biblicism" and on the utter dispensability of ministers is the result of his rejection of natural man. In his view, if public, organized forms of religious worship cannot show that they have divine credentials, they would be better abolished; religious life cannot run the risk of contamination by the "world."

This assumption should, in keeping with the common intellectual patterns of the time, also lead him to condemn secular reason as an element of natural life. And indeed Boreel's main work would seem to entail such a condemnation.[3] But there is a little treatise he wrote called

Leben und seine Schriften, Giessen, 1911. Almost all his extant writings may be found in *Scripta Adami Borelli posthuma*, Cosmopoli, 1683.

2 Galenus Abrahamsz de Haan (1622–1706), medical doctor and Mennonite activist, one of the central figures (along with the mystic and hebraicist Adam Boreel, the Chiliast Daniel de Breen, and Michael Comans) of the non-denominational Collegiant movement and the cause of a notorious split, in 1664, within the Mennonite community of Amsterdam. In 1657 he wrote, together with David Spruyt, nineteen articles in which he questioned the existence of the visible community of Christ on earth. In 1660 he was condemned for his opinions by the Mennonite community. In 1664 he broke with it entirely and the Mennonites split into two distinct communities, one rigorously conservative, the other non-denominational. (The weakened Mennonite movement did not begin to regain something approaching unity until the eighteenth century.) He published a variety of theological, catechetical and polemical texts and continued until his death to teach in the community. There is no trace of any "rationalist" leanings in his writings; he did not consider himself a philosopher and scorned speculative theology. His arguments are based only on the Bible and he quotes only established Christian authorities. Paradoxically, it is only in his mystical treatise on religion experienced through reason - and even then only in the title and in the first few sections - that one can discern arguments which attempt to go beyond the Bible.

3 In addition to condemning denominations and the symbols of faith, Boreel also condemned universities, as hotbeds of non-legitimate, extra-Biblical and

The Golden Chain of Christianity, where we find a curious attempt – curious but very characteristic of its time – to set out "rational" arguments for the mystical doctrine of unity with God.[4]

The *Golden Chain* promises to provide knowledge of God "through reason, Holy Scripture and internal divine approval." This it attempts to do by a lengthy proof, set out in the form of syllogisms. Its conclusion is that man's pre-eminent goal, the only goal both of his reason and of his heart – the goal of unity with God – can be achieved only if he purges himself of his (human) nature and assumes a nature similar to God's. Only by eliminating everything that divides him from his Creator can man assimilate all the divine qualities and achieve perfect and lasting unity with God[5] – "*unio constans atque perseverans cum Deo*"; and the way to achieve this is by following the example of Christ. The whole proof is intended to demonstrate that the practice of religion is not only man's highest but his most rational duty: "*rationalissimum et excelentissimum hominis officium.*"

This little treatise, in which the cult of "reason" is combined with the ideal of mystical deification, is very different from the most common forms of classical mysticism: there is no principle of passivity, no ideal of *caritas pura,* no contempt for natural cognition as an instrument of unity. The combination of rationalism and Christian spiritualism is undoubted testimony of the "Cartesian invasion" in religious life. Its progress can be observed in various forms in non-denominational Dutch theology in the second half of the seventeenth century.

    therefore anti-Biblical "theologizing." See also Gottfried Arnold, Kirchen und Ketzer-Historie, Vierter Teil, Frankfurt a.M., 1700, ch.III, p. 68).

4 *Concatenatio aurea christiana, Sive cognitio Dei, ac Domini nostri Jesu Christi. Proposita secundum Rationem, S. Scripturam, atque internam divinam Approbationem. Exacte ac simpliciter composita per Adamum Boreel,* Amsterdam 1678. This is a posthumous work and we do not know when it was written. The Dutch text has not survived. In Boreel's Scripta posthuma the *Concatenatio* appears under a different title and in a different translation.

5 *Concatenatio aurea christiana,* A2, v.: "Quare, cum hinc manifestum sit, quod fortis ille appetitus secundum intellectum prorsus, et debeat, et possit in Deo acquiescere, tanquam in unico, planeque sufficienti bono, ea etiam de causa homo satis capere posset, quod illa, quae diversi generis sunt, sese invicem plena cum sufficientia frui nequeant; et propterea, quod ista Deo dissimilis natura humana arcenda sit, et in eius locum Deo similis natura succedere debeat, in qua homo semper plena sufficientia acquiescere desiderat . . . et consequenter homo removere debebit omnia illa, quae huic naturae ex rationali applicatione contraria sunt atque praeterea sibi, suisque actionibus acquiret divinam illam naturam ex applicatione istorum attributorum divinorum rationali, quo possit, se ipso iam in similitudine cum Deo existente, in sufficientia plena cum Deo uniri."

Daniel de Breen and Non-Denominational Chiliasticism

Another example of the influence of this "Cartesian invasion" on religious thought in Holland is Daniel de Breen, co-founder of the Amsterdam Collegiants and prophet of *parousia*, which would restore the true Church of Christ on earth.[6] De Breen's education had been shaped by the early Remonstrant movement, and he retained certain elements of it: his ideals of toleration, his aversion to fanaticism and his dismissive attitude towards all churches (which ultimately led to his break with the Society) all testify to this. He had certainly read the classic Remonstrant texts: he quotes Castellio in the introduction to his main Chiliastic treatise. But the Chiliastic expectations harbored by De Breen were not a part of authentic Remonstrantism; it is possible that he was infected with Chiliasticism in Strasbourg, by the Strasbourg sectarians, who retained old Anabaptist traditions. But neither the Remonstrants nor the Strasbourg sectarians could have been the source of his rationalist phraseology; this, too, must be considered as symptomatic of the Cartesian trend which had been exerting an increasing influence over Dutch theologians over the past forty years.

Chiliastic imaginings are a central theme in all de Breen's writings, both in his extensive commentaries on both parts of Scripture, amounting to almost 600 folio pages, and in his other texts; they form the basic substance of his thought. In the *Treatise on the Glorious Kingdom of the Church which will be established on Earth through Christ*, in the *Treatise on the Nature of Christ's Kingdom*, in the *Brief Demonstration of the Truth of the Christian Religion* (a polemical text against the Jews), in his dialogue about the truth of Christianity – in all of these the hope of restoring the Savior's kingdom on earth is the main theme.[7]

6   Biographical information (citing van Slee, pp. 135–38): born in Haarlem in 1594, Daniel de Breen joined the Remonstrant movement at an early age. At the time of the Dordrecht synod he was secretary to Episcopius; after the synod and the setback suffered by the Remonstrants he left . . . Haarlem and went to Strasbourg, where he may have encountered Schwedenkfelders, and where he remained until 1621, when he returned to Haarlem and soon afterwards left the Remonstrants – probably because, like Camphuysen, he was disenchanted with their denominationalist tendencies and their views on the relationship between the church and the secular world. He himself held Mennonite views on the subject. He met Boreel in Amsterdam, and together they founded a private collegium, unaffiliated to any church. He died in 1664. See also Sandius, pp. 135–37; S. Kot, *Ideologia polityczna i spoleczna Braci Polskich zwanych Arjanami*, Warsaw, 1932 (English translation: Socinianism in Poland, Boston, Star King Press, 1957), pp. 112–14.

7   Daniel de Breen, *Opera Theologica*, ed. Frans Kuyper (Amsterdam, 1664), contains 1. Breves in vetus et novum testamentum Annotationes; 2. Tractatus de regno ecclesiae glorioso per Christum in terris erigendo; 3. De qualitate regni

Thus to call de Breen simply a "rationalist," even in the religious sense, would be a colossal exaggeration. True, the guidelines for the interpretation of Scripture which he sets out are indeed examples of what is popularly known as "religious rationalism": he sets out a number of technical principles of interpretation, such as the comparative study of texts, the consideration of the author's purpose and of the historical circumstances in which the given text was written, stylistic and linguistic analysis, and so on (all this of course assuming the fundamental recognition of the holiness of the Bible), and formulates the following general principle: "We may not adopt any interpretation of Holy Scripture that contradicts either itself or common sense or the clear evidence of the external senses."[8] Similarly, in the *Brief Demonstration* he writes that of all religions, "the most authentic and truly divine is that whose rules about serving God are the most perfect and in the best accord with the sources of common sense,"[9] and that among the ways in which Christianity demonstrates its superiority to other religions is that "it does not prescribe anything that is not entirely in accordance with reason."[10] But these and similar declarations turn out to be the extent of his rationalist fervor.

If by religious rationalism within Christianity we mean embracing the principle that canonical literature is to be interpreted in such a way as to adapt its content to the demands of "natural" reason, then the above-cited prescriptions do indeed come under that heading. From this point of view they are far more "rationalistic" than the principle, common in peripatetic variations of scholasticism but also encountered in Socinian writings, of *"non contra, sed supra rationem"* – for this principle does not admit the mysteries of the faith among the things that can be brought under the control of reason. But they are less rationalistic than the approach (of which Spinoza's *Tractatus Theologico-Politicus* is an example) which treats Biblical texts as ordinary historical documents, and must consequently renounce any attempt to reconcile the opinions contained therein with secular knowledge and the demands of secular reason.

domini nostri Jesu Christi; 4. Amica disputatio adversus Judaeos; 5. Colloquium inter duos de veritate religionis christianae; 6. Brevis demonstratio religionis christianae veritatis. Tractatus de regno ecclesiae glorioso, together with a commentary to the Book of Revelation (Annotata in Apocalypsin S. Johannis) and a few minor commentaries on the Gospels. Quotes are taken from the earlier, anonymous edition.
8   Breves . . . annotationes, Introduction, p. 8.
9   Brevis demonstratio, p. 100.
10 *Ibid.*

De Breen's principles are analogous to those published two years after his death by Ludwig Meyer in his notorious treatise *"Philosophia S. Scripturae Interpres,"* but in de Breen's case they remain mere phrases; his exegetical commentaries are not organized around them, and indeed are no different in their methodology from the work of the dozens of theologians of his day who were quite free of "rationalist" aspirations of any sort. De Breen made no attempt to argue that the content of Biblical stories and prophecies can be confirmed independently of the Bible: that it can be established as true by "the evidence of the senses" or by "common sense." His exegetical principles remain on a superficial level; unlike Meyer, de Breen seems to have no more than brushed against the "Cartesian invasion." It left its mark on his phraseology but did not fundamentally alter his way of thinking.

But De Breen's chiliastic longings deserve attention as an attempt to reformulate, with the aid of different conceptual categories, the same critique of churches that other nondenominational writers made directly, without a "futuristic" context. His writings are also noteworthy because, like Boreel's but unlike Galenus's, they are permeated with the idea that the natural world and the Christian life are fundamentally, radically opposed and utterly irreconcilable.

De Breen, arguing from Biblical evidence and appealing to the authority of the early church fathers – Justin, Iraeneus, Tertullian, Lactantius and others – to lend weight to his arguments, predicts the Second Coming of the Messiah: Christ (whom, like both Boreel[11] and Galenus,[12] he interprets in the unitarian spirit: as a man who in reward for his obedience was given the power to cleanse us of our sins and our weaknesses[13]) will come down to earth in order to destroy the kingdom of the oppressors in the name of God and establish the rule of Christian people; and when the kingdom of God is established, it will last until the end of the world, when Christ will hand it over to his Father.[14] This king-

---

11 *Annotata in Apocalypsin*, 241: "Qui pro potestate sua, quam per obedientiam qua patri obediens fuit usque ad mortem, accepit, purgavit nos a reatu et culpa omnium peccatorum nostrorum ac porro purgat et tandem penitus purgabit ab omnibus infirmitatibus naturae huic mortali annexis."

12 Galenus, Korte Grondstellingen, pp. 24–25 (Jesus as a demiurge, created before the world and mediating in its creation); Anleyding, 2 (only the Father is truly God); Korte Grondstellingen, 69 (denial of the individuality of the Holy Spirit).

13 See *Concatenatio*, p. A3v, where Jesus is an example of deification.

14 *Tractatus de regno*, p. 12: "De hoc autem regno dicit Daniel quod non relinquetur alteri populo, sed semel sanctis traditum perpetuo apus illos manebit, hoc est donec Christus supremus hujus regni administrator illud patri suo tradiderit, quod non nisi cum caeli terraeque interitu futurum constat."

dom, according to de Breen, will be a spiritual, not a material one, and its subjects will have mastery over their bodies and their bodily desires. However, it will be established on earth, not in heaven; it will destroy all false religions and topple all earthly kingdoms; it will encompass the globe, utterly and entirely. The people of God will wrest power away from the beast and keep it forever, and rule over all earthly kings and nations.[15] Those who claim that Christ's Second Coming means the Last Judgment are false interpreters, says de Breen, for it means nothing of the sort: the end of the corrupt world will not be the end of the world altogether, but the triumph of God's spirit on earth. It is not clear exactly how long this kingdom of God on earth will last (De Breen's "a thousand years" should not be taken literally); we are told, however, that it will last a long time, and that the holy people in it will live much longer than people live nowadays – a thousand years or more. The whole of Israel will be converted and will come to Christ, and will be accepted. Christ himself will remain at his Father's right hand and will not come down to earth in visible form (it would in any case detract from his majesty to assume a body for a second time); he will rule over the earth spiritually from the heavens, doing his work through the agency of angels and through the heavenly powers bestowed upon him by his Father.[16] The Messiah will subdue the whore of Babylon (the Church of Rome) and all her daughters (the other false churches), and the beast of the Apocalypse (the Pope), and all the false prophets. He will not do this through the just, for the disciples of Christ are commanded to love their enemies; thus he will not order the just to cut them down with the sword and wreak bloody revenge on them, but, just as God brought about the destruction of Babylon not at the hands of the chosen people, but by the Persians and the Medes, so he will cause the whore of Babylon to be destroyed by those who committed acts of depravity with her. Having passed judgment on the godless, Christ will transfer rule over his kingdom to his people, gathered together from all nations, and those who sowed with tears shall reap the fruits of their faith with joy. Satan will be cast into the abyss, and those who refuse to worship Christ in their

15 *Ibid.*, p. 37: ". . . occidi bestiam et potestate sua privari, sic tamen ut propterea non cesset imperium omne inter populos mundi, sed populus sanctus in bestiae locum succedeus, accipit imperium, dominationem, maiestatem, regnum super reliquas linguarum omnium nationes, ut obediant ei sicut olim bestiae: haec quae potestas nullo unquam tempore ab illo auferenda, nec alteri populo tradenda dicitur, quemadmodum bestiae ademta dominatio eaque sanctis tradita fuerat. . . . Est igitur hujusmodi majestas, dominatus et amplitudo, quae non in coelis sed sub coelis hoc est in terra constituetur, seque extendet super omnes ejus habitatores tam principes quam subditos," etc.

16 *Ibid.*, pp. 176–79.

hearts will be forced to bow to his rule. In this new kingdom peace will reign; the faithful will enjoy the constant protection of God, and will be granted knowledge of divine mysteries; there will be health and plenty, and children will be born to hundred-year-olds. There will be no more use for prophets, doctors or ministers; the universal spiritual ministry of the faithful will supplant the old religions, as well the old material laws.[17] All the external signs of religion – temples, rituals, fasts, holy days, dietary laws – will be abolished, and God will be worshipped only in spirit.[18] Justice will reign without the need for laws, for the law of God will be engraved forever in the hearts of the faithful. The houses will be of crystal and precious stones and the people will all be splendid (the least of them will be like David); there will be moderation in the use of material goods and perfect happiness will reign. We cannot know when or where God will establish this earthly paradise, but the coming of the New Jerusalem will be heralded by terrible signs – war, famine, plague, floods, earthquakes, falling stars and solar eclipses.

What we have here is the very model of a Christian utopia. In religious life the function of such utopias is the same as that of secular utopias in secular life: they express a negative attitude towards the existing state of affairs by positively describing an ideal state of affairs. Thus to say that Christ will establish his kingdom and true church on earth is tantamount to saying that no existing religious community is under his care (and hence the natural suspicion with which all organized churches treat millenarians). For de Breen, the idea of a non-denominational Christianity, utterly purged of all church affiliations and organizations, all ministerial institutions and external signs of religion, is linked, in a curious way, with dreams of a quite worldly nature: an end to states and laws and wars, an abundance of worldly goods, and mortal people showered with the joys of mortals – good health, knowledge, longevity, peace and even richness and splendor. Of course there are considerable differences between de Breen's utopia and Rabelais: material pleasures are moderate, in keeping with customary Christian principles. Nevertheless, it is hardly ascetic, and its temporal qualities are made to sound extremely alluring.

17 *Ibid.*, p. 215: "Non indigebunt amplius Apostolis, prophetis, Euangelistis, pastoribus et doctribus ut in principio, qui introducant eos in cognitionem filii Dei" and p. 218: "Cum carnalium sacerdotum abrogatione, etiam carnales leges quae sub eorum ministerio obtinebant et quarum respectu instituti erant, abrogari oportuit."

18 *Ibid.*, p. 220: "Imo totus eorum cultus erit spiritualis ipsique universi et singuli, utpote quod Deus in templa et sanctuaria sibi consecraverit, neque lapideis templis, neque corporalibus ullis signis, ut in viis ejus ambulent, indigebunt."

There is a reason for this: here, the opposition between the natural world and the Christian life, between natural man and man as the subject of Christ, the Community of Christ and the Gospels, between "nature" and "spirit," differs in scope from its Spiritualist equivalent. It encompasses mainly the authority of ecclesiastical institutions, and does not involve a fundamental rejection of physical life. Its limited scope is clearly evident in de Breen's extensive commentaries on the Apocalypse and his treatises on the kingdom of Christ. After some lengthy railing against the harlot of Rome and the Pope as Antichrist, who claims divine attributes for himself,[19] and after an assurance that those who remain faithful to Christ will receive the prophetic spirit and will become equal to him,[20] de Breen proceeds to extol the glories of the spiritual kingdom in its present form. All the laws of this kingdom, all its weapons, its courts and its punishments are purely spiritual. No one has physical authority over anyone else: "Our Savior does not simply condemn secular authorities; he makes it plain that they will have no place among the subjects of his kingdom, whom he has called to a different sort of greatness. But apart from this they will remain as before."[21] Christ's commandments do not abolish the authority of parents over children, husbands over wives or masters over servants; but Christian masters must abandon their rights over their servants and treat them as their equals and free men.[22] For while the Christian religion does not abolish differences of status, it does abolish constraints: Christians should voluntarily renounce the rights with which earthly laws have endowed them. For their kingdom is not of this world, and they are but pilgrims on this earth. Hence they want no dealings with earthly authorities. The earthly and Christian kingdoms should not come into contact with each other, for they are based on conflicting principles.[23] Nevertheless, regardless of the *parousia* which is to come, they can continue to co-exist without risk

---

19 See *Annotata in Apocalypsin . . .* , pp. 303–37.
20 "Nam qui testimonium Jesu habet, hoc est qui facultatem praedicandi, aut palam profitendi euangelii a Deo consecutus est, sicut omnes Christiani, alii magis, alii minus consecuti sunt, is etiam spiritus prophetiae habet, plusque videt et sapit in rebus Dei absconditis quam prophetae ac reges. . . . Hac ergo in parte conservum se agnoscit et aequales sibi facit credentes. N. Testam., utpote quos communis Dominus Jesus ad aequalem secum honorem in arcanis hisce cognoscendis assumserit."
21 *De Qualitate regni. . .* , p. 389.
22 *Ibid.*, p. 392: "Utcumque ergo leges hujus mundi potestatem dent cogendi, Christianus hoc suo jure lubens cedit, propter communem domunum servos habens tanquam homines quos natura liberos sibique aequales fecerit . . ."
23 *Ibid.*, p. 395: ". . . regnum istud its opponi regnis hujus mundi, ut nullo modo inter se misceantur . . . omnia contrario modo se habent ac in mundo."

of mutual contamination. The laws of Christ's kingdom are stricter than earthly laws, for they equate the intention with the act, and thus punish mere anger and impure desires, independently of the acts they might lead to; such laws would destroy all "external communities," and hence cannot be applied in secular states.[24] The kingdom of Christ in this sense already exists – it is the church of Christ, but it is not any particular church or collectivity: its faithful are scattered throughout the earth, subjects of its spiritual authority.[25] The law which governs them differs in fundamental ways both from the law of Moses and from secular law: it commands them to forgive trespasses and forbids them to engage in war and to hold official positions in the secular world. At the same time it commands them to abstain from revolting against secular authorities, however tyrannical or idolatrous – not from fear, but because this is what the Christian conscience dictates.[26] It also encourages material as well as spiritual poverty (this latter being humility), but as something voluntarily assumed, not simply accepted when it is sent by fate.[27]

From the whole of this long argument the following conclusions can be retained: that with regard to the existing, corrupt world de Breen advocates a radical non-denominationalism and the idea of an invisible church, without ministers and without external forms of worship or religious symbols. He evidently regards existing church institutions as belonging to the corrupt secular world – to the realm of those "earthly powers" which he scorns; and although only the Church of Rome, an object of particular loathing, is singled out by name and favored with curses, other, less sinister churches and religious communities also fail to achieve inclusion in the kingdom of Christ. And since the subjects of the invisible kingdom are enjoined to avoid contact with temporal powers,

24 *Ibid.*, p. 400: "Hae sunt fundamentales regni Christi leges, quibus positis prudentissimi, quique politici censent, societatis omnis externae fundamenta convelli protinus ac labefactari debere, ut quae sublata malorum resistentia et defensione corporali neutiquam stare posse credentur. Ideo nullus unquam legislator its desipuit ut hujusmodi praecepta cum politicis suis misceret."

25 *Ibid.*, pp. 402–3: ". . . si Ecclesiam intellegimus, ut par est, non de particulari alique coetu aut congregatione, cujusmodi plures esse possunt in uno regno unave repub., sed de Christi regno hic in terris constituto, aut de populo illius per orbem universum disperso, quem ubique uno semper modo gubernat, non est extra ecclesiam quod in Christi populo fit, et quocumque in coetu seu publico seu privato fidelem constituas, considerari semper debet ut subditus hujus regni."

26 *Ibid.*, pp. 421–34.

27 Daniel de Breen, *Brevis explicatio quinti, sexti et septimi capitis Mat.*, p. 446.

the prohibition presumably includes existing churches. De Breen seems to be implying that the truly faithful will cut themselves off from all visible religious communities, as he himself has done; certainly they will not want to hold positions as ministers in them.

In this regard De Breen clearly goes much further in his non-denominationalism than Galenus, who restricts himself to the suggestion that existing religious communities should not be acknowledged as charismatic, i.e., that their ministers and priests should not be considered as divinely ordained. De Breen considers that in the temporal world the opposition between Christian and secular values is absolute; nonetheless, Christians may express their rejection of the latter only by a passive refusal. However, the promised kingdom of the Messiah on earth will abolish almost all *institutions of political power*, including the church, while providing its Christian people not only with spiritual freedom but also with an abundance of earthly goods.

Thus the temporal paradise prophesied in de Breen's utopia does not involve an opposition between "natural" and reborn man; it seems, on the contrary, to imply the possibility of reconciling the two. It is, of course, a passive utopia, for we have no means of hastening the longed-for *parousia*, and can only wait patiently for its advent; but it promises ultimate fulfillment both in body and in spirit. De Breen's rejection of "natural" man is more radical than Galenus's as far as the existing world is concerned, but it melts away in his vision of the future world – along with something that de Breen really did strongly condemn in the "natural" world, namely the spiritual and secular systems of power. This, too, is melted away in the future world. There is also (at least in his extant writings) no trace of any ideal of *theosis* or mystical union with God. He writes in praise of reason, and even if his praise does not go beyond general declarations, still it imposes a degree of moderation on his condemnation of the "natural" world. De Breen's chiliastic visions, irenic and involving no force of arms; his passive rejection of the existing world with no prospect of its reform; his Christian ideal of estrangement from a world which by nature must be such as it is – all this betrays a consciousness of loss: it is a dream proper to people who have been removed, or are conscious of gradually being removed, from their "temporal" positions, with no hope of return. It is a form of anti-denominationalism of which it may reasonably be supposed that it expresses, in all its various and individual forms, the religious consciousness of the old, educated, urban patrician class, pushed out of its old positions in the social hierarchy and searching for ways to regain its lost paradise through mysticism or through hopes of a New Jerusalem. The difference between this and Galenus's program is evident, despite their surface similarities. Nor is it surprising, in light of this, that Galenus eventually left the Boreelist circle.

Balling, Irenic Mysticism and the Problem of the "Spinoza Circle"

The name of Pieter Balling has been immortalized in the work of Spinoza scholars, for Balling, like Jelles, was part of the young Baruch's circle: a set of friends who used to meet in Amsterdam in the second half of the 1650s, and continued to meet (as we know from Simon de Vrees' letter of 1663[28]) even after Spinoza moved to Rijnsburg in 1660. It was within this "collegium" and its atmosphere and discussions that Spinoza's first work, discovered only two hundred years later, was composed: *A Short Treatise on God, Man and his Happiness*. It was also in this circle that successive chapters of his *Ethics* were debated as Spinoza sent them to Amsterdam. The ideological stance of the "Spinoza circle" has been the subject of debate ever since Meinsma[29] collected the basic facts about it (little augmented since then). Carl Gebhardt, persistent in his efforts to interpret Spinoza's doctrine as a form of *"religio metaphysica,"* attributes great significance to Spinoza's contacts with the Collegiants (among whom he numbers both Balling and Jelles) and tries to demonstrate fundamental similarities of thought between the *Ethics* and the mystical treatises of his friends.[30] Madeleine Francès,[31] in the interpretation she published in 1937, tends to the contrary view: her conclusion (based on documents already known at the time) is that the "Spinoza circle" did not consist of Collegiants or even, more generally, Christian reformers, but of freethinkers, *esprits libres*, free of any religious affiliation and interested in scientific rather than religious matters. With regard to Balling and Jelles her argument may be summed up as follows: they were not Collegiants, but they were connected with Galenus's party in the Mennonite community (which as far as we know they never left); thus Gebhardt is wrong to consider Spinoza's friendship with them as proof of a Collegiant influence on his thought. Moreover, neither Balling nor Jelles – both more interested in religious matters than other members of their circle – was among Spinoza's closest friends: Spinoza's letters to Jelles are rather official in tone, and do not touch on any fundamental issues of his philosophy.

28 See Spinoza, Epist. VIII, *Opera* IV, ed. Gebhardt.
29 K.O. Meinsma, *Spinoza en zijn kring*, The Hague, 1986.
30 Carl Gebhardt, Die Religion Spinozas, *Archuv für Geschichte der Philosophie*, vol. XLI, 1932.
31 M. Francès, *Spinoza dans les pays néerlandais de la seconde moitié du XVIIe siècle*, Paris, 1937.

These arguments do not seem very strong. Spinoza's letters to Jelles survive only in printed form, where, as is the case with all the letters in the *Opera posthuma*, all personal elements have been expunged from them; and they seem no different in tone from the correspondence with Meyer. It is true that they do not touch on any of the central themes of Spinoza's philosophy, but it is unclear what this is supposed to prove: there is no trace of any correspondence between Spinoza and the libertine Adrian Koerbagh, for example – who, according to Frances, *was* a member of Spinoza's circle – and, conversely, no doubt that Spinoza discussed issues central to his philosophy in his letters to Blyenbergh, who definitely was *not* one of his friends. As for the question of whether Balling and Jelles were Collegiants, it must be considered in light of the same arguments which apply to Galenus's separatist church in general. To wit: the Collegiant movement defined itself negatively, through its protest against all the institutional means whereby exclusive and dogmatic elements of positive religion, such as churches, official creeds and the ministry, were created and perpetuated. If Galenus's church, Mennonite at the outset, was influenced by Collegiant ideals and transformed in their spirit, there are, in the absence of any central authority, no criteria for determining whether it was "still" part of the Mennonite movement or "already" a sort of Collegium. Internal reform or schism? The question is easily settled in the case of both the Catholic and the Calvinist church, but in the case of the Mennonites it is often a pointless one.

Finally, distinguishing between freethinkers and Christian reformers is a delicate matter, especially in Protestant countries. The escape from denominational bonds was characteristic of reformers, who were preoccupied with religious questions: writers like Boreel and de Breen, or mystics and prophets like Rothe, Serrarius and Brill, none of whom were affiliated with any church. They can hardly be considered products of a rationalist current. Scholars, on the other hand, preoccupied with scientific rather than religious study, tended mostly to remain with their churches, but gravitated towards deism, which allowed them to go on with their studies or experiments while maintaining their faith – tolerant, free from fanaticism and modest in content – in the basic dogmas of Christianity. Of Spinoza's correspondents, Oldenburg is an example of this current. Thus if the members of Spinoza's circle no longer considered themselves Christians, as a letter from de Vries seems to imply (their task being to "defend the truth against Christians"), this is no grounds for assuming that they were non-believers and libertines or scholars with no religious interests. On the contrary: by a peculiar paradox, it is precisely those that declare themselves to have abandoned Christianity who are often passionately interested in religious questions.

They can be people who, having taken their anti-denominationalism to its furthest point, do not feel bound even to an irenic form of "general Christianity," but want to practice Christianity in their own way, independently of the great collective church bodies. Ludwig Meyer was involved in medicine, philology and the theatre, but it was his work in biblical exegesis that brought him fame. Jan Rieuwertsz published the writings of Descartes, but also treatises by Camphuysen and Galenus. Adrian Koerbagh was undoubtedly a libertine, but we know that his younger brother Jan studied theology and went on to be a theologian.

Religious and reformist passions could, and often did, invade even the most illustrious scientific minds. This, after all, was an age when people of the caliber of Komensky or Swammerdam bowed in prostrate admiration before the ravings of the mad visionary Antonina Bourignon; when Nils Stensen, the creator of modern paleontology, became a Catholic fanatic, and Newton wrote commentaries on the Apocalypse; the age both of the chemist and mystic van Helmont and of an astrologer named Kepler. Hence neither the presence or absence of church affiliation nor the presence or absence of religious interests are good criteria for distinguishing between scholars and religious reformers. The first would place Spinoza with the mystical prophets and the most zealous fanatics of the New Jerusalem; the second would place Descartes on one side and Grotius and Leibniz on the other.

Thus in order to distinguish between reformers and scholars we must seek, among the approaches to religion typical of the time, a different model as a criterion. One possible such model is provided by the deist idea of *religio naturalis*. This deist approach was popular among natural scientists, but also among some theologians. It was characterized by a kind of denominational adiaphorism: an indifference toward all creeds arising not from a rejection of religion altogether (this was very rare), but rather from the belief that in the domain of religion one should accept only that which can be established by natural reason and reject entanglements in the incomprehensible dogmas of particular religious communities. Exponents of this approach were not, as a rule, prone to reformatory zeal; they were content to remain in their church communities, albeit without taking their catechisms literally, and did not fight openly for their principles.

Another possible model is provided by those whose non-denominationalism, rather than springing from an intellectual spirit of indifference, was dictated by religious principles. These were people who wanted the reform of religious life as a whole, not just the reform of some particular church. This group comprised both irenists, with their principles of "general Christianity" based on ecumenical ideals, and individual Spiritualists, prophets, mystics and saviors of the world who rejected all organized communities on principle, as well as founders of new sects (such as Gichtel or Labadie). While some of them (like Boreel and de Breen) were susceptible to rationalist influences, their primary motivation was religious; the rationalist spirit could modify their arguments or their way of thinking to a greater or lesser extent, but it did not define their goals. The early "Spinoza circle" was made up largely of people from this group. They remained within the sphere of Cartesian influence, but their interests were not those of the Cartesian-influenced doctors and physicists of the period: they were preoccupied with "ultimate questions" – questions inspired by religion, though sometimes couched in the indifferent language of metaphysics. Of this circle, Ludwig Meyer and Adrian Koerbagh were certainly among the most emancipated in terms of their religious interests; but Balling, Jelles and Rieuwertsz all fit the type of the non-denominational reformer, with religious questions enjoying undoubted predominance in their intellectual life. Balling and Jelles's writings and papers, the latter's in particular, testify to this "rationalist invasion" into the Christian world.

Pieter Balling,[32] an Amsterdam merchant, was an educated man. He knew Spanish, which came in useful on his business trips to the Iberian Peninsula; he also knew Latin and Greek, and translated Spinoza's *Principia* into Dutch. In spite of this he was not entirely free of popular superstitions, visible among other things in his questions to Spinoza about prophetic signs. His little treatise *The Light upon the Candlestick*, published anonymously in 1662, was for some time thought, because of its ambiguous title,[33] to be the work of the well-known Quaker activist Wilhelm Ames, and indeed a year later an English translation of it appeared under Ames's name. It also appeared, with the same attribution, as an appendix to the fifth and sixth editions of Wilhelm Sewel's apologetic history of the Quakers.[34] Sewel, a friend of Ames's (Ames had converted Sewel's parents to Quakerism), is firm in his assurances that Ames approved of the treatise, though he was not its author. Sewel himself suspected that the author was Boreel, whose *Opera Posthuma* (1683) were augmented by the inclusion of a Latin translation ("*Lucerna super*

---

32 Balling's biography is almost entirely unknown; all we know is that he was dead by 1669. A letter from Spinoza from July 1664 (Epist. XVII) provides no biographical information except that a child of Balling's died at around that time.

33 Peter Balling, Het licht opt den Kandelaar Dienende tot opmerkinge van de voornaamste dingen; in het boekje genaamt De verborgentheden van het Rijke Ghodts, etc. tegen Galenus Abrahamsz en zijn Toestemmers etc. verhandelt en beschreven door William Ames, 1662.

34 See William Sewel, *The History of the Rise, Increase and Progress of the Christian People called Quakers*, 5th ed., London, 1811; 6th ed. London, 1834.

Candelabrum").[35] It was not until 1684 that the original Dutch version was reissued, published, together with Jelles's *Profession*, by Rieuwertsz, with a preface explaining past misattributions.

This mystical treatise, written in obscure and convoluted language, does indeed bring to mind Quaker writings, mainly by its symbolic references to "inner light." Balling advocates a mystical, non-discursive contact with God, who according to him lives in us as an inner light. He dwells on the imperfections of language and the conflicts and misunderstandings to which it inevitably gives rise, unavoidable because we have no other way of communicating with each other. Most people, he says, uncritically accept everything they are told about their faith, and just as uncritically reject all that comes from other faiths; and yet every faith, because it is expressed in language, is prone to the same errors and gives rise to the same conflicts and disputes – disputes where the advantage lies not with those with a clearer understanding, but with those more skilled in the use of words. Balling offers a road to salvation that by-passes language and nullifies the power of words: "We do not wish," he writes, "to take you away from one human community only to draw you into another. . . . we offer you a way of achieving happiness and salvation by and through yourself."[36] For, he goes on, this highest and most precious of all things that we seek – the inner light of truth, the source of infallible knowledge, Christ, the Spirit, the Word; whatever we call it, we all mean the same thing – exists in all of us; we should therefore seek it by looking within ourselves, and we shall find it. This inner light removes all possibility of doubt: it gives us certainty about things and their qualities, about truth and falsity and good and evil; it reveals our sins, justifies us and leads us to union with God. It exists in us all, even in those who have never heard of Scripture; only circumstances prevent us from seeing it. Our worldly cravings, our sins, our daily lives, our sensory contact with the things of this world, the memory of finite, transitory objects and our longing for them – all these screen from us its full shining glory, though they cannot destroy it. And it is from this light alone that all religion and knowledge of things divine can flow; it is the only source of sure instruction about life and about the path to salvation, and of our power to do good. We may be led and helped along the path to salvation, but we must first show ourselves willing to change within ourselves: we must cast off our attachment to the things of creation as in adulthood we cast off childish toys. Conversion begins from within, and it is from within, through the light which is in us, that we can reach divinity. Only through it can we understand the real meaning of words

---

35 *Ibid.*, vol. I, pp. xv–xvi.
36 Het licht . . . , p. 4.

and religious signs; without its illumination they are merely letters, empty and devoid of meaning. Whoever would understand the word of God must come into God's light. True Scripture is not letters and signs but meaning, and this meaning is revealed only to those who stand within the light from which Scripture arose, and through it experience the same illuminations that were granted to the authors of inspired books. The divinity of the Bible can be comprehended only through inner light, when we see that its content agrees with what we have witnessed for ourselves through its illumination; then we understand that both must flow from the same source. Without this light there can be no understanding of Scripture and no knowledge of God. All the signs we have express only what has been learnt directly, but by themselves they cannot reveal the truth to us; we cannot "learn" God through reading. In addition, words, which belong to the world of finite creatures, cannot adequately encompass infinite reality;[37] God cannot be described in words. We also cannot grasp Him through the visible results of His work, for these are limited in the same way; even if we see something we cannot explain by the workings of nature, this is evidence merely of our own weakness, not proof of its divine origin. Moreover, knowledge of God precedes knowledge of created things; they cannot be grasped without Him.

What places Balling within the mystical tradition is his belief that the experience of non-discursive contact with the absolute – *experimentum divinum* – is possible at all. The non-denominational nature of his mysticism is apparent in his conviction that God is revealed to us only through our inner experience: no other way of seeking and grasping Him, neither the Bible nor the creeds of particular churches nor rational proofs, has any intrinsic value. Words are secondary to experience and cannot communicate the nature of experience to anyone who has not himself experienced what they describe; everyone must make his own path to God. And what distinguishes his mysticism as specifically Quaker is, in addition to the "inner light" metaphor, his assumption that this supra-natural contact with God is in fact natural, in the sense that it is accessible to

37 *Ibid.*, p. 7: "En dewijl alle uyterlijk teken, deze kennise nootwendich moet voor onderstellen; zoo moetze onmiddelijk zonder enich uiterlijk teken wezen. Dat de tekenen een zodanigen kennisse moeten voor onder stellen, is onwedersprekelijk, want deze tekenen zouden, of woorden of uit werkingen moeten zijn. Zoo het woorden zouden zijn, man zeit voor eerst een onmogelijkheid, in de zak zelve: want woorden zijn geschapen, eb bepaalt; Ghodt di zich hier door te kennen zoud geven, is ongeschapen en onbepaalt: en derhalven is hier een oneindich verschil; alzoo dat'r geheel geen overeenkominge, noch iets is in de woorden waar doorze daar toe bequaam zouden konnen zijn."

everyone without exception, regardless of any previous knowledge they may have, even their knowledge of Scripture, and independently of exceptional grace: everyone can reach God through his own efforts, for God lives in everyone through His Word. The idea of passivity, typical of mystical writings, is absent from Balling's work, as is the idea of mystical experience being granted through exceptional, undeserved grace. Nor does he speak of deification. Lastly, what gives Balling's mysticism its Spinozan (and in a sense also Cartesian) flavor is his belief that knowledge of God necessarily precedes adequate knowledge of finite things, and that infinity cannot be grasped through its finite products.

The desire to reduce faith to its empirical foundations – not in the sense of rationalizing it by empirical evidence, but in the sense of experiencing the divine directly – was common in seventeenth century approaches to religion, and it is striking here. It is difficult, admittedly, to discern in Balling's program even the faintest trace of rationalist inspiration, and yet there are good grounds for supposing that it owes much to the influence of Descartes and Spinoza. Inner experience is a fundamental element of Descartes' metaphysics; and the Spinozan "intuition," defined in the *Treatise on the Improvement of the Understanding* as a strictly rational process, acquires different characteristics in the *Short Treatise*, where it unquestionably involves elements of non-discursive experience of the absolute. And later, in the *Ethics*, it retains this dual nature: it is both an existential and a cognitive process – an act of intellectual identification with the infinite.[38] The idea that the finite is grasped as the negation of the infinite appears both in Descartes and in Spinoza, and while in Descartes' doctrine its presence is contingent, in Spinoza's it is an essential, constitutive element. And a metaphysics where the absolute has cognitive priority over finite things naturally involves the view that this prior knowledge of the absolute cannot be articulated or communicated (or simply that it belongs to direct experience). Balling espouses a simplified form of this metaphysics and uses it as the foundation of his non-denominational, mystical approach to religion.

The (inevitable) consequences of this mysticism for religious life – the rejection of all creeds and all dogmatic content, all positive assertions, in religion – are set out by Balling in two independent texts, polemical and purely circumstantial, in which Balling supports the Galenists in an internal dispute within the Mennonite community. The dispute was between the "innovators" (*nieu-gezinde*) and the traditional-

---

38 For a detailed treatment of this question see L. Kolakowski, *Jednostka i nieskonczonosc: wolnosc i antynomie wolnosci w filozofii Spinozy* ("The Individual and Infinity: Freedom and Antinomies of Freedom in Spinoza"), Warsaw, PWN, 1958, pp. 51 ff., 218 ff.

ists (*out-gezinde*) – or, as Balling calls them, the "moderates" (*moderate*) and the "rigorists" (*precijse*) – and concerned the special powers of ministers and the autonomy of a particular community. Balling argued, in support of the liberals, that the Mennonite tradition demands complete and unqualified democracy in the community;[39] everything must be decided by a majority of votes, and all votes, whether of the deacon or minister or any of the other brethren, are of equal weight. This equality lies at the very foundations of the Mennonite movement, he argued, and means that ministers (*dienaren*), appointed and dismissed by the whole brotherhood, must bow to the will of the majority in every decision. Nor do ministers from outside have the right to interfere in the affairs of the church or infringe its autonomy: the college of ministers is not a separate body, he said, and cannot decide anything without the agreement of the brethren.[40]

In a long reply to the conservatives' rebuttal of these arguments, Balling condemns abuses of power and inveighs against ministers who claim the right to govern the souls of the faithful.[41] His arguments here appeal not just to tradition but to the community's founding principles: he stresses that the Mennonite movement was created by people who in good faith set out their own interpretation of Scripture and consists of people united by a belief in certain principles (adult baptism, the symbolic nature of baptism and the Lord's Supper, the prohibition against the swearing of oaths and the use of weapons, the prohibition against holding office) who gather together and from among their body choose ministers for the carrying out of purely formal functions. Here, very much in the spirit of Galenus, is an interpretation of the church as a purely human, non-charismatic community, with an emphasis on the principle of tolerance towards the different opinions within it. Balling expresses particular contempt for denominations and official creeds, and in a

39 See Verdediging van de Regering der Doopsgezinde Gemeente, Die men de vereenigde Vlamingen, Vriezen, en Hooghduytsche noemt, Binnen Amsterdam, Zijnde een Wederlegging van het zoo genoemde Notwendig Bericht, etc., Amsterdam, 1663 (the text is signed "P.B.")

40 *Ibid.*, p. 17: "Het Collegie der Dienaren is geen Lichaem apart, beneffens noch in tegenstellig der gemeente, vermag ook in generley wijze enige de alderminste ordre, of wet te maken, zonder kennisse en aprobatie van de Gemeente; of ingevalle zy het doet, de Gemeente vermag die te vernietigen, en hen na gelegentheit van zaken te censureren."

41 See Nader Verdediging van de Regering der Doopsgezinde Gemeente . . . etc., Amsterdam, 1664 (signed, as above, by the initials "P.B.") The attribution of this text to Balling is confirmed by, among other things, a sentence on p. 34, about the difference between sign and meaning, which repeats almost word for word a phrase in Het licht . . .

lengthy argument against them criticizes a proposed formulation, in twelve articles, of Mennonite dogma, presented to the Galenists by a group of conservative ministers. He analyzes this proposed catechism word by word, pointing out its ambiguities and the questions and different interpretations to which certain of its phrases might give rise. How, he asks, for example, are we to understand God's "unity"? Is "eternity" an eternal present or an infinite succession? What is "incomprehensibility"? In what way have we inherited the sins of our ancestors and does the acceptance of this inheritance as a fact entail a belief in predestination? Can we avail ourselves of what Christ has done for us without believing in him? What are the external signs by which a visible church can be recognized? Can we be saved if we are not baptized? What does it mean to exclude someone from the church on the strength of the authority of God's word? What is heresy? And so on, with as many questions as there were words and every answer giving rise to new questions. His conclusion was that the new catechism, far from uniting the community, would give rise to new disputes, and that all attempts to formulate denominational dogma were doomed to failure. The only solution was to abandon them and practice tolerance towards all views.

Balling's writings are perhaps more striking than Galenus's *apologia* in the clear insight they provide into the essence of the dispute within the Mennonite church. It was a dispute about the autonomous authority of the priestly caste: this latter, invoking in its support the idea of the charismatic visible church of Christ, the charismatic qualities of rites and the divine nature of the faith, had arrogated to itself certain powers which defenders of the church as a democratic community questioned, insisting that ministers had no more authority than ordinary elected administrators. The essential issue was one of authority: all the internal controversies in which the members of the community were engaged – "human" interpretations of the church versus the principle of the Apostolic Succession, rites as symbolic versus rites as soteriologically essential, faith as the expression of private opinion versus faith as an official holy creed – could be reduced and traced back to their origin in the basic conflict between the natural tendency of the church apparatus to affirm its authority as an independent organ of power and the democratic opposition to its arrogation of that power. The Apostolic Succession, for example, was a principle which it clearly lay in the interest of power-seeking ministers to uphold, for it sanctified their role as the bearers of a divine legacy. It was similarly in their interest to insist that the rites they performed were divinely ordained and necessary to salvation, and that the tenets of the faith of which they were the keepers were divinely inspired (thus giving their church a monopoly on infallibility). The mystical currents within the church were also embroiled in this controversy, and fuelled it: it is hard to imagine that an active minister, eager to strengthen his own position in the community by enveloping it in a nimbus of divine authority, could have written Balling's little treatise *Light Upon the Candlestick*, with its idea of "inner light" which denied the possibility of any true contact with the divine save an internal one, achieved and experienced only through individual effort.

However, to interpret these conflicts in terms of a struggle for power is not to deny them meaning; we may perceive the genesis of certain religious phenomena in interests of an entirely different kind, but this in no way negates their genuineness or seriousness as religious issues. Indeed, when conflicts of power in a religious congregation arise, we must presuppose that their participants take their involvement in religious life seriously and consider it as a value in itself; otherwise there would be no reason for them to express their views as religious views. The defenders of the idea of the church as a secular institution were not less "religious" than their opponents. On the contrary, their aim was to reduce religious life to a purely religious form: to purify it of all secular pollutants. The traditional slogan of the Spiritualists was: "We obey only God; we reject human systems of authority." They wanted to reduce as much as possible the part played by secular life in realizing religious values; it was to this end that they wanted to reduce pseudo-charismatic institutions to their secular origins. They wanted the church to remain a voluntary congregation of people who – together but independently of one another – held similar religious opinions; they wanted to free religious life from material constraints. Thus their attempt to secularize the church was an attempt to purify religion by purging it of all secular intrusions.

From this point of view the issue of tolerance is a secondary one. When Balling demands tolerance from his opponents, for instance, he is not just demanding that they tolerate his views, on the principle of mutual toleration, but that they abandon their own. The very idea of a charismatic church inevitably entails intolerance: if one church and one faith is considered to have the monopoly of truth, its leaders cannot accept into the community people who do not acknowledge that faith as the only true faith. One can only preach tolerance towards different views if one considers one's own views as no more sacred than those of others. Thus Balling can extend tolerance towards his opponents, but in demanding their tolerance he must demand that they abandon those of their beliefs about their faith and their church which entail intolerance. He is, in effect, demanding either that they accept a patent internal contradiction in their views or that they accept his own position. The conservatives, too, can similarly defend their position: their intolerance is consistent with and entailed by their ecclesiological principles, in just the same way that the tolerance of the liberals is consistent with theirs. Thus it is pointless to demand tolerance from them without demanding that they alter their principles, for tolerance on their part would necessarily involve a rejection of those principles. Hence the futility of the whole dispute. Hence, too, the fact that it took the form of a conflict between divergent theological opinions rather than between opponents and proponents of tolerance. The infallible cannot be tolerant of falsehood, nor the holy of Satan. Tolerance would require that the church authorities renounce the theory which confers holiness and infallibility upon them; such a renunciation would imply, on their part, a consciousness open to the possibility of self-criticism. And such a consciousness would naturally run counter to the interests of the church apparatus of power.

Jarig Jelles and Unitarian Pseudo-rationalist Mysticism

About Jelles, the second of Spinoza's Mennonite friends, we have a little more information, thanks in part to Rieuwertsz's afterword and in part to Spinoza himself.[42] Jelles was a grocer, and perhaps it was in this capacity that he met the young Spinoza before the latter's expulsion from the Jewish community. But in the mid-1650s, as a result of a religious crisis, he left his shop to devote himself to the study of religion and metaphysics. His material resources made up for his lack of education (he knew no languages other than Dutch): he paid for the translations of various writings which interested him, and it was owing to his support that Spinoza's first work, *The Principles of Descartes' Philosophy*, was published, as well as Dutch translations of Descartes. He also wrote a preface to Spinoza's *Opera Posthuma*.[43] His interests, as we can see from Spinoza's surviving replies to his letters,[44] ranged far beyond theological questions: he was interested in, among other things, optics, geometry and hydromechanics. Since he was a member of the Mennonite community, he was presumably connected with the Galenists. In 1684, a year after Jelles's death, Rieuwertsz published his *Profession of General and Christian Faith*, a sort of *apologia* in which Jelles defends himself, at some length, against a number of accusations of ill-defined content and unspecified source, and takes the opportunity to expound in detail his own views on all controversial religious issues. We know that as early as 1673 Jelles sent this work to Spinoza, who in a brief reply gave it his full

42　On Jelles, see Meinsma, *op. cit.*; M. Francès, *op. cit.*, pp. 48–49, 169–85, and 235–42; Gebhardt, *op. cit.*; and Hylkema, *Reformateurs*, vol. II, pp. 211–42.

43　In the past doubt was cast on the authorship of this anonymous text, but the attribution is now generally accepted by Spinoza scholars. A comparison of Jelles's *Profession* with this preface leaves no room for doubt: the style is identical, the same phrases are repeated, the same passages from the Bible are quoted.

44　Spinoza, Epist. XXXIX, XL, XLI, L.

approval, expressing reservations with regard only to one sentence (which in any case does not appear in the published version).[45]

As an illustration of the rationalist invasion of the non-denominational Christian world, Jelles's example is incomparably more eloquent than Balling's. Jelles's writings are a rich mixture: alongside all the elements that make up the Erasmian tradition of religiosity (the attempt to return to the simplicity of the Gospels, a moral interpretation of faith, a literal interpretation of Scripture, the refusal of denominational particularities), they display the influence of Protestant theology (the theory of irresistible grace) and are couched in a rationalist phraseology that is clearly taken from Descartes, but chiefly from Spinoza; and the whole is enveloped in the "inner light" of northern mysticism. From these heterogeneous elements arose a work that was nevertheless quite homogeneous in its initial reformist aims (and which in any case was intended as a personal profession of faith rather than a theological treatise). The first part consists of articles of faith, abundantly supported by appropriate verses from the Bible and occasionally supplemented by a meager scrap of commentary. The second, which contains fewer quotations, consists of reflections on a few basic theological terms and a critique of the Roman Church. The whole contains over six hundred quotations from the Bible, of which about fifty are from the Old Testament, mainly from the Psalms – a proportion typical of reformers. Jelles occasionally cites Erasmus and Acontius, but he also cites Calvin and Luther; he also refers to Jodocus Lodenstein, who may have been one of the sources that inspired his mysticism.

The whole of Jelles's theology can be arranged around, and explained by reference to, his image of Christ. It is a twofold image, an amalgam, as it were, of two separate images: on the one hand there is the image which corresponds to the anti-trinitarian interpretation of Erasmian reformers; on the other, there is the mystical image dear to worshippers of the neo-platonic *logos*. All the quotations from the Bible that support the Unitarian position, scrupulously chosen and collected, speak for the view that the historical Christ was a man of David's line. But Christ as the Son of God and as the Holy Spirit is a kind of impersonal emanation of God – divine wisdom or reason which at its highest intensity inhabited the historical Christ, Christ the man, but with which the faithful can also communicate internally on the path to salvation. This divine wisdom or light, or word/reason (this being the best ren-

---

45 Jarig Jelles, *Belydenisse des algemeenen en Christelyken Geloofs vervattet in een Brief aan N.N.*, Amsterdam, 1684. (The addressee of the book was not Spinoza, as is evident from the preface, in which the unknown "N.N." maintains that followers of Descartes have succumbed to old pagan beliefs and thus harm the Christian faith.) See Spinoza, Epist. XLVIII bis.

dering of the meaning of *"logos"* in the Gospel according to John) is a sort of demiurge through whom God created the visible world. Furthermore – and this is a crucial point – knowledge of the historical Christ, of Christ "according to the flesh," is not essential to salvation;[46] to that end only knowledge of the divine spirit which animated him is indispensable. Christ revealed to us the light of eternal truth given to him by God, and that light is, in fact, God Himself, for there is no difference between God and His wisdom except one of reason.[47] Divine wisdom is God's knowledge of Himself,[48] but we, too, can partake of that knowledge within the limits of our cognitive capacities. In this divine spirit "there can be no cognition except of a purely rational kind, and no emotions or passions save those which flow from that reason and are of a purely rational nature."[49] Similarly, human cognition of the regenerative kind – that knowledge which alone leads to salvation – is a "purely rational form of knowledge," independent of all sense perception, but also independent of any "verbal" knowledge we might have.[50] Sin is the result of ignorance, and freedom from sin the result of knowledge. We are born without knowledge, and although we are not evil by nature – for God's work cannot be evil – we are by nature prone to base emotions; spiritual regeneration takes away our capacity for sin, as it were, for our lives are guided by divine reason, the Son of God – the same that was with God at the beginning and animated Christ. It is only through participating in God's

46 See Belydenisse . . . , pp. 11–12: "Ik geloove en belijde datter een Soon van God is, en dat onze Heere Jesus Christus, wie so veel hat vleesch of lighamelijke van hem angaat, uit Davids zaat geboren en des Menschen Soone is . . . Gods Soon: naar of ten opsigt van de heiligmakende en levendig makende Geest, die in hem woonde, en die God hem zonder mate gegeven had . . . dat het tot verkrijging der zaligheit niet nut is Christus naar 't vleesch te kennen," etc.

47 *Ibid.*, p. 23: "Gods innerlijke Reden of verstant niet iets van Gods verscheiden, en dieshalven in 't begin aller dingen by God, en God zelf geweest is."

48 *Ibid.*, p. 21: "De waarheit . . . dat Gods Zoon of Gods eewige Wijsheit, Gods Beelt en 't uitgedrukte beelt van Gods zelfstandigheit is, zal ook verstaan worden als men aanmerkt, dat Gods eewige en oneindige wijsheit gantschelijk in de kennis bestaat, die God van zig self heeft, en dat hy ('t welk mede niet geloochent kan worden) zich zelf voolmaktelijk kennt, of zich kent gelijk hy in zig is . . . God even zodanig in zijn verstant moet wezen, als hy vormelijk is; te weten, op een voorwepinge wijze, en zodanig, als de voorwerpen gemeenlijk in 't verstant zijn; en dat dieshalven zijn oneindige wijsheit, het denkbeelt of de bevatting die God van zig heeft, volmaaktelijk het vormelijke wezen van God Vertoont, of uitdrukt, dat is, een volmaakt Beelt van Hem is."

49 *Ibid.*, p. 25.

50 *Ibid.*, pp. 35–36.

eternal wisdom that we can attain that kingdom of grace which is freedom from passions.[51]

The knowledge that leads to salvation is faith; but faith is not simply conviction. If it were, our knowledge of the written Word could justify us before God. True faith, true knowledge or reason, comes only from participating in that knowledge which is the Son of God: from direct communication with eternal wisdom, with the regenerative spirit. This is what enables us to free ourselves from being slaves to the Law; for although those who live according to the spirit of the Gospels act, externally, in the same way as those who live in bondage to the ancient Law, they do what they do from love, not because the Law obliges them to do it. Law and faith do not differ as to their effects, only as to motives; and we are saved not by our deeds but by our faith, of which deeds are the natural fruit. Christians have an obligation to do good deeds; a mask of ostensible internal faith will not conceal their indolence. But in order to fulfill this obligation in a truly Christian way, they must act from faith. Evil desires as well as evil deeds must be eradicated; and good deeds must not only be done, they must be done from love.[52] Only in this way can we "become one with Christ, just as Christ is one with God";[53] and this oneness is a perfect oneness of reason, will and emotion. Those who live under the rule of the New Covenant have no need of religious rites, which were established for the benefit of the immature.[54]

Once faith is attained, we cannot depart from it; grace is inalienable. It is also (Jelles places great emphasis on developing this purely Calvinist theme) irresistible; for the attractive power of God's light is irresistible, and when it acts as an efficient cause, we do not have the free will to reject it. The objects of human desires are of distinct kinds; we act according to a strict causality. There is no general power which is "the will," only particular "acts" of wanting or not wanting something – just as there is no general "reason," just particular acts of affirmation or negation. Furthermore,

51 *Ibid.*, p. 34: "By het Rijk der Genade versta ik de heerschapy of macht die wy menschen over de begeerlijkheden verkrijgen."

52 *Ibid.*, pp. 44–57, 122 and 143. See also p. 56: "Deze Werken der Wet zijn dan, naar mijn gevoelen de werken van liefde of barmhartigheit, van rechtvaardigheit, van matigheidt, van kuisheidt, en andere zedige werken, die van Moses, en de Propheten voorgeschreven worden, en de Christenen verplicht zijn te doen; te weten, voor zo veel zy gadaan worden door Wet of Gebod, en zonder dat de nootzakelijkheit en 't goet, daarom de mensch verplicht is de zelve te doen, gekent word. Want men zal hier na toonen, dat deze werken ook uit kennisse, of waar geloove gedaan konnen worden."

53 *Ibid.*, p. 82.

54 *Ibid.*, pp. 147–48.

". . . although each of our acts of wanting or not-wanting has its immediate efficient cause, and although for this reason we necessarily want or do not want the things we want or do not want and cannot alter the fact of our wanting or not-wanting, nevertheless the things we want, we want freely and voluntarily: we are not coerced into wanting them by any external power . . . on the contrary, the greater and stronger are the causes [of our wanting something], the more freely or voluntarily we want it; and the weaker and smaller those causes, the weaker their effect on us."[55]

However, Jelles does not think that acknowledging the irresistibility of grace and the determination of human actions entails acknowledging the principle of double predestination. On this question he does not commit himself, since an answer one way or the other is not among the truths essential to salvation. But he also believes that the question is better left unanswered, for it is good for people to believe that the question of their salvation is open: it encourages them to practice virtue.

Since the truth that leads to salvation is revealed to us only when we are touched by grace – a touch we experience internally – we cannot attain it by merely listening to or reading the written Word. The meaning of Scripture is revealed to everyone through his inner light; no congregation, no synod or other authority can have the power to judge what is and is not a true interpretation. It is for this reason that the false practices of the Church of Rome, which wants to subjugate the meaning of Scripture to its authority, only serve to reveal the illegitimacy of this institution. Unfortunately, the Reformation, which in its fundamental principles aimed to free divine knowledge from the shackles of church authorities, has itself embarked on the Roman path and is attempting to subjugate the Christian conscience to ecclesiastical resolutions.[56] The truth is, however, that binding creeds lead only to error, for "truth – as all those who know it are aware – can be known only through itself, and in no other way; it makes itself known, infallibly";[57] and "purely rational cognition, or understanding, contains within itself the proof that what is known or understood is and always will be, in its essential nature, just such as it was known."[58] This understanding, where, in accordance with Spinoza, "veritas est index sui et falsi," is accessible to all those who seek it with good intentions; it requires no special learning or knowledge. Those who judge his *Profession* according to their own official creeds will surely find that on many points it does not accord with Scripture, Jelles

55 Belydenisse . . . , p. 156.
56 *Ibid.*, pp. 97–111.
57 *Ibid.*, p. 94.
58 *Ibid.*, p. 120.

says; but those who judge it according to the truth, which is its own measure, will find no cause for disagreement.[59]

The origins of Jelles's central themes are easy to trace. The idea of justification through faith and the role of deeds is a continuation of the thought (also embraced by Dutch Erasmians such as Camphuysen) which the young Luther imposed upon the Christian world – that first attempt to subjectify religious values and shed the ballast of ritual, denomination and creed. The separation of Jesus into two figures – on the one hand the historical Christ, Christ the man and the person, and on the other the mystical Christ of faith, the emanation of divinity who reveals himself in inner light and can illuminate everyone just as he illuminated the protagonist of the stories in the Gospels – this, too, is a familiar idea, present in the second German Reformation and above all in the writings of Sebastian Franck. The association of Anti-trinitarianism of the Erasmian variety with the mystical idea of *logos* is a well-known one.

Two motives or aims can be discerned behind Jelles's critique of the historical Christ's divinity. First, it enables him, without questioning the divine spirit that breathed in David's descendant, to undermine the eternal divinity of the institution of the church which he established: the institution itself need not inherit the personal attributes of its founder. In particular, those who claim to have inherited Christ's charismatic legacy – ie., church authorities – cannot justify their claims, for Jesus's special participation in divine wisdom was bestowed upon him as an individual human being, and thus can be bestowed only upon other individual human beings. Second, it brings out the moral motivation behind the Unitarian idea: the exhortation to follow the example of the Savior is a discouraging one if the example we are to follow possessed, as a person, divine attributes to which no one else can aspire. In other words, if we are to consider Jesus's paradigmatic qualities as the real qualities of a real person, we must be able to believe that his example can be followed by human effort; a model that possesses divine powers does not inspire imitation. The Christ of faith, on the other hand – the impersonal emanation of divine wisdom – is manifestly connected with the anti-denominationalist position: the divine power at work in each of us brings salvation through our individual contact with it, a direct contact, without the mediation of church or ceremony.

But there is another influence at work behind Jelles's thought. If he places such emphasis on the "rational" nature of our communication with God, it is because of his acquaintance with Spinoza. The formulations he uses when discussing divine wisdom, the wisdom which manifested itself most fully in Jesus, are taken almost literally from the

59 *Ibid.*, p. 160.

Tractatus Theologico-Politicus. If Jelles understood them in the traditional mystical sense, it is reasonable to assume that here, too, he was fulfilling Spinoza's expectations: after all, the same Spinoza who wrote to Boxel that he could not commend him to God without laughing, and whose students did not call themselves Christians, also told his landlords to remain true to their Lutheran faith and approved Jelles's *Profession.* Spinoza couched his metaphysical ideas in a language that those who were morally pure but intellectually weak might associate with traditional religious notions; he translated his metaphysical terminology, as it were, into something people could understand. His metaphysics was for the intellectual aristocracy; but his language, especially in the *Tractatus Theologico-Politicus,* was for all those who wished to practice love of their fellow men in accordance with ancient mythologies, without fanaticism and without crass superstition. Thus hell was presented as destructive emotion, grace as the control of one's passions, Christ as the moral example to follow and divine love as adequate (in Spinoza's sense of the term) metaphysical knowledge.[60] Jelles adopts a good deal of this phraseology. And although he remarks, at the beginning of his *Profession,* that Cartesian philosophy has no bearing on the sphere of religion (as can be seen from the fact that it is accepted by people of various faiths, even Catholics[61]), he was clearly drawn by the fascinating radiance of rationalist slogans, and the pull they exerted is evident in his work. Not only does he constantly repeat that we come to know God through "purely rational cognition," make lavish use of the word "reason" and the phrase "clear and distinct understanding," proclaim ethical rationalism (the idea that sin results only from ignorance) and equate knowledge with faith; he also believes, generally, that Scripture, in the way he understands it, is entirely in accordance with natural knowledge,[62] that God's perfection can be established with certainty through reason alone, independently of Scripture,[63] and that Scripture can contain nothing that cannot be encompassed by reason or that contradicts reason.[64] However, these were no more than the trappings of rationalism. Jelles's rationalism was ostensible only, restricted almost entirely to the rhetorical level.

Traces of Spinoza abound throughout Jelles's *Profession,* but the content of Spinoza's thought has been assimilated to an unreconstructed, intellectually unsupported mysticism. When Jelles repeats after Spinoza that truth is its own measure and that "the truth of an adequate idea con-

60 For a more detailed justification of this interpretation see my *The Individual and Infinity,* cited above.
61 Belydenisse . . . , p. (4).
62 *Ibid.,* p. 92.
63 *Ibid.,* p. 10.
64 *Ibid.,* p. 96.

tains perfect certainty within itself,"[65] he takes this to mean simply that inner illumination requires no further proof: it suffices by itself to provide an unshakeable sense of certainty. When, in keeping with Spinoza's nominalism, he treats divine attributes, and in particular "eternal wisdom," as essentially identical with God, the only distinction between them being a *distinctio rationis*, it is as part of his general tendency, characteristic of mystics, to treat everything good as identical: God, Christ, reason, light, knowledge, good, wisdom, grace, salvation, love – for those who profess mystical union, all these are one and the same. When he talks, like Spinoza, of "purely rational affects," he attributes them, vaguely, to God. When he talks of the "state of grace" which is control over the emotions, in his argument he does not go beyond the traditional Christian recommendations of restraint. Like Spinoza, he identifies happiness with knowledge, but reduces the latter to inner illumination. Like Spinoza (but of course without mentioning him), he expounds the Stoic principle of virtue being its own reward and sin its own punishment,[66] but what he most likely had in mind by this was the mystical idea of God's disinterested love – an altogether different idea. In general, while Spinoza regarded the Bible as a historical document and a highly useful tool in the moral instruction of the uneducated, Jelles treats it as a divinely inspired work whose hidden meaning is revealed only by inner illumination – although in principle this illumination is accessible to all. And while Spinoza intended his metaphysics as fare for the intellectual elite and recommended the Bible as a way of teaching unschooled minds the principles of justice in an easily digestible form, Jelles – although for him, too, the content of religion was primarily a moral one – stops at the level which Spinoza deemed appropriate for the morally pure but unenlightened.

Most noteworthy, however, is Jelles's adoption of Spinoza's determinism (very often with its literal terminology) and his transformation of it into a theory of irresistible grace. Here Spinoza's influence is manifest in the doctrine as well as the vocabulary, for the Calvinist theory of irresistible and inalienable grace is in glaring contradiction with the entire religious tradition to which Jelles belonged – Erasmian, Mennonite and Spiritualist. Jelles's assimilation of it can in some measure be interpreted as being simply an expression of the traditional spirit of mystical passivity (grace as an unmerited gift). This is the more likely in view of his refusal to commit himself on the question of predestination, for it is difficult to see how a serious theory of irresistible grace could avoid entailing it. In other words, there is a lack – unsurprising in

65 *Ibid.*, p. 90.
66 *Ibid.*, p. 158.

a poor theologian – of coherence and consistency. Jelles probably intended, in keeping with the Erasmian spirit, simply to stress the unmerited aspect of grace; but since in doing so he adopts Spinoza's terminology (the necessary and infallible action of causes), the result is a Calvinist principle the full consequences of which he is loath to embrace.

Jelles insists that while his *Profession* is intended only to express his own opinions, it fulfils (in its first part, where there is no mention of irresistible grace or free will) all the requirements listed by Acontius for a universal symbol of Christian faith. There is no doubt, however, that Jelles tried to give it an irenic slant, deluding himself that he was only repeating what Scripture says and what all Christians must accept (or rather all Protestants: for despite his criticism of the Reformation, he unequivocally rejects, like De Breen, only the Church of Rome, and is convinced that he himself is reconstructing the original, abandoned ideas of early reform). In fact, for the most part he tries to preserve the general idea of reform as it was before it became the "reformed church." His opposition to the latter is evident in many elements of his program: a tolerant religion, free from obligatory creeds, rituals and temples, based on "rational" mystical experience and communication with the "inner light." (He cites almost every instance of the word "light" in the Bible; perhaps his insistence on this symbolism is connected with his interest in optics, as was the case with the thirteenth century Oxford metaphysics of light.)

There are no grounds for supposing that Jelles was Spinoza's guide or inspiration in metaphysical questions. The mystical themes in Spinoza's thought are disciplined by his metaphysics (for example, the idea of intuition as an act of intellectual identification with the absolute, which ultimately must be considered the only genuine reality). Moreover, they are unlikely to have been inspired by people of Quaker tendencies; more likely by Jewish Neoplatonists. Nevertheless, one can well imagine that he felt a certain affinity with people who wanted – as he did in his political thought – to reduce public religion to moral education and free society from the constraints imposed by organized churches. In this they were also expressing, albeit in a more primitive form – one far closer to popular Christian mythology – a longing that was not alien to his philosophy: the longing to be free of the bonds of finitude.

Zwicker: "Reason" as an Ecumenical Slogan

Daniel Zwicker[67] showed greater susceptibility than the other non-denominational reformers described here to the influence of the "ratio-

---

67 Born in Gdansk in 1612, by profession a doctor, Zwicker owed his Apostolic
    ideals about life in a community of goods to the influence of the Moravian

nalist" trend, for he tried to apply the general idea to his arguments. He thought that Reason, Scripture and Tradition must be reconciled in common conclusions which would provide a basis for uniting all of Christianity. But his irenic treatise[68] of 1658 begins, somewhat arrogantly, with an unequivocal denial of Christ's divinity, arrived at through purely rational arguments – for "everything that is contrary to reason must always be impossible and false, in matters divine as well as natural."[69] Having shown that the idea of human divinity contradicts common sense, Zwicker proceeds to support his claim with the standard array of quotations from the Bible, familiar from their abundant presence in all antitrinitarian tracts. He then goes on to demonstrate that none of the Church Fathers until the end of the second century believed in Christ's divinity, that his deification was begun by Simon Magnus and that the first Christian to accept it was Justin, who, however, did so in the spirit of the pagan tradition which treated all distinguished people as gods. He stresses that, in keeping with reliable traditions, he regards Christ as simply a man and not, for example, as having been created before the world;[70] and, with astonishing self-assurance, he presents this thesis as an infallible foundation of ecumenical endeavors.

Attempts to harness "reason" in this way were not, of course, a rarity among Socinian writers. But in the Second Reformation as a whole they were slow to clear a path for themselves, and far inferior in their argumentation to the Scholastics. The Reformation, especially in the north, had abandoned logical skills together with Scholasticism, and the return to them during the Second Reformation, this time from different traditions, was a lengthy and difficult process.

Brethren and tried to effect a rapprochement between them and the Polish Brethren. From 1656, when he was expelled from Gdansk, he lived in the Netherlands. He died in Amsterdam in 1678. See Sandius, *Bibl. Antitr . . . ,* 1684, pp. 151–56; S. Kot, *Ideologia polityczna i spoleczna braci polskich (The Social and Political Ideology of the Polish Brethren),* pp. 107–11 and 136–37.

68 *Irenicum Irenicorum, seu Reconciliationis Christianorum hodiernorum Norma Triplex, Sana omnium hominum Ratio, Scriptura Sacra, et Traditiones . . . ,* n.p. 1658 (the Dutch translation appeared in 1678).

69 *Ibid.,* p. 7.

70 *Ibid.,* p. 68: "Verae Traditiones Apostolicae non tantum Solum Patrem summum Deum esse testantur, sed ne Filium quidem, paulo ante mundum conditum a Patre genitum esse (prout prima plerorumque Christianorum a fide aberratio vult) permittunt; imo, omnibus aliis Veterum, tam pro Filii divinitate, quam pro eiusdem cum Patre aequalitate, allatis Traditionibus, et antiquiores, et certiores sunt, adeoque eas falsas prorsus, fictasque esse, clarissime docent."

Zwicker expresses his anti-denominational position with character-istic clarity: "I am neither a Lutheran nor a Calvinist, nor a Remonstrant, nor a Greek, nor a Papist, nor a Socinian, nor a Mennonite; I belong to no sect that exists today . . . but what I want for each and for all is a reform according to divine truth, which is the only teacher I follow."[71] Zwicker insists that he takes from each sect what is good in it: the beginning of reform from the Lutherans, the belief in the necessity of good deeds from the Papists, clarity and integrity of judgment from the Socinians, and so on. Whereupon he declares, unexpectedly, that he considers all these sects as part of Christ's church, for they all believe in Christ as the Son of God and their Lord. This declaration, at first sight startling, is in fact quite in keeping with other anti-denominational programs. For to say that all churches are "genuine" is the same as saying that they are all "false": that despite a certain common core of beliefs, they all cultivate, with no justification, the exclusivity of their creed. All are in need of basic, far-reaching reforms, which according to Zwicker must involve the elimination of a number of faults, among which are: ignorance, the spirit of particularism (their *"partium nimium studium"*) and the condem-nation of others, greed for temporal things, pride, indifference to progress, contempt for truth, lack of Apostolic discipline, confusion between Christ's kingdom and the realm of earthly things, the use of the sword, persecution of those who hold different opinions and fear of per-secution for their own.[72] After listing these ingredients of his "unification platform," he proceeds to list the order in which particular sects should unite. Until they do so, he says, he considers himself simply a Christian: God has His faithful in every sect; why should He not have them outside the sects as well? After all, Elijah and John the Baptist led solitary lives. In his concern to return to the Apostolic tradition, he condemns every-thing that, in his view, has been corrupting Christianity, since the Council of Nicea, with the spirit of power, greed and war: the false Donation of Constantine, the false primacy of the Bishop of Rome, and so on. He also recalls the community of possessions of the first Christians and by recalling these principles hopes to awaken an ecumenical impulse in the Christian world.

Zwicker's writings, as well as what we know of his activities in Holland, display a tendency to obsessiveness. He seems totally indiffer-ent to earthly realities, and he strives for absolute consistency. When he proclaims tolerance, he does not hesitate to include atheists among its beneficiaries; when he emphasizes the strict opposition between the "world" and Christianity, he reproaches the Mennonites for the fact of their not being persecuted, hated and killed off by the authorities, as

71 *Ibid.*, p. 79.
72 *Ibid.*, pp. 81–86.

befits true Christians.[73] He declares his categorical and uncompromising opposition to all states and all institutions, thus bringing persecution upon himself. He resembles an extremist visionary with no regard for the consequences of his utterances: the kind of person least likely to exhibit rationalist tendencies. And yet, despite this, and despite the disdain for "scholarly learning" which had become customary among reformers, it is here, in Zwicker's writings, that the idea of a religion perfectly adapted to the demands of reason but at the same time democratic and accessible to all, in all its claims, finds its strongest expression.

Conclusion:
Cartesianism and the Second Dutch Reformation

Let us sum up. At the beginning of the second half of the seventeenth century, the second Dutch Reformation faced a serious problem. Nurtured until then (in some of its variants) by St. Paul's Epistles, selected works of Patristic literature and Erasmian or Coornhertian traditions, or (in others) by the Book of Revelation, Dutch translations of Jacob Boehme and the tradition of Dutch mysticism, the non-denominational movement was suddenly confronted with the volcanic explosion of Cartesianism, which with extraordinary speed – within the space of a few years – transformed the intellectual life of the whole country. Indeed, attitudes to Cartesianism for a time became the main criterion by which different positions within academic philosophy were distinguished. For more or less freethinking theologians, non-denominational prophets, anti-clerical apostles of early Christianity, for mystics, Chiliasts, Quakers, Socinians, Collegiants, liberal Mennonites and Remonstrants, for sects which rejected the label of sect while condemning the sectarianism of all the other sects – for them Cartesianism and its influence were different than for, say, philosophers and scholars on the one hand and reformers on the other. Direct answers to the questions which preoccupied them – Christ's divinity, the resurrection, deeds and grace, the kingdom of God on earth, the literalness of the Bible, the sacredness of the ministry, the Apostolic Succession – were not to be found in the *Meditations* or the *Principia*. Conversely, laws governing the collision of bodies, stellar vortices and the circulation of the blood were not among the subjects of dispute which preoccupied reformers, who were far more interested in the method of achieving salvation than in reliable methods of discovering scientific truths. And yet Cartesianism seeped through to all of them, in each case differently, according to their interests. Among scholars weary of the old Aristotelian conceptual apparatus its rapid rise to popularity, despite the efforts of the clergy, was nat-

73 See Hylkema, *Reformateurs*, vol. I, p. 170.

ural enough; but it soon became apparent that it was also exerting its influence on the heralds of the new reform – unexpectedly on the face of it, given how different were the questions which preoccupied them. Among the latter, however, it was not adopted in its entirety, as a systematic structure; one word above all spoke to them from it – "reason." "Reason" became a general slogan: for some reformers the leading slogan expressive of their creed, for others a stumbling-block. The debate between these two camps had nothing to do with the problems raised by Cartesian physics or metaphysics. It concerned the role of "reason" in salvation: does the voice of God speak to us through our "reason," our acts of reasoning, or is "reason" merely part of our degenerate, fallen nature, as powerless and indeed harmful from the point of view of salvation as human will?

The issue of the relation between secular reason and faith, between philosophy and revelation, was hardly a new one in Christian controversies; Scholastic literature had been devoting considerable space to it for centuries. But the new religious formation which was the Protestant movement had to deal with the problem from scratch, in its own way. And in its early days the way it went about dealing with it was unequivocal: through Luther's attacks on Erasmus, through utter condemnation in Calvin's *Institutiones*. The passionate desire to lay low the proud hydra of reason did not spare even that most venerable tradition, the writings of the Church Fathers, if any of them seemed to be displaying excessive faith in the possibilities of human reason: Luther thundered that there was "no writer more hateful" to him than Jerome;[74] Calvin declared that Saint Chrysostom had "exceeded all bounds" in extolling human powers and that, with the exception of St. Augustine, all the old Fathers of the Church (not to mention Duns Scotus) expressed views on the subject that were dubious or vague.[75] And indeed, he says, had not Jeremiah, Isaiah, the Psalmist and Solomon all warned against excessive faith in human powers? The reason of fallen humanity is, for Calvin, a "distorted ruin" and a "blind man feeling his way in the dark"; if reason can achieve something in the mechanical and liberal arts, if medicine, rhetoric or law owe something to it, it is utterly powerless when it comes to knowledge of God and divine providence: here the most subtle minds are "more blind than the blind." The "little drops of truth scattered here and there in the books of philosophers" are covered over by a flood of "dreadful falsehood"; we can understand of divine mysteries only as much as God, in His grace, deems fit to reveal to us.[76]

74 From: Lucien Febvre, *Un Destin: Martin Luther*, 1952, p. 90.
75 See *Institution de la Religion Chrétienne*, II.2, para.4.
76 *Ibid.*, paras. 10–21.

It was in the 1520s, with the polemics between Luther and Erasmus, that the movement of church reform – until then undifferentiated, for the mass of criticism against which it struggled covered it like a mist – began to manifest its first, and ultimately incurable, internal divisions. The conflict between those who believed that "reason" alone was capable of plumbing divine mysteries and the proponents of organized reform, incarnated in the new church institutions which were being created, seemed firmly established. For the latter, the concept of "natural theology" was anathema; the very words seemed to conceal a blasphemous and outrageous purpose. "Reason" could be a useful thing for man, in the building of ships, for instance, the study of anatomy, the construction of calendars – although here, too, it should take care not to conflict with the word of God; but woe betide it if it dared to approach things sacrosanct and divine, for then it would be in the grip of the sacrilegious purposes of the devil.

In this way the Reformation, through its opposition both to Scholasticism (with the exception of late nominalism) and to Christian humanism, defined the limits of human intellectual effort: the capacities of natural human ingenuity could be exploited in the practical sphere of everyday life; but in matters concerning the knowledge necessary for salvation we are entirely dependent on grace, and no exertions of natural reason can help us.

The standpoint from which theoreticians of the Reformation criticized Scholasticism was of course quite different from that of humanists engaged in the same pursuit: for the latter, Scholasticism, especially since Duns Scotus, was a bizarre and loathsome monstrosity, an example of the corruption with which theologians had contaminated the faculties of reason; it was a mockery of reason. For the former, it was a genuine child of reason, and an example of the monsters reason can breed when its powers are unchecked; a monster born not in spite of reason but of it, and in spite of God's light. It was also, but not only, in the name of common sense that the humanists called for a return to the simplicity of the Gospels: for them it was a return to the salvaged remains of what was good in human nature, in which they trusted. The reformers, on the other hand, liked to quote the curse of Jeremiah: "*Maledictus homo, qui confidit in homine*": "Cursed be the man that trusteth in man . . . and whose heart departeth from the Lord." (Jeremiah XVII.5)

But corrupt "reason" held its own. The Erasmian tradition did not die out in the Netherlands, and manifested its distinctness from the Calvinist movement of reform first in the Remonstrant split and later in the Collegiant movement. This latter kept the insistence on the principle of freedom of speech and the radical anti-clericalism and anti-denominationalism, but it also retained, at least in its dominant variants, the cult of rationalist religion and the conviction that the idea of the essential rationality of human nature was in accordance with the precepts of the Gospels. The Collegiants parried Calvin's quotations from the Old Testament about the poverty of innate human possibilities with St. Paul's remark that serving God is *"rationabile obsequium vestrum"* (Romans XII.1) and tried to put a literal interpretation on John's words in the First Epistle to the effect that love of God and of one's fellow man is indissociable from knowledge of our Creator, and thus from intellectual effort: *"et omnis qui diligit, ex Deo natus est et cognoscit Deum"* (I John, 4.7) The van der Kodde brothers, organizers of the Rijnsburg collegium, were educated men; they knew Latin and modern languages, and one of them, Guiliemus Coddeus, was an illustrious Dutch orientalist, professor of Hebrew and Oriental Languages at Leiden until he was suspended as a result of the purge which took place after the Dortrecht synod.[77] Later supporters and organizers of *collegia* also tended to be highly educated men;[78] doctors, like Galenus or Laurens Klinkhamer, theologians, like Daniel de Breen or Adam Boreel, or lawyers, like Adriaan Paets. Their faith in "reason," combined with their rejection of any symbols of faith save Scripture and their belief in the principle of freedom of speech for all, made Collegiants very susceptible to the penetration of Cartesianism, which promised an infallible method for the guidance of reason without in any way encroaching on the fundamental principles of the Christian faith. In Collegiant circles there was no rigid wall of Calvinist dogma (which plainly could not be reconciled even with Descartes' physics, much less his metaphysics): the principle of exegetical freedom made it possible to reconcile the new cosmology with Holy Writ; the antitrinitarian tendency which was widespread among them allowed them to dispense with convoluted speculations about the physical aspects of incarnation; and the symbolic interpretation of the sacraments allowed them to accept Cartesian mechanics without getting stuck on the question of transubstantiation, which could perhaps be fitted into Aristotelian categories, but could not possibly be dealt with if bodies were defined in terms of extension. Cartesianism sometimes also acted as a stimulus which strengthened existing currents of thought, in particular all the principles which had been inspired by the Erasmian spirit and were in opposition to the ruling church: the principle of the clarity

77 See Paul Dibon, *La Philosophie néerlandaise au siècle d'or,* vol. I, Amsterdam, 1954, pp. 72 and 89.

78 An 18th century German observer (M.S.F. Rues, *Aufrichtige Nachrichten von den gegenwärtigen Zustände der Mennoniten oder Taufgesinnten wie auch der Collegianten oder Reinsburgers . . . ,* Jena, 1743) writes: "Die Collegianten sind vernüftige Leute, und haben ingemein wenigstens einige Kenntnis von Sprachen und Wissenschaften."

and comprehensibility of Scripture in all matters concerning salvation; the aversion to the Scholastic variety of theological speculation; the demand for doctrinal simplicity; the belief that Christianity was in accord with common sense; the belief in free will. Thus for activists in the second Dutch Reform movement, Descartes was not so much a source of new ideas in physics or metaphysics as the confirmation of a few general rationalist slogans which were already there, having been nurtured by a different tradition.

But the influence of Cartesianism on Calvinist theologians was also marked. Jan Coccejus protested when his critics accused him of succumbing to the influence of the new philosophy, but the writings of his many students, who continued his attempts at a rationalist exegesis of Scripture, display very clear Cartesian sympathies. The extent to which Cartesianism managed, despite all opposition, to influence even Calvinist thinkers becomes evident, indeed striking, when we read the following passage:

> Quod revera sint duae distinctae et creatae substantiae, quarum altera spiritualis est, altera corporalis; et quod hae duae substantiae distinctae, quibus nihil est inter se commune, sint cogitantes et extensae; quod cogitans spiritualis est, et extensa corporalis; unde etiam corpus et anima res duas distinctas constituunt.

This declaration, the genealogy of which leaves no room for doubt, appears in a list of articles which the consistory of the reformed church in Zwolle presented in 1704 to one of its preachers, the famous Frederik van Leenhof, accused of professing the doctrine of Spinoza. This, however, was not one of the condemned beliefs he was accused of holding. On the contrary: it was *one of the articles he was asked to sign to prove his Calvinist orthodoxy* and show that he had renounced his Spinozist errors.[79]

Nevertheless, there were a number of factors, in addition to differing purposes and interests, that limited the extent to which Cartesianism could influence these groups, Calvinist and Collegiant alike.

It is important to stress, once again, the fundamental conflict between the use of "reason" in matters divine and the demands for democracy within churches: the rationalization of dogma, strongly associated with the Scholastic tradition, was a tool used by theologians and ministers, one which distinguished the learned caste from the people; it therefore tended to perpetuate the authority and power of the church and worked against its democratization. It is for this reason that the ide-

---

79 The text of these articles can be found in Fr. Jenichen, *Historia Spinozismi leenhofiani . . .*, Lipsiae, 1707, pp. 120–53. The quoted passage is from p. 129.

ologists of the non-denominational movement were obliged, when trying to revive the original ideals of the Reformation – as embodied in the main ideas of Erasmus and the young Luther – and decrying the corruption of a Protestantism that had become "churchified," to regard attempts at reviving Scholasticism in the new church institutions as a symptom of Christianity's contamination by the spirit of secularism. The very nature of their protest necessarily involved a distrust of all "rationalist" enterprises in religious life.[80]

80 In the Lutheran world this protest may be more visible and more radical, for there it also involves repeated attacks on the universities as hotbeds and disseminators of pagan, anti-Biblical ideas. Among the many testimonies of this is Arnold's (*op. cit.*, chapter IV, pp. 469–71), which quotes a long poem by Johann Werdenhagen against philosophers. Below are some excerpts:

> Humana quid scientia?
> Annon furens dementia? . . .
> > Carnalis est scientia
> Semper Deo contraria;
> Abstrusa sacra Mystica
> Sunt captui non consona . . .
>
> Quod Socrates pronunciat
> Non Christus illud approbat.
> Est Christus ipsa veritas,
> Et Ethnici sunt vanitas . . .
> > Mentitur hostis omnia
> Dicat licet verissima . . .
>
> Omnino mendax dicitur
> Homo nisi renascitur.
> Innata lucis claritas
> Est summa mentis caecitas.
> > Carnalis ipsa veritas
> Est ima cordis falsitas. Etc.

Arnold also quotes, still in the context of attacks of the universities, a song by a certain Johann von Kötteritz:

> Exul Aristoteles nostra a pietate facessat,
> > Atque tibi cedat, spiritus Alme, locum.
> Qui sapis, ante alios amplectere Biblia libros
> > Rebus ut inde sacris sola medela fluat:
> Non Tibi Aristoteles nili, non unius assis
> > Profuerit: non si venerit ipse Plato. Etc.

These and many other similar written testimonies confirm that for these "Savonarolans" secular knowledge was false not in the traditional sense, but in the sense of being fundamentally harmful; since they thought that only faith and salvation was of any importance, they condemned secular wisdom

And yet they, too, in their appeals to Cartesianism, succumbed to some extent to the pathetic snobbery of "rational religion." They could invoke Cartesianism because it did, after all, "take off" in intellectual life as an appeal for democratic common sense and for authority that was universal, applying equally to all, and did not require "scholarly learning" or syllogistic training. The effect of these appeals, however, was feeble – necessarily so, for even though it was theoretically possible to use Descartes in an attempt to "rationalize" faith without incurring any of the anti-democratic and hierarchy-perpetuating consequences of such a rationalization, there was no real need for "reason" in the non-denominational enterprise. Such a need existed in other, quite different circumstances, among those for whom the issue of the separation between religious and secular life was of an entirely different kind. In intellectual circles the goal was to free the sphere of secular life, especially secular thought, from dogmatic control, and *"religio rationalis"* was one of the tools employed to this end: its purpose was to allow the intellectual elite to reduce religion to a side-aspect of life – a separate domain that would not constrain or encroach on other parts of it. But among those whose preoccupation was almost exclusively with religious issues and projects of reform there was no need for such a tool. If they called for a separation of the "world" from Christianity, it was not in order to preserve their secular lives from religious encroachments; their aim was to ensure a place for themselves on the "anti-world" side of the division. As for the "world," either they regarded it, together with organized churches, as fundamentally unreformable and were happy to leave it in the hands of Satan, or they tried to improve it in a Christian spirit – namely, by denying that it had any legitimate charismatic claims. The first of these attitudes (the principle of unreformability) was typical of people trapped in hopeless social positions (penniless aristocrats and members of the nobility, for example); it found its expression either in extreme forms of individualism or in sectarian impulses (which gave rise, for example, to communities of "saints" rigorously cut off from the world). The second was more characteristic of people who were well integrated in society or in the process of integrating themselves, but who resisted the growing autonomy of the church authorities; it found its expression in attempts to democratize the religious community as a secular gathering, and on the assumption that it was accepted as such. Non-denominationalism

not because of its content but because of its origin (similarly, they held that knowledge cannot save devils; the devil lies even if he tells the truth). The difference between the Reformers and Erasmus in their attitudes to "pagan knowledge" is more clearly visible here. Wherever the Erasmian tradition retained some influence, anti-intellectual attitudes tended on the whole to be less aggressive and less extreme.

typically accompanied the second of these attitudes and in some cases (namely those of individualist Spiritualists) the first. Mystical tendencies, too, often appeared in both, mostly as an element of non-denominational aspirations. As did antitrinitarianism, bound up as it often was with attempts to "secularize" the religious community: the writers discussed above all had a vague feeling, a suspicion they found it difficult to justify or even articulate, that belief in the Trinity was in some way – not just historically – connected with the system of persecution, intolerance and religious coercion. Their "Socinianism" (the term "Socinian" was universally used in polemical writings to refer to all those who questioned Christ's divinity) was part of their non-denominationalism. But nothing in their aims and aspirations could justify the ideals of "rationalist religion." The second Reformation had neither the need nor the strength to expend its efforts on trying to inculcate rationalism in intellectual life.

However, even this generalization is not entirely accurate or adequate. For the same religious attitude which checked the influence of Cartesianism on reformers or restricted it to a superficial, rhetorical level, also contained the element that facilitated its spread, and this element was absent from organized churches. The intellectual elite who remained within the Calvinist Church and tried to reconcile their faith with Descartes' methodic rationalism found that at some point they came up against a barrier they could not cross: a clear limit which their faith set upon their speculations. But the non-denominationalists had no such limits. The limits of the freedom of thought and expression which was the basic principle of the Collegiant movement were so loosely defined that a particular individual could in practice stretch them almost to infinity if he so wished. At the same time, however, excessive consistency in applying the rules of the new method could – as we know from a number of examples too familiar to need mentioning – lead to conclusions that could not possibly be reconciled even with the most liberal interpretation of Christianity. The problem of the acceptable limits of rationalism could not be satisfactorily resolved within the *collegia* because there were no official dogmas or creeds; people participated in the faith *"op eygen proef"* – according to the dictates of their own conscience. The only official basis of the faith was Scripture, and this, given the principle of freedom of exegesis, could be made to accord with any doctrine one liked. Thus among non-denominationalists, secular, non-denominational "reason" encountered no barriers of creed to impede its progress.

Moreover, and conversely, Cartesianism attracted not only Christians who wanted a "rationalist religion"; in time it also became popular among atheists and libertines. Which of course provided critics of Cartesianism with grist for their mill; and they pointed to Spinoza's writings as proof of its corrupting effects. Look, they could say, *this* is the real fruit of the Cartesian method – this undoubted blasphemer, atheist and enemy of Christianity! Cartesians were quick to attack Spinoza's doctrine in order to protect themselves against dangerous presumptions of guilt by association. But the destructive work of "reason" continued: Spinoza's circle of friends consisted of people who in one way or another were connected with the evangelical reform movement and who had been brought up on Cartesianism; for some of them his doctrine was a new synthesis of the two tendencies – rationalism and evangelism – which coexisted within them and which until then they had found it hard to reconcile. But it was a far more dangerous synthesis than anything Descartes' pupils had ever attempted: a synthesis in which the Christian God and Christian salvation could have no place. When "reason," in this new version, launched its attack, evasive compromises became increasingly difficult to sustain. As a result, those who had experienced the Spinozan revelation began to see reason without God on the one hand, and Christianity without reason on the other, as exclusive alternatives. Cartesian "reason" could be reconciled with the Christian tradition in a number of ways; but the "reason" of the *Ethics* imposed a choice between two radically opposed possibilities. And very often the paradoxical outcome of this pressure to choose was a forced escape into extreme irrationality; for some it seemed the only option, for it was their sole protection against the inescapable but to them unacceptable consequences of the demands that Spinoza's method placed on reason.

Translated and edited by Agnieszka Kolakowska

The Mystical Heresy and the Rationalist Heresy in Dutch Calvinism at the End of the Seventeenth Century

The Ideal Model of Counter-Reformation

Ecclesiastical reformation movements, if they genuinely reflect the feelings of the faithful, can as a rule be brought under control only by a counter-reformation which succeeds in assimilating certain slogans and ideas of its adversaries while imposing on them an interpretation and a well-defined area of application; in this way they can be maintained within the bounds of canonical discipline. In other words, an effective counter-reformation is nourished by certain ideas of the very reformation it wants to stifle. It must assimilate and bring under control the spiritual substance which threatens to destroy the fabric of the religious body, neutralize the foreign bodies within it and impose a new direction on them: in order to prevent a schism, the structure of some of the spiritual elements of the reformation movement must be undermined and its reformatory energy paralyzed. But since this process is carried out by individuals, who may articulate the assimilated ideas in a way that is more or less resolute, more or less restricted, and more or less colored by their personal preferences, it is often hard, especially in periods of upheaval, to distinguish reformation from counter-reformation by doctrinal content alone.

This state of affairs is not, of course, news to historians, and I mention it here only to emphasize the enduring and invariable three-stage rhythm of all religious conflicts. One might say that their structure, when simplified, obeys a law of dialectical logic: the law of the synthesis of action and reaction.

This regularity, however, is only the first stage of another, wider cycle. Reformatory ideas have a momentum of their own: even when they appear to have been neutralized and assimilated into the ecclesiastical organism, they exhibit a dangerous propensity to spill out of the area to which that organisms's interests have restricted them and provoke new separatist or heretical tendencies. Whenever the Church attempts to restore order and cohesion, the risk of generating a new separatist conflict is always present; no matter how orthodox its strategy, how rigorously adapted to the re-establishment of the order that can preserve its identity, its continuity and its "social individuality," the danger of creating a new fissure is always there. A counter-reformation, being a particular instance of reformation, is not immune to these risks. Thus counter-reformation movements sometimes gave rise, by the force of their own momentum, and especially in their second phase, to new separatist movements. These in turn required a new response, and so on. The process was progressively destructive, weakening the fabric of the main organism each time it was repeated.

This, then, is the general – rough and simplified – model of the dynamics of reform and counter-reform. At some stage in its development, an ecclesiastical organization produces a movement of reform (its antithesis); the conflict gives rise to a counter-reform, which attempts to assimilate and control it. This counter-reform, being a purely defensive reaction, reaches a point of hypertrophy; this is when it gives rise, in its turn, to heretical or schismatic movements (a successive antithesis). Again the organization must respond. As it attempts to eliminate this new threat (the new pathogen produced by its own immune reaction), it produces another counter-reform. Thus movements of counter-reformation can be seen as an organism's defensive reaction to a sickness – a reaction so strong that it destroys the organism itself. The antibodies it secretes to fight the attacker turn on it and attack its own tissues.

It would be rash to claim that this is a verifiable hypothesis; it is merely a model, but one that seems to reflect quite well the evolution of the various Christian movements and trends of the sixteenth and seventeenth centuries. For example, the Spanish Illuminism of the 1520s contributed to the development of a rich current of Catholic mysticism; this current, despite its teething difficulties, finally established itself within the Church, and in its turn succeeded in identifying, and neutralizing, a new threat to the Church – the subjectivist movement which wanted to internalize all religious values and questioned the need for the visible Church and its mediating role. This mystical current, transplanted to France and cultivated in Oratorian and Carmelite brotherhoods, went on flourishing for a long time, until the shadow of suspicion cast upon it by the scandal of Quietism – in a sense its natural product, but at the same time a return to the same primitive form of heterodoxy it had wanted to tame and control – brought it to an end. Another example is the trend, widespread in Lutheran Germany during the first half of the seventeenth century, to return to the original sources of the Reformation. This trend, in both its versions (for it found expression in both evangelical and mystical movements), provoked a counter-reformation in the form of pietism; this pietism in turn gave rise to phenomena, groups and communities whose Erasmian or mystical leanings clearly exceeded the acceptable limits of Protestant orthodoxy, thus forcing the Church to take defensive action.

Most likely the history Jansenism, too, can be seen in the same light: as a movement of counter-reform which in the end became contaminated, as such movements inevitably are, by the enemy it had wanted to destroy. Indeed, the three versions of French Counter-Reformation in the seventeenth century – Berullian mysticism, Jesuit culture, and Jansenism – may all be seen as (mutually opposed) responses to the different kinds of heterodoxy which were threatening Catholic integrity at the time. These three reformatory currents differed from one another no less than the enemy movements which they wanted to control: the Spanish Illuminists in the first case, secular and naturalist humanism in the second, and the strict, "Flemish" form of Protestantism in the third.

The Spiritualist Counter-Reformation

To descend for a moment from the dangerously cosmic scale of these generalities and move to something less risky and more concrete, let us examine in detail a specific example from the history of Dutch Protestantism: a double counter-reformation which arose from a double ideological danger and doubly failed, thwarted by the internal logic of its own development.

The national Church of the United Provinces, theologically more and more tightly held in the clutches of a progressive "Calvinization" and stagnating in its rigidly disciplined clericalism, found itself faced, at the beginning of the 1620s, with a large opposition movement, expressed both in a Remonstrant faction and in an abundant literature. The literature advocated a non-denominational Christianity and condemned the formalism and rituals of the dominant community, seeing in them the abandonment of Apostolic ideals. These attacks were reinforced by similar criticism from liberal factions within the Mennonite community. As an antidote to them, the Calvinist Church produced the "Reform Party," concentrated mainly in Utrecht and led by the energetic Voetius. Its aim was to assimilate certain elements of the criticism aimed at the Church and transform them into a form of self-criticism. It stressed the need for individual moral discipline and exalted internal religious values and an existential conception of "faith," but did not attack ritual or organized discipline. Its *"praecisitas"* – sometimes accompanied by mystical tendencies, sometimes limiting itself to emphasizing the moral aspects of religious life, the moral mission of the Church and the practical nature of theology – was adapted to assimilating a specific and well-defined form of external criticism of the Church: criticism from the mystical and Erasmian traditions, which shared a disdain for the organizational and denominational aspects of religion and wanted to restore its internal and individual character.

The theology of the Reform Party, inspired by the doctrines of the famous English puritan William Amesius, glorified the ideal of the Church, the community of saints and the assembly of the chosen. Aggressive and anti-philosophical, it precluded the possibility of any ethics or metaphysics except that which a theologian could deduce from Scripture; there was no place in it for any autonomous metaphysics, natural ethics or natural theology. It insisted on our organic incapacity to apprehend spiritual things or to understand the true meaning of Scripture without the aid of divine Grace, and it saw this incapacity as the expression of the inevitable flaws of human nature after the Fall. Theology itself, in its legitimate forms, was seen as a practical rather than an intellectual activity: a domain of faith (in the Lutheran sense) rather than reflection, of art – *ars Deo vivendi* – rather than knowledge. In stressing that it is the devil who is the best metaphysician and that the object of theology is not reason but the will, Amesius wanted to dignify the idea of faith as spiritual regeneration through Grace and personal trust in the Creator. At the same time, the radical opposition of Nature and Grace in his theology entailed an insistence on the total and indivisible sanctity of all true participants in the body of Christ; hence the strict obedience required of the faithful and an austere rigidity of approach to divine law and their submission to it. For Voetius there is no opposition between the Gospels and the law; the idea of sin and forgiveness is understood within the religious framework of the Old Testament. There is, on the other hand, a deep opposition between the sacred and the profane, one consequence of which is the view (rejected by radical anti-denominationalists) that the visible Church (situated in the domain of the sacred) must preserve its autonomy and resist submission to temporal powers. This attitude unequivocally defined the Voetian party's political position in the conflicts which arose between magistrates who considered that their powers extended to organized religious life and clergymen of a theocratic bent, jealous of their autonomy or even seeing themselves as the personification of divine law and its superiority to the civil variety.

The Voetian counter-reformation rejected both the premises and the anticlerical and anti-denominationalist conclusions of the spiritualist anti-Calvinist movement which it wanted to contain and assimilate. Its violent anti-rationalism could not shock its intended audience, for the anti-denominationalist spiritualism which they professed was no champion of profane reason; on the contrary, it was notoriously hostile towards natural theology, which it saw as serving only to deepen the alienation of the clergy from the faithful – an attitude which emphasized its anti-clericalism.

This was how things stood until the Cartesian invasion – the moment when the influence of Cartesianism became sufficiently strong to spread beyond the world of learning and affect, among others, liberal religious reformers, scattered throughout the cities of the Netherlands. At the start of the second half of the century it took the form of a sort of pseudo-rationalist snobbery, which infected the Collegiants and those connected with them; even the most mystically inclined were not immune to its influence. Its expression in religious tracts and pamphlets tended to be superficial and purely verbal: the magic word "reason" was repeated like an incantation; some even went so far as to identify reason with divine Grace, or with the mediating Logos of the Gospel according to John. Bizarre combinations of rationalism and mysticism sprang up; there were those who hoped that all the mysteries of Christianity could be made to conform to the requirements of scientific method. But even if these attempts on the part of mediocre pious souls to rebel against the official religion in the name of free and direct access to divinity were often clumsy and superficial, they reflected the influence of the rationalist pressure which was increasingly shaping the spiritual atmosphere in cultivated circles. The distinction between revealed truth and natural science was in danger of becoming blurred as "reason" extended its control to both, encroaching upon the territory of the former, which until then had been the preserve of theologians, and setting itself up as arbiter in dogmatic disputes. A counter-reformation movement aimed at containing this pressure appeared in the form of Coccejanism – a powerful theological school whose name requires some explanation, for Coccejus's doctrine itself contains little to justify hopes of its harmonious alliance with Cartesian rationalism. We know, however, that such an alliance did take place; we also know, thanks in great measure to the research of Ms. Thijssen-Schoute, that its dimensions were considerable. So it is naturally tempting to try to discover what, in Coccejus's theology, might have inspired it, in spite of his avowed ignorance of the works of Descartes.

On the crucial question of predestination Coccejus was orthodox but moderate. He agreed with the Voetians' purely practical interpretation of theology and shared their idea of the Church as a community of the chosen, but he was opposed to any definition of the Church by its institutional features. This opposition sprang from his adherence to the "federalist" doctrine, which radically opposed the Covenant of Works to the Covenant of Grace, considering the two to be qualitatively different and incompatible; and it is on this incompatibility that the Covenant of Christ, after stripping away all elements of Jewish law (the great dispute with Voetianism over the Sabbath was a small part of this conflict), built its model of religiosity: one whose values were almost all contained and expressed in practical obedience to the commandments of the Gospels. Coccejus's millenarist hopes are expressed in a theory which opposes spiritual and profane government in such a way that it questions the legitimacy of the Church's wielding any temporal power at all – an idea which is tantamount to a political declaration against the Voetians, who accepted the charismatic values of the visible Church. The Coccejean principles of Biblical exegesis, although inflexible, intolerant of the liberties of interpretation taken by the "Enthusiastic" prophets, and insistent on attributing a rigidly univocal meaning to the sacred texts, allowed the interpretation of Scripture through Scripture alone (thereby denying that any creed could be binding), and were thus particularly vulnerable to the charge of "Biblicism", which was often made against them.

All these ideas turn around an ideal of the Church defined by its moral, not institutional, characteristics; a Church which on principle renounces temporal power or even, more radically, all temporal forms of organization. Coccejus, Calvinist in his theology and Lutheran in spirit, proposes what one might call a "de-laicizing" of the Church, convinced that its visible aspects are accidental, or indeed just *adiaphora*; but in fact his apparent de-laicizing turns out to be a deep and radical laicization: for if the external aspects of religion – i.e., the visible Church – are not part of the essence of Christianity, it follows that they belong to the domain of the State. His doctrine, with its reduction of the religious to the moral and the ecclesiastical to the political, could almost be regarded – in its practical consequences, not in its theology – as a belated substitute for Arminianism, whose original structure, determined by its situation as an internal faction, was naturally lost after its expulsion from the body of the Church.

The Rationalist Counter-Reformation

Coccejus, less Coccejean than his disciples, bequeathed to these latter neither a sympathy towards Cartesianism nor a theological system which could evoke such sympathy by any positive remarks. If they were open to rationalist influences, and if they later integrated Cartesianism into their theology, it was thanks more to Coccejus's silences than to his words. His very failure to express an opinion about such things as the heliocentric hypothesis, the circulation of the blood or the interpretation of comets attracted students of an enquiring disposition, curious about the world and its novelties. Voetius explicitly condemned the work of Copernicus and Harvey, preferring to explain comets as omens and seeing Scripture as the complete treasury of medical, astronomical, physical, legal, economic and other knowledge. But Coccejus, without being excessive in his belief in the value of metaphysics or natural theology, did not share this aggressively anti-philosophical stance; his ambiguous and sometimes contradictory remarks concerning faith or, as he was fond of repeating, *logike latreia* – the rational cult – may be taken as an affirmation of natural theology and natural philosophy. Moreover, the question of how far their domain might in future be extended was left open. But here Coccejus's followers may have permitted themselves more flexibility their teacher intended: where his own writings had been equivocal, judiciously vague and hedged about with restrictions, they expressed their views with a dangerous clarity. The belief in the total autonomy of reason in the domain of nature; the subjection of Holy Writ to independent rational interpretations; the violent criticism of popular superstitions about comets, witchcraft, satanic possession, etc.; the almost total acceptance of Cartesian physics and anthropology, and the attempted proofs of their integral harmony with the reformed faith; the proclamation of the sovereignty of civil powers and of their right to govern the Church – these were the Coccejean themes. In their struggle against theocracy in both civil and intellectual life, the Coccejeans, while condemning excessive rationalism (Spinoza comes in for a fair amount of criticism here) and abstaining from any attack on the articles of faith, hoped to assimilate Cartesianism to Calvinism and from this mixture forge a tool to promote a moderate laicization of life; at the same time they sought a way of assimilating Cartesianism into the religious culture, so as to bar the way to its libertine, atheist and anti-Christian offshoots, which were already springing up.

The Voetian and Coccejean schools, whose conflict represents a fair-sized chunk of the annals of the Church and of reformed Dutch theology, can both be seen as versions of the Calvinist counter-reformation, each oriented towards the assimilation of different phenomena in the spiritual culture of its time. Mutually hostile in content, distinguished by the material they assimilated, they also differed in their aims, the one wanting to reconquer the Church's lost possessions, the other tending to concede them. But in the end both were defeated by the external enemy they had sought, with some initial success, to assimilate; and both, finding themselves in an impossible situation, succumbed to an internal crisis whose germ is already discernible (*a posteriori*, of course) in their initial ideas.

The Failure of Coccejeanism

The crisis of Coccejeanism began with Frederik van Leenhof – minister of Zwolle, militant Coccejean and writer of mediocre and unfailingly unoriginal texts who had probably breathed some French libertine air during his time at the court of Louis XIV as preacher at the Dutch embassy. His abundant literary output contains all the elements which make up the "standard" form of popular Coccejeanism: the rationalist exegesis of Scripture and the belief that its meaning can only be grasped in the natural light of reason; Descartes' proofs of the existence of God, his clear and distinct ideas and the "occasionalist" interpretation of his dualism; an approach to the Church which, while accepting the need for its "visible" organization and for the priesthood, rejects all its charismatic values; an irenic program based on an appeal to our autonomous reason; curiosity about science and praise of earthly pleasures. He defends Coccejus against the attacks of the Voetians and also directly attacks the "Reform party", which by its strict asceticism, its rigidity, its pedagogy based on fear and its stifling of individual liberty, terrorizes the faithful and breeds superstition. In practice his attitude is tantamount to a popular form of deism: a vision of the world that is almost totally devoid of any references to eternity and where religious values are subordinated to temporal requirements. It is a primitive form of Cartesianism, watered-down and reduced to rationalism – a rationalism which wants to restrict visible religious life to the minimum and weaken as much as possible the importance of revealed truth in thought and daily life. Leenhof succeeded for quite a long time in maintaining this impoverished Cartesianism within the limits of orthodoxy; the crisis came with the publication of his book *Heaven on Earth* (1703), which left no doubt that its author, in his personal intellectual evolution, had followed the path taken by rationalist philosophy in its progress from Descartes to Spinoza. The forbidden name of Spinoza does not appear, but the signs of his influence are unmistakable; they could not possibly have passed unnoticed. It was a flat, miserable kind of Spinozism, devoid of any metaphysical sweep and tailored to a pale and enfeebled libertinism; but Spinoza's naturalist and secularized vision of the world clearly shines through its thin, bloodless religious declarations.

These reveal a religion reduced to a few "fundamental truths", chiefly of a moral nature. It is a religion purged of all theological speculation and "sterile" dogmatic controversy, indifferent with regard to "secondary issues" and trusting in the independent power of profane "reason", which is glorified as the criterion *par excellence* of human perfection and the unique source of moral values. Scripture is treated as a historical text, subject to the ordinary, rational critique of the philologist;

its importance lies principally in its use as a popular catechism for the ignorant. Man is regarded as a part of nature, and as such dependent on nature's immutable order; his aim should be to master the passions with the aid of "adequate ideas" about things. The Church is viewed as a civil institution, and as such subordinated to the power of the State; its tasks are almost entirely confined to the moral realm. The book condemns Calvinist teaching as being based on fear, melancholy and the oppression of individual freedom; violently attacks ignorant and fanatical theologians who impose their prejudices on the faithful and torment them with excessively rigorous demands and rituals; and defends the Stoic idea of virtue as its own reward.

Such, roughly, was the content and program of "heaven on earth." There is no need to interpret the author's position as veiled atheism; it is, rather, a popular form of deism, where the divinity, although not rejected, is present only in name, and loses all practical importance for life, morals and our understanding of the world. The Coccejean movement, in its attempts to integrate faith with rationalist values, finally adopted this libertine re-interpretation of Spinozism – with disastrous results, for it was this that brought the whole enterprise to a spectacular end. There was a lengthy controversy which involved the national Church at almost every level; Leenhof had a rough time of it, and was finally forced into a humiliating recantation. His story symbolizes the final defeat of a counter-reformation undermined from within: by the internalized enemy who wreaks his own brand of havoc as the body that assimilated him congratulates itself on its success.

The Failure of Voetianism. Conclusion.

The Voetian counter-reformation collapsed in a disarray that was analogous in form, although of course opposite in theological content. Here the culprit was the fantastic figure of Jean de Labadie: ex-Jesuit, ex-Jansenist, and soon an ex-Calvinist, who brought about the final disintegration of the "Party of the Reformed" by his insistence on dragging his principles through to their logical conclusion, thereby exposing the internal contradictions of Voetianism. His conflict with the Walloon community in Zeeland, which ended in his establishing a separatist sect, can no doubt be explained by his ambition and his manifest greed for power; but it can only be understood in light of theological controversies concerning the idea of the Church.

Labadie believed in what is traditionally known as a converted rather than a converting Church; and this former, although implicit in the fundamental ideology of the Voetian party, turned out, in its practical consequences, to be incompatible with the status of a socially active, indeed militant, organization. The crisis was sparked off by Labadie's critique of a book by Wolzogen, a well-known Coccejean. Labadie claimed – rightly, in fact – that Wolzogen, while ostensibly attacking the Biblical rationalism of Louis Meijer, in fact accepts all the fundamental principles of the enemy and allows "natural reason" to hold sway over revealed truth. The details of the long controversy which ensued cannot be gone into here, but it turned on Labadie's spiritualist conception of the Church. In the deep and incurable division between the sacred and the profane, he – like the rest of the Reform Party but unlike individualist spiritualists – placed the visible Church firmly within the former camp: in the realm of the divine. This being so, he deduced, with unimpeachable logic, that the Church should be completely separated from earthly things. Such a church – a church of saints regenerated by the touch of divine Grace – clearly could not find its conditions satisfied within the organization of the Dutch Calvinist Church. Hence the need for a profound reform. But such reform, in elevating the Church to a status of integral sanctity, would inevitably reduce it to a closed sect, indifferent to the fate of sinners – since it is only thanks to the operations of an undeserved Grace, and not through any human efforts, that these latter can be brought into the saintly Christian body of such a church. It is precisely this Church of the elect that Labadie wanted to establish, imposing rigorous demands of absolute sanctity on the members of his sect: a Church closed in upon itself, totally separated from the world, whose members concentrated on cultivating the gifts of the Holy Spirit and lived in the constant hope of an imminent second Coming. This fanatical sectarianism, accompanied in practice by all the typical features of a sect closed in upon itself – the rigid internal hierarchy, the dependence on the intangible authority of its leader – plainly precluded any work of conversion on the part of the church; but for a church well established in national life, with aspirations to power, renouncing such work was, just as plainly, out of the question.

The latent contradiction inherent in the Voetian program – the incompatibility of its theocratic aspirations with the idea of a Church of saints – was forced out into the light of day by the Labadie affair, and its emergence virtually paralyzed the Reform movement.[1] The idea of a living faith (an assimilated but essentially anti-Protestant spiritualism, however genuinely Protestant its intentions), when taken to its logical conclusion and consistently applied, led to sectarian consequences

---

1   Goeters provides a convincing analysis of the crisis in his history of Dutch pietism (W. Goeters, Die *Vorbereitung des Pietismus in der reformierten Kirche der Niedrlande bis zur labadistischen Krisis 1670*, Leipzig/Utrecht, 1911).

which were incompatible with the idea of an active church, a converting church, working towards the salvation of the faithful through ritual and form.

Thus the failure of the Voetian movement followed the same pattern as the failure of Coccejeanism: that of a counter-reformation destroyed by its own internal logic – or by an external logic which it wanted to assimilate. Its history is a cautionary tale about the perils of applying excessive logic to religious life (logic, in this case, meaning more the logic of social processes than the logic of individual thought). But it is also grounds for suspecting that, in the end, neither mysticism nor rationalism could be fully assimilated into Protestant religiosity: even when apparently assimilated, they would invariably transform themselves into heresies. And it imposes the conclusion that in all forms of mysticism, and all forms of rationalism, there lurks an ineradicable anti-ecclesiastical element which the course of events will sooner or later reveal.

Translated by Agnieszka Kolakowska

The Tragic Career of Uriel da Costa

The causes of Uriel da Costa's fame are twofold. The first is his unsuccessful revolt against tradition: his life was the classic example of a rebellious mind crushed by the pressure of a fanatical orthodoxy, and it is to this that he owes his place in the pantheon of European freethinkers. That place was more firmly established after Carl Gutzkov's play about him (based on a story published earlier) was first performed in Dresden in 1847; the play (still occasionally staged in Europe) was an element of the battle for toleration and freedom of conscience waged by German radicals just before the 1848 Revolution. Gutzkov made the Jewish rebel into a romantic hero against the background of the conflict between freedom of conscience and the dogmatic cruelty of established religion, quite independently of the content of the ideas which this conflict involved.

The second cause of Uriel da Costa's fame is the study of Spinoza. Spinoza scholars, investigating the genealogy of his philosophy, naturally sought its roots in the Jewish intellectual life which both taught him the rabbinical tradition and spurred him to overcome it; it seemed a likely source both of Spinoza's familiarity with the Hebrew Bible and Talmud and of his critique of them. As a result of this, scholarly studies of Uriel da Costa tend to be offshoots of studies of Spinoza. The twentieth century's most illustrious (alongside Dunin-Borkowski) Spinoza scholar, Carl Gebhardt, collected the extant fragments of Uriel da Costa's writings and published them, along with what remains the most penetrating analysis they have received to date, as volume two of the Spinoza Library.[1]

---

1   *Die Schriften des Uriel da Costa, mit Einleitung, Ubertragung und Regesten, herausgeben von Carl Gebhardt*, Amsterdam-Heidelberg-London, 1922. This collections contains, as well as a long introduction, *Da Costa und das*

Gebhardt, along with a few other historians who took an interest in Uriel da Costa's life and writings, managed to reconstruct both the essential corpus of da Costa's ideas and the reactions to them, Jewish and Christian. Their work also provides an insight into the intellectual background of that deplorably ended conflict, the situation within which it arose being marked chiefly by the sea of intellectual vicissitudes engulfing Portuguese Marrano Jews who, bereft of their Sephardic culture, were struggling to adapt to the traditions of Jewish communities in the Netherlands.

The Marranos – forcibly Christianized Iberian Jews who professed conversion but secretly kept faith with their religion – were flooding into the Netherlands in flight not only from the terror of the Inquisition, which after the edict of 1492 scrupulously hunted out doubtful converts and tortured, imprisoned or burnt at the stake all those who betrayed signs of continuing attachment to the religion they had been forced to renounce, but also from the economic policies of the Spanish rulers, which placed harsh restrictions on trade initiatives and made life hard for merchants while according privileges to the gentry. The hope of both religious and economic tolerance brought some of the refugees to Holland, where they could practice their religion openly. By the start of the seventeenth century they were a well-organized community. But it was not easy to return to a tradition which, after a century of persecution, many of them had forgotten; they found, in the attempt, that the extent of their assimilation to Renaissance European culture was perhaps greater than they had suspected. For their initiation into Jewish customs and rituals they had to rely largely on Ashkhenazi rabbis, and while these represented the continuity of the Jewish tradition, they also embodied its dogmatic stagnation – its rigid, petrified form, preserved in complete isolation from the development of European culture and untouched by anything that had taken place in the intellectual life of the non-Jewish world in the course of several centuries. For Spanish and Portuguese Jews steeped in Renaissance culture, the return to the faith which persecution had forced them to abandon but about which they had, by then, no more than the vaguest idea, was something of a shock; and when, on closer acquaintance (and especially in the form in which it was taught by Talmudic scholars from the East European tradition), this faith turned out to consist in a mixture of superstition, obscure cabbalis-

Marranenproblem, all the extant fragments of da Costa's writings, with German translations of the Portuguese and Hebrew originals; documents concerning his life; and a selection of polemical texts attacking the author of *Propostas contra a Tradicao*.

tic lore and endless, equally obscure rituals, their discouragement was profound.

The lengthy conflict which the history of Uriel da Costa famously (though not uniquely) illustrates arose out of this confrontation and its disillusionments. It ended in a victory for the Ashkhenazi spirit in the Amsterdam Jewish community – the victory of strict northern orthodoxy over the secular culture of the south. Most likely it could not have been otherwise: the elements of secular culture brought by the Marranos had little chance of survival in the isolated conditions in which the Jewish communities in Holland chose to live, with no external impetus to further development. The cultural emancipation of those Jews who refused to accept the beliefs and rituals of the community could not be achieved through the reform of that community; it required – as in the case of Spinoza – a total break with it. Those who did not feel ready for such a step, or had no means of support outside the Jewish community, had no choice but to conform; otherwise they were doomed. Would-be reformers and renegades had almost no place to go after breaking with the community. But the Marranos found themselves cut off from Dutch society not only as Jews but also as Spaniards or Portuguese – southern people set apart by a different language and different customs; they were already isolated, and because of this the break from the religious community was in a sense more natural for them.

From this point of view the fate of Gutzkov's protagonist was a model of its kind. Gabriel da Costa (Acosta) was born in Porto before 1585. He studied canon law at the Jesuit university in Coimbre and probably intended to embark on a career in the Church. But soon he began to have doubts, which finally led him to leave the Catholic faith and return to the forgotten religion of his ancestors. At the same time he left the Iberian peninsula. It was sometime between 1612 and 1615 that Gabriel, along with his mother and his siblings, emigrated to the Netherlands and in Amsterdam assumed, along with the Jewish religion, the new name of Uriel.

He became critical of his new faith very soon after assuming it, for his first text, entitled *Theses against Tradition*, was written in 1616, when he was in Hamburg on trade business. He sent it to the elders of the Jewish community in Venice, whose pronouncements in matters of faith were treated with particular respect in the Jewish world. As might be expected, the reaction was unequivocal: Rabbi Leon da Modena of Venice wrote back attacking Uriel's heretical opinions, condemned him as an Epicurean and an atheist, and threatened to have him excommunicated if he persisted in his mistaken views. He did persist, and in August 1618 was officially excommunicated by the Jewish community of Venice.

But the place of his excommunication was apparently too distant to influence his own community and lead to his casting out at home, since he returned to Amsterdam and remained there several more years, until the next conflict.

The *Theses Against Tradition* in fact contained nothing to justify the charge of Epicureanism contemptuously flung at da Costa by the Rabbi of Venice. Its approach was, so to speak, of the Protestant type: it attacked certain established religious customs and rituals as being without any foundation in the Bible. Among the things criticized were the use of tefillin; various details of the rite of circumcision; the interpretation of the principle "an eye for an eye" (which according to da Costa should be taken literally: a murderer or other criminal should not be able to get away with just a fine); the number of days required for the celebration of Passover; and a few other things of this type. Da Costa expressed alarm that belief in superstitions was becoming more and more prevalent among Jews, and attributed this state of affairs to the fact that, over time, "human inventions" had supplemented the only true and binding source of the Jewish religion, which is the Torah and the rest of the Hebrew Bible; the Talmud in particular he rejected as being the work of man and therefore of no real consequence. In other words, he defended the unique authority of the Hebrew Bible against later innovations. In this sense his position in the Jewish world might be seen as analogous to the position of those Protestants who, in the Christian world, struggled to defend the unique authority of Scripture against such human products as Councils and later pontifical decrees. In this early period Uriel da Costa was a Jew who defended the original canon against later interpolations and accretions unsupported by divine authority.

But his criticism soon went beyond this. Around 1623 he came to the conclusion that the Bible says nothing about immortality or resurrection, and that we should therefore reject belief in eternal life. He wrote a book on the subject, but the manuscript fell into the hands of his opponents, and not long afterwards (still in 1623) was attacked in print by Samuel da Silva, in an article entitled *Tratado de Immortalidade*. Da Silva quoted extensively from da Costa's manuscript, and the passages he selected for condemnation – three chapters – constitute the only extant evidence of what da Costa wrote. Da Costa, far from retracting his views, replied with a polemical treatise, of which we know only the title: *Examination of the Pharisaic Tradition and the Written Law*. Da Costa's rejection of immortality – a crime punishable by law even in a country as tolerant as Holland – cut him off not only from the Jewish but also from the Christian world. His enemies in the Jewish community brought charges against him before the Amsterdam magistrates; he was imprisoned, then released, but forced to pay a fine of 300 florins – a huge sum. His manuscript was destroyed and da Costa himself officially excommunicated; all the members of the community received strict orders to have nothing to do with him.

Those three surviving chapters of da Costa's treatise on the mortality of the soul are a curious document. They contain no evidence that their author abandoned his faith in God and his belief in the authority of the Bible. On the contrary, he bases most of his arguments on passages in the Bible, directs the brunt of his criticism against the Pharisees and their false and superstitious interpretations of sacred texts, and presents himself as an upholder of the Saducean tradition. The Sadducees, as we know from Josephus Flavius's *Wars of the Jews* and *Antiquities of the Jews*, rejected the belief in the immortality of the soul and in rewards and punishments in the after-life, and accepted only the authority of the written law, which they accused the Pharisees of distorting. Da Costa, then, saw himself as the reviver of what he considered to be the only genuine and orthodox Jewish tradition, and presented his conflict with the Jewish community as the old quarrel between Pharisees and Sadducees. His purely naturalist interpretation of man was based on that original Biblical somatism which Spinoza was to remark on in his *Tractatus Theologico-Politicus* and which, according to his biographer, Lucas, was what first incited him to adopt a critical stance towards the beliefs of Judaism. And indeed many books of the Old Testament – Job, Ecclesiastes, the Psalms – seem to indicate that their authors did not believe in eternal life; de Costa had ample Biblical material to quote in support of his position.

It is apparent, however, that the conflict between "Pharisees" and "Sadducees" is a smokescreen put up to mask the true controversy, which was connected with the changes taking place in the intellectual culture of European Jews. The passages da Costa quotes from the Bible serve to justify his animalistic view of the soul: the belief that the "soul" is part of the material world – a material element of the body (made up of blood and "the life spirit") whose death is as natural as its birth; that there is no other life, no spirits of the dead, no ghosts and no angels; that rewards and punishments are meted out on earth; that divine justice, too, whose intentions no mortal mind can fathom, operates only on earth; that there is no resurrection when our earthly lives come to an end. (The book of Daniel, which claims otherwise, is rejected by da Costa, in accordance with Saducean tradition, as a Pharisean invention.) But his criticism goes beyond the theoretical; its true aim, revealed in the last of the three surviving chapters of his book, is in fact a moral and highly practical one, and has to do with what he saw as the deplorable practical consequences of the beliefs he attacks. He condemns belief in the immortality of the soul because it gives rise to superstitious practices, such as prayers for the dead, sacrifices, asceticism, eremitism and celibacy, and serves to maintain an absurd morality, swathed in the mists of superstition and based on the illusory hope of rewards in the world to come. We must cast off these illusions, he says, and organize our life on earth in the full awareness that it is the only life we have. And he adds that the Pharisees are wrong to argue that belief in immortality is an effective deterrent to wrongdoers: the criminal fears a scaffold he can see more than he fears the unknown terrors of an invisible hell; if the prospect of earthly punishment does not deter him, he will not be influenced by the thought of punishment in the afterlife. We should therefore rejoice in the life we have and give thanks to the Creator for endowing us with reason; instead of building castles in the sand, we should praise God for the joys of our earthly, finite existence.

We can see the direction in which da Costa's thought was developing by tracing its progress from the early *Theses against Tradition* to his treatise on the mortality of the soul. The transition from the first to the second is, to resort to another analogy from the Christian world, rather like a transition from Protestantism to deism. The *Theses* were simply an attempt to defend the purity of the Bible against the "human additions" which distorted its message. The treatise on mortality still defends the divine authority of the canon, but the slant has shifted; the aim and direction of the criticism are different. It defends morality rooted in life on earth against a morality based on eschatology, the idea of man as a reason-endowed part of the material world against the idea of him as a participant in eternity, and the uniqueness of our life on earth against the idea of an imaginary life in the hereafter. The Sadducean tradition is a pretext – used to support and disguise the true direction of da Costa's thought, which was evolving in roughly the same direction as European secular thought at the time.

Our only source of information about subsequent stages of this evolution is da Costa's autobiography. It tells us that after his excommunication he did not renounce his views, but developed them in an even more radical form: he arrived at the conclusion that Mosaic law is the work of man like any other legal code, and many of its precepts are contrary to the laws of nature; consequently God, the creator of nature, would be contradicting Himself if he set down such laws for us to follow. In this way, by questioning the divine provenance of Holy Writ, da Costa arrived at a position which in European thought was usually described as deism; and the road he traveled to arrive there was the same as that taken by the intellectual culture of Europe in the course of its two hundred years of development within the Christian tradition, from

Luther to the early Enlightenment. He did not lose his faith in God, but he lost the faith that His existence had any practical meaning: the faith in Revelation, in eternal life and in eschatological morality.

With time, however, his total isolation became intolerable, and he caved in. Ten years after his excommunication he returned to the Jewish community and asked to be taken back. Against the dictates of his conscience, he wrote and signed a renunciation of his heretical opinions. There is nothing surprising in such a step: he was fifty years old; for ten years he had suffered contempt and ostracism, had been cut off from his friends and family. The moral and material pressures were too great, and he finally bowed before them. He signed the renunciation with no self-delusions, no crisis of a divided conscience; he signed it in the full awareness that it was a lie from start to finish, and he did so only because his life since his excommunication had become beyond bearing. Gebhardt's interpretation of this act is astonishing: he thinks that da Costa stopped believing in the truth of Revelation, became a libertine and rejected all moral principles, and for this reason had no qualms about in signing a false renunciation. But the harsh circumstances of his life are surely explanation enough; we can understand da Costa's action perfectly well without the aid of anti-libertine ideology.

At the very end of his life, when he was writing his autobiography, da Costa regretted his decision. But he was already a broken man; signing the renunciation had destroyed him. The false reconciliation with the Jewish community had been short-lived – not because da Costa committed any new offences against orthodox doctrine, but because he was accused of violating the dietary laws. He had been denounced by an informer. It was still 1633 – the year of his return to the fold. There was another trial, another excommunication. But somewhere da Costa found a new courage – or perhaps he simply could not face another humiliating ceremony of contrition. Whatever his reasons, he did not repent. Once again he found himself isolated and abandoned. The remaining years of his life were spent in utter solitude and dreadful poverty – seven wretched years, which ended in a death that was as tragic as his life. For at the end of this period da Costa weakened once more. He decided to try again: once more he went back to the community; once more he agreed to abase himself in a public act of repentance. This degrading spectacle, described in detail in da Costa's autobiography, took place in the Portuguese synagogue in Amsterdam. He did not survive his humiliation for long. He wrote his autobiography, in which he expressed all his loathing for his persecutors; then, in April of 1640, he shot himself.

The autobiography, like his other writings, was written in his native Portuguese. But the original is lost; the only surviving version is a Latin translation, published in Gouda in 1687 by the Arminian theologian and activist Philip van Lomborch, in his work *On the Truth of the Christian Religion*.

Uriel da Costa's wife died in 1622. He had no children.

* * *

At the time of da Costa's suicide Baruch de Spinoza was eight years old. There is a painting by Hirschenberg which shows the two of them together – the philosopher with the dying defeated reformer. Historians have often wondered to what extent Uriel da Costa's failed rebellion was a source of inspiration for the young Spinoza. Spinoza's objections to Judaism also began with a critique of the Torah. But he was luckier, and probably more prudent as well. He did not break under pressure from the Jewish community; his excommunication was to be permanent. But unlike da Costa he had friends outside the community; it was thanks to their support that he was able to lead an independent life, and to go further in the direction in which da Costa's thought seemed to be heading: towards a naturalistic picture of the world as an autonomous whole, governed by its own laws, and the idea of an autonomous morality, created by people for use on earth. In this light the story of Uriel da Costa is more than just the story of a personal defeat – the defeat of a freethinker crushed by organized orthodoxy. It is also part of the history of the never-ending conflict between tradition, which is the affirmation of the world as we find it, and innovation, which is the rejection of that world. And it is testimony that while there are no ultimate triumphs in this conflict, nor are there ultimate defeats.

Translated by Agnieszka Kolakowska

Pierre Gassendi
Christian, Materialist, Skeptic[1]

Gassendi, long ignored by all but a very few textbooks in the history of philosophy, has only recently become the subject of serious historical study. As the literature about him grows and he begins to attract the attention of historians, the ambiguities and ambivalences in his work become increasingly apparent, and conflicts of opinion about him multiply. It was not only because of the company he kept, but also because of his philosophy, that Gassendi was – and still is – traditionally considered a "libertine"; Friedrich Lange, in his history of materialism,[2] allotted him a privileged position in the pantheon of materialist thinkers – an honor he denied to Descartes. And yet if the label "materialist" seems a trifle rash, to say the least, in the case of Descartes, privileged object that he was of violent attacks from the Jesuits and honored with a permanent place on the index of banned books, how much more inappropriate in the case of his antagonist, Gassendi, whose life was spent in blameless execution of pastoral tasks without any conflicts either with the Jesuits or with the censor. Some Christian historians, eager not only to erase the

1   This essay, published in Warsaw in 1962, was written as an introduction to the Polish translation of Gassendi's *Logic*.

    Citations from Gassendi's works are from the 1658 six-volume collected edition, *Opera Omnia*, Lyon.

    Citations from Descartes' works are from Charles Adam and Paul Tannery (eds.), *Oeuvres de Descartes*, 2nd edition, 11 vols., Paris, Vrin, 1974–1986. This is abbreviated to AT. Citations in English are from J. Cottingham, R. Stoothoff, D. Mardoch and A. Kenny (eds.), *The Philosophical Writings of Descartes*, 3 vols., Cambridge University Press, 1984–1995. This is abbreviated to CSM.

2   A. Lange, *Geschichte des Materialismus*, 2 vols., 1865; vol. I. English trans.: *The History of Materialism*, 3 vols, Harcourt, Brace, London, 1925.

traditional stigma of libertinism from "Gassendi the Epicurean" but also to reconcile the philosopher with the man, duly undertook the task of rescuing both biography and work, in the hope that a picture of complete and unadulterated orthodoxy in all areas of life would emerge. The label of libertine did not, however, stick without good reason. Resolving the conflict may depend more on a clearer formulation of the question than on unearthing either new facts about Gassendi's life or hitherto unknown philosophical texts; in both areas there is plenty of material to be going on with.

I. Gassendi's life
His name
Pierre Gassendi was born on January 22, 1592, in Champtercier, near Digne. His family was of peasant stock, and his was the first generation to abandon the land for professions in the city or for the Church. The name Gassendi is often wrongly considered as the genitive of a presumed Latin 'Gassendus,' but there is no evidence that the form 'Gassendus' was ever used. According to Bernard Rochot,[3] the foremost Gassendi scholar, the '– i' ending (used by all Gassendi's friends) was not a Latin genitive but an italianization – a suffix considered elegant at the time of Marie de Medicis and Mazarin.

His studies and first writings
Gassendi divided his time between Provence and Paris. He began his studies in Aix and continued them in Digne, where, at a very young age, he started lecturing on rhetoric in the local college. In 1609–1612, back in Aix, he studied theology and classical languages, and in 1612 went back to Digne as the director of the local college, a post in which he remained for three years. In the same year he also took holy orders. In 1614, in Avignon, he became a doctor of theology. The following year he went to Paris for the first time, and in 1616 he was ordained as a priest. He became a professor of philosophy at Aix, where, in accordance with custom, he taught Aristotelian doctrine; but he was soon discovering its defects, and indeed the defects of Scholastic philosophy in general, with its peripatetic conceptual framework. It must have been after his return to Digne, where he became a canon of the cathedral chapter, that he began to write down his critical observations about the pagan philosopher most honored in the Christian tradition. The fruit of his dissatisfaction was his first publication, printed in Grenoble in 1624 under the title *Exercitationum paradoxicarum adversus Aristotelos libri duo priores*. It was

3 Bernard Rochot, *Pierre Gassendi, 1592–1655, Sa vie et son oeuvre*, Paris, 1955, p. 11. Reprinted from *Journées gassendistes*, 1953.

conceived as a work in seven parts, but the *Exercitationes* of 1624, despite its title, contained only the first of these; Gassendi may well have feared the consequences of too violent an attack on Aristotle. It was not until after his death that an unfinished manuscript of the second volume found its place in editions of his collected works, and as for the remaining five, it is not known whether any of them were ever written.[4]

At this time Gassendi belonged to a certain well-defined type: the humanist-scholar infected by a deep skepticism and mistrust of authority. He had digested the whole written tradition, classical and Renaissance, which made up the humanist's equipment of his age: Cicero, Seneca, Sextus Empiricus and Lucretius; Ramus, Lipsius, Vives, Montaigne and Charron. He attacked Aristotle mainly from the "Pyrrhonist" standpoint, as it was then called, demonstrating the uncertainty of his proofs and the uselessness of his conceptual categories; for good measure he also condemned him for all the sins and errors which history or legend recorded him as having committed. But his criticism clearly goes beyond Aristotle. It is a critique of dialectics in general, of metaphysics in general, of investigations into "the nature of things" and of absolute morality in general. The spirit which pervades his first published work continue to pervade his thought until his death (although in later writings he was to exhibit more prudence and restraint in articulating it): disbelief in the possibility of a rational approach to metaphysics or theology; the conviction that human knowledge is irremediably faulty, probabilistic, and indeed pragmatic; the denial that there can be any infallible criteria of truth. He was thoroughly steeped in the erudite skepticism characteristic of his age: the doubt of the scholar whose historical studies, supplemented by a knowledge of the world acquired by reading and hearsay, instils in him a profound conviction of the changeability, impermanence and instability of all opinions, all customs, all beliefs and philosophical doctrines. It would be a mistake to see him as an atheist who simply concealed his opinions or failed to follow them through to their conclusion, mindful perhaps of the still-recent terrible fate of Vanini. A skeptical attitude towards natural theology had long been associated with faith that was irrational on principle; in humanists it was usually an undenominational kind of faith, so to speak – a faith reluctant to engage in arguments about dogma, a faith that was general and restrained, free of denominational fanaticism, suspending judgment – on principle – on questions relating to specific points, and at the same time conformist with respect to the rites of the prevailing religion, which it accepted as a necessary element of social order or as a necessary condition for moral education.

4   Lange says that they were but that Gassendi burnt them. However, there is no evidence for this.

It was in the 1620s that Gassendi formed the friendships which were to have the greatest influence both on his life and on his later reputation: his ties to the circle of scholars considered the example *par excellence* of "French libertinism." In Aix he was befriended by Nicolas Fabri, sieur de Peiresc – great scholar, collector of esoterica, correspondent of men of learning throughout Europe; native of the pagan city of Padua; skeptic and anti-cleric, friend of Galileo and patron of Campanelli; a man fascinated no less by natural science and astronomy than by history and studies of antiquity; an encyclopedic mind, although not a creative one. The years 1624–25 witnessed Gassendi's second trip to Paris, where he met Mersenne. This learned Minimite could not, of course, by any stretch of the imagination be considered part of the libertine circle of Gassendi's friends. At the time he had just published his *Quaestiones celeberrimae in Genesim* (1623), where he did his best to demolish the whole of Italian naturalism – the main intellectual source of French libertinism; soon afterwards he went on to publish two further works, in which he attacked deists and skeptics (*L'impiété des déistes*, 1624, and *La vérité des sciences, contre les sceptiques ou pyrrhoniens*, 1625). Nevertheless, he was the person through whom men of learning throughout the world, with their conflicting views, made contact with one another, and without him nothing in the world of scholarship could function. And his unquestioned orthodoxy did not prevent his becoming the chief propagator of Galileo's physics, nor from contributing to the new, quantitative interpretation of the physical world – an interpretation both mechanistic and phenomenalistic. What linked him to the libertines was an attitude shared by the whole avant-garde of natural scientists at the time: an anti-metaphysical approach to physics and an aversion to occultism.

During his next trip to Paris, this time a lengthy one (1628–1632), Gassendi cemented his friendships with the libertine circle in the strict sense of the word: with Elio Diodati, Gabriel Naudé, François Luillier and François de La Mothe Le Vayer. Whether we should take account of these friendships when interpreting his writings is the main question that has divided historians – most often according to what their own ideological preferences and prejudices happened to be.

The return to natural science

It may have been his friendship with Peiresc and Diodati, but above all with Mersenne, that sparked Gassendi's interest in the natural sciences, around which a great philosophical debate was developing. He began to keep a journal of astronomical observations, which he was to continue until the end of his life; he familiarized himself with the latest discoveries in physics and astronomy. His first letter to Galileo dates from 1625.

The long list of his publications, in which he set out observations, theoretical speculations and polemics with other scholars, begins in this period and continues throughout his life. In 1632 he published *Mercurius in
sole visus*; in 1636, *De apparente magnitudine solis*. In 1640 and 1642 he published further observations on the same subject. 1642 saw the publication
of his *De Motu impresso a motore translato*, as well the letter *De proportione
qua gravia decidentia accelerantur*. In 1643 there was *Novem stellae circa
Iovem visae*, and in 1647 a collection of lectures, *Institutio astronomica*. In
1654 he published the biographies of some astronomers and a work entitled *Sentiments sur l'Eclipse qui doit arriver*. But this list, far from complete,
does not reflect the full extent of his interest in natural science. Gassendi
was curious about everything; he knew doctors and physiologists, and
took part in anatomical demonstrations; he defended Harvey's theory;
he was interested in questions of nutrition (and advocated vegetarian-
ism as the healthiest diet). He soon forgot his youthful interest in astrology, and began to take an active and eager part in the battle then being
waged by the republic of scholars against the "sciences of the occult" –
fortunetelling by the stars, alchemy and cabbalism – which had become
extremely popular. In 1630, at Mersenne's suggestion, he wrote an attack
on the doctrines of the well-known English occultist Robert Fludd
(*Epistolica exercitatio in qua praecipua principia philosophiae Roberti Fludi
deteguntur*,[5]), and in 1642 he tackled the astrological doctrines of Jean-
Baptiste Morin, a sworn enemy of Copernicanism and the only person
who in Gassendi's lifetime ever accused him of atheism.

At the same time, Gassendi did not neglect his priestly duties; he
approached them with the same eagerness and scrupulousness which
characterized his astronomical observations and elicited the admiration
of other scholars. In 1629 he was made provost of the cathedral chapter
in Digne, but it was not until his return from Paris in 1634 that he took
up his position. He was a staunch and conscientious guardian of the
interests of the diocese, and energetically defended its rights of owner-
ship to various disputed buildings and pieces of land. He also made a
study of its history, and the fruit of his investigations, based on a considerable amount of detailed archival research, was a brief work entitled
Notitia Ecclesiae Dinensis, which he published near the end of his life, in
1654.

It was in the mid-1620s that Gassendi first took an interest in the
philosopher to whom he was to devote so much of his life's work, and
whose name came to be linked, in popular memory and in the consciousness of philosophers, with Gassendi's own – Epicurus. "My phi-

5   In the *Opera* (vol.III), this essay is entitled *Examen philosophiae Roberti Fluddi
    medici*.

losophy of Epicurus" was how he later referred to his own work; others were to think of him as the man who "resuscitated Epicureanism."

Within the Christian tradition, Epicurus enjoyed the worst possible reputation. Given the atmosphere of the age, Gassendi's attempts to elevate him to the distinguished position occupied (in his view unjustifiably) by Aristotle seem astonishingly risky, even reckless. And yet Gassendi's most important philosophical works are devoted to exposing and defending Epicurus's doctrine. It was a doctrine which in his view lent itself much better than pointless peripatetic speculation to an assimilative treatment within Christianity. But his work on Epicurus did not appear until in the second half of the 1640s: *De vita et moribus Epicuri* appeared in 1647; *Animadversiones in Decimum librum Diogenis Laertii, qui est de Vita, Moribus, Placitisque Epicuri* (which included his *Philosophiae Epicuri Syntagma*) was published in 1649. Gassendi's own *Syntagma Philosophicum* was not published until after his death.

In 1632 Gassendi returned to Provence, where he regularly visited Peiresc until the latter's death in 1637 and kept up a voluminous correspondence with men of learning throughout Europe. The list of his friends and correspondents is extraordinarily long and includes, apart from those already mentioned, almost all the most illustrious European names of the age: Campanella, Hobbes, Descartes, Kepler, Galileo, van Helmont, Sorbière, Grotius, Saint-Evremond, Guy de la Brosse, Beeckman, to mention only a few (and excluding those who became famous chiefly through their association with Gassendi).

In 1643, at Peiresc's request, Gassendi wrote a polemical essay about a recently published but already famous book by Herbert of Cherbury, *De Veritate*. (An incomplete version, which is all that survived, was published posthumously with his other papers.) This critique, like his attacks against the Aristotelians, was written in a spirit of what one might call skeptical pragmatism. It ridicules the idea of consensus as a criterion of truth, denies the possibility of a "philosophical" Christianity – a Christianity reducible to natural knowledge – and repeats arguments purporting to demonstrate the inaccessibility of the hidden secrets of nature.

In 1633 the European world of learning was shaken by the sight of the seventy-year-old Galileo, condemned by the Holy Office and forced to recant his work, kneeling to recite the statement of retraction prepared for him by the inquisitors and listening as his sentence of life imprisonment is pronounced. Descartes was quick to interpret Galileo's recantation as a sign that he, too, was in danger of being condemned, and renounced the publication of the work he had just finished. Gassendi, a convinced Copernican, wrote to Galileo expressing his support in matters scientific but advising obedience towards the judges; his conscience was salved by the knowledge that he had served the cause of truth.

In 1641 Gassendi again came to Paris, and remained there for seven years. It was to be his longest stay in the capital. On his previous visit he had stayed with François Lullier; this time Lullier was absent, and Gassendi found lodgings with a canon of his acquaintance. He took up again with his libertine circle of friends, which in the meantime had admitted a new member: Guy Patin, a physician, anti-clerical and free-thinker. That year, in addition to a biography of Peiresc – a homage to the memory of his dead friend – Gassendi wrote (at Mersenne's request) the work for which he is best known: the objections to Descartes' *Meditations*. They appeared, together with Descartes' response, along-side a number of other objections, written from a variety of philosophical standpoints; the resulting polemical document was to become one of the most famous texts in the history of philosophical thought.

He was also gathering pupils; and the group of young followers who attached themselves to him contributed no less than his friends and peers to his reputation as a libertine. They included Claude Chapelle, illegitimate son of Luillier, as notorious as his father for his loose ways and more than doubtful faith; Bernier, the future propagator of Gassendi's doctrines; the young La Mothe Le Vayer; Rostand's colorful eponymous hero Cyrano de Bergerac – playwright and trouble-maker, godless cynic and malicious mocker; and – at least according to Gassendi's first biographer, Grimarest – Molière. Grimarest was not known as the most accurate of biographers, and since there is no corrob-orating evidence in other sources, this claim has been disputed. Nevertheless, it is quite possible that Molière was indeed part of Gassendi's circle; we certainly know that he counted Gassendists among his closest friends. We also know that in his views he was a Gassendist himself, and his comedies provide plentiful indications of this (as does the fact that Molière also translated Lucretius into French, although the manuscript of his translation was destroyed by a servant who made it into curl-papers.) In addition to giving private lessons to his pupils, Gassendi also lectured in public: in 1645 he became professor at the Collège Royal, where he lectured on Astronomy – clearly enough so as to leave no doubt that he was a Copernican, but prudently enough so as to be able to pass, if necessary, as a proponent of the more moderate cos-mology of Tycho Brahe. Some time before the beginning of these lectures Sorbière, without Gassendi's knowledge, announced the publication of his reply to Descartes' Response to the Objections to the *Meditations*. This work, entitled *Disquisitio Metaphysica, seu Dubitationes et Instantiae adver-sus Renati Cartesii Metaphysicam*, appeared in Amsterdam in 1644.

The Last Years

In 1648 Mersenne died, Gassendi fell ill with tuberculosis and the Fronde broke out. Gassendi went back to Provence, first to Aix for a few months, then to Digne. Here he worked on "his" Epicurus and reproduced the famous vacuum experiments which Périer, inspired by an idea of Pascal's, had carried out in September of that year in Puy de Dôme.

He was by now a famous man. Queen Christina of Sweden, determined to persevere in her quest for men of learning, invited him to Stockholm shortly after Descartes had breathed his last at her court. Gassendi declined: he was ill, he wrote in an elegant reply, and could not undertake such a journey.

He did undertake one last journey, however – to Paris. He traveled up in 1653, accompanied by the ever-faithful Bernier, and was taken in by a new protector, whose hospitality he enjoyed until his death – the aristocrat Habert de Montmor. It was under the patronage of de Montmor that the "Academy for the Study of Natural Causes" – the precursor of the future Academy of Sciences – was formed.

His last years were extraordinarily fruitful. In addition to biographies of famous astronomers (Tycho Brahe, Copernicus, Peurbach, Müller-Regiomontanus), a treatise on musicology, a history of the church in Digne and a small work entitled *Romanum Calendarium*, he wrote his *Syntagma philosophicum* – a kind of synthesis of his own philosophical thinking – and prepared a complete edition of his works, which included a number of texts not previously published, among them part two of his *Exercitationes*.

However, he did not live to see them published or to complete his editing. He fell ill in November 1654 and died less than a year later, in October 1655, having received all the rites which the Church bestows upon the dying. His end may have been considerably hastened by the intensive medical care he received, in which – according to the detailed descriptions left by his secretary, La Poterie – the main form of therapy seems to have consisted of copious bloodletting at frequent intervals. He was looked after by Patin, who remarked after his friend's death, "I would rather ten Roman cardinals had died." He hated cardinals with a passion.

In 1658 the efforts of his friends – Sorbière, Poterie and others – resulted in the publication, in Lyons, of a six-volume edition of Gassendi's works. The dense, heavy Latin tomes could not be expected to attract huge numbers of readers, and the next edition was not until 1727, in Florence. Nevertheless, Gassendi's doctrine spread, promoted in the writings of his friends, and it was not long before the existence of a clearly Gassendist and anti-Cartesian circle made itself felt in the intellectual world of Paris. "Gassendism" received more publicity when

Bernier began publishing his "concise" (seven-volume) version of Gassendi's philosophy (1674–1678). By the end of the seventeenth century, syncretic views in which Gassendism and Cartesianism were combined were much more common in the intellectual world of France than pure, orthodox Cartesianism. The watered-down libertinism popular in "good society" owed more to Gassendi than to his infinitely more famous antagonist. But apart from the objections to the *Meditations*, which appeared in countless editions of Descartes, Gassendi's works were neither reprinted nor translated. It was not until 1959 that a critical edition and French translation of the *Exercitationes* was published, prepared by Bernard Rochot, who intended it as the first volume of Gassendi's collected works. Recent years have seen a certain amount of renewed interest in Gassendi and the development of an ideologically laden debate about how his doctrine should be interpreted.

II. Gassendi's milieu

What were they like, all those people who made up the circle of Gassendi's closest friends? René Pintard, the author of a monumental work on libertinism in the first half of the seventeenth century,[6] provides a detailed account of this milieu and its ways: the habits, interests and inclinations of its members and the characteristic features of the group as a whole: its areas of weakness and stubbornness, its hesitations, equivocations and silences.

There is of course no libertine catechism, no collection of doctrinal assertions representing the views of every libertine and summing up the essentials of French libertinism. This is because among its salient characteristics are flexibility, an aversion to closed systems and a disbelief in the possibility of definitive solutions to metaphysical problems. Intellectual libertinism is more an attitude than a doctrine: a kind of calm skeptical detachment towards the age in which one lives, often ironic and tinged with a certain melancholy. But the irony is not combative, the skepticism is not militant or doctrinal, and the melancholy is not despair. Libertines were a by-product of Christian culture: more than a hundred years of violent doctrinal conflict, religious wars, schisms, sects, heresies and theological speculation had instilled in them in a total indifference to issues of creed and a conviction that any kind of established faith, if it is free from internal conflict, is better than the pointless bickering of theologians which can only be stilled with the aid of firearms and gunpowder. The libertines combined wide historical learning and humanist culture with a passion for scientific discoveries, which they discussed and

6 René Pintard, *Le Libertinage érudit dans la première moitié du XVIIe siècle*, vols. I–II, Paris, 1943.

commented on quite independently of whatever their particular religious point of view happened to be. Their writings were rarely polemical or belligerent; they preferred to withdraw rather than engage in decisive conflicts. They were ever mindful of the experiences of the old church, which had seen everything and been through everything and which few things could surprise or outrage. They had none of the spirit of missionaries, no wish to convert the masses to their truth. An enclosed, elite group, they thought of themselves as aristocrats of the spirit. Indeed, they condemned atheism among the people, for they were convinced that an established faith was essential for the maintenance of social order. According to Naudé, Cesare Cremonini, a leading figure in the movement, confided to his friends that although he believed neither in God nor in the devil nor in the immortality of the soul, he saw to it that his valet was a good Catholic, for otherwise the man might one day slit his throat.[7] Cremoni is also said to have ordered the epitaph *"Hic iacet totus Cremoninus"* to be engraved on his tombstone.

So it was not only the fear of persecution, and the fact that blasphemy, sacrilege and godlessness were punished by the law (which in any case dealt much more severely with libertine behavior than with speech; in cases of purely verbal expressions of atheism it tended, in practice, to be less harshly enforced), that led the libertines to moderate their skepticism and atheism in their public utterances; if their motto was *"Intus ut libet, foris ut moris est,"* it was also because they believed that a morality freed from religious motivations was accessible only to a select few, and that the masses must receive its commandments in the more readily digestible form of traditional faith – a conviction voiced clearly and honestly by La Mothe Le Vayer in his early dialogues. The libertines also believed that good government requires religious unity, and on this point found Machiavelli's advice of enduring value. Sorbière, Naudé and La Mothe Le Vayer knew perfectly well how religious pretexts can be used as political instruments. But their program was not one of emancipating religion from politics; they were all inclined to favor absolutism, especially after experiencing the Fronde. Pintard even called them the avant-garde of the absolutist movement.[8] Their principal concern was simply to free society from the uncomfortable weight of religious conflicts and doctrinal disagreements. Naudé hated the Reformation, but he viewed with equal distaste the endless squabbles of the Jansenists and the Jesuits. The libertines deplored and saw little point in the multiply-

7 Pintard, *op. cit.*, p. 172.
8 *Ibid.*, p. 560.

ing of sects and points of disagreement in a hopeless effort to discover an ultimate, divine truth which in any case is inaccessible to man. They thought that religious faith, if it was to be of any use to society and public morals, should be formulated as generally as possible, without detailed explanations; and that, having reaped the benefits that accrued from it, people should be encouraged to occupy themselves with activities more useful than reflecting on the nature of the Trinity or of efficient Grace.

Thus the skepticism of the libertines was not aimed against religion in general. It did, however, have political consequences. The libertine program, involving as it did a form of religion which, reduced to the basic, most important beliefs, would serve the state by helping to maintain social unity, effectively supported the principle of subordinating religion to the state. This is not to say that all libertines were simply convinced atheists. Most of them probably tended towards a deist view of the world, although they did not expect to be able to establish the existence of God with the aid of "natural" reason, believing rather that it should be accepted through fideism alone. On this issue Pintard identifies three distinct viewpoints among the libertines:[9] there were Catholics with ties to the Church (Bouillau, Gassendi himself) who had, almost against their will, progressed farther than they would have liked in their atheism; emancipated Protestants (Diodati, Sorbière) with philosophical interests outside religion, who lapsed into heresy and finally into atheism; and genuine atheists (Naudé, Le Vayer, Luillier, Bouchard), devotees of a pagan humanism, by character, instinct and nature deeply non-Christian, who sought a solution in calm irony. But they all of them felt out of tune with their age, and distanced themselves from it through their own private, proud secret.

Skepticism bolstered by historical erudition can serve as a weapon against unjustified attempts to rationalize religion; against metaphysical speculation and the Scholastic tradition; and against common superstitions, beliefs in omens and visions, and the occult sciences. The libertines attacked the last of these in particular quite openly and unequivocally, since here they had Catholic orthodoxy largely on their side. They could with impunity indulge in unrestrained mockery of pretenders to secret wisdom, hermeticists, masters of esoteric techniques, Rosicrucians, sorcerers, astrologers and the like, and against these they gleefully directed their venom. Ostensibly, in attacking gullibility, childish credence and superstition they were supporting a cause which the Church, albeit for

9   *Ibid.,* p. 565 n.

somewhat different reasons, considered its own. But to readers the analogy was plain: their criticisms of pagan priests, seers and soothsayers, oracles, prophecies and miracles relied rather too heavily on examples which bore striking resemblance to popularly known Christian legends. They also cast doubt, openly and directly, on many miracles in the history of Christianity. No one denied the existence of miracles, of course, or said outright that he didn't believe in them; on the contrary, general declarations of a perfectly orthodox kind were made. But they questioned particular instances of miracles and cases divine intervention, individually, one by one, and gave no contrary examples. In principle miracles could happen, but it seemed that in each individual case the purported miracle was shown to be either explicable by natural causes, or demonstrably a sham, or patently derived from legends and myths.

Thus skepticism attacked Scholasticism, natural theology and common superstition. It did not, however, attack historical or scientific investigations, as long as they were conducted in a spirit of detachment, with permanent reservations, without appeals to authority or dogmatic assumptions. It involved no contempt for "natural" reason and had no sympathy whatsoever with criticisms of scientific or historical studies as a pointless waste of time. On the contrary, it was a skepticism imbued with the spirit of endless curiosity about the world, a skepticism that shaped and propagated new methods of historical criticism and emphasized the importance of careful observations and experiments. (It is remarkable how closely some of its main tenets resemble the rules later formulated by the logical positivists.) Its chief concern was simply that we should not waste time on fruitless disagreements over problems which cannot be solved by any experimental means available to us; and that, in matters where our knowledge *can* progress, we should consider no solution as definitive, but always be prepared to change our opinions, maintaining towards them that attitude of constant detachment and reserve which is essential to the scholar and scientist if he is not to sink into a permanent, frozen self-satisfaction, clutching stubbornly at the results he has achieved and unwilling to let them go.

Ever since the 1560s, when Stephanus and Hervet published Latin translations of Sextus Empiricus, the spectacular career of Pyrrhonism overshadowed this kind of skepticism. There is a vast difference between the Pyrrhonists' stiff, all-encompassing dogma that we can know nothing and the attitude of prudence and moderation in judgments advocated by the libertines; and it is this latter which seems to have interested the Renaissance skeptics and their seventeenth-century followers. This is apparent in the works of Charron, and even more in those of Sanchez, whose notorious tract *Quod nihil scitur* was not, as its stark and somewhat brutal title seemed to proclaim, an attempt to question the possibility of knowledge, but only to oppose the cult of authority and put a stop to pointless investigations of insoluble problems.

There is ample evidence of this. Gassendi's own works, the writings of his libertine friends and the works of Montaigne and Charron all contain frequent assurances that this kind of skepticism not only does not undermine real faith but actually serves it, for by proclaiming the powerlessness of reason in the face of things divine it protects the mystery of faith from the criticism and curiosity of our feeble human understanding; it makes the nature of divinity a question of faith alone and puts sacrilegious debates to rest.

However, there is an important distinction to be made here. When Christian mystics or apologists for the Counter-Reformation abandon Scholastic realism and reject rational arguments in favor of faith alone, they seem, on the face of it, to be making a very similar point: that we must distinguish between the realm of things accessible to reason and the realm of the mysteries of revelation, and that faced with latter we must bow to authority and abandon the subtle arguments of reason. But the similarity is superficial and misleading. Their argument is quite different, because the framework of values within which they situate it is quite different. For them, while the mysteries of faith are indeed inaccessible to reason, they are also the only things worth thinking about – the only area of life that is genuinely important. Consequently, if "reason" is powerless in matters of faith, it is powerless altogether: its defects and its fallibility are so far-reaching that it cannot help us to realize the only values which matter and are worth striving for. While the fideism of the Counter-Reformation was an attempt to rescue faith from the pressure of rationalist or heterodox criticism by declaring the content of revelation to be essentially (*sit venia verbo*) "unrationalizable," libertine skepticism, on the contrary, wanted to establish the independence of secular knowledge and free it from theological control, and – no less importantly – to eliminate dogmatic conflicts which are "in any case" impossible to resolve. Its aims, despite some ostensible similarities of formulation, were quite different.

Indeed, a skepticism so conceived may be seen as part of a more general, irenic current of thought, where the emphasis was on eliminating religious discord and, in matters concerning revelation, being content with the accepted formulas, without trying to fathom more than can be fathomed by human reason. It was a skepticism which masked a complete religious indifference, in particular to disagreements in matters of dogma; a conviction that the existing religion is always the best, just because it exists; and a belief that all attempts at religious reform are doomed to end in religious wars, persecution and intolerance. Hence the libertines' absolutist program in religious matters and their advocacy of a state religion – a good thing regardless of its content, in their view, as long as it brings about the desired outcome: an end to dogmatic controversy. La Mothe Le Vayer is quite explicit on this point, like Hobbes: "Insofar as the truths which heaven has revealed to us are, in their entirety, undemonstrable principles, they are spiritual medicines, which should – if we care about our own salvation – be swallowed at one gulp rather than savored with an excess of curiosity about their taste; but in every other area we may make use of our reason."[10] This, then, would seem to be a skepticism that is anti-theological and anti-metaphysical in its attitude to knowledge and cognition, absolutist in its attitude to politics, and modern and scientific in its approach to methodology.

But such a description would not be entirely accurate. For while it is true that these skeptics love and value knowledge, learning and scholarship, that they are curious about novelties, interested in the world and eager to amass information about all variety of things, nevertheless their eagerness, interest and curiosity are counterbalanced by an excessive preoccupation with the mutability and uncertainty of all general principles, so that they lack any enthusiasm for a broader and more vigorous approach and are averse to scientific generalities, syntheses or universal constructions. This attitude gave rise to men of great learning and encyclopaedic collectors of information, to critics of legend and polyhistorians, such as Bayle or Fontenelle; but it did not give rise to Galileos.

The French libertines were generally favorable to the new astronomy, but the trend towards the mathematization of knowledge which was beginning to make itself felt in physics and astronomy was alien to them. They remained in large measure men of the Renaissance; and, like the Renaissance freethinkers, they were born into a Catholic atmosphere. Libertinism was a product of Catholic culture, and could not really find a firm foothold within the sphere annexed by the Reformation; one might say that the Reformation was too young to permit itself the luxury of tolerance towards what was a barely veiled religious indifference. Whereas the Catholic Church, even (or perhaps especially) during the Counter-Reformation, succeeded in maintaining a pluralist attitude, permitting so great a diversity of religious spirit, so many different forms of religious life, that its flexibility was often advantageous to, and exploited by, people whose religiosity had decayed and faded away almost to nothing, even if they retained some modest, private measure of faith in Providence. Heretics, militant atheists, critics of dogma and reformist zealots who lived only by Christ (albeit a Christ conceived according to

10 *Ibid.*, p. 526.

their own rather singular design) could not hope for indulgence; but those who looked to religion for peace rather than martyrdom and approached it in a spirit of ready, open-hearted toleration, with equal indifference to everything – to atheism no less than to all varieties of religion and creed – stood a far greater chance of acceptance within the sphere of influence of Catholic culture. These were people who, although they believed in the progress of knowledge, doubted the value of great social and religious reforms; they accepted – like Guy Patin or Naudé – the existing forms, in the full knowledge of their imperfections and without much hope that they could ever be fundamentally changed, or that political life could ever be governed by moral principles. They did not construct utopias. They firmly believed that human life just was the way it was, and that this should be accepted.

III. The skeptic; the two phases of Gassendism

It is generally agreed that the radical skepticism of the *Exercitationes* gave way to a much more moderate attitude in Gassendi's later works, particularly in his *Syntagma*. Henri Berr, who in 1898 wrote a treatise on Gassendi's skepticism, thought that this mellowing was simply the result of Gassendi's gradual accumulation of knowledge: the more he knew, the more he was convinced that knowledge was possible; as he observed his own progress, his critique of the value and possibilities of human cognition was weakened.[11] Pintard, however, thinks that Gassendi, like many people, simply became more conservative with age; it was age that naturally blunted the edge of his arrogance, his élan and his philosopher's fighting spirit. Both these analyses share the distinction of being utterly unverifiable. Putting psychological speculation aside, let us see what can be said for certain about Gassendi's change of position towards skepticism, and how, in spite of this change, the spirit of Pyrrhonism nevertheless permeates all his work.

When he wrote the *Exercitationes* Gassendi already had a considerable amount of philosophical learning under his belt, acquired by readings in ancient philosophy but also by the study of Renaissance thinkers (such as Vives, Pico della Mirandola, Ramus and Charron). In volume two he is explicit and unequivocal about his Pyrrhonism, and makes use of it – mainly to attack the philosophy of Aristotle's *Organon*, which seems to him, in its basic conceptual framework, to be badly flawed and full of contradictions. (Nor does he spare Aristotle himself, painting him in his biography as an ungrateful, intriguing hypocrite, a traitor to his country and a poisoner.) But it was not his intention to discourage his

11 Henri Berr, *Du scepticisme de Gassendi*, French tr. by Bernard Rochot, Paris, 1960.

readers from study; he merely wanted to convince them[12] that in order to acquire knowledge they had no need of dialectics, only of the right mental and physical conditions, reliable teachers and good will. He is forceful in his condemnation of the cult of authority, but when he exalts independent thought, it is not in the belief that all striving after truth is doomed from the start, and that the emancipated spirit, powerless in the face of this fact, can do nothing except affirm its own freedom; his often quoted phrase, "*quod nulla sit scientia, et maxime Aristotelea*," does not mean that all knowledge is impossible, only that a certain kind of knowledge is impossible – namely the kind of knowledge hoped for by traditional dogmatists. Gassendi agreed that the experience of our senses can never reveal to us the true nature of things; that philosophical argument is powerless to prove the existence of God and the immortal soul; that general consensus, even if it could be shown to exist, is not an adequate criterion of truth in any matter; that human judgment is infinitely changeable and dependent on all sorts of factors – temperament, climate, race, upbringing, education, age, etc.; and that there is no "natural instinct" which could be seen as the source of universal moral or legal norms, but that justice and morality are the products of human decisions, and just as unstable as human conditions: actions condemned as contemptible and wrong in one place will be considered laudable and right in another. But he believed that knowledge is nevertheless possible, and that it has two sources: revelation and sense experience.

According to Gassendi, all we can know of metaphysical matters – including the nature of substance or mind – is what revelation tells us; the mysteries of faith are not subject to proof. Gassendi is radical in rejecting metaphysics as well as theology as irrational; metaphysics is for him by definition beyond the reach of discursive reason. As for his attitude to sense experience, he is an Epicurean: *sensus nunquam fallitur*. He accepts the Epicurean principle that our perception cannot be wrong, only our judgments. Perception by itself gives us no insight into the real nature of things; it only tells us about phenomena: how such and such a thing appears to us. In other words, within the sphere of knowledge accessible to us there is no difference between how things appear to us and how they really are, for only things as they appear to us can be the object of human cognitive endeavors. But even this kind of knowledge – circumscribed in its goals, conscious of its own limits and humbly resigned to abandoning higher aspirations – is worth cultivating, and even merits our enthusiasm. In a letter to Galileo written in 1625, Gassendi expresses his wholehearted admiration for Copernican astron-

12 Petri Gassendi . . . *Opera omnia*, Lugduni MDCLVIII; vol. III, p. 156 (*Exercit.*, II.1.IX).

omy, which "allows the emancipated spirit to wander freely through infinite spaces now that the obstacles of the traditional (*vulgaris*) world and its conceptions have fallen away."[13]

There are many similar passages in Gassendi's later writings, where the same motif returns again and again. In his critique of Herbert of Cherbury, written in 1634,[14] he attacks the English irenist's proposed criteria of truth, objecting that neither our allegedly innate instincts nor general consensus are of the slightest value as cognitive tools. "The truth is concealed from human sight," he says; our infallible sense experience tells us only how things appear to us, not how the things our senses perceive really are; I can state with certainty that honey appears sweet to my palate, or, to put it another way, that I am experiencing sweetness, but I can have no certain knowledge about the true nature of honey. There is nothing clear about the idea of the immaterial soul, despite Herbert's apparent understanding of it; and his belief that the truths of Christian faith are compelling, and must strike every human reason as evident, derives simply from the fact that he was brought up on those truths from childhood. There is no such thing as general consensus; and even if it could be established on any question, it would prove nothing. For even if it is true to say that everyone desires happiness, and that there is general agreement that everyone desires happiness, nothing follows from this agreement, since everyone's conception of happiness is different. The only things we can know are the things we can do.

This last statement of Gassendi's seems to suggest a pragmatic conception of knowledge; and indeed he comes back to it several times his later writings. We should content ourselves with the knowledge we can make use of, he says; that is what our cognitive skills are for. We should not seek to learn the true nature of things. This approach – according to Fludd's critique, written in 1630 – may be seen as a sort of "return to things," to use a Husserlian phrase. Metaphysical speculation imposes on the world a fictional design which exists only in our imagination, whereas knowledge based on experience and experiment, free from grand aspirations and extravagant claims, is "thought based on reality itself." It "reads directly from the book of nature," and precisely for this reason is able to put an end to sterile arguments and allow us to attain such certainty as the human mind is capable of. The view Gassendi is expounding, then, is a phenomenalism that is very close to Mersenne's: somewhat differently expressed, but in its content (at least as far as science is concerned) basically the same. Its main skeptical principle is that

13 *Opera* III, and reprinted in *Tricentenaire de Pierre Gassendi, Actes du Congrès,* 1955.
14 *Opera* VI, p. 4.

theology and metaphysics should give way to knowledge in the Comtean sense of the word. Gassendi's letters and astronomical treatises abound in disparaging remarks about the meager penetrative capacities of human reason, and in each instance he stresses that since the truth about the nature of things is inaccessible to us, we must be content with probability, which was created only because of the weakness of our reason.

Both Berr and Pintard observe a change in Gassendi's skeptical orientation at the beginning of the 1640s. In his *Disquisitio* concerning Descartes Gassendi remarks that the ancient skeptics distinguished between the world of phenomena, which was accessible to our senses, and the noumenal world, about which we must suspend judgment; and also between our practical activities and the search for truth. They did not question our cognitive capacity to assimilate the world of appearances, but cautioned that the knowledge we accumulated about that world was not to be ascribed to anything beyond phenomena. However, this distinction is still entirely in keeping with the skepticism of the earlier treatises: Gassendi simply wants to defend skepticism against the objection that the Pyrrhonist *epoche* leads to practical paralysis, making all activity impossible. His argument is that it does nothing of the kind, for we can perfectly well act even when we know that the results of our cognitive efforts can be measured only in terms of probability and can never go beyond appearances. Even his remark that, contrary to Descartes' view, the external world is more certain and better known to us than our own inner world, does not exceed the limits of his previous skepticism: there is no suggestion that the external world can be known on any level other than the phenomenal. In fact we know that Gassendi did not abandon his phenomenalism: in his Objection to the *Meditations*, commenting on Descartes' example of the wax, he says, ". . . the concept of the wax or its substance can be abstracted from the concept of its accidents. But does this really imply that the substance or nature of the wax is itself distinctly conceived? Besides the color, the shape, the fact that it can melt, etc., we conceive that there is something which is the subject of the accidents and changes we observe; but what this subject is, or what its nature is, we do not know."[15]

In questioning the Cartesian distinction between what is evident in fact and what is evident to us subjectively, Gassendi is still well within the limits of his old Pyrrhonism: he is repeating his objection that there is no way of establishing that something which appears evident to us is evident in reality. Even the axioms of mathematics, which seem evident to our reason and impose themselves on it with an irresistible force, con-

---

15 *Fifth Set of Objections to the Meditations*, AT VII, p. 271; CSM II, p. 189.

tain nothing that compels us to believe them to be true "in themselves." And Gassendi's criticism of other Cartesian arguments, such as Descartes' proofs of the existence of God and the immaterial soul, is made in the same stubbornly skeptical spirit as in his previous work: within the domain of what we can know about the world, all statements about supernatural reality must be consigned to parentheses. There are no innate ideas, no clear idea of God or of the soul, no direct knowledge of ourselves, but only indirect, through external things; the God of philosophers, including Descartes' God, is constructed entirely out of human attributes which have simply been enlarged, and any other kind of God must remain hopelessly elusive to our reason. "You say *that it is reasonable to believe that you are made in the image and likeness of God*. This is certainly believable given religious faith, but how may it be understood by natural reason, unless you are putting forward an anthropomorphic picture of God?"[16] Gassendi's nominalist criticism of Cartesian ideas, his almost Berkeleyan sensualism (apparent in his remark about the "false nature of the triangle"[17]), his purely negative and very Hobbesian conception of infinity, his critique of the ontological argument for the existence of God and his dangerously far-reaching program of complete tolerance towards all opinions, since all are equally justified – all these views and arguments fit quite comfortably within his earlier program, and are quite befitting for a pupil of the Academy.

In one charge he makes against Descartes, however, Gassendi does diverge markedly from his previous position. He accuses Descartes of abandoning the teleological path to God – the path of final causes. His arguments seem to indicate quite clearly that he accepts the argument from God's existence *ex gubernatione rerum*, and indeed his later texts fully confirm this. In his letter to Louis de Valois[18] he distinguishes "acataleptic" skeptics, who thought that all truths were ungraspable and inaccessible, from those who simply advocated suspension of judgment in matters which were uncertain, while continuing their search for knowledge. However, he still insists that we can know only the "surface" of things.

In the *Syntagma* there is a marked difference of approach – a general change of style and emphasis, but on many specific issues also a significant shift of position. Where the Gassendi of the *Exercitationes* might say,

16 *Ibid.*, AT VII, p. 306; CSM II, p. 213.
17 *Ibid.*, AT VII, p. 322; CSM II, pp. 223–24:. ". . . the false nature of the triangle, which is supposed to consist of lines which lack breadth, to contain an area which has no depth, and to terminate in three points which have no dimensions at all."
18 *Opera* VI, p. 135.

"although the world of appearances is there for us to see, we cannot know the nature of things," the Gassendi of the *Syntagma* would shift the emphasis and say: "although the hidden mysteries of nature are inaccessible to us, there are no limits to how far we can extend our knowledge of the world on the phenomenal level." This contrast roughly sums up the difference in general approach: we may not be able to penetrate into the inner sanctuary of the cosmos, but we can participate in its external ceremonies. In other words, in the *Syntagma* Gassendi concentrates more on what we can know rather than on what is hidden. On some issues, however, such as that of truth criteria and evident truths, there is a substantial change of position. He now thinks that certain *"propositiones necessariae"* – the axioms of mathematics and of the mathematical sciences, the first principles of cognition – impose themselves irresistibly upon our reason, compelling our assent: "propositions to which we assent as soon as we have grasped their meaning."[19] He gives as examples not only common tautologies ("the whole is greater than its parts," "something either is or is not," "the same thing cannot both be and not be"), but also statements of a metaphysical kind, or which at least would be instinctively considered as such today: "Neither nature nor art can make something out of nothing," "God and Nature do nothing in vain." It seems clear that he now accepts the criterion of purely intellectual evident truths which he had firmly rejected in his critique of Descartes. He also admits the possibility of deducing the existence of God from its observable effects in nature, and even accepts the validity of the argument for general consensus as a criterion of truth.

In spite of this, however, Gassendi remains at least partly faithful to his Pyrrhonist past. The philosophical program of the *Syntagma* divides philosophy into physics, logic and ethics; metaphysics is conspicuous by its absence. So is natural theology: although some of his remarks might seem to belong to this domain, it has no allotted place, and in general Gassendi is very little concerned with it. Epicurean physics, in which his presentation of the material world is grounded, attracts him precisely because it maintains knowledge within the limits of experience, and especially because it involves no speculation about the metaphysical structure of reality. Thus the essence of his phenomenalism remains, despite some concessions to natural theology. In the domain of ethics, too, his arguments are very much in the spirit of his old relativism, and presuppose Epicurean principles. And the pragmatic or utilitarian nature of philosophy is stressed in an initial declaration: "*Nisi qui eo spectat, ut felicius vitam traducat, haud revera philosophatur.*"[20]

19 *Opera* I, p. 104.
20 *Ibid.*, p. 3.

One might hazard the claim that the same God once considered by Gassendi as an object of blind faith, utterly excluded from the realm of rational thought, has now become a reality which manifests itself, through the order of the visible world, as the guiding principle and efficient cause of that world, but in no way influences our thinking about the structure of nature and the ways in which it reveals itself to us. God is not an explanatory principle without which the world is incomprehensible; we need not invoke divine intervention in order to explain the causes of individual events and the workings of nature. Our faith requires us to believe that prayers are sometimes answered; but God does not change His mind as a result of human entreaties. God, in His infinite wisdom, anticipates all our prayers and fits His response to them into the causal chain of events; if the particular event which is the response to our anticipated plea comes about, we see it, wrongly, as the result of His intervention in that individual case. Nor does our understanding of nature require God as an explanatory cause. The aim of philosophy is happiness in this world, not knowledge of things divine. God is not substantial but "supra-substantial"[21]; His nature is such that it cannot be grasped with the aid of our conceptual tools, and our knowledge bears no imprint of His existence.

There is no doubt that Gassendi's skepticism softened considerably in the course of his life. But he remained wedded to a dualism in which faith and rational thought, secular life and prospects of eternity coexist quite comfortably, separated through an amicable arrangement. The metaphysical questions which in Descartes' thought are apparent at the heart of every discussion are consigned by Gassendi to the heterogeneous realm of faith – even if parts of that faith can be grasped by our reason. Gassendi is both a Christian and a philosopher, but he is not a Christian philosopher. The conviction – expressed in his letter to Herbert of Charlbury – that his Christianity and his philosophy belong to two strictly separate spheres remained a firm and enduring principle in Gassendi's thought until the end of his life.

IV. The physical world and our knowledge of it

It is hardly a new discovery that the backbone of Locke's doctrine is derived from Gassendi – indeed, its essentials repose entirely on Gassendi's thought.[22] We know that Locke read Gassendi and Bernier, although he never referred to them in his writings. The radical sensualism of this philosophy, one of its best known elements, remains

21 *Ibid.*, p. 299.
22 See Gaston Coirault, *Gassendi et non Locke créateur de la doctrine sensualiste moderne sur la génération des idées*, in *Tricentenaire de Pierre Gassendi*, pp. 69–94.

unchanged throughout its evolution; its simple, textbook-like formulations, found in Locke, in Condillac and in countless others, have been so often repeated that they have come to sound banal: "All ideas in the mind are derived from sense experience"; "All things are in the world, and those that can be recognized by the senses are individual things, such as Socrates, Bucephalus, this rock, this bit of grass, and other suchlike things that can be pointed to."[23] Our basic ideas are individual; we form abstractions from them either by putting together certain properties common to a number of objects ("*aggregando*") or by ignoring those properties in which they differ ("*abstrahendo*"). Similarly, we form general ideas from less general ones; and the most perfect ideas are those which most fully and clearly represent the common properties of a certain number of particular things. Moreover, the ideas we obtain through our own direct sense experience are better than those which have been described to us by others. Thus the sensualist position opposes the cult of authority and supports direct empirical evidence. And if our thoughts should wander off down some path of their own and result in an idea which conflicts with the evidence of our senses, it is to these latter that the final decision belongs.

As we have seen, Gassendi's nominalism and radical sensualism are often expressed in a way that is reminiscent of Berkeley: there is no such thing as a purely intellectual representation in our minds, for even the abstractions of theology or mathematics always appear to us as objects of our imagination, endowed with properties which material objects possess. We cannot conceive of a geometrical point in the way that geometry defines it; we always imagine it as something extended and colored. Nor can we conceive of God except in human form. There is no rational means of formulating the distinction between our faculty of sense perception and our faculty of intellectual comprehension that would allow us to analyze the activities of this latter in some kind of purified form. There are no ideas innate in our minds, and no difference between existence and essence: it is not possible, for instance, to grasp the idea of "human nature" without reference to the existence of particular humans.[24] Nor do we have any idea of our own soul, for we know ourselves only through the reflection of things; pure self-reflection is impossible, just as it is impossible for the eye to perceive itself or for the leg to kick itself. Unlike Descartes, who thinks that we understand finite things through the negation of the idea of infinity, as limits or determinants or modes of infinity, Gassendi agrees with Hobbes that we have no

23 *Opera* I, p. 92.
24 Fifth Set of Objections to the *Meditations*, AT VII, p. 319; CSM II, p. 222: ." . . it is impossible to grasp how there can be a human nature if no human being exists, or how we can say a rose is a flower when not even one rose exists."

idea whatsoever of infinity: the word conjures up only a vague and murky image of something negative relative to things that are limited.

If we accept this, then the entire structure of Cartesian metaphysics turns out to be built on sand. If there is no real difference between existence and essence, the ontological argument for the existence of God is clearly impossible; if there are no innate ideas, the psychological argument, based as it is on the idea of a perfect being, an idea allegedly injected into our minds by Nature or God, likewise collapses. And if our knowledge of ourselves is always derived from our perception of external things, the *cogito* is groundless.

Gassendi's critique of Descartes is ultimately the revolt of common sense against essentialist metaphysics. Gassendi appears not to have grasped the existential content of the *cogito*, and the organizational idea behind Descartes' thought – the idea of seeking an epistemological absolute – seems to be alien to him. He is interested in how the world is: in those of its qualities which can be logically organized, classified, formulated as causal laws and put to practical use. Descartes, on the other hand, is preoccupied by metaphysical questions: by the question of the existence of the external world and our knowledge of it through our own existence and God's. Despite the vastly greater role he went on to play in the annals of "positive" science, utterly overshadowing Gassendi, Descartes is much more of a pure metaphysician than Gassendi, whose questions and concerns remain within the limits of empirical knowledge. And there is food for thought in that "despite."

When we look at the physical doctrines of these two antagonists, we find some equally striking contrasts. One can say, of course, that both Descartes' and Gassendi's physics remain within the limits of what is generally called mechanicism: the belief that all the events which occur in the world may be seen as the movement of bodies in space according to the laws of mechanics. But for Gassendi, Descartes' non-atomistic physics is in glaring conflict with common sense and with the rules of empirically constructed science.

Gassendi's negative starting-point is of course not Descartes but Aristotle. The atomism of the Epicureans which he adopted and modified was intended above all to supplant peripatetic metaphysics; the chimeric categories of Aristotle's *Organon* once disposed of, its purpose was to describe the physical world in terms of clear, precise and comprehensible physical units. Physics – that "broadest and noblest area of philosophy"[25] – has no use for concepts that do not correspond to anything in empirical experience. It is based on a few simple and easily acceptable principles, of which the most important can be succinctly for-

25 *Opera* I, p. 125.

mulated: "Space that is not occupied by a body we call vacuum or a void ... All space, whether or not occupied by a body, remains unchanged and motionless ... There is no part of a body that does not inhabit a corresponding part of space ... Space itself is infinite and conceived as extending beyond the limits of the world ... In the natural world, matter is neither infinitely divisible nor destructible: in any division or diminution of it there is a limit beyond which no force of nature can further divide or diminish it. The ultimate particles obtained after such a division are not mathematical points without extension or parts. Such ultimate particles are called atoms – indivisible bodies (*"individua"*); not because they have no parts, but because there is no force in nature which could divide them further."[26] Thus atoms, although imperceptible to our senses, are extended bodies of a certain size, and differ from one another both in size and in their shape and position; hence the qualitative diversity of the bodies which present themselves to our senses in everyday experience. "Time is not dependent on movement; for time flows whether or not there is movement, and whether or not the sky is at rest. For this reason, too, although time is eternal, we cannot deduce from its eternity anything about the eternity of movement or of the world."[27] And while all movement is "the movement [of something] from one place to another," some movements take longer than others – the longer ones being more readily evident to our senses, the briefer ones less so; for this reason we call only the former of these by the general name of movement, and the latter we call change. But there is no difference between movement and change except a qualitative one (*secundum magis et minus*)."[28]

Thus it is not extension (a property bodies share with empty space) but indivisibility or impenetrability that is the constitutive property of matter; and indivisibility is not the result of human limitations but a property of atoms "in themselves." Atoms of various shapes move about in empty space according to the laws of mechanics, and their motion does not change or diverge from those laws. Epicurus assumed that it did, but this, if we are to believe Lucretius, was chiefly in order to salvage the possibility of free will. Gassendi rejects Epicurus's assumed *clinamen* and accepts strict determinism in the physical world. But he parts company with Epicurus wherever the latter's doctrine cannot be reconciled with Christian tradition. He insists, for example, that the number of atoms, although extremely large, is not infinite; that only atoms, and not the infinite space within which they move, make up what can properly be called the "world"; and that atoms are not eternal but created by God – together with the motion which is their immanent property.

26 *Ibid.*, p. 131.
27 *Ibid.*, p. 167.
28 *Ibid.*, p. 363.

Although Gassendi believes motion to be an inherent property of atoms from the moment of their creation, nowhere does he formulate the principle of the conservation of motion which plays such an important role in Cartesian physics. On some issues he hardly goes beyond the naive imaginings of Democritus: the variations we perceive in the density, hardness, weight and other material properties of bodies result from the diversity of atoms; our acts of perception, too, are nothing other than the motion of atoms, which "break away" from the objects they compose and attach themselves (with the aid of hooks, with which they are conveniently endowed) to certain parts of our minds, creating images. A different kind of explanation is required, however, in cases where certain combinations of atoms – namely, animals and people – are endowed with the capacity of experience, or simply with organic life. Here Gassendi takes the hylozoist approach, common in Renaissance philosophy and variously expressed by, among other, Cardan, Paracelsus, van Helmont, Bruno and Bacon: "We may then suppose that God, in creating the heavens and the earth and commanding animals and plants to be brought forth, also created the seed-sac, so to speak, of all things that can bring forth new life; that is to say, from selected atoms He created the first seeds of all things, and all that was born from these seeds would then multiply and continue the process of birth."[29] There is a sort of "principle of sensitivity" in atoms, he thought, activated in response to certain complications; and in some combinations, atoms are endowed with progenitive powers, creating beings which are capable of reproducing. It has admittedly been pointed out that Bernier, for long the main source of information about Gassendi, was somewhat excessive in his emphasis on this aspect of the master's doctrine, even going so far as to attribute to him a theory of a "soul of the world" – not a theory Gassendi explicitly formulates anywhere in his writings. Nevertheless, Gassendi certainly considered the capacity of organic generation as a kind of universal quality disseminated throughout the physical world. One might add that in his time this was almost the only way of interpreting the phenomenon of life without resorting to supernatural explanations, and the only way of integrating organic beings into the material world. On this approach the Cartesian theory of animals as machines also collapses; indeed, Gassendi sees nothing absurd in attributing a certain kind of reasoning capacity to lower species: "I am rendering reason unto the animals," he even says in the *Exercitationes*. The crucial question then arises of the extent to which purely natural, physical changes and combinations of atoms can also explain human thought.

29 *Ibid.*, p. 280.

Gassendi was neither the only nor the first person in his age to "resuscitate" ancient atomism; Claude Bérigard and Jean Magnien also published treatises that were meant to restore respectability to corpuscular physics. But only Gassendi expounded the doctrine in such depth and detail. Most importantly, only he expounded it in a way that was both free from speculation and concerned with connecting and reconciling the atomistic interpretation of the world with modern scientific knowledge.

For Gassendi, the world of atoms – discontinuous, dynamic, quantitatively diverse, governed by natural causality and organized according to the laws of mechanics – is the only proper object of our natural curiosity. God created the world, and because of God the order of the world is a teleological one, governed by a final cause; but creation *ex nihilo*, or *post nihilum*, although it is an article of faith, is nowhere accepted by Gassendi as a postulate of physics. Science, from this point of view, is self-sufficient. It is in this sense, and in this sense alone, that one can speak of Gassendi's "materialism." This use of the term may not be strictly literal, but then neither was Gassendi's Christianity.

V. The soul and the body

The *Objections* to Descartes' *Meditations* are the main source of ammunition for defenders of the materialist interpretation of Gassendi, and certainly the text most frequently invoked by them on the issue of the relationship between the soul and the body. Gassendi is at pains to stress, at the very beginning of the Objections, that he is not questioning the substance of the propositions whose truth Descartes is concerned to demonstrate, i.e., the existence of God and the immaterial soul, only the validity of his proofs. But since the argument which follows is plainly intended to show that the idea of an immaterial and unextended soul has no place in rational thought, this declaration strains credulity, and is easily dismissed as nothing more than a precautionary measure.

In the *Exercitationes* Gassendi already treats the existence of a non-embodied soul as an article of pure faith, but in the *Objections* his critique is more detailed. Descartes, he says, has utterly failed to demonstrate that the faculty of thought requires a special kind of substance, and cannot be a property of bodies organized in a certain way; to say "I am a thinking thing" is to say nothing about the nature of the thing which thinks. And since our only contact with and knowledge of the world is through the senses, as it is in the case of animals, why should we not assume that human reason is a faculty peculiar to the same human organism on which the operations of the intellect depend? The difference between human and animal reason seems to be purely quantitative; nothing in our experience proves that our faculty of reasoning is made possible by some entirely different sort of thing, independent of our bodies. We can also imagine (as Locke was to assume) that God endowed matter with the faculty of thought. Gassendi does not, of course, explicitly suggest that the soul is identical with the body, but he demolishes every argument one might make to the contrary, and fails to indicate any rational way of solving the problem. Moreover, it follows unequivocally from his argument that the claim in question – the claim asserting the existence of the immaterial soul – is not only unprovable but incomprehensible; we may therefore suppose that it can be believed only through revelation, and that any scrutiny of its meaning would be useless.

Both in the *Syntagma* and in the commentaries on Epicurus, however, Gassendi very clearly sets out a theory of the duality of the human soul. In addition to our animal soul (*anima*), whose functions are directly connected with sense experience and which the human race shares with animals, we also have a peculiarly human soul (*mens*), which manifests itself through the workings of our intellect. This latter is endowed with the ability to contemplate immaterial things and the faculty of abstraction and self-knowledge – faculties with which the animal soul is unequipped. But Gassendi has not jettisoned the assumption that the intellect expresses itself by refining the raw images it receives from sense experience; this assumption still holds. Consequently, it is unclear how the non-embodied soul can exist independently of its union with an embodied organism; and the nature of this union is no clearer.

The problem, in this general form, was not a new one; Aquinas, too, had tackled it. But there is no trace in Gassendi of any solution even remotely resembling Thomist anthropology (which is hardly surprising, since in rejecting hylemorphism he also rejects Aristotelian conceptual categories, and therefore cannot express any solution in such terms). The idea of the higher soul, called into being outside the natural order of the world, by a separate act of creation, is at odds with the rest of his doctrine, which denies that any clear distinction between acts of reasoning and acts of perception can be made and certainly admits no phenomenon that would require us to posit the existence of a separate soul to explain it. Indeed, Pintard dismisses this second soul as an epiphenomenon with no true raison d'être in Gassendi's doctrine; it is, he says, an evasion, a simple precautionary measure: the *"subterfuge d'un hérésiarque aux abois."*[30] An exaggeration, no doubt, but it is hard to escape the impression that the "second soul," far from being an essential feature in Gassendi's philosophical interpretation of the world, is a heterogeneous element, even more at odds with the whole than divine providence, and can be understood only within the framework of his earlier position – as

30 Pintard, *op. cit.*, p. 490.

an object of blind faith. Bernard Rochot, at pains to interpret Gassendi's thought as being in complete accordance with Catholic orthodoxy, remarks that Gassendi considerably extends the functions of the animal soul to the detriment of the higher, but nonetheless insists that the role of the higher is too great to permit of a "materialist" interpretation on this issue.[31] To the Church's Thomist dogma on the unity of the soul, formulated at the council of Vienne, Gassendi contents himself with a declaration of agreement; there is no sign of any genuine effort to reconcile his own opinions with Catholic dogma. Such declarations only exacerbate the problems in which his theory of the soul is enmired – problems which he never suceeded in solving. There is no doubt that Gassendi's associationist empiricism requires no "second soul"; it is quite capable of dealing with human intellectual activities in such a way that they turn out to be a natural extension of the perceptive activities common to men and animals. But there is no reason to believe that his "higher" soul was mere subterfuge, and that Gassendi himself simply did not believe in the immateriality and immortality of the human soul. Here, as elsewhere, his own beliefs ran counter to the natural logic of his philosophy. The two were not to be reconciled: Gassendi never found a position that would accommodate both his personal faith and his philosophical doctrine and integrate them into one harmonious whole.

VI. Virtue and happiness

For those who cling to the view of Gassendi's philosophy as irreproachably Christian in all its aspects, his ethical doctrine is a particularly ungrateful object of study. It is here, in his moral thought, that his Epicureanism finds its expression in what one might call its pure form, unencumbered by any of the reservations which inevitably accompany his cosmological or anthropological arguments. Gassendi had planned to expound his position on moral questions in the *Exercitationes*; he did not get that far, but one can gather from his brief declaration of intent that his views then were no different from those expressed in his later writings. While his views on human cognition and the soul evolved, on moral issues his Epicureanism remained unchanged.

Gassendi thought that moral customs and opinions were changeable things, dependent on the climate (both social and meteorological) and the historical period. One feature only he finds to be invariable and ubiquitous: the pursuit of pleasure, or happiness. About this predominant human aim there is general agreement; opinions differ, however, on the best methods of achieving it. The Stoics were wrong, Gassendi thinks, to see virtue as a value in itself, the supreme and final aim of human activ-

---

31 Bernard Rochot, in *Pierre Gassendi . . . , op. cit.*, pp. 94–95.

ity; it is not virtue we should be pursuing but happiness, in the pursuit of which the virtues are indispensable instruments. The human tendency to pursue pleasure is a fact so evident as to require no proof; likewise the fact that all human activities are and must be subordinate to this pursuit. But the moral theory of pleasure, which Gassendi accepts and adopts *in toto* from the Epicurean doctrine, must deal with the false stereotypes which present Epicurus as a eulogist of crude sensual delights: pleasure, the supreme human good, means (both for Gassendi and for Epicurus as interpreted by him) inner harmony and tranquility, freedom from passions, and moderate contentment of body and soul.

In his *Philosophiae Epicuri Syntagma* Gassendi sets out Epicurus's views and recommendations in the domain of ethics with no critical comments whatsoever, and we may safely assume that they correspond to his own. Indeed, he anticipates and refutes objections wherever he thinks they might arise. In addition to this, and to correcting the false assumptions commonly associated with Epicurus's moral doctrine, he also takes pains to paint the man himself in the most glowing colors, whose brightness derives in large measure from the contrast with Aristotle. The openness and directness of his approach seems remarkable when one remembers that Epicurus, burning in his flaming coffin in the sixth circle of Dante's hell, was hardly a graceful candidate as an apologetic object of admiration in the Christian world, and that his ethical doctrine contributed no less to this state of affairs than his teachings about gods and the soul.

Epicurus's recommendations can be summed up in the following rules: pursue pleasure without any admixture of pain; avoid pain if it is not associated with any pleasure; avoid pleasure if it stands in the way of greater pleasure or if it is likely to result in greater pain; accept pain if it allows you to avoid greater pain or if it is essential to the pursuit of greater pleasure. It is clear that for Gassendi, too, any good worth pursuing is a function of pleasure. Philosophy, too, is such a good; accordingly, we should, and do, engage in it only in order to lead a happier life. Similarly with faith. The principle of disinterested love, so widely discussed in the Christian moral writings of his day, is absent from Gassendi's philosophy. The only good worthy of the name is the happiness of the individual.

The spirit of libertinism is particularly evident in Gassendi's ethical doctrine. It is a doctrine at once secularized and conformist, commonsensical and unheroic. When Gassendi describes Epicurus's conformism with regard to the accepted religious customs of his time, customs to which he himself attached no significance and with which he felt no connection through faith, one senses strongly that he is also describing his own attitude – especially since such an attitude is not only in perfect accordance with the moderate hedonism of his doctrine, but indeed one of the distinguishing features of the libertine way of life.

Gassendi's vision of man and the world is a serene and optimistic one. He recommends putting our trust in human nature, and does not think that the good life requires deeds of heroism. In his vision of man there are no signs of corruption by original sin. Grace and its operations have no place in the human world, just as God and his operations have no place in the physical world; the fact that He created it does not mean that we must resort to His intervention in explaining events. There is no trace in Gassendi's attitude of the "terror of the infinite," the terror of sin and condemnation. Nothing was more alien to him that the Jansenist religion. There is no doubt that if he had to choose between the different religions available in his time, he would choose Catholicism in its gentle, Jesuit form.[32] His philosophy, in all its aspects, is indulgent, flexible and tolerant. He is the advocate of a gentle conformism: adapt to the world as it is; make use of its goods with prudence and moderation; do not abandon your natural curiosity; value harmony, peace and order. There is no trace in his thought of any kind of fanaticism: no hatred, no fear and no tragedy.

VII. Gassendi's scientific work

Despite the scrupulousness of his observations, his love of precision and his indefatigable efforts in carrying out experiments, Gassendi did not, contrary to Sorbière's predictions, achieve a distinguished place in the annals of science. Alexander Koyré attributes the poverty of his scientific results to his excessive empiricism, which prevented him from assimilating the spirit of mathematization that inspired the new physics.[33] His own physics, although anti-peripatetic, remained qualitative in its principal aims. But in Koyré's view he succeeded elsewhere: in providing physics with the atomistic ontology it needed, and in hastening the demise of many traditional Aristotelian concepts in physics which had been hampering its progress.

R. Dugas and P. Costabel, co-authors of the great history of science edited by R. Taton (in which Gassendi plays a very modest role), see Gassendi's physics as a precursor of the Cambridge School, which in turn was a source of inspiration for Newton.[34] And indeed, in Gassendi's

---

32 It is worth remarking that in their philosophical writings the Jesuits abstained from attacking Gassendi, indeed frequently praised him, and always contrasted him favourably with Descartes. Louis Andrieux (*Pierre Gassendi*, Paris, 1927) cites many authors whose works confirm this: Tournemine, Bourdin, Daniel, Duterte, Harduin, Regnault, Rapin, Buffier.

33 A. Koyré, in *Pierre Gassendi* . . . , *op. cit.*, pp. 60–69.

34 *Histoire générale des sciences publiée sous la direction de René Taton*, Paris, 1958; vol. II, p. 248.

doctrine time and space have an existence of their own, independent of material objects. A finite number of atoms in an infinite space, time which was not created and which flows independently of movement – these make up the broadest framework of the physical world. Movement is not a transition from potentiality to actuality, as it was in Aristotelian physics, but rather a displacement in space: *"nullum esse alium re ipsa motum, quam localem,"* he says in the fourth book of his *Syntagma*. Gassendi also arrived at a correct formulation of the law of inertia. According to Crombie,[35] he was the first to abandon the concept of impetus as the cause of movement and determine that bodies move in a straight line, requiring external force only for changes of direction or increases in velocity; a body in a vacuum remains at rest, and once set in motion continues indefinitely in a straight line. Movement, according to Gassendi, is not continuous: it is composed of successive intervals of motion and rest. If movement is continuous, its speed is always the same; the differences in speed we observe are the result of differences in the number of intervals of rest.

In 1641, in Marseille, Gassendi carried out an experiment intended to refute the charges leveled at Galilean physics by the Peripatetics, who objected that if the earth moved, as Galileo claimed, then a body thrown up into the air should land in a different place. Gassendi refuted this by an experiment on a ship: he showed that a weight thrown down from the mast comes down in exactly the same way as it does on land, despite the vessel's motion. However, he disagreed with Galileo in claiming that weight is not a property of bodies but the result of the earth's gravity.

Gassendi's experiments and observations encompassed a large number of issues. He measured the speed of sound (arriving at a result that was greater by about two fifths than the true value) and observed that the speed at which sound was propagated did not depend on its pitch. He reproduced Torricelli's and Pascal's barometric experiments and interpreted them atomistically. And he carried out a host of astronomical experiments. In 1631 he confirmed Kepler's predictions concerning Mercury's transit in front of the Sun and helped Peiresc to draw the first map of the Moon. His corpuscular physics, known in England thanks to Walter Charleton's *Physiologia epicuro-gassendo-charletoniana* (1654), had considerable influence on English natural sciences – on Boyle, Cudworth and Newton. But for all that, Gassendi does indeed seem firmly to have believed that physical theories were accounts of observations and experiments.

35 A.C. Crombie, *Augustine to Galileo: the History of Science AD 400–1650*, London, 1952.

Gassendi's Copernicanism is unquestionable, in spite of the fact that when he lectured on Copernicus and Tycho Brahe in his course on astronomy, he did not clearly come out in support of either. Indeed, he thought it was possible to accept both heliocentric cosmology and Scripture, as long as one assumed that the Bible is concerned with the purely phenomenal aspects of the movements of heavenly bodies. In general he maintained his independence of thought in his scientific studies just as he did in philosophy, and was aware of the clashes and contradictions which could arise between the opinions of the Holy Office and the search for truth. It is just this awareness that he expresses in his famous letter to Galileo: "*Si quid fortassis adversum te, hoc est adversus placita tua Sanctissima Sedes definit, aequo animo aquiesce, ut virum decet prudentissimum; satisque esse reputa, quod animatus non fueris nisi in gratiam solius semper creditae tibi veritatis.*"[36]

VIII. His pupils

Gassendi's relative neglect, and the tendency to dismiss him as unimportant, is generally attributed (e.g., by Berr[37]) to the fact that he wrote in Latin, which made his works inaccessible to a wider readership. But this seems an insufficient explanation. Spinoza wrote in Latin; so did (in large part) Descartes; so did Grotius. Ideas thought deserving of an audience beyond exclusive learned circles quickly found translators and were disseminated in different languages. It is more likely that the way in which Gassendi's thought exerted its influence was connected to the nature of his doctrine: it was propagated through individual ideas and the mode of their expression, not through a closed system presented to the reader in a lump, to be accepted or rejected as a whole. This propagation was often anonymous: many of Gassendi's ideas were spread and absorbed without any clear link to his name, or any awareness, on the part of those whom they influenced, of their authorship. They shaped a certain way of thinking: a way that did not involve "systems" or require universal metaphysical constructions. Gassendists were not Gassendists in the (dogmatic and systematic) way that Cartesians were Cartesians. Because of the tolerant, pluralist and common-sense nature of Gassendi's philosophy, it is unlikely that those who were influenced by it felt themselves bound to a strictly defined doctrine; rather they must have felt free to preserve their independence with regard to all existing doctrines.

In spite of this, as a philosopher Gassendi was undoubtedly the most distinguished figure in libertine circles. He also had pupils of his own, who identified themselves with varying degrees of outspokenness as fol-

36 *Opera* VI, p. 67.
37 Henri Berr, *op. cit.*, pp. 17–18.

lowers of their master; and here, too, there are questions to be asked. For when one wants to interpret a philosopher's thought in a certain way, a way that clearly diverges from the interpretation supplied by his intellectual progeny, one can always say that his followers "betrayed" him and distorted his "true" intentions. Sometimes this can indeed be the case; but in general a philosopher's intellectual progeniture tends to be a better guide to understanding his thought than biographical facts, at least when one is engaged in the history of philosophy. It is worth remarking that defenders of Gassendi's image as a philosopher of unblemished orthodoxy attribute great weight to the scrupulousness with which he fulfilled his priestly obligations, insisting that this is the light in which he should be read; but when faced with those of his pupils to whom the label of Christian orthodoxy cannot by any stretch of the imagination be applied, they content themselves with declaring that these are untrue and unworthy heirs to his thought. Yet there is no apparent reason to consider a philosopher's biography to be a more reliable criterion in the interpretation of his work than the influence exerted by his thought. A philosopher is surely whatever his readers think he is; and for historians of philosophy his role in the history of ideas is certainly more significant than such testimony of his beliefs as the details of his life can provide – testimony which, moreover, can never be unequivocal, and which plays no role in the posthumous history of his thought.

Among Gassendi's private pupils the best-known (as a Gassendist) is Bernier (born in 1620), who propagated his doctrine in French. Georges Mongrédien[38] regards Bernier's Epicureanism as unquestionable: his hedonism was so far-reaching that he believed abstaining from pleasure to be a sin. It is also certain that his version of Gassendi's philosophy had much a stronger materialist tinge than interpretations of Catholic historians today. Hence Rochot's opinion[39] that Gassendi was falsely perceived as a libertine and a materialist because his work was rarely read: people read Bernier's *Abrégé* instead.

Luillier's illegitimate son Claude Chapelle (born in 1626) rejoiced in the reputation of a thoroughgoing libertine, both in his mores and in his opinions. He did not distinguish himself as a writer, but, as historians have noted, he remained true to his mentor until the end of his life.

As for Molière, his Gassendism, too, is unquestionable. The targets of his mockery were precisely those at which Gassendi's philosophy was (explicitly or implicitly) aimed: Cartesianism, Jansenism, Scholasticism, popular superstitions.

Cyrano de Bergerac, from the point of view of Christian orthodoxy, is among the least edifying examples of Gassendi's influence. His

---

38 Georges Mongrédien, in: *Pierre Gassendi . . .* , *op. cit.*, pp. 122–23.
39 Bernard Rochot, *ibid.*, p. 71.

Epicureanism is most striking in his famous utopia about the moon; it is an undiluted Epicureanism, unsoftened by Christian elements of any sort. Cyrano was notorious for his mockery, and beyond any doubt quite free of religious faith. Most likely he was the instigator of the syncretic trend, popular in the French intellectual world at the end of the century, which linked Gassendi's thought with the Cartesian tradition, or rather pruned Cartesianism to fit Gassendi's common sense.[40]

Gassendi's immediate circle of pupils and followers (which included, in addition to those mentioned, Royer de Prades, Dassoucy and Le Vayer junior) is perhaps less significant a guide to the nature and extent of his influence than are exponents of Gassendism in the second half of the century. In addition to its considerable impact in England, briefly discussed above, Gassendi's Epicureanism had some very concrete effects in France, where it was instrumental in weakening the hold of Cartesian orthodoxy and gradually influencing Cartesians towards some quite far-reaching concessions to empiricism. La Fontaine, Sorbière and Cureau de la Chambre, to mention only some of the more famous names, were generally known as Gassendists. But the Cartesian Cordemoy, too, betrays signs of Gassendi's influence, as does, in even greater measure, Rohault. As does Pierre-Sylvain Régis.[41] Many of the next generation of libertines, such as Saint-Evremond and de Méré, were Gassendists in their moral views and their general outlook on the world. Antoine Adam describes a group a Gassendists formed in the second half of the 1650s, which included such names as Mme. Deshoulières, Déhenault, Lignières, and the abbé de Marolles. Gassendist inclinations have been observed in some of the leading writers of the Enlightenment, among them Montesquieu and Diderot.[42] And while the gulf between Gassendi and Descartes must have seemed vast during their lifetimes, they were united with respect to the chief and most deeply divisive conflict of ideas of the age, where the opposition consisted of epigones of Scholasticism and keepers of the faith in substantial forms. As exponents of the "new science," both were antagonists within the same scientific circle. After their deaths, when the conflict between them lost its personal aspect and attempts were being made to syncretize their thought, their agreement on some fundamental issues struck the next generation more forcibly. Just as Gassendi himself had recognized that the main idea animating

40 This, at least, is what Rachmiel Brandwajn seems to be suggesting in his *Cyrano de Bergerac Among Libertines and Pedants*, Warsaw, 1960 (in Polish).

41 See Paul Mouy, *Le dévéloppement de la Physique Cartésienne*, 1646–1712, Paris, 1934, p. 145 n.

42 Antoine Adam, *L'influence de Gassendi sur le mouvement des idées à la fin du XVIIe siècle*, in: *Tricentenaire de Pierre Gassendi*, op.cit., and in *Pierre Gassendi . . .* , *op. cit.*, pp. 165–69.

the thought of Descartes and Bacon was essentially the same, despite all their differences,[43] so Leibniz hardly discerned any differences between Gassendi and Descartes.[44] Such issues are always complicated by the difficulty of finding the right perspective on another age and deciding which of its aspects are most significant.

The example of Fontenelle seems symptomatic of the way in which Gassendi's influence operated. In his *Entretiens sur la pluralité des mondes*[45] he confesses his Cartesianism, although many (sometimes quite significant) elements of Descartes' philosophy strike him as utter aberrations. For him, to be a Cartesian meant above all to believe in the possibility of a natural, causal interpretation of the world, to value clarity of thought and intellectual independence, and to distrust the authority of tradition. He accepts Cartesian physics, together with its theory of vortices (by then completely rusted over), but he is unquestionably an empiricist: he rejects the theory of animals as machines, the theory of the subjectivity of the senses and the theory of innate ideas. In the *Dialogues des morts* (1683) he turned his traditional libertine skepticism on the metaphysical edifice built by Descartes,[46] and his *Histoire des oracles* (1687) and *L'origine des fables* (1724) are both typical of libertine literature in presenting their opposition to explanations of the world in terms of miracles and supernatural events as a critique of pagan superstitions. Although Fontenelle's historical pessimism distinguishes him from Gassendi, in the final analysis his philosophy probably owes more to Gassendi than it does to Descartes. And yet Fontenelle writes about Descartes, but not about Gassendi. But this is understandable, for what he took from Gassendi was his *pars destruens*, his uncertainty and distrust of ultimate solutions and all-encompassing constructions. For him Gassendi was a negative tool, one that allowed him to single out for attack anything that smacked of dogmatism, unverifiable metaphysics or extravagance – in Scholasticism, Aristotelianism and the occult sci-

43 See *Opera* I, p. 65: "*Is videlicet* [i.e., Descartes – L.K.] *Verulamium ea in re imitatus est, quod novam quoque Philosophiam a fundamentis excitaturus, omne omnino praeiudicium exuere imprimis voluit; ac invento subinde quopiam Principio solidissimo, ipsi ut fundamento superexstruere totam molem. Non eandem tamen viam est, quam Verulamius ingressus; sed cum Verulamius auxilia a rebus ad perficiendam Intellectus cogitationem petierit, ipse omni rerum cogitatione ablegata censuit in ipsa cogitatione satis esse praesidii, ut Intellectus possit vi sua in omnium rerum etiam abstruissimarum, hoc est non modo corporum, sed Dei etiam, ac Animae notitiam perfectam venire.*"

44 See Paul Mouy, *op. cit.*, pp. 218–19.

45 Bernard le Bovier de Fontenelle, *Entretiens sur la pluralité des mondes*, 1686; published in England in 1688 as *A Discovery of New Worlds*.

46 See Krzysztof Pomian's introduction to the Polish edition of *Dialogues des morts*: *Rozmowy Zmarlych*, Warsaw, 1961.

ences, but also in Descartes. In the *Dialogues des morts* Descartes finds favor only because he abandons his philosophy in the end; and Molière, in his conversation with Paracelsus, is plainly speaking in the author's voice when he derides the occult sciences and pronounces the creations of our minds to be no less changeable and subject to fashion than the cut of our clothes.

In this way Gassendi's thought as interpreted by his followers gradually pared down Descartes' system and instilled in the next generation of pupils a spirit of caution and skepticism towards ultimate truths and metaphysics, trust in common sense and a feeling of affinity with relativists and conformists. But this skepticism and relativism was not part of a completed, fully and deliberately elaborated doctrine. Gassendi taught skeptical thinking, but constructed no skeptical system or anti-system on the model of Sextus Empiricus. He inculcated relativism by practicing it, but he was not a theorist of relativism like Protagoras. Because of this his influence, like that of all the libertines of his generation, was for the most part negative, anonymous and elusive. The teachings of the libertines are resistant to efforts to distil them into a collection of clear statements, a systematic whole like a Cartesian construction. Their general statements (e.g., "truth is fundamentally inaccessible," "no certainty is possible," etc.), taken on their own, would seem excessive when attributed to a "classic" of libertine thought from the first half of the century. Their main method of proceeding was by example, by a consideration of details and careful critical analysis. It is for this reason that their influence was often nameless and hard to define. But towards the Christian tradition it was, in Gassendi's case no less than in others, almost entirely, unambiguously negative. Catholic historians may, of course, claim that Gassendi's pupils misinterpreted his intentions. But if all or almost all of them were mistaken, their very numbers turn the mistake into a truth; for what counts in the life of an idea is not the intention behind it but the way in which it is generally understood. In other words, might, in this domain, is right.

There are, in fact, some concrete examples which justify that "almost all." One such is Huet, bishop of Avranches, generally considered to have been a follower of Gassendi and unquestionably a Christian skeptic. His efforts, in which he deployed the entire arsenal of Pyrrhonist arguments, were directed to showing that given the feebleness of human reason only faith in the truths of Revelation can satisfy our need for certainty. But Huet's attempt at a Christian assimilation of skepticism seems to have failed in the same way that Malebranche failed in his attempt at a Christian interpretation of Cartesianism – "failed" in the purely historical sense, insofar as neither skepticism nor Cartesianism were successfully assimilated by Christian culture. Both trends could make their presence felt and have a real historical impact only in areas uninfluenced by or even hostile to the Christian view of the world.

IX. Gassendi and Gassendism

Christian efforts to "rescue" Gassendi have concentrated on undermining the historical picture which presents him as a materialist and an atheist, or at the least a man of doubtful faith, concealing his disbelief under a mask of orthodoxy. If such a picture does indeed exist, it is not my intention to defend it. Everything seems to indicate that he was quite the opposite: a Christian with the philosophy of a godless libertine. Pintard's description of him as a "pagan mind in a Christian soul" seems on the whole apt. In interpreting his philosophy we are not compelled to ask whether it was orthodox or heretical from the point of view of Catholic dogma; there is no reason to organize our approach to the history of philosophy around the opinions of the Holy Office. In any case, it was certainly not heretical, for the simple reason that it was never condemned as such: one is a heretic, in the only sense of the word that is meaningful outside a strictly religious viewpoint, if and only if one has been declared a heretic by that part of the Church hierarchy whose task it is to issue such declarations. On the question of heresy the only verdict that matters is the verdict of the Church, and in this case no such verdict was pronounced. In this, the only meaningful sense of the word, Gassendi was not a heretic, nor was his doctrine heretical.

But nor can we form an opinion about Gassendi's philosophy by asking questions about his belief in God or in the immortality of the soul, and uncritically accepting the assumptions behind them. For such questions concern only his life, not his philosophy or his place in the history of philosophy; and while they are of course relevant to his biography, the answers to them are no guide to interpreting his doctrine. For the historian of philosophy the right questions to ask concern the content of his doctrine and the way in which faith and philosophy coexist within it. One can then go on to ask how this content relates to what we know about Gassendi's own inclinations and beliefs.

We may assume that Gassendi's declarations of faith were sincere, not mere precautionary measures. We may assume this not just because he was a priest and exercised his priestly duties – Jean Meslier, too, was a priest until the end of his life – but simply because there are no sufficiently strong grounds to believe otherwise; in their absence, the burden of proof clearly rests with his accusers. This is the more obviously the case when those accusers cast doubt on the genuineness not only of his public declarations but also of his expressions of faith made in private conversation.

Given this, however, there are two areas in which questions can usefully be asked. The first concerns the relationship between Gassendi's personal faith and the institutionalized faith of the Roman Catholic Church; the second concerns the relationship between his faith and his philosophical doctrine. A hypothesis concerning each of these things comes to mind.

At the end of his Objections to the *Meditations*, Gassendi writes: "When some dish pleases my palate but I see others do not like it, I do not defend my taste as being more perfect than anyone else's; and similarly, when an opinion appeals to me but is unwelcome to others, I am very far from supposing I have managed to come closer to the truth. I think it is more correct to say that everyone is satisfied with his own views, and that wanting everyone to have the same view is as unfair as wanting everyone's tastes to coincide."[47] Everything indicates that the attitude of tolerance, uncertainty and pluralism expressed here may be understood as applying not merely to philosophy but to all opinions, including religious ones. At the same time, the explicit Christian elements in Gassendi's philosophy – the existence of God the Creator and of an immortal soul – are not particular to Christianity; these are general beliefs, religiously undefined. Gassendi's is clearly not a fideist position, within which all beliefs can be accommodated. In Gassendi's philosophy God and the soul are present only as God and soul *simpliciter*; moreover, as we have seen, there is no organic link between these two concepts and the rest of his philosophy. There is no trace of any specifically Catholic, or even specifically Christian, elements: Grace, Christ, redemption, original sin – none of these things are present in his writings. It is insufficient, indeed absurd, to argue that Gassendi was not a theologian and was simply uninterested in such issues: he was a priest of the Catholic Church, and he lived at a time of violent religious conflicts. Silence is significant in philosophy, and the extent of its significance naturally depends on the circumstances in which that philosophy comes into being. Everything indicates that Gassendi's personal religious beliefs were of a very broad and general kind, unconnected with any particular religious persuasion; and that he, like other libertines, believed that one could worship God in a variety of ways, through whatever rites one thought fit and in whatever church one chose, regardless of its denomination and according to the customs of one's country. Denominational distinctions were irrelevant to the basic truths of faith. Like Charron, whom he had studied in his youth and whom he greatly admired, Gassendi stressed the extent to which our opinions depend on the circumstances of our lives and our religious beliefs on our upbringing; he even remarks that God, in His goodness, allows the existence of various religious currents adapted to historical changes.

47 *Fifth Set of Objections to the Meditations*, AT VII, 346; CSM II, 240.

This attitude – denominational indifference combined with what was in fact a kind of deism, although not in the sense of deism as a "religion of reason" – crops up frequently in libertine texts. Assuming that Gassendi shared it, his scrupulous exercise of his priestly functions is perfectly explicable; but it provides no evidence as to the content of his religious beliefs. Gassendi, and all his libertine friends, embraced the principle that one must adapt to local customs. This belief was also shared by perhaps the most distinguished (and in those times extremely rare) example of the absolute and unquestionable atheist and materialist, a philosopher for whom Gassendi had the greatest respect and who was no less fervent in his admiration of Gassendi – Thomas Hobbes. Both in Gassendi's doctrine and in Hobbes's political theory, the established religion of the state deserves deference and respect; participation in its ceremonies is the duty of every good citizen. There is no hypocrisy here: it is simply assumed that the domain of public life to which organized religion belongs, with its rituals and its institutions, is separate from the domain of personal beliefs, and that there is no need for any arrangement or reconciliation between them; taking part in religious ceremonies is like paying taxes or, to modernize the analogy, obeying the rules of the road. Such a separation may seem extraordinary today, but at the time it was quite commonly expressed as a principle, and even more often put into practice. It was considered quite natural not only by theoreticians of absolutism, like Hobbes, but also by sympathizers of democracy, like Spinoza; and the assumption that Gassendi shared his friends' view on the matter is entirely justified. From the time of Machiavelli, the view of the church as an institution in the domain of public as opposed to philosophical life had become so widespread in enlightened circles, so firmly entrenched and so often repeated, that accusations of cynicism or hypocrisy are out of place. We may be shocked and incredulous today that Giordano Bruno, a man beyond doubt quite free of any positive religion, accepted the religion of the country in which he lived, or that Justus Lipsius changed his religion five times, adapting himself to the customs of wherever he happened to be; but such things were neither shocking nor incredible then, even for genuine believers, for they accorded with the belief that salvation was not linked to any particular religious persuasion: God, who did not reveal to us every detail of His secrets, and whose specific qualities we cannot know, saw fit to allow different peoples to worship Him in their different ways, according to their customs, their character, their temperament and the climate of their country. The same tendency to generalize religious values, to sever the connection between church and salvation and to separate real, personal belief from public ceremony can be seen in Erasmus, in Morus and in the overwhelming majority of Renaissance Christian humanists. In

Gassendi's time this tendency was still very much alive, especially among followers of Montaigne and Charron.

This much can be said about the relationship between Gassendi's personal faith and established religion. What can we say about the relationship between his faith – understood in the above sense – and his philosophy? There is no doubt that his philosophical thought tends naturally towards materialism. In his theory of knowledge pure sensualism (but sensualism of the Epicurean, not the Scholastic kind), unencumbered by any theories of substantial forms or species, provides sufficient explanation of our intellectual life, without the need to posit unembodied substrata of thought; the intellect has no independent cognitive functions. In his view of the physical world there is nothing that requires God as an explanatory principle, no part of reality that would be incomprehensible without Him. And in his ethical theory God has no place at all: Gassendi's morality is totally independent from religious values. God and the soul, presented in the earlier stages of Gassendi's thought as objects of pure faith, and as such irrelevant to philosophical enquiry, do make a late appearance in his doctrine, and this is undoubtedly a significant development; but they remain a heterogeneous element in Gassendi's picture of the world as a whole.

Gassendi as an individual in a historical community of men was a Catholic; as an individual *simpliciter*, a holder of opinions about the world, he was a believer in God and the soul; as a scholar and philosopher he was a positivist and a materialist. How were these three aspects of his existence reconciled? On the psychological level they certainly managed to coexist without difficulty: there is no evidence that this learned priest was unhappy and torn by inner conflict. From the logical point of view, too, one can see how they could have coexisted, given a suitable interpretation of Gassendi's expressed opinions in each of those three domains. But we need not attempt to fill in the details of what such a suitable interpretation might look like; there is no reason to construct a synthesis of Gassendi's thought which he himself – at least in the writings we have – did not construct. And any such reconstruction, if it were full enough to be worth presenting, would have to consist mostly of pure fantasy. We must assume that Gassendi's life as a priest, a believer and a philosopher was a harmonious one for him, and that it was a good life, in the sense of being what a good life ought to be according to the principles of his philosophy. Whether it was coherent from our contemporary point of view we cannot say; the question is pointless, for we have no other point of view at our disposal. A Christian might say that we should consider whether it was coherent from God's point of view, but he would add (unless he had the tendencies of an inquisitor) that this is a question only God can answer. More than that one cannot say.

Translated by Agnieszka Kolakowska

The Philosophical Role
of the Reformation
Martin Luther and the Origins of Subjectivity

I

Discussing the question announced in the above title might seem a pointless exercise. One could easily argue that the Reformation brought to the history of thought no new ideas deserving of the attention of the historian of philosophy, but simply revived, according to well-defined principles of selection, certain motifs present in Christianity since its inception; that it was, to a greater extent even than the so-called Philosophy of the Renaissance, merely a "renaissance," in the literal sense of the word, with, consequently, no place in the history of philosophical ideas; and that is was notable at most for its destructive role in breaking the monopoly of Roman dogma or catalyzing social transformations which are of interest to historians of philosophy only as historical "events."

This objection, however, strikes me as beside the point. All the variants of Christianity, all the heresies and sects were, in intention, interpretations of one and the same canon; none of them claimed to be discovering anything new. Almost all the fundamental differences of interpretation had been articulated in the first centuries of Christianity. Adopting a principle whereby we exclude from the history of philosophy anything not clearly new would force us to ignore huge areas of Christian philosophy and theology; Christian culture would be of interest to the historian of ideas only in his research into the social consciousness of a given time, not because of the specificity of its content. There are at least two arguments against adopting such a principle. The first is the well-proven and generally acknowledged fact that the meaning of philosophical ideas is determined by the intellectual and cultural climate in which that idea occurs. The same thoughts seem to recur in philosophy, but each time they must be differently formulated; they must change the language in which they are expressed and adapt themselves to the style of the day. This has consequences for their meaning. They lead to different conclusions and spring from different motives. The second argument is that philosophy itself, as a panoramic view of its history will easily show, contains the very flaw which is to serve as the pretext for excluding religious conflicts from the sphere of the history of philosophy: in the history of philosophy, too, the same fundamental concerns crop up again and again, each attired in different verbal costume. The contrast between the monotony of religious ideas and beliefs on the one hand and the changeability and variety of philosophical reflection on the other may well prove reducible to a purely verbal level; it may not have the remotest connection with the essential ideas of either.

We know to what extent the selection and way of arranging the same ideas can make a philosophical project seem startlingly innovative – in accordance with Pascal's well-known dictum. For instance, when the Reformation took an appropriate selection of the ideas of St. Augustine, contrasted them with the Scholastic systems, and cast the resulting opposition upon the waters of philosophical reflection, by this alone it created a significantly new situation, important not only in the history of the Church, but also in the history of ideas.

II

Let us try to define the question that is involved here, and let us begin by listing what it is not.

First, it is not a question of the philosophical sources of Reformation doctrines. For instance, it is not a question of the support which Lutheran theology found in the writings of the late German nominalists and mystics; it is, rather, a question of the role of that theology in the later evolution of philosophical thought.

Second, it is not a question of the general negative role of the Reformation: obviously, we know that the reform, quite independently of its original intentions, created a tension which unleashed a general spirit of criticism, thereby fostering a long-enduring illusion that the freedom of individual religious life had been its basic principle. I say "illusion" because the liberating effect of the reform in intellectual life did not derive from the fact that – in its "great," classical forms – it proclaimed the principle of free criticism (it did so only where and only as long as it was in opposition to something); it was not through its intentions, but through its acts – through the act of questioning Rome's monopoly of dogma and breaking down the doctrinal monolith – that the Reformation enabled religious experience (as well as subsequent philosophical ideas which in spirit were quite alien, or even starkly opposed, to the intentions of the reformers) to be articulated. This general destructive role of the upheaval which was the Reformation is outside the scope of this essay – partly because it seems fairly self-evident, and partly because it can be discerned throughout European spiritual culture, and is not limited to the specific content of the ideas of the Reformation. Clearly, from this point of view all that happened in European culture in subsequent centuries can be regarded as the result of the Reformation – simply in the sense that we cannot imagine its happening without the Reformation. But it is precisely the universality and totality of this negative influence that allow us to ignore it when considering the Reformation's specific philosophical role.

Third, it is, obviously, not a question of considering in what respect the work of particular philosophers may be interpreted in such a way as to justify speaking of a "similarity" between some of their ideas and some idea considered characteristic of the theology of sixteenth century reform.

Fourth, and finally, it is not a question of considering only the ways in which this or that particular philosopher drew his ideas directly from the doctrines of the reform, since many philosophers whose ideas we regard as essentially defined by the tradition of the Reformation probably never came into contact with those doctrines.

Having eliminated what the question is not, we are now in a position to define what it is. It is, namely, a question of the substance, the positive content, of the ideas which the Reformation, both as a theological movement and as a doctrine, introduced or resuscitated, and of the nature of their influence on the course of philosophical thought. When the question is put this way, it becomes clear that we should concentrate on the fundamental ideas which defined the Reformation's doctrinal form in clearest contrast to the existing body of dogma and were peculiar to the reform movement. This means directing our attention particularly to the beginning of the Great Reform (that is, to the years 1517–1523). We also want to concentrate on ideas which concerned essentially philosophical questions: questions arising directly out of theological and anthropological concerns, and not those connected with such issues as the organizational reform of the Church, changes in the liturgy, typical features of morality or the rules of social life, the interpretation of the sacraments, etc. All these issues, however important for our understanding of the Reformation, must be considered secondary in the hierarchy established by a purely philosophical point of view. It is true that reforms such as the dissolution of monastic orders, or the abolition of fasts or of simony, might seem, from the social point of view, more significant than purely theological issues. Moreover, it was precisely such concrete and well understood reforms, with their visible impact, that can be regarded as a significant basis for the Reformation's first triumphs. They might even seem, to the historian, to be the fundamental thing about it, defining its basic meaning. But if what we are interested in is the history of philosophical ideas, these issues are secondary, and must be seen as consequences of theological and anthropological (and thus ultimately philosophical) positions.

The philosopher or historian of philosophy must not abandon his purely philosophical point of view, even though he knows it cannot provide answers to questions about the historical significance of the Reformation as a whole; if he abandons it, he will be giving up the autonomy of philosophical thought altogether. For if philosophical thought is to be regarded as no more than a form of mystification, a complicated way of expressing other, allegedly uniquely "real" intentions or interests, it would cease to be thought at all, and become an instrument of expression for entirely different realms of life. The philosopher or historian of philosophy may be aware that such and such a German burgher looked approvingly on Luther's reform because he wanted to be able to eat meat on Fridays, or that such and such a priest went over to the new faith because in it he could legally satisfy his sexual needs. But in the philosophical perspective these and similar reforms must be considered secondary to the principle of justification through faith, even though for some people they may have been more important as motivations. And the principle of justification through faith must in turn be considered secondary to general assumptions about the nature of the connection between man and God.

The meaning of a philosophical idea cannot be reduced to the motives which determine its spread, or even its genesis, if the history of philosophical thought is to preserve its distinctness from, for instance, the history of technology – in other words, if it is to exist at all. It ceases to exist the moment it renounces the belief that the logic of thought is different from the logic of vested interests – in other words, the belief that the uses of philosophical and religious ideas do not exhaust their meaning.

I have said that what we must concentrate on at this point are the fundamental ideas which gave the Reformation its specific shape in its initial phase; and indeed they are the philosophically important ones. Once the new faith was codified in the form of a series of dogmas, gradually stiffening within the collar of its own catechisms, its own organization and liturgy, the Reformation proved philosophically more barren than the Roman Church. Insofar as it did continue to produce philosophically stimulating ideas, it was only thanks to those who made a conscious effort to break out of its rigidity, went back to its original sources, to the ideas by which it had initially been inspired, and attempted to inject new vigor into its forgotten early ideals. This process, as we know, began very swiftly – as early as the 1520s, when the new reformers (like Sebastian Franck) attempted to take Luther's doctrine further (in philosophical as well as social terms) than Luther himself had intended.

III

The philosophical barrenness of the organized and catechized Reformation – doubtless connected to its fundamental dislike of philosophical justifications of its own doctrine – is obvious and indisputable. Neither the sixteenth nor the seventeenth century produced Protestant philosophers – that is, philosophers whose thought was clearly connected with a denominational religiosity, defined in a Protestant way – of any distinction. There was no Protestant Suarez, no Protestant Pascal, no Protestant Malebranche. If the Catholic Church produced eminent philosophers in the seventeenth century, philosophers who consciously linked their philosophical thought with the Roman faith, not just with a general belief in God and immortality, it was mainly because the form of religiosity which emerged victorious and established itself in Catholicism involved, in principle, an acceptance of nature. The essential difference between Rome and the Great Reformed Churches is connected with the much greater philosophical fertility of the former: the Protestant belief that human nature is fundamentally corrupt, and thus that reason is powerless in the face of ultimate, metaphysical questions, naturally had a paralyzing effect on philosophical thought. Neither Locke, an Anglican, nor Grotius, a Remonstrant, nor Leibniz or Pufendorf, both Protestants, can be called Protestant philosophers. Deistic doctrines in particular are quite alien to the Protestant religious spirit, despite the undeniable fact that they could never have developed in European culture had it not been for the intellectual developments set in motion by the Reformation. It is true that Leibniz's philosophy is strongly and clearly marked by Protestant religiosity, in the sense that much of it (above all its attempt to reconcile free will with pre-existing harmony) is concerned with reconciling Catholic and Protestant dogma about the relationship between nature and grace. This has often been pointed out. Nevertheless, in no possible sense can Leibniz be regarded as continuing the thought of the reformers – chiefly because of the extremely marked rationalism of his philosophy, and his unshaken conviction that all problems can be resolved with the aid of the instruments available to discursive reason.

In considering the philosophical significance of the Reformation, we do not, then, want to know about Protestant philosophers – those whose philosophical program was connected with and limited to one denomination or another. What the Reformation accomplished for philosophy, it accomplished in spite of itself, through thinkers who not only grew out of the social climate it created but were also inspired by its values. It is these we are interested in. One might say that philosophy repaid the Reformation handsomely for its disapproval: by drawing on the raw material it supplied.

In considering the general historical or cultural role of the Reformation – as Max Weber, Troeltsch, and Holl do in their classic works – it makes sense to adopt a broad definition of it, encompassing all the reformist currents in the Church from the beginning of the fifteenth century to the end of the Council of Trent (after which denominational divisions became, in a sense, petrified), and thus including Erasmus and the Erasmians, the Illuminists, and so on. But if our interest is limited to specifically philosophical influences, we should narrow it, concentrating on the theological and anthropological ideas which were the clearest distinctive features of the reform movement. In other words, we should ignore ideas motivated chiefly and directly by a concern with reforming ecclesiastical customs and organizational structures, the role of the clergy and their position within the Church, moral and economic injunctions, and so on, and take into account only those which, by their content, influenced philosophical thought.

IV

Contempt for philosophy was in fact so natural and inevitable a part of the religiosity proclaimed by the reformers that it does not occupy a great deal of space in their writings, and is rarely expressed explicitly. For it is evident that the corruption of the human will, incurable by any natural means, manifests itself in the depravation of reason, which, if it tries to fathom divine mysteries by itself, only succeeds in multiplying the fruit of pride and the chances of damnation. "... *nec rectum dictamen habet natura, nec bonam voluntatem,*" says Luther in his 34th thesis[1]: human nature has neither good precepts nor good will. These words, drafted shortly before October 31, 1517, say all that needs to be said about philosophy. They are supplemented by explanations which strikingly reflect the process of Luther's final break with Aristotelianism and Scholastic theology. Anyone who says that a theologian must be a logician is a heretic, proclaims thesis 45; syllogistic reasoning cannot apply

---

1 *Disputatio contra scholasticam theologiam* (Theses against Scholastic Theology), 1517 (Thesis 7 reads: "Without the grace of God the will produces an act that is perverse and evil.") *D. Martin Luthers Werke. Kritische Gesammtausgabe* (Herman Böhlau: Weimar, 1883 [1966 reprint]), vol. 1. Cf. Luther's thesis against philosophy in his *Disputatio Heildelbergae habita* (April 25, 1518).

to things divine (*"Non tamen ideo sequitur, veritatem articuli trinitatis repugnare formis syllogisticus"*; thesis 48), and anyone who tries to use such reasoning to investigate the mystery of the Trinity will cease to believe in it (*"Si forma syllogistica tenet in terminis divinis, articulus trinitatis erit scritus et non creditus"*; thesis 49). In thesis 50 Luther sums up by saying that all the writings of Aristotle are to theology as darkness is to light (*"Breviter, totus Aristoteles ad theologiam est tenebra ad lucem"*), and in thesis 41 he adds that almost the whole of Aristotle's *Ethics* is the worst enemy of grace.

The same alternative – *either* trust in reason *or* believe in divine mysteries – crops up again and again in Luther's attacks on Erasmus, who, despite his coolness towards metaphysical speculation and despite the *Praise of Folly*,[2] is placed by Luther in the Scholastic camp because of his basic trust in the possibilities of human nature and reason. This in spite of the fact that Erasmus had no intention of trying to fathom divine mysteries, nor did he enjoin others to do so; nor did he claim that the content of Christianity could be rationally justified. What he said was that we should content ourselves with the words of Bible, without attempting minute analyses of their meaning in disputes over dogma. Nevertheless, Luther's hatred of him is understandable. For Erasmus, everything that is essential in Christianity is simple and easy to accept for the natural world, and entirely sufficient to provide the Christian with practical guidelines in life; the rest is of little importance. But Erasmus's preference, in matters of dogma, for the least complicated solutions, and the least offensive to common sense (above all on the questions of the Holy

---

2   For example: "Then they [the Scholastics] let fly at the ignorant crowd their syllogisms, major and minor, conclusions, corollaries, idiotic hypotheses and further scholastic rubbish. . . . The Apostles knew personally the mother of Jesus, but which of them proved how she had been kept immaculate from Adam's sin with the logic our theologians display? . . . The Apostles baptized wherever they went, yet nowhere did they teach the formal, material, efficient and final cause of baptism. . . . I fancy the Apostles themselves would need the help of another holy spirit if they were obliged to join issue on these topics with our new breed of theologian." *The Praise of Folly*, translated by Betty Radice (Penguin Books: London, 1971), pp. 171, 157, 156. And in his "Letter to Martin Dorp," 1515, Erasmus writes: "What, I ask you, has Christ to do with Aristotle, or the mysteries of eternal wisdom with subtle sophistry? What purpose is served by that maze of debatable issues, so many of which are a waste of time or a noxious evil, if only because of the strife and dissension they create? . . . In short, we have come to the point when the basis of the issue involved rests not so much on Christ's teaching as on the Schoolmen's definitions and the power of the bishops, such as they are. Consequently everything is now so complicated that there is not even a hope of recalling the world to true Christianity" (pp. 230–31).

Trinity, the divinity of Christ, and original sin), is so well known that it needs no further elaboration. In short, Christianity, for Erasmus, neither violates nature in its moral precepts nor offends reason in its theological content. For Luther, on the contrary, the unintelligibility of divine mysteries is essential, above all for imbuing us with contempt for ourselves and our powers, since "to love God is to hate oneself."

Calvin's anti-philosophical stance, based on the same premises, was perhaps more strongly expressed. The words "philosophy" or "philosophers" rarely occur in his texts without a context of contempt and hatred. And he expresses an idea which is not, I think, explicitly formulated in Luther's writings, though it is in keeping with his intentions: that God gave us just as much natural knowledge of ourselves as to make it impossible for us to plead ignorance at the Final Judgment. In other words, natural light in divine matters is merely an instrument which deprives sinners of their alibis and excuses. But it is neither necessary nor sufficient for attaining faith; Christianity cannot be strengthened by reason and logical argument. If pagan philosophers achieved some knowledge of God, it was to their greater damnation, for they erred immeasurably. Philosophers' notions of divine and human matters are as dust, worthless, before the Bible.

The fury with which the creators of the Reformation persecuted philosophy, and the immediate practical results of their activities – above all the desolation of the German universities a result of the Lutheran reform – might raise doubts about the point of asking about the role of the Reformation in the history of philosophy, if the question concerns something other than its purely negative results. But historians of philosophy as a rule consider almost all explicitly anti-philosophical programs as part of their domain. Moreover, such programs are a significant and fairly considerable part of the philosophical history of Europe. The condemnation of philosophy on the grounds that it is *rational* – and therefore opposed to divine light – is a continually recurring phenomenon, from the early Church Fathers to Kierkegaard and some twentieth century existentialists; its condemnation on the grounds that it is *irrational* – that it cannot justify itself scientifically – is, in turn, an essential component of the history of positivism, from its earliest days. Both these lines of attack belong to the history of philosophy just as fully as all the systems of the great metaphysicians. In fact, nothing is more common than the process whereby an obsessive dislike of philosophy becomes the root that nurtures new philosophical ideas.

V

We have, then, a process of fission, as it were, whereby the basic religious tenets of the Reformation branched off, as they developed, in divergent directions, giving rise to philosophical ideas whose fruit was often radically different from the root, and yet in some real, genetic and indeed positive way connected with that root. This is the process we must now consider.

To put it briefly, Luther's interpretation of Christianity, taking off on an independent life of its own, bifurcated and followed two quite different and mutually incompatible paths: a *mystical* path and an *existential* path. The starting-point for both was the same; and the possibility of just such a bifurcation is contained in the very idea of justification through faith. This dual development should not be all that surprising. We may be able to reconstruct the personal motives which underlie Luther's doctrine; we may even understand, through empathy or intuition, his experience of the Christian hope of salvation. But once that experience is expressed in theological language and becomes a doctrine, it inevitably loses the coherence of the original experience and begins to show signs of internal contradiction.

From the psychological point of view, the initial act of Lutheranism is the experience of *resignation*: an awareness of our powerlessness in the struggle against our innate wretchedness. This brings the illumination that we must trust divine omnipotence, entrusting to it not only our external life, but also our ability to merit God's praise for our spiritual life – our will, in other words, which no human efforts can cure of its corruption. "Doubt in yourself" is the the first commandment; it outweighs all others and constitutes the core of the true act of faith. In its theological, non-normative form, this commandment says: *a corrupt nature does not lead to God*. And the principle of justification through faith is a particular consequence of this general belief: since our nature does not lead to God, no effort based on our innate abilities can make us just according to divine criteria; therefore only God (if we reject the terrible possibility that all mankind is damned), through His freely given grace, can acknowledge us as just, despite our sins, and save us from eternal perdition. Thus the principle which says that a corrupt nature does not lead to God (which Luther did not express in these words, but which sums up his reply to the question of the relationship between nature and the supernatural) entails two things: that it is impossible to merit God's praise by deeds inspired by natural desires, but also that our innate reason cannot by itself attain knowledge of divine things.

This principle, on the face of it clear in its intentions, contains within it contradictory possibilities. It can be understood (and certain texts by Luther suggest this possibility) to mean that *all forms of human self-affirmation* – all human motives, all cares of which we are the object – are contrary to God. Including, in particular, the desire for redemption, if it stops at the hope of eternal happiness as the ultimate goal: for then it, too, is a private sin, a form of self-interest unbefitting the true Christian, who should be thinking about the glory of God for its own sake, and should love God for Himself, not because He is the source of the hope of salvation. This interpretation of Luther's principle can be developed further, in the classical spirit of mysticism: all that gives man his uniqueness as a being, preserves his distinctness and maintains his activity (all individual human activity being the work of "nature," and as such contrary to God), is an evil. Consequently all individual existence is an evil, and the true fulfillment of human destiny must be loss of individuality and oneness with divinity, *theosis*: an existential transformation into the infinity of the original source of being – what the mystics called *annihilatio*. As time went by, Luther increasingly forgot the inspiration he had drawn in his youth from mystical writings; and as the organizer of a new congregation and a new denomination, he could not base himself on an idea of Christianity where the only value was the goal of existential fusion with divinity. Nevertheless the development of his thought in a mystical spirit was by no means an aberration, but an interpretation both legitimate (though questioned by Luther himself) and in keeping with the nature of the stimuli which had initially influenced him.

Moreover, Luther's basic premise allows not only for a mystical interpretation but for a mystically pantheistic one. A theory that proclaims the powerlessness of creation, the absolute omnipotence of God, and the corruption of nature easily leads to the conclusion that man's revolt against divine will, expressed in the desire for a distinct activity of his own, is what distinguishes human will, uniquely and negatively, from the rest of the world; but since what is created is powerless and passive, everything that happens happens not by nature but through the agency of God. Thus not only is the world the revelation of God through creation, but all that happens in it is divine activity – it is the body of God. If this reasoning is pursued further, it can lead to a pantheistic belief in the divinity of creation – despite the fact that the point of departure was the radical dichotomy between the divine world and the world of nature. The view of all natural existence as the life of God is also rooted in Luther's doctrine of the powerlessness of nature; and the whole of German pantheistic philosophy, though it goes counter to Luther's intentions, springs from his thought and derives its driving force from it. From Sebastian Franck (the first pantheist produced by the Reformation) through Jacob Böhme (who, as Holl points out, developed Luther's idea of the contradictory ways in which God reveals Himself, as love and as revenge, into a metaphysical cosmogony of the contradiction of being), through Weigl and, finally, Silesius, the German pantheism of the Reformation passed down this aspect of Lutheranism to German Romantic philosophy, and ultimately to Schelling and Hegel. Nothing was more remote from Luther's ideas than pantheism. Nevertheless, he was, in a real sense, the mediating link in the process whereby the heritage of medieval pantheistic mysticism was passed down to the German culture of later centuries. Schopenhauer's metaphysics, which treats the particularization of being as the original sin of creation, as the true source of evil, has its roots in the same tradition.

The social background of Luther's reform is well known and we need not go into it here. But it is worth considering the consequences of this "revolution" (the word is misleading insofar as the new faith was in fact – and in Luther's own view – a return to the Pauline version of Christianity).

The rejection of nature as a way to God also has, as we know, moral consequences: it entails the abolition of the "good deeds" aspect of religion, which is seen as a glaring example of those ineffective attempts to amass merit for oneself for the Day of Judgment. To condemn as ineffective (at best) all initiatives deriving from nature is to deny that the path of righteousness is worth following (from the point of view of redemption). The dethroning of righteousness in favor of love is an idea that has had an astonishing career since Luther's time, and crops up widely as a motif. It became the inspiration for explicitly antinomist movements, which used principles proclaiming the uselessness of good deeds and of all "external" actions as a pretext for advocating moral anarchy and the abolition of all discipline (something entirely unconnected with Luther's intentions). But it was also – as has often been remarked – the source of Kant's moral doctrine – *via* the pietistic Renaissance. The view that true moral qualities can be attributed only to the will is of Lutheran origin; in this sense, the Kantian, anti-utilitarian position in ethics may be regarded as the heritage of Lutheranism. Kant's moral philosophy is a secular version of Luther's anti-works theology.

In a certain restricted sense, the principle that nature is not a path to God can also be seen as a source of the deist tradition (although here the gulf between the original ideas of the reform and their later fruits is a vast one). For this principle certainly operated in two different directions: it denied the efficacy of natural reason in religious matters and condemned "*usus rationis in divinis*" as a usurpation; at the same time it proclaimed its indifference to the use of natural cognition within the bounds of the natural world, as long as it did not lead to conflict with the word of God. It thus allowed one to accept, without closer examination, a fundamentally irrational faith while also acknowledging the autonomy of secular reason in the natural order – an attitude later widespread among Protestant scholars. The reason I say that this can be considered an example of the philosophical influence of the Reformation only in "a restricted sense" is simply that this influence was largely a negative one.

Nonetheless, it is not only Protestant deist thought that is genetically linked with the essentially reformist separation of the natural world from divine reality: the belief that there is no way from nature to God also links Descartes with Pascal (as Alquié points out in his *La découverte métaphysique de l'homme chez Descartes*), although the meaning of this principle, and the reasons for which it was arrived at, are different in each case.

VI

Of the two essential paths which branched out from the ideas of the Reformation and influenced philosophical thought, the mystical one described above, although of unparalleled importance in the history of European culture, is nevertheless a side branch from the point of view of the issue under discussion here. The other is, as I have said, the existential path. The existential sense of Lutheranism is more clearly discernible than its mystical sense, but its substance is more difficult to formulate.

It is clear, however, that the idea of justification through faith has a dual polemical aim in Luther's writings: it is directed against the principle of justification through *deeds*, but at the same time against the principle of justification through *doctrine*. The world of faith is radically different from the world of discursive thought; it springs from the sharp rift, the gap, that separates all things natural from all things divine. On the one hand, true Christianity is achieved by overcoming nature – that is, overcoming human will and human self-affirmation; and it is possible only when we have overcome false Christianity – Christianity conceived as an extension, perfection or ennoblement of natural human inclinations. This is the point around which the *mystical* variant of the Reformation principle develops. On the other hand, true Christianity also means overcoming Christianity conceived as doctrine – as knowledge of God; it means overcoming the blind nonchalance with which the believer puts his hopes of eternal life in his orthodoxy alone. Satan also believes in God, and he trembles, in the marvelous words of James[3] (a text, as it happens, which Luther considered – for other reasons – as the most suspect of the Biblical canon). Being a Christian does not mean amassing all the knowledge of God that is accessible to us; Christ's mission was neither to inform nor to promise redemption as a reward for the proper learning of doctrine. Being a Christian means living in faith; and faith is not belief but total spiritual regeneration: total renewal, which involves the eradication of the old, "outer" self. It is an act of entering a new reality, an act which no natural mediator – neither the organized

---

3   James 2.19: "Thou believest that there is one God; thou doest well: the devils
    also believe, and tremble."

church, nor the saints, nor learning, nor any externally administered sacraments – can perform for us. ". . . *Deus pater omnia in fide posuit*," writes Luther in his *Freedom of a Christian*; God has made all things depend on faith. And that faith "*non nisi in homine interiore regnare possit*." In the act of faith, the Christian stands before God stripped of everything. Only there, in the "inner person," in each one individually, does Christianity fulfill itself.

Speculative, abstract Christianity, in which the human individual is also an abstraction, is thus contrasted with Christianity as a living faith – *theologia regenitorum*, Christianity which is achieved only through the purified soul's contact with divine grace.

Here too, as with mystical *kenosis*, we have a process in which the Lutheran mission is distorted, indeed lost, in the later evolution of "ecclesiasticized" Lutheranism, while its original intentions develop and spread beyond the organized congregation. Indeed, Christianity conceived as a purely "internal" value, with no possible support in any visible reality, cannot be the basis of a congregation; by its very nature, it cannot create a collectivity. In faith, human individuals are unreckonable: they cannot be totted up into the sum of them all. Each stands alone before God, and their combined faith does not produce any doctrinal unity or organized collective. Thus the whole *raison d'être* of the visible Church is put in question; this kind of message can be preached by a lone prophet, but not by the organizer of a social movement and the architect of a reformed congregation, for he would be cutting down the tree he had planted. So it seems natural that the idea of faith as the non-transferable property of the individual soul, closed to the world and visible only to God, had to yield to collective forms of Christian life which could be passed on and proclaimed. Nor is it surprising that the idea of justification through faith spread among the faithful in the very form which Philipp Jacob Spener and other Pietists so often attacked for being the exact opposite of what Luther had intended: as the idea that we are the children of God and can be certain of redemption because of the true doctrine handed down by Christ, a doctrine corrupted and perverted by the Papacy but extracted from oblivion by Luther.

VII

We can now define more clearly the difference between the two very divergent interpretations of the principle that establishes the fundamental separation of God and nature – the mystical and the existential. In the former, the emphasis is on eliminating nature; this involves (in milder variants of the mystical interpretation) eliminating human individuality or even (in pantheistic variants taken to their logical conclusion) eliminating absolutely all particularization of existence. In the latter, the emphasis is on eliminating all "natural" forms of support: the individual must strip himself of everything, both temporal and abstract, in order to attain the state of the "inner person"; only then will he stand, in his full concreteness and his non-transferable subjectivity, before the world of grace. These two currents go in opposite directions: the essential idea and ultimate goal of the former is all-encompassing absolute existence, in which all individual existence sheds its appearance of ontological autonomy; the essential idea and ultimate goal of the latter is, on the contrary, the irreducible *Jemeinigkeit* (to borrow Heidegger's expression) of every human being separately, and the unreckonability of all of them together.

The existentialist path created by Luther, or rather the path he revived – for here, too, he resuscitated an extinct but very real Christian tradition – lacks the visible continuity of the mystical path, which can be traced almost from generation to generation in German culture, down to the nineteenth century. But it is no less real. Obviously, it would be absurd to see the Jansenist strain of Augustinian Catholicism in the seventeenth century as an intentional prolongation of Luther's program; nevertheless, the Jansenists' attempt at counter-reformation was of a similar kind: they wanted to defeat the opponent with his own weapons, appealing to and claiming for the Roman Church the very values – the values of early Christianity – which the heretics had proclaimed as their own. From the point of view which interests us here, Jansenism was an attempt to invest Catholic religiosity with the same distrust of nature and of natural paths to redemption that was preached by the Reformation (all the while of course trying – unsuccessfully, as we know – to stay within the bounds of dogma on the question of grace). But the Jansenists' distrust of nature did not lead to the doctrine of mystical annihilation (though in the earliest phase of Jansenism, in the writings of St. Cyran, the anti-mystical current is not yet explicit). For them, rejecting nature did not mean mystical union with divinity; it meant preserving, through an act of contrition and faith, full human subjectivity – resigned, humbled and awaiting grace. Reason was considered an aid to this, as a negative force: because it could voluntarily deny its own value and renounce itself. Pascal's religiosity, in contrast to that of the mystics, leaves us with a heightened awareness of our own individual existence. It is an awareness which manifests itself as a penetrating insight into our wretchedness and corrupt nature, and at the same time allows us to glimpse the path to salvation, open to us not as a result of human efforts but by the mercy of God, manifested in Christ.

This is the path we can call the existential version of Christianity. Mysticism is not a "subjectivization" of religious values; on the contrary, it wants to abolish human subjectivity in the all-consuming night of the absolute. Existential religiosity, on the other hand, while it also wants to stifle the individual will and curb its desire to defy God in self-assertion, nevertheless preserves the full distinctness and existential irreducibility of the human subject. Enjoining constant awareness of our instinct to yield to our natural inclinations, it wants to reduce the self-knowledge gained through this vigilance to a consciousness of our sinfulness and wretchedness; but it does all this in the name of saving the individual. In the existential version, the mystics' extreme act of resignation – the abandonment of the hope of eternal salvation; resignation to the prospect of damnation, if such were to be God's will – is unthinkable. The existential consciousness wants to preserve the hope of personal redemption as the supreme value while maintaining the belief in the omnipotence of grace, which ultimately determines the question of redemption, independently of any natural efforts. And because it wants to preserve both these things, it is condemned to an eternal anguish of uncertainty; it cannot lead to the final peace which mysticism brings, after long tribulations, to its chosen.

In the nineteenth century, Kierkegaard was rightly considered the true prophet of existential Christianity. His link with the tradition of Luther's theology seems unquestionable. His critique of Hegel and his critique of "objective Christianity," as he called it, are both argued from the same position and in the name of the same values – the values of concrete subjectivity grasped in the act of self-humiliation, through an awareness of sin and guilt. He gives expression to the true principle underpinning the young Luther's religiosity – a principle impossible to express in this form in the language of the sixteenth century: that faith is the negation of all "objectivity," of all values in which men can participate jointly, as a collectivity, as members of a species. Individual subjectivities are absolutely unreckonable; there cannot be "two" consciousnesses, since to classify consciousness by number, which is an abstraction, is to deprive it of its unique specificity, and that means taking away its reality. "The difference [between Christianity and Hegelianism]," says Kierkegaard in the *Postscript*, "is that philosophy teaches that the way is to become objective, while Christianity teaches that the way is to become subjective, i.e., to become a subject in truth." And he directs at Christianity – Christianity as a doctrine, as an organization, as a collective fact – the same fundamental objection he directs against Hegelianism: "If Christianity were a doctrine, our relationship to it would not be a relationship of faith, since the only relationship we can have to a doctrine is an intellectual one. Christianity is not a doctrine; it is the fact that God existed." In other words, Christianity does not rest on a belief in the historical reality of the story of Christ in the Gospels, nor on the belief that such and such a dogma is true, nor even on obedience to divine law, set out in the Bible for all men to follow. Christianity is only for one; "only one attains the goal." And this one can be anyone. Faith – in accordance with Luther's idea and Abraham's example – is not a belief, but a complete transformation of the inner person. It means consenting to the absurd, to crime, to impossibility; it means going beyond everything that can be formulated as equally directed towards all men, towards a collectivity. It means going beyond reason and suspending moral law. To live in faith is to preserve one's full subjectivity, whose only reference is divine subjectivity. Kierkegaard's attack on Lutheranism is a repetition of Luther's attack on the Church of his age. It questions a Christianity whose subjects are abstract constructs (human individuals seen as members of a collectivity) fulfilling their faith in abstractions (by asserting doctrinal orthodoxies or carrying out rites); it is an attack in the name of the one concrete thing which is truly concrete: the concrete subjectivity of the human individual.

The recognition of subjectivity as, first, ultimate and irreducible, inexplicable by anything else and inexpressible in "objective"" language, and, second, coming to know itself through an awareness of its own evil and wretchedness, and discovering its need of a justification which the natural world cannot provide, is the crux of the existential experience of Christianity. This is the form in which Luther's challenge, for him a renewal and continuation of the mission and message of St. Paul, revived in the nineteenth century, distinguishing itself by opposition to three things simultaneously: Hegelian rationalism, romantic pantheism, and institutional Christianity. And Kierkegaard in turn passed this current of thought down to our century, to philosophers who, from Miguel Unamuno to Karl Jaspers and finally to Martin Heidegger, have tried to express in roundabout ways what cannot be expressed directly: the irreducible concreteness of human subjectivity. Kierkegaard is a particularly important link in this chain: his presence and place in philosophy show that the connection between modern existentialist philosophy and Luther's thought is not an artificial construct based on mere coincidence, but a genuine and powerful link. This is true despite the obvious fact that modern existentialism has scarcely any knowledge of its genealogy and feels little connection to the Lutheran tradition, or indeed to any Christian tradition whatsoever: it is hard to imagine Sartre acknowledging that his denial of God the law-giver, and thus of any norms and rules that might be binding on the human subject apart from its own free decisions, contains even the glimmer of a reflection of Luther's denial of the Law which Christ's religion of grace abolished. And yet this connection is not entirely fictitious. Furthermore, Luther's condemnation of philosophy as a doctrine, his rejection of it as not only alien but harmful to the world of Christian values, reappears in the Kierkegaardian – and generally existentialist – conception of philosophy as an act of self-knowledge which must be constantly renewed by everyone individually, and which cannot be transformed into an abstract theory or doctrine aspiring to general validity. This theme is particularly striking in the work of Jaspers: since existence, at each moment renewed at its source, cannot be conceived as an object, as a collection of qualities which can be enumerated in abstract terms, philosophy as an attempt to catalogue or describe a collection of particular existences is not possible, at least not in the form of theory; philosophy is rather a continually renewed challenge in which the individual existence tries to come into contact with another, although it knows that through this contact it will never be able to communicate itself in the sense that an idea can be communicated or a thing passed on. This essentially existentialist negation of philosophy also has its roots in Luther's Christianity.

VIII

Let us sum up. Luther's idea of reform was a new interpretation of Augustine's confession: *Deum et animam scire cupio.* It expressed a striving that has characterized philosophical and religious efforts almost from the very beginning: the desire to define the human in opposition to the rest of nature. Deprived of its natural support and confronted with the overpowering attraction of grace, human subjectivity was to define itself through an awareness of its own wretchedness and corruption. This fundamental break with nature allowed a development along two different paths, which I have called the mystical and the existential response to the challenge of the Reformation. In the mystical response, man, when he attempts to define himself in opposition to the world, finds nothing but the corruption and evil which is inherent in his particular, separate existence; he thus abandons individual existence, believing that this act of self-destruction, of dissolving himself in an absolute, will be a way back to that root of being from which his diseased individual existence had the misfortune to spring. In the existential response, this deprived human subjectivity discovers itself as absolutely irreducible: not explainable or analyzable in terms of anything in the world of things or the world of ideas. If it discovers God, it will try to engage in a private dialogue with Him – a dialogue no one outside it can hear or understand or judge. If it does not discover him, it must see itself as a sterile absolute, with neither root nor ultimate aim; being for itself, pure negativity, *"passion inutile."*

In this sense, one might say that Luther's call for reform entrusted to posterity the discovery of the seed which lay within it – subjectivity, the embryo of modern philosophy. And indeed, philosophy is constantly striving to return to a primary, unmediated human subjectivity – a subjectivity which will inevitably dismiss philosophy as metaphysical speculation, as system-building. The Lutheran hatred of philosophy can be discerned in all the persistent attempts to forge philosophy out of its self-negation.

Translated by Agnieszka Kolakowska

Richard Avenarius and the Apparent Suicide of Philosophy

In philosophical writing, the search for literal expression always conflicts with the need to be didactic and suggestive. Avenarius opted for the former. At the risk of being almost unreadable, he tried to write as plainly and literally as possible: no metaphors, no allegories, no memorable aphorisms. We must assume that he was conscious of the risk; he must have known that his deliberately rigid and arid style was discouraging to his readers. And yet he never succeeded in being as literal as he would have liked. His writings teem with quotation marks; on crucial points he can be ambiguous, just like everyone else. However, he left us what is perhaps the clearest account of a certain fundamental philosophical intuition which he was neither the first nor the last to try to formulate.

Avenarius wanted to eradicate our sense of the mystery of the world; he wanted to explain away its mysteriousness. That, generally speaking, is the aim of all positivist programs. Some philosophers – those who constructed metaphysical "systems," for example – have believed that the world's hidden significance is inaccessible to us through scientific research, and only theoretical meditation or a particular kind of experience can reveal it. Others thought that all our cognitive efforts and the knowledge that comes from them must encounter an impregnable barrier which will always separate us from the "true" reality, which is deeper and more authentic than anything science is capable of revealing. Others still rejected both the hope of one day solving the enigma and the idea that such an enigma existed at all; they considered cries of "ignorabimus" as poison to the development of knowledge and culture, dismissed them as consequences of linguistic abuse or excessive imagination, and tried to get to the root of the confusion in order to extirpate the misguided beliefs which had arisen from it. They wanted to show that the very idea of the enigma of the world, even if we think it a problem impossible to ignore, involves false assumptions about the way we come to know things; and that once these assumptions are brought out, we will no longer waste our energy on the futile investigation of pseudo-mysteries.

It was to this last category of philosophers that Avenarius belonged. It is a radical position, because it not only dismisses as futile all attempts to construct great ontological and epistemological syntheses, but also rejects, on principle, all ontological and epistemological research, considering it to be worthless and doomed from the outset. There have been many variations of it, differing in the way in which the source of the error and its consequences were identified.

According to Avenarius, the root of the error lay in what he called the act of introjection: this was the source of all misleading philosophical and religious constructions, and also all the faulty ideas of our common sense.

Here, says Avenarius, is a stone; I take it in my hand. Nothing mysterious about the feel of it. But philosophers want us to believe it contains some enigma worthy of supreme attention. They want to persuade us that the tactile impression of the stone is somehow in us, while the stone itself is something different from that impression; consequently, we need to explain the relation between our experience and the thing we experience: in what way our "impression" of the stone is "like" the stone itself, and in what way, if at all, it gives us access to the stone as it "really" is. But a mind uninitiated into these mysteries will not naturally pose such questions. What we have is just one thing, not two: the stone, not the stone and our impression of it. If we let ourselves be bamboozled into believing that our world consists not of things but of impressions of things, we will fabricate an insoluble enigma; we will go around multiplying everything in the world by two, and then torment ourselves with the question of whether the copy is "really" like the original in some inaccessible realm "beyond" our experience. This question being patently unanswerable, since we have no way of comparing the copy (the impression) with the original (the thing) and studying the relation between them, we will either conclude that the thing-in-itself lurks mysteriously somewhere behind the veil of experience, or end up succumbing to the idealist fallacy, which consists in identifying things with the mosaics of mental "content".

And yet nothing forces us to accept this extravagant vision; to avoid it, we need only avoid the primitive error of doubling the world by distinguishing between "external" things and an "internal" mental reality in which those things, in some unfathomable way, become impressions. However, we still need to explain why it is that we succumb so easily to the idea that the world has a mental double which is "in us". For we do succumb to it; the double vision which produces a world of "physical" and "mental" things is not an ailment restricted to philosophers, but is encountered everywhere, in many different forms. How is it, then, that the pure, untrained experience of ordinary people, uninfluenced by philosophy, allows itself to be distorted in this way? And how can its purity be restored? It with these questions that a good part of Avenarius's work is concerned.

Introjection, he says – the mental operation whereby we convince ourselves that physical things exist in our minds in the form of copies – consists of several stages, each of them producing new illusions and more and more bizarre beliefs. But our original error is "justified," because the process provides us with an interpretation of they way we come to know things, which, although false, is perfectly intelligible.

The process is as follows. We naturally, and rightly, attribute meaning to people's behavior; we treat people as persons, not as stones or automata. Since we cannot participate directly in other people's experience and feel it as they do – we cannot, for example, feel their pain, although we are allowed to say that it really is pain, and not merely behavior indicative of pain – but must deduce it from their behavior, we attribute to them an "interior" in which all their experiences – pain, thoughts, impressions – are located. We see them as a sort of receptacle where objects are collected in a special "mental" form. Thus we divide people into two parts: a spiritual interior and its external manifestations. This is the first stage of introjection.

The second stage consists in performing the operation on ourselves: we project on to ourselves a model originally designed to explain other people's behavior and enable us to interpret them as persons. Assuming ourselves to be essentially similar to other people, we attribute a similar "interior" to ourselves. Having divided ourselves up in the same way, we begin to treat our own experiences as collections of mental impressions caused by "external" influences. We now have two realities, subjective and objective, and have convinced ourselves that the subject, or interior, is fundamentally different from the external object.

The germs of all the fantastic ideas ever produced by the human imagination are there in this double vision. Having created two distinct, totally heterogeneous worlds, we already have the idea of the spirit as something separate from the body, and can manipulate this idea at will: we can transpose it to different objects, produce the concept of the immaterial soul, fabricate spirits, ghosts, gods and so on. And if we are philosophers, we can go one step further and perform the operation again, doubling experience itself to obtain two kinds of experience: internal and external. Once we do this, everything "external" becomes an enigma, which we can deal with in one of two ways: we can either express it in the form of an agnostic doctrine or dispose of it by invalidating the results of our introjection. The latter option leaves "interior" experience as the only valid kind and leads us to epistemological subjectivism.

On this path of error, according to Avenarius, lies the origin of all forms of idealism, agnosticism, and also religious belief. If we trace it back to its beginning, we can free ourselves of our illusions. We need not, in order to recognize that other people are like us, divide them (and ourselves) in two; nor need we believe that what we experience is not the object itself but the object-for-me, or the impression of an object. All we need to do is identify our initial error and undo it. We will then discover the futility of all the controversies between realists and spiritualists; the conflicts between determinists and voluntarists; the debates around the ideas of force, cause, substance and attribute. For all these categories have their source in introjection, and are dispelled along with it. If we rid ourselves of the illusion that everything – other people, objects, we ourselves – have an interior and an exterior, the problem of the relation between these two worlds will not arise; if we refuse to believe that things as they are "given" to our senses become, through a form of mediation, part of our "internal" experience, we shall stop asking what these things are like independently of being "given". The question of being-in-itself will disappear, and philosophy itself will (apparently) cease to exist; it will commit suicide, having revealed itself to be no more than a collection of pointless questions originating from a misinterpretation of experience.

This is the *pars destruens* of Avenarius's analysis. But there is also a positive part. Being a philosopher, Avenarius had to ask about the "purified" world that remains after introjection is done away with. What is it like, and how can we explain it? We *are* – we experience our being – in a certain way; we cannot stop believing that we are different from the things we experience, even if we accept the non-introjective interpretation of experience – the "presentationalist" interpretation, as it is awkwardly called. When we "know" or "feel" something, we want to be able to say what it is that does the knowing, and what it is that is known, and what the relation is between them. In asking about the knower and the thing known, I am already presupposing a distinction between them, and this distinction demands clarification.

Avenarius's positive side, his epistemological analysis, is based on the notion of what he calls principal coordination. "I exist in a certain environment," he says, and that environment also contains my body. I can distinguish between the things I "find" in the world and the way I describe them to myself: as pleasant or unpleasant, ugly or beautiful, true or false. Among the things I "find" are other people and myself – my own "I". Other people and my "I" have an equal status; both belong to the relatively stable resources of experience, and are "found" in the same sense as things are "found". In other words, my "I" is not something that experiences, but something that is experienced. All that remains after we have cast off the illusions of introjection belongs to the realm of our experience.

We know, then, that the "I" is not an interior where copies of objects exist in the form of "mental" content. But it is indissolubly linked to the other elements of my experience – defined as "counter-terms" in their relation to the "I," which is the "central term". The counter-term and the central term are equal, in that neither has logical or causal priority over the other; and both are present in every experience. Principal coordination describes their necessary connection and the relation that obtains between them.

Avenarius does not think that this purified image of the world, purged of its superfluous flotsam of objects-as-mental-content, changes the meaning we attribute to our scientific and pre-scientific understanding or in any way impoverishes our knowledge. He does believe, however, that it eliminates the very possibility of epistemological idealism and agnosticism. In order to understand how principal coordination contributes to this outcome, we must consider three things.

First, the central term in principal coordination is the the human individual, and for any number of different central terms there is only one of any given counter-term. In other words an object is not multiplied according to the number of people perceiving it: it is always one object (although it may not have identical properties for everyone). Thus recovering the "natural" image of the world, which is what Avenarius believes he has succeeded in doing, is not done at the price of solipsism; on the contrary, principal coordination precludes the very possibility of solipsism, since we have admitted that what we perceive is the thing and not the thing-as-mental-content, and that thing is one and the same thing for every human individual perceiving it.

Second, we cannot, without abusing language, ask questions about the thing-in-itself that is hidden beyond experience. There is only one of each object, and that is the experienced object; there is no second object that is different from the object of experience. So it is absurd to ask questions about the thing-in-itself; asking "What is the thing-in-itself?" is tantamount to asking, "What is a counter-term that is not a counter-term?" The question cannot be formulated without contradiction. Thus we have also eliminated the possibility of agnosticism.

Third, when we ask about the reality that lies outside our experience, we are addressing ourselves to that reality, and the very act of asking about it places it in a situation of principal coordination. For example, we cannot ask what the world was like when there was no one there to observe it: a question about the world-in-itself, the "world-for-no-one," cannot be meaningfully formulated. Instead, we mentally project ourselves into the world that lies outside our experience and ask how it would be altered by our presence there as observers. But the very act of asking such a question places the world we are asking about in a certain relation to us; it gathers up that world, as it were, and encloses it within the question, so that it automatically becomes a counter-term in principal coordination. But the possibility of knowing things outside our direct experience remains unchanged. What Avenarius seems to be saying is that the act of asking such a question cannot be separated from the question's content. The question about the thing-in-itself cannot be formulated because the act of formulating it already produces the dependence which our question was an attempt to avoid; the thing-in-itself ceases to be in-itself once the question about it is asked. In short, to ask about the thing-in-itself is to ask how we can know the world without entering into a cognitive relation with it – or, to put it more simply, how we can know the world without knowing it.

Avenarius's polemical intention is clear. His target is the European metaphysical and epistemological tradition, with its meaningless questions that derive from an unjustified division of the world into mental and physical ingredients. He wants to invalidate the questions posed by Locke, by Descartes, by Kant; to do away with the theory of ideas according to which things are either copies or forever hidden; to demolish the very distinction between subject and object; to exclude the very possibility of a theory of knowledge or a metaphysics. He also attacks the idea that the cognitive act is part of the search for "truth" rather than a biologically necessary part of an organism's behavior, which is how it should properly be viewed. "Truth" is not an element of experience; it is not a quality "found" in experience. It is a secondary interpretation of experience: one of the "qualities" we add on to the content of our experience, like pleasure, beauty or ugliness. This is the negative result of Avenarius's analysis.

The positive result is that we have dissolved the artificial heterogeneity of subject and object while salvaging the possibility of science and knowledge. We can now see that the human individual is made up of the same stuff as all other things and, like them, is part of "experience" – which is itself ontologically undifferentiated. The universal reality of "experience" is common to all individuals, but this does not mean that there is some absolute truth about reality which this universality reveals. It means only that all human individuals are linked to it in the same way, by purely biological conditions: given the structure of our organisms and the structure of the world, there are certain stable circumstances in which the conditions of our exchange of energy with the environment cannot vary. Our experience of the world contains elements of varying durability: some are relatively stable, others fleeting, others still universal and immutable, valid under all conditions and for all human beings; and science is the classification of these elements according to their degree of durability. Thus science and cognition *are* possible, indeed they are a necessary part of our world, for they are simply the form which our biological reactions take. What is *not* possible is traditional theory of knowledge, of the kind that deals with questions about the relation of mental content to the world.

One thing, however, remains puzzling: if it was hostility towards idealism that inspired Avenarius's critique of introjection, why is it that his philosophy is so often and so easily interpreted as a form of subjectivism? For this is how most of his critics, from Wundt onwards, have interpreted the idea of principal coordination.

On this crucial point Avenarius did not succeed in expressing his intentions with the clarity he prized; he seems to have been unable to free himself from the deeply entrenched habits of human thought. A semantic interpretation of his idea might be expressed as follows: the content of what we say about the world necessarily includes an observing "I". The statement "There is a green tree outside the window" can only be understood to mean "I see a green tree . . ." or "I think there is a green tree . . . ," or "I know there is a green tree . . . ," or "It seems to me that there is a green tree . . . ," etc. The observing "I" is given, necessarily present in the content of everything we say, and cannot be eliminated except by cutting out the corresponding part of the statement; but such a cutting out is a purely superficial operation, for it only conceals the statement's real meaning, without changing it. The observer can be eliminated from the world only on the linguistic level. Such elimination can be either insignificant and superficial – a consequence of habit, when we leave out a term that is constantly present in our expression and thus always understood – or symptomatic of the illusion of introjection.

But what is this "I" that is always and irrevocably there in everything we say? Avenarius says that it is an element of experience like any other: it is experienced, but does not experience. This answer, however, involves enormous difficulties.

If I am not the subject of experience but an element of it, we have an act of experiencing with no one doing the experiencing: perception without a perceiver, an experience without a subject, belonging to no one. Something is given, but it is not given "to" anyone: it is just "given," *simpliciter*, by itself. Now it is logical that for Avenarius the perceiver should be secondary to the perception, for he is just like any other thing in the world; he is distinguished only by his (relatively great) degree of durability. But if so, then it is illegitimate, or at least misleading, to use the pronoun in the first person singular; for in its everyday meaning, the statement "I see a green tree" does not presuppose any cognitive equivalence between the "I" and the tree as two "givens" of the same kind. On the contrary, in its everyday meaning the phrase implies that I am experiencing the tree as an element within my field of perception; the relation between me and the content of my perception is one of perceiver to perceived: I am the perceiver, while the tree is the thing perceived.

But Avenarius says that the "I" is a thing that is experienced, just like any other kind of thing; the "I" is not an experiencing thing. If so, my statement should read, "The green tree is experienced and "I" am experienced with it" – with no subject to experience the experienced "I". I cannot say, "I experience both the tree and my "I" at the same time," since the phrase "I experience" contains an illegitimate "I," an "I" which has no right to be there. This "I" must be eliminated, reduced to one of the experienced elements of the world. But then, if the phrase is to be intelligible, we need to presuppose another "I," a higher-level, experiencing "I". But this "I," too, must then be reduced to an experienced thing, so we need to presuppose another, higher still. And so on, *ad infinitum*.

It turns out, consequently, that when I say "I am experiencing such-and-such," what I really mean is "Such-and-such is being experienced," or, more awkwardly, "There is an experiencing". This is the key to the epistemological enigma. But it is an elusive key, hard for our minds to grasp, for that is not how we talk: we do not know how to use verbs in such a way as to *exclude* the possibility of putting them into active or personal form while remaining intelligible. When we say things in an impersonal or passive form, things like "It's dark in this room," or "There are no bananas today" or "Dresses like that aren't being worn any more," we understand them in a way that allows for their translation into sentences with subjects, like "This room is dark," "We have no bananas today," "Women don't wear dresses like that any more," etc. We cannot understand them in any other way; we cannot grasp how a statement about the way something is experienced could be untranslatable *in principle* into a statement involving the (literally understood) subject of those experiences. When defined in this way, the category of experiences which belong to no one, experiences which precede the distinction between subject and object, is no more comprehensible to us than that habitual source of philosophical perplexity – dualism. On the contrary, it seems, if anything, even less accessible. To this Avenarius might reply that the prejudices instilled by the habit of introjection have robbed us of the capacity to understand the meaning of our own words. But how do we convince ourselves that the meaning he would ascribe to them is the right one?

Let us assume for the moment that we do understand his interpretation, and accept his category of ontologically undifferentiated experience in which the "I" has same status as other things and is "found" in the same way. It follows that the two terms – the counter-term and the central term – are both "given" (*simpliciter*, not "to me") in the same way; they are objects constructed according to the same principles, and are called "objects" in the same sense. The "I" is the object of psychological investigation, not a subject which absorbs the other elements of experience. But what, in that case, does "principal coordination" consist of? How are we to interpret it? And why should we accept that the "I" is given in every experience? If it is an *object* of experience (which has precedence over everything else), why should it be present in every experience? My "I" (or rather the "I" which I can no longer consider my own: I am no longer allowed to say that I possess an "I" as an element of experience, because saying "I" launches me on the infinite regress mentioned above) is no different, in its ontic constitution, from any other object in the field of my experience. It is merely one item in that neutral field, and consequently may at any given moment be present in it or not, according to the circumstances; its presence there is contingent, not necessary. The "I" as an object of experience leaves no room for principal coordination.

We therefore have two options left to us. We can agree to the total destruction of subjectivity (which is Avenarius's aim) and admit that "experience" is a universal, ontologically neutral category. On this interpretation it is absurd to ask how experience is related to its subject, for it *has* no subject. Within the field of experience so conceived, only empirical and specific questions may be asked; they cannot have epistemological aspirations. However, if we accept this, we must abandon principal coordination. Or, if we want to salvage principal coordination, we can return to the view of the "I" as an experiencing subject – the view Avenarius rejects. But then we cannot salvage the priority of experience and the equivalence between the central term and the counter-term. Principal coordination or equivalence: we must renounce one or the other. We cannot coherently retain both, for doing so would commit us to accepting the truth of two propositions which, taken together, lead to an absurdity: we would have to assert both that a certain finite object of experience is necessarily present in every experience, as the central element of that experience; and that this finite object, the human individual, is just one object among many, a "physical" thing in the same sense as all the other objects of our everyday experience. In other words, we would have to believe that that my "physical" presence (physical not in the sense of my ontic status but in the sense that "I" belong to the same category of objects which I encounter in everyday life, and which are the objects of scientific study) is the condition of the existence of the whole world, considered as a collection of counter-terms – which is absurd.

Avenarius wanted to salvage both, but he would certainly not have accepted this result. (Nor has it ever been accepted in any idealist philosophy: no idealist has ever maintained that the "I" is the same kind of object as the stone which is perceived, and that by its presence it is the condition of the world's existence.) He seems simply to have been unaware of the fact that his two central ideas were mutually contradictory. And yet the absurd consequence is not difficult to spot; it is clearly visible when Avenarius identifies the central term of principal coordination with the central nervous system. This entails admitting that a physical object – a collection of nervous cells – is the necessary condition for the existence of other objects. Avenarius did not, of course, make this absurd claim, but it is unavoidable unless we renounce either principal coordination or the ontic neutrality of the "I" and its equivalence with other objects.[1]

The Polish philosopher and Avenarius scholar Adam Wiegner (1889-1967) tried to save Avenarius from the absurd consequences of his theories by distinguishing between two senses of coordination. He accused Wundt of failing to distinguish between ontological and semantic coordination and thus establishing Avenarius's image as an "immanentist". According to Wiegner, Avenarius was concerned with the latter: the semantic connection between the two terms; and what he meant was that coordination takes place in experience itself, in the *act* of experienc-

---

1 From this point of view Mach's philosophy is more consistent, for it does not involve anything resembling principal coordination. Mach (Ernst Mach, *Beiträge zur Analyse der Empfindungen*, 1886) tried to be consistent in maintaining the ontological neutrality of all the elements of experience and rejecting as meaningless questions about the subject and its relation to objects and perception. In the end he recognized as legitimate only empirical questions about particular items of experience. He wanted to invalidate all epistemological questions in one fell swoop, and to reduce the meaning of scientific questions to their practical or technological applicability. He also renounced the transcendental (and everyday) concept of "truth". In his philosophy there was only the *pars destruens*. Avenarius, on the other hand, wanted to salvage the possibility of asking epistemological questions (in his theory of coordination) while at the same time questioning it (in his theory of the equivalence of the two terms of experience).

ing, not in the *things* which participate in that experience. In other words, the "I" and of the environment are equivalent in every particular experience, but this does not entail their equivalence on the ontic level. Wiegner thought that Avenarius had taken the idea from Fries[2], whose work he certainly knew (he quotes from it in his *Kritik der reinen Erfahrung*), and who had used arguments similar to those later used by Nelson to demonstrate the impossibility of a theory of knowledge.

But this is not a plausible explanation. It is by definition impossible to distinguish between the empirical and the ontological level of discourse in Avenarius, for the simple reason that no question on the ontological level can even formulated; the thing-in-itself, whatever the cognitive situation in which it appears, cannot legitimately be the object of any question. So when we analyze coordination in experience, what we are analyzing is the mutual dependence of its two terms in the only reality we can legitimately talk about; Avenarius would think it absurd to say that coordination takes place within the limits of experience but is not present beyond those limits, i.e., in the thing-in-itself.

Wiegner is right to stress that the main target of Avenarius's attack was epistemological subjectivism, and that his attempt to abolish the idea of "mental" content as the subjective form of objects was instrumental in that attack. But Avenarius was not content with invalidating just the idealist response; he wanted to eliminate the idealist question itself. This is why he refused to provide a different answer to that question, in particular a realist answer. And it is also why he cannot escape the alternative outlined above: either a radical neutralization of experience and the abandonment of principal coordination, or a return to the "I" as the experiencing subject and the abandonment of equivalence – in other words, a return to the subjectivist interpretation of experience.

Another point which exposes the incoherence of Avenarius's theory is his insistence on interpreting cognition as a physiological process while reducing the category of "truth" to a biological level. It was Husserl who pointed out the *petitio principii* which this involves. If "truth" is merely a kind of quality we attribute to the things we find in experience (Avenarius calls it a "character"), not an "element" found in experience itself, then our truth criteria are biologically determined, and thus purely pragmatic. In other words, our knowledge can only be measured by its practical usefulness – its biological advantages or disadvantages. Avenarius accepts this result. At the same time, however, he justifies his concept of truth by an appeal to physiological studies of perception, accepting their results as true in the ordinary sense of the word

2   Jakob Friedrich Fries (1773–1843), *Neue anthropologische Kritik der Vernuft*, 1807.

"true" – which traps him in a vicious circle. In this he is far from being uniquely privileged: he shares his imprisonment with all those who apply the theory of evolution to epistemology but justify the resulting theory by an appeal to a non-evolutionary criterion of truth. One cannot at the same time reduce the meaning of knowledge to a purely pragmatic one, interpreting it as an instrument in the service of the human race, and justify this interpretation by an evolutionary model which one considers "true" in the ordinary sense of the word. Husserl pointed out that any biological or psychological theory of epistemology will inevitably lead to a vicious circle, since it will have to justify its interpretation of experience by appealing to some particular result of that same experience, to which it must attribute a different interpretation, with a different – transcendental rather than pragmatic – criterion of truth. Such theories are therefore impossible on principle.

One is tempted to ask whether phenomenalism or subjectivism is the stronger tendency in Anevarius's writings, but it is unlikely that we will ever be able to reach a definite conclusion on this point. His conscious intention was certainly scientistic: to push philosophy towards suicide. He wanted to destroy philosophical questions by destroying the superfluous and misleading subjectivity which, in his view, creates them. But he did not succeed in destroying it totally, for he was hampered by the theory of principal coordination. Nevertheless, his efforts were not in vain. He demonstrated the insurmountable difficulties involved in any attempt to interpret the content of perception as a reproduction of the perceived object. He argued convincingly that we do not find, in experience, any distinction between the object and the perceptive content relative to that object; and he abolished this distinction by abolishing not the object, but the "mental interior". His anti-philosophical doctrine opened up an important area of epistemological exploration where Lockean and Cartesian questions can no longer be accepted as spontaneously thrown up by experience alone; he exposed their hidden presuppositions. His work shares the fate of all important philosophical projects: examined closely, it reveals its incoherence, but it also creates a new duty for philosophy, which is forced to reconsider traditional questions and once again question its own legitimacy. Philosophy seems condemned to this constant, relentless questioning; but this, paradoxically, may be what nourishes it and keeps it alive.

Translated by Agnieszka Kolakowska

Karl Marx and the Classical Definition of Truth[1]

Practical Activity and Truth: Two Viewpoints

The end of the nineteenth century gave birth to two different, though often ill-differentiated, theories in which human practical activity was a principal epistemological category. One of them, which we may call Marxism of a positivist bent, is found in the philosophical writings of Engels. It adopts the *effectiveness* of human actions as a *criterion* for verifying the truths of our beliefs about particular activities when we undertake them. The second, which found its classic (though with regard to rigor and precision somewhat nonchalant) expression in the works of William James, introduces the concept of practical *utility* as part of the *definition* of truth. This utility, however, is not a tool for establishing the truth about things as they are, independently of our beliefs; it is part of what *creates* that truth. Thus truth turns out to be relative insofar as it is applied in daily life.

The two sets of terms that underline the opposition between these theories are italicized.

---

1 This essay was originally written in either German or French (I do not remember). A shortened version was delivered as a lecture at the University of Tübingen in December 1958. A Polish version appeared in the journal *Studia Filozoficzne* in 1959 and, later, in a collection of essays, *Kultura i Fetysze* (1967). It was included in a collection of essays in English translation by Jane Zielonko Peel, published by the Pall Mall Press, London, called *Marxism and Beyond* – a title not devised by the author – but the translation, unfortunately, was full of horrible errors. The following year a corrected version of the same volume was published by Granada Publ. The present translation is an extensively corrected and revised version of the version which appeared there.

The first of these theories treats truth as a relation between a proposition or statement and the reality to which it refers, and this relation is independent of our knowledge about it. It is not *created* by our practical activity; it merely obtains, whenever we engage in any such activity.

The role of human practical activity as a criterion, and thus as a method of verification, depends on our acting on our beliefs in the hope of attaining a certain result. Success proves the truth of our beliefs, failure forces us to reject or modify them; but these measures do not in any way affect the truth or falsity of the propositions involved. If, for example, we are not certain today whether rational beings exist elsewhere in the solar system, it is nonetheless certain that the proposition "Rational beings exist in places other than on earth" is, today, either true or false. Propositions possess the (relative) attribute of being true or false independently of whether or not we know or can prove them to be so. From this standpoint the classical definition of truth remains valid: a statement is still true or false if and only if what is says is in accordance with what is the case in reality, regardless of whether this has been, or indeed ever will be, established through the criterion of practice or any other criterion. So conceived, the relativity of truth can easily be accepted: we apply the concept when we speak of progress in human knowledge in areas where that knowledge can never succeed in formulating scientific generalizations with sufficient accuracy as to the scope of their validity or applicability.

This doctrine, commonly accepted in Marxist circles, was popularized, but also generalized, in Lenin's *Materialism and Empirio-criticism.* Lenin thought it could be applied not only to propositions but also to sense-impressions, claiming that they "copy," "photograph" or "reflect" the objects of the external world. These vague expressions were not warmly received by the positivists; but with certain refinements they would fit quite well within the framework of the classical definition of truth that the Marxist tradition has relied on ever since Engels. What is clear, in any case, is that both Engels and Lenin saw in the development of the human conceptual apparatus an attempt to achieve ever greater faithfulness in copying the external world, which they regarded as a pre-existing model for the former. They believed that human cognition, though incapable of absolute mastery of its object, makes constant progress, as it evolves, in approaching such mastery, and that the perfection towards which it strives is to become more and more *like* reality, and better and better at imitating the qualities and relations which exist (independently of human cognition and the striving of the human mind) in the external world.

In the second of the two theories, human practical activity is raised to the status of an epistemological category. Its role is not limited to *ver-*

ifying the correspondence between human knowledge and a pre-existing model; it is broadened to encompass *defining* the very concepts of truth, falsehood and nonsense.

My aim here is not to reconcile the various formulations – often vague and sometimes mutually contradictory, apparently or in fact – in which the pragmatists expressed their thought. It will be enough to recall the main idea which the first modern version of pragmatism left as its distinctive mark.

In this version of pragmatism – and of course it is not the only one – the truth of a statement is defined as a function of the practical useful-ness of accepting or rejecting it, while its meaning is literally identical to the practical benefits it brings to the person who adopts it and acts accordingly. We may regard a statement as true if as a result of our accepting it our needs are better met or our lives change for the better, and false if its acceptance causes those needs to be less well satisfied or seems to us to be the cause of our failure to achieve certain goals or aspi-rations.

From this doctrine it follows that, since its logical value is relative not only to the individual but also to the time and circumstances of its expression, a statement can turn out to be true or false depending on the individual and on the sum total of the needs that define his aspirations at a given time. Thus for a statement to be "true" does not mean being in accordance with a pre-existing model to which our beliefs can be referred and compared; it means fulfilling the criterion of usefulness.

Consequently, to apply this criterion of truth to a statement is not to *verify* or establish its (independent) truth or falsity, but to *bring it about*: it is to *make* that statement true or false. Truth is not a relation independent of its establishing; to establish the truth of something is also to create that truth: to bring about the fact that it is true. If idealism is reducible to the view that all statements, or at least all existential statements, are mean-ingless unless we posit, implicitly or explicitly, some consciousness with regard to which they are true or false, then this theory of truth can be considered one possible formulation of idealism.

Unlike the first theory, provisionally described above as Marxism of the positivist variety, the pragmatic concept of truth is clearly not com-patible with the classical definition of truth. According to the first theo-ry, human knowledge, although largely defined by our biological and social needs, nevertheless strives to copy reality, gradually and endless-ly progressing towards its aim of copying it absolutely; and that reality, albeit changing, is pre-existing and always prior to cognition. Knowledge is a means of satisfying human needs only insofar as it is also a tool which enables us to describe the world as it is "in itself." According to the second theory, however, cognition is a biological response which permits the best possible adaptation of individual organisms to their environment. Indeed, the classic pragmatic concept of cognition is purely biological. Just as we can reasonably talk of an organism's response to a stimulus as being adequate or inadequate, by which we mean that it is either useful or detrimental to the organism's survival, so the pragmatic theory allows us to evaluate cognition from the same point of view, and consider statements to be true or false according to practical results. But to ask if a statement is true or false in the commonly accepted sense, i.e., to ask if its content corresponds with the world "in itself," would be as pointless as asking if our knee reflex is true or false: it is hard, on this view, to see what "similarity" between objects and the content of knowledge might mean. But it is perfectly possible to ask if the sum of biological responses that is called cognition effectively orients the organism in its environment and satisfies its needs or innate instincts – such as the instinct of competition, war, play and so on.

If we discern in Engels's doctrine the optimistic scientism that characterized European intellectual life in the last decades of the nineteenth century, we may consider the first pragmatists as advocates of the philosophy of individual success that for so long nourished the minds of the New World in its rapid economic development. Some of James's formulations are repeated almost verbatim in the writings of Henry Ford.

Nature as a Human Product: Marx

There is nothing particularly new in this is summary of two different views of cognition – as a reflection of the world and as a form of organic adaptation. It is justified only by its aim, which is to bring into sharper focus the view of human cognition – of "cognizing" man – that I discern in the writings of the young Marx – a view whose sources and inspirations are, I believe, quite different from those that lie behind contemporary Marxism.

The writings I want to discuss are Marx's Manuscripts of 1844. They have been much studied, but their epistemological content seems to me as important as the general theory of human alienation that most historians concentrate on. They had no direct influence on the growth of dialectical thought, but after their publication they threw new light not only on Marx's own intellectual development but also, and to an even greater degree, on the relationship between contemporary Marxism and its original source.

It seems to me that the vision of the world presented in the *Manuscripts* is the result of an attempt to consider human practical activity as a factor that defines our behavior as thinking beings. As such it can be likened, from the point of view of historical tradition, to some of Spinoza's ideas, and also to some of Bergson's. Needless to say, this strange "lineage" is a purely conceptual construction, not a historical one in any strict sense.

The premise of Marx's epistemology as a whole was the belief that the relation between man and his environment is a relation between a species and the objects of its need, and this is also true of man's cognitive relation with things. Marx's thought can be summarized in the following points:

a) The world of things exists for man only as a totality of possible satisfactions of his needs.[2]

b) ". . . and *nature*, conceived abstractly, in itself, independent of man, is *nothing* to him."[3]

c) If various objects, like the objects of science or art, are only a part of his consciousness, then in practice they are only a part of his life and his activity. Nature is man's nonorganic flesh.

d) For Hegel, nature is the alienation of the consciousness; consequently, overcoming alienation means overcoming the "objectness" of objects. But for Hegel it is not the "definiteness" – the specificity – of the object that creates the alienation, but its very quality of being an object."[4]

Of the principal themes of early Marxism, the idea of humanized nature is the one we shall take as the starting-point of this discussion. Man, according to Marx, was unquestionably a product of nature. In what sense, then, can nature itself be considered as the alienation of man, or as alienated man? In other words, how can man, who is a part of nature, regard nature as a part of himself?

Being-in-itself certainly cannot, according to this theory, be obtained from the data of consciousness. But nor can it be an object of cognition, for it is not an object of human activity. Our assimilation of the external world – at first biological, then social and thus human – consists in organizing the raw material of nature in order to satisfy our needs; cognition is an element of that assimilation, and as such it, too, is thus determined, like every other element. Thus to ask how the world would be seen by an observer whose essence was pure thought, his consciousness

2 "Man is essentially a child of nature . . . the objects of his impulses exist outside him, independently, but these objects are necessary to him to allow him to bring his energies into operation and affirm them, and are indispensable and significant. To say that man is a being that is corporeal, has natural strength, is alive, real, sentient and objective means that real, material objects are the object of his being and of the expression of his life, or that he is capable of expressing his life only in relation to real, material objects." Marx, *National Economy and Philosophy*, in *Early Writings*, von Siegfried Landshut, Stuttgart, 1953, p. 274 (this and all subsequent quotations are taken from this edition).
3 *Ibid.*, p. 285.
4 See *ibid.*, p. 276.

wholly defined as disinterested cognitive effort, is to ask a pointless question, for all consciousness is born of practical needs, and cognition itself is a tool designed to satisfy those needs: "The dispute about the reality or non-reality of thought in isolation from practice is a purely scholastic one."[5] Nature manifests itself as the resistance that human drives encounter; cognition is our awareness of the confrontation between consciousness and that external resistance. No other kind of cognition is possible; this relation is the only object we are capable of mastering intellectually. It is futile to hope that, by making the two elements of this relation independent from each other, we could come to know either pure consciousness – i.e., ourselves as an independent consciousness – or pure "externality" – i.e., being-in-itself, which is not "given" to anyone, although it is "given," and mirrored, in our imagined, illusory contemplative consciousness.[6]

If we accept this, we can also accept as valid the traditional idealist argument that it is impossible, indeed self-contradictory, to think of an object that is not thought (of). But it does not follow from this that "to be thought" is the same things as "to be." Furthermore, this argument does not adequately describe the relation between subject and object, because being can never really be "thought" in the positivist or idealist sense. If, on the one hand, being can be the object of thought only as "thought being" – which is clearly tautological – then, on the other hand, thought itself is a function of human existence and thus of the practical behavior of the species. We cannot conceive either of ourselves as independent from nature, or of nature as independent from us – from our practical contact with it and its resistance to our efforts; for it is this contact which gives birth to and defines our cognitive faculty. On this assumption, the materialist view may be expressed as the view that the world of known phenomena – the field of our social consciousness or the force of resistance we experience – does not define the entire potential of resistance which human activity must overcome; that there is always the possibility of resistance not yet experienced; and moreover that this experience of resistance is what makes up and defines all consciousness.

If we now ask how we can define that determination of the world by human consciousness – by a social being pursuing its activity on recalcitrant material – we are tempted to discern the answer in Marx's objection that Hegel treats objectness itself, rather than the definiteness of the object, as a product of alienation. For a given object to be "defined" in

5   Karl Marx, *Theses on Feuerbach*.
6   This is my interpretation of Marx's remark that the reality of all beings is defined by the fact of their both being objects for others and having others as their objects (see *Early Writings*, op. cit., pp. 274–75).

this sense means that it possesses properties by which it can be differentiated from the rest of the world as an individual object. But it is impossible to comprehend the properties of a thing before one has formed a general concept with the aid of which one can grasp that thing as being in some respects similar to other things; and forming such a concept involves either inventing a name to designate that thing or describing its properties with the aid of existing names. If things are not composed of their abstractly understood properties – it the individual cannot be reconstructed out of an amalgam of a number of specific properties expressed in general terms – it is nevertheless equally true that only those general terms enable us to describe the individual. The world as it is given to discursive human cognition is a world composed of abstractions; the individual can be reached only through the intermediary of abstract and general concepts. Traditional empiricism, where cognition is the creation of general concepts from the observation of individual cases and the properties which, as a species, they have in common, fails to take into account a basic fact about consciousness: that knowledge of the general is essential for the perception of the specific. Every object of cognition presupposes the conceptual apparatus which allows us to differentiate that object from the rest of the world. If cognition, as it develops, allows us to grasp increasingly abstract qualities of the world, then our perception of the specific cannot dispense with either abstractions or generalities: both are needed if we are to grasp reality and describe it concretely, definitely, and specifically.

Human consciousness – the practical mind – cannot get at being-in-itself, but it can reconstruct reality in terms of individuals and divide it into species and genera. From the moment that man, as a being and as a species, begins to dominate the world of things intellectually, creating instruments to organize it and then expressing this organization in words, he finds that world already constructed and differentiated, not according to some alleged natural classification but according to a classification imposed by the practical need for orientation in one's environment. The species into which this world has been divided are not the result of convention, nor something consciously agreed upon by society; they were formed by the natural, spontaneous human effort to overcome the resistance of things. It is this effort to subdue the chaos of reality that defines not only the history of mankind, but also the history of nature as an object of human needs – and it is only as such an object that we can grasp it. The world cut up into species – collections of individuals endowed with particular traits that can be separately defined and perceived – is the product of the practical mind. Given this, the very idea of an opposition, or even so much as a distinction, between the practical and the theoretical mind becomes meaningless.

This is the point at which Marxism diverges from the Aristotelian conception of the world, or, more precisely, from Aristotelian realism. This latter presupposes that the categories into which the sciences divide reality are merely copies of the categories which exist in that reality, reflected, more or less exactly but with ever-increasing precision, in the mirror of consciousness. But "humanized nature" knows no substantial forms inherent to it or preceding human (and thus social) consciousness and its effort to organize matter intellectually – an effort which must necessarily precede the attempt to organize matter practically. By the time people have enough leisure to engage in epistemological reflection, the main result of this effort – the biological apparatus of human cognition – has long been achieved. The habit of dividing up the world in a particular way, selecting its constituents according to human needs – the most basic of which is survival – is an integral part of the most elementary activities of the human mind. It is a delusion to imagine that we perceive "sensuous qualities" as "reflections" in our brains: "The eye has become the *human* eye, and its *object* has become a social, *human* object, produced by man and destined for man. Thus *the senses* have, directly through practice, become *theoreticians*."[7] The qualities of things exist as human products – but not in the idealist sense: if pure consciousness, given as primary, created them from nothing, if they were immanent or at least wholly dependent on consciousness for their existence, like divine creation, the existing world would be, from the theoretical point of view, even more difficult to understand than the theological world, and its existence even harder to justify. (In fact, man has far fewer rational motives than God for creating a world *ex nihilo*.)

But nor are the qualities of things forms or attributes of reality "in itself." They are "natural" insofar as they are constantly present in the substance given to man as his place of origin. They are subjective – or rather, socially subjective – insofar as they bear the imprint of the organizing intelligence we impose upon the world according to the aspect from which we perceive it (which is in turn determined by human needs, such as the need to adapt to the world and transform it in useful ways). Once we realize this, it becomes clear that to ask what absolutely independent reality is like is to ask the wrong question: if knowledge of such reality were possible, man would no longer be possible.

This is one interpretation of the view of the world presented in the writings of the young Marx – of "humanized nature" and matter which, divorced from man, is "nothing" to him. From the point of view of this anthropological, or rather anthropocentric, monism, the picture of reality given by everyday perception and scientific thought is a form of

7   *Ibid.*, p. 240.

human creation (not imitation); since both the linguistic and the scientific division of the world into particular objects arise from man's practical needs, in this sense the results of this division must be considered man-made products. In this world the sun and stars come into being because man is able to make them *his* objects, differentiated in matter and conceived as "corporeal individuals." In theory, there is nothing to prevent us cutting up the matter which surrounds us into chunks constructed quite differently from those we have become accustomed to. (For instance, we could construct a world where there would be no such objects as "horse," "leaf," "star," or others allegedly devised by nature. Instead, there might be, for example, such objects as "half a horse and a piece of river," "my ear and the moon," and other similar products of a surrealist imagination. Such a surrealist world seems strange to us only because we do not have names for its components and do not use it in technology. Hence our common sense considers it "unreal" or divides it up into parts with familiar names, thus preventing itself from perceiving it properly.) No division, not even the most fantastically remote from what we are used to, is theoretically any less justified or less "true" than the familiar one we accept. The problem is just that it is hard for us to imagine what such a world would look like, since it would be composed of objects we have no words to describe, and would therefore be inaccessible to our discursive cognition.

What justifies our belief that the visual world of a fly, made up of light and dark spots of neutral colors, is less "authentic" or less "true" than ours, except the fact that ours is better adapted to our needs? True, we are able to reproduce the visual world of the fly in our sense apparatus, and the fly cannot do likewise with ours, for the fly's reality is not only different from ours but also poorer: we imagine that the reality we have at our disposal is blessed with an objective richness. But this does not make the fly's reality any less authentic. Reality "in itself," since it is beyond our practical perception, is also beyond our knowledge. Its parts, its species – and thus also its properties, which allow it to submit to classification – have only an *"esse concessum,"* an existence bestowed upon them, granted not by arbitrary convention but as a result of the eternal dialogue between human activity and the object's resistance to it. The components of language, and thus of our cognition, are also the components of the world; language is not a transparent pane of glass through which the "objective" richness of reality can be contemplated, but the tool we use to adapt ourselves to reality and adapt reality to our needs – an active tool: a tool of construction, not exploration.

This vision of the world is not the consequence of a Kantian position; it does not claim that things as they are "in themselves" are inaccessible to the speculative mind, but rejects the whole concept of things-on-themselves, and says that the Kantian question is wrongly put. For in order even to ask if "things as they are in themselves" can be revealed to the mind, we would first have to come up with some concept of them. But this is precisely what is impossible; the very nature of concepts contradicts such an attempt. Only "things for us," not "things as they are in themselves," can have conceptual counterparts; and they come into existence simultaneously with their appearance as a picture in the human mind. Agnosticism might have a chance of success if it could succeed in formulating its question; its weakness lies in its inability to do so without abusing words. It can verbally phrase the question, but it cannot convey any meaningful content; thus the doctrine under consideration does not affirm something agnosticism denies, but rejects the question. Thus, once again, "the dispute about the reality or non-reality of thought in isolation from practice is a purely scholastic one," and matter divorced from man is nothing to him. In this sense, to ask about matter "in itself" is to ask if nothingness exists – a question to which all possible replies lead to contradictions, since it involves flawed concepts.

It is true that one of Kant's basic ideas has been retained here: the belief that the object cannot be grasped without the subject that constructs it. But for Marx the "subject" can be conceived only as a social subject, and "objects" no longer stand in opposition to a metaphysical world of which we know nothing except that it exists and that it is not the world of matter, since it is free from temporal and spatial determinants. Marx's world cannot be other than material – by definition, because it offers resistance to human activity, and it is precisely this resistance that defines matter as we understand it. Speculative reason, whose various categories apply to the objects of all possible experience, does not need to be complemented by practical reason as a separate realm which would allow us to grasp objects inaccessible to theoretical speculation in the form of moral postulates: since speculative reason is ruled by practical considerations, the objects it cannot grasp, or the concepts that are "unconstruable" within its framework, cannot be accessible to a distinct practical cognitive faculty. On this view no criterion to distinguish between practical and speculative reason is possible.

It follows that there is no such thing as a real (as opposed to imaginary) problem that is fundamentally unsolvable. Only questions in an understandable language can be formulated and considered; questions about things or situations that are wholly unknown to us only have the appearance of real questions. In order for us to know that a question is fundamentally unanswerable, that question would have to contain, in one form or another, conceptual counterparts of objects that are absolutely unknowable. And for all the above reasons, such concepts cannot be formulated.

It also follows that it is hard to imagine, from Marx's point of view, an enduring, "pure," universal and non-historical theory of knowledge – to imagine, in other words, how we might go about studying the cognitive capabilities of man, with respect to the common and universal properties of human existence, or human nature in its immutable elements. Cognition can be investigated only as history: analyzed not in its universality but in the changes and interdependencies that occur in the history we know – in social life, in the mutable elements of people's contact with nature, in social conflicts and social classes. These are the only things accessible to us. A general theory of knowledge could only be a general awareness of the immutability of human nature, and as such its role would be nugatory. In other words, the enduring element in human nature is also the fundamental and final datum of all analysis: the only absolute starting point. We cannot judge the influence of this "absolute" on our vision of the world; we can examine only what can undergo change, otherwise we would have to be able to shed our own skin and observe ourselves from outside. This is possible for the individual because of the existence of other individuals, but it is not possible for the social subject as a whole.

The Boundaries of Analogy

A few more brief points are needed to bring into clearer focus this hypothetical reconstruction of the early Marx's view of cognition. It will be useful to try to establish some lines of demarcation to distinguish it from theories that are, or seem, akin to it.

In evoking the name of Spinoza earlier I did not intend to consider the difficult question of whether his attempt at a comprehensive view of the world could in fact, through the intermediary of Hegelian thought,[8] have left its mark on early Marxism. It was merely to note a striking convergence – one whose immense role in the history of ideas exceeds the limits of this essay. One of the most salient characteristics of Spinoza's thought is the opposition between a world conceived as a whole, as a single substance, and a world composed of parts, as a collection of particular *modi*. For Spinoza, metaphysical reality cannot be reconciled with any sort of division into parts: acts of distinguishing particular things,

8 The early Marx was familiar with Spinoza mostly through Feuerbach; because of this, his knowledge of Spinoza's thought was limited to issues dealing with God, pantheism and religious alienation, which was what Feuerbach was almost exclusively concerned with. Spinoza's thought concerning the integration of elements into the whole and of finite things into the infinite has no echo in Feuerbach's original writings, at least not in a general way (although the significance of the latter in Hegelian logic is unquestionable).

species, and individuals – quantitatively limited and qualitatively differentiated from one another – are procedures that belong to a purely subjective realm. They are determined by practical needs – the necessity of using things in everyday life. The world thus divided is also the field in which scientific activity takes place; the achievements of science, though extremely profitable for the human species, have nothing to do with the need to engage in a disinterested contemplation of reality. Such contemplation, liberated from the images imposed by imagination and experience, succeeds to the degree that the thinker manages to penetrate that indivisible whole of substance, through an effort which ends in a total identification with its object. Theoretical reason cannot be separated from practical reason; it is the surgeon who cuts up the indivisible whole of reality into discrete parts accessible to human operations. And it is only through abstraction that we can grasp individual, finite objects, for the bonds and interreactions that exist between things, their universal "concatenation," are such that every part of reality is *literally* identical with the whole. All that we call "the concrete" must be considered a product of abstraction – made possible by our distorting perception of the world. Our perception of the world is an abstraction precisely *because* it is empirical: it takes as its point of departure particular objects of the senses. In reality only the cosmos as a whole is "concrete" in the true sense; all its parts are abstract figments, created to fulfill the demands of everyday life, not disinterested curiosity about the world.

This view of the world is one of many themes in Spinoza's heterogeneous system. There is no room here to attempt to justify this interpretation of it; nevertheless, I think it is possible to discern in it the essential idea put forward at the beginning of this essay as the hypothetical basis of the young Marx's epistemology: the idea that nature as composed of separate parts and species is an "artificial" creation arising from human practical needs and from our effort to master nature. In other words, it is an extreme form of overcoming Platonism, if the essence of Platonism can be summed up in the claim that there is a natural classification of the world.

But it is only up to this point that the analogy holds. Integral to Spinoza's thought is the belief that this determination by practice of human intellectual activity and our everyday imagination prevents both intellect and imagination from attaining authentic knowledge of reality; and, further, that this knowledge can be attained by "intuition": that alongside the intellect and the imagination, or rather above them, there is an instrument of intuitive knowledge that is free from the distortions which are inevitable in the activity of the theoretical mind. Spinoza's intuition, in at least one version (I think there are several, mutually contradictory), carries out in a different fashion the work of Kant's practical reason: it allows us to penetrate reality "in itself," the reality hidden behind the distorted pictures we have from the imagination and the empirical sciences. In Marx, this enigmatic world of reality in itself is reduced to nothingness, rejected as a problem that cannot be intelligibly formulated. One is tempted to say that this is a human nothingness, just as the reality in which we live is human: that the act of creating the object "for us" is identical with the act of destroying the object "in itself." In this sense one can say that Marxist metaphysics is impossible. For if metaphysics is, by definition, knowledge of the world that is absolutely independent of all human coefficients, then clearly from Marx's point of view it must be considered as internally contradictory, since such coefficients cannot be eliminated from cognition. That is why Marxism, so understood, cannot set out to construct a transcendent metaphysics, whether as an intellectual enterprise yielding results in the form of discursive knowledge, or as a purely intuitive effort culminating in its integration into or identification with the reality that it wants to reach.

If it is Marx's rejection of the deceptive images produced by a cognition which imitates reality "in itself" that distinguishes his epistemology from positivist or scientistic theories, his rejection of the possibility of knowledge by assimilating reality in an act of intuitive integration undermines a possible analogy with Bergson. Bergson, like Spinoza, is concerned to overcome the inevitable limitations and distortions of discursive cognition – to strip this cognition, precisely because of its practical origins, of that validity which a disinterested inquiry into truth aims to find. But Marx rejects the antithesis between the world shaped in the human image and the world that pre-exists "in itself," the world we want to grasp in a futile effort to go beyond our humanness. He would not stigmatize cognition by calling it "distorted": even if we disregard the word's pejorative implications, we can show something to be distorted only with regard to a true and accurate model to which we can compare it, and we do not have such a model, for we cannot go beyond the world as given to the human species. Since we have no grounds for supposing that pre-existent reality is in any way like human reality, we also lack the tools to plumb nature and the kind of distortions it undergoes when it throws off its transcendency to reveal itself to us. Without denying its existence or declaring it unknowable, we reject it as a possible object of study. It is worth adding that although Marx saw human knowledge as incapable of overcoming its limitations through intuition, at no point did he consider it was doomed to create an inescapably mechanistic picture of reality.

It hardly needs stressing that this reconstruction of Marxist epistemology reveals how superficial is its supposed kinship with voluntaristic doctrines like that of Maine de Biran, later resuscitated by Wilhelm

Dilthey. No act of pure will is raised to the status of a primary fact of consciousness. The resistance of nature experienced in human activity simultaneously creates both cognizing man and nature as the object of his cognition. There is no epistemological absolute: neither reality in itself "reflected" in consciousness, nor sense impressions, nor a *cogito*, nor innate categories of the mind, nor pure, non-mental phenomena. The only accessible world is the endless interplay between human needs (our needs as social beings) and the natural environment as the possible means of satisfying them. In this interplay there is nothing we may interpret as "given" absolutely, nothing obvious or elementary or requiring acceptance as a "primary fact." Nor is there any technique of epistemological analysis we could apply to break down the contents of our knowledge into its primary elements, into indivisible and irreducible atoms of consciousness.

It would be rash, however, to push this exegesis too far, especially if we also want to maintain that it is completely present, or pre-formed, in Marx's thought. Of course all this is supposition, based on texts that are unfinished and not unequivocal. An over-detailed interpretation of aphorisms runs the risk of ascribing to their author claims he would have found surprising. So in discussing the difference between Marxist epistemology and the two above-mentioned doctrines with respect to the concept and the so-called "classical definition" of truth, we must proceed with the *caveat* that it should be regarded only as the consequence which seems to follow from the above reconstruction.

Indeed, there is an important point of resemblance between the Marxist doctrine and the ideas of the pragmatists, and it is worth pointing out, despite the opposition between the two. Both manifest the same hostility to theories that see consciousness as an ever more accurate imitation of an external model, and the action of this model on the mind as achieved through some sort of *"species"* – an image or vision which, imprinted upon the sensory organs, introduces into the mind progressively more exact replicas of reality. Both, as we have seen, see cognition as essentially functional – as a tool that allows us to master the circumstances of our life, not a photographic plate that reproduces the pictures it receives. Practical activity determines consciousness through selection (steering our interest towards particular objects in the world) and control (allowing us to verify the knowledge we have gained), but above all through organization, in that it allows us to introduce into matter a certain system of intellectual classification.

If it is accurate to say that for Marx consciousness is the world presented (to it as object), then would be all the more apt to generalize this idea by saying that the world is reified consciousness. The first statement concerns only the origins of consciousness in the struggles of the human species with the resistance of its environment, considered as a whole or as pre-existing "chaos"; the second takes into account the world of things already shaped and differentiated from each other. The first of these worlds is the primary *universum* "in itself" – the Spinozan substance. The second is composed of objects with various properties organized by species – by the categories fixed in human thought and speech.

This pre-existing "chaos" is significant in epistemology, for it is this that defines the opposition between the Marxist and the pragmatist theories of knowledge. In the Marxist view of the world, truth cannot be a relation of "resemblance" between human beliefs and a wholly independent reality; but nor is it defined exclusively by a relation of biological correspondence, i.e., by the relation between those beliefs and their practical usefulness for the individual who holds them. If it were, it would follow, as indeed it does for pragmatist relativists, not only that reality is produced *ex nihilo*, in its entirety, for each separate individual, but also that the act of production must be renewed at every moment for that individual: for it is possible, and indeed probable, that a belief recognized as true at a given moment on the basis of the criterion of utility can become useless a moment later, and thus nonsensical or even harmful, and thereby false.

Pragmatist relativism, which does entail this view of reality (the form in which it is expressed here may be extreme, but if we take James's "classical" pronouncements seriously and literally, it is an unavoidable consequence of them), is irreconcilable with Marx's thought for two major reasons. The first is the impossibility, in the latter, of creation *ex nihilo*; the second is Marx's conception of human consciousness as a social instrument that is not reducible to the behavior of particular organisms. This is why the Marxian reality is neither the sum of the phenomena in whose existence some individual thinks it useful, at a given moment, to believe, nor the sum of responses an individual's consciousness makes to the stimulus of his needs at a given moment. There is, for Marx, a reality that is common to everyone, though it is a reality in an eternal state of incipience; a reality in which creativity certainly occurs, but in which there is also a constant, and that constant corresponds to what we call "human nature" – that totality of human qualities, biological needs and social relations which can rightfully be termed immutable. And the concept of human nature has a valid place in the Marxist view insofar as that view also accepts the concept of an enduring reality as an epistemological category (i.e., the reality that is accessible to us, and thus the only reality worth taking into consideration). Finally, this reality is one to which the Aristotelian concept of truth is also applicable: the correspondence between a belief statement and reality is not a relation of "resemblance" that obtains between the belief or statement and the world in itself; the statement *refers* to the world – albeit a world on which human consciousness has already imposed a "substantial form."

But this classical definition of truth has acquired a sense that is not entirely classical. For when we adopt it in the traditional meaning in which it was intended, we take on with it a large part of Aristotelian metaphysics: we presuppose that the language we use to describe reality according to certain categories has exact correspondences in reality itself: that forms, accidents and predicates exist in things just as they exist in language. But if we believe that this reality, divided up into species in the way that human language has divided it, comes into existence together with language, we presuppose that the relations which obtain between things, and which we describe in statements we call true or false, are relations between "artificial" objects that have been extracted from matter according to a system of classification which makes reality amenable to human practical activity. The subjects and predicative expressions of statements to which we ascribe logical value – conformity or non-conformity with reality – must be names of things that are absolutely independent if truth or falsity in the traditional sense is to be applicable to those statements; and in that case, individuals and species must be considered to exist in matter itself, in the same way they exist in words (where they are reflected not only in nouns and adjectives, but also in verbs and other parts of speech).

Man may have replaced God the Creator in Marx's doctrine, but he is still not like the God of St. Augustine or the God of Aquinas – a God creating the world *ex nihilo*; he is more like the God of the Averroists, who organizes the world from pre-existing matter, whereupon this world becomes the only world; the act of its creation destroys the pre-existing chaos. However, an awareness of this state of affairs does not lead to positive atheism – to the conviction that God does not exist:

> Atheism as a negation of this dependence [man's] loses its meaning, for it is the *negation of God* and affirms, by this negation, the existence of man; but socialism as such no longer needs this intermediary. . . . It is the *positive self-knowledge of man* which is no longer conditioned upon the abolition of religion, just as *real life* is the positive reality of man no longer conditioned upon the abolition of private property, i.e., communism.[9]

Thus the difference between material objects, which man creates, and God, whom he also creates, becomes a functional one: the existence

9 *Op. cit.*, p. 248.

of God is a form of man's enslavement, for God is a thing man cannot assimilate and adapt to his needs; moreover, it is a thing which itself exists by virtue of the very fact that there are certain things man cannot assimilate. According to Marx, consciousness freed from alienation abolishes God in abolishing atheism – which it does by refusing to answer the traditional question: was the world created by someone outside it? The discovery of the world as a human product is in fact a kind of social quasi-*cogito*: it requires no further justification, for it is not a theoretical postulate but a state of social consciousness which confirms its own autonomy. Accordingly, freedom, once achieved, does not need to justify itself; it can defend itself against threats, but the task of searching for justification belongs to those who threaten it.

Historical Cognition

I will not extend this interpretation to Marx's theory of alienation and his analysis of the situation of man – that of having lost control of a world he himself has called into being. But in this embryonic epistemology, which I think is not only present in Marx's thought but philosophically worth pursuing, there are a few points that require clarification, and two of them are particularly significant.

The first concerns the continuous nature of the process of creating the world through cognition, and above all the continuation of that process in historical cognition.

We have seen that in this epistemology the relativity of cognition is limited by a constant, which is human nature. This is the coefficient which introduces into reality certain permanent divisions, correlatives of the permanent elements of human nature. Thus historically immutable reality (on the scale of human history, of course) is conceivable insofar as immutable human needs and relations exist. But this constant, though it constitutes the primary matter of our cognition – all the things, like the material objects of everyday life, that seem obviously "natural" – is by no means the only thing that makes up the object of our cognition. The creation of the world, which is connected with the unchanging characteristics of man as such, precedes creative activity and further distortions, which are connected with all the changing elements of history: epochs, social classes, political situations, national feeling – all that comprises the sociology of knowledge. It is inconceivable that the human world, the world humanized by human nature, could be overcome in the cognition of man, who shaped it. And yet we sometimes believe that we can free ourselves completely from all that is imposed upon our vision of the world by changing historical conditions – in other words, that we can achieve an absolutely objective vision of the world (within the limits set by immutable "human nature").

This is a problem that has been much and long discussed, especially with regard to how we apprehend human historical reality. The approach Marx takes to it when he considers the matter of cognition in general seems a possible one: we could consider historical cognition as a function of the tasks imposed on the historian by *his own epoch*: slicing up the material of history and selecting the conceptual tools appropriate to it, according to the criteria and scale of values provided by the era and environment in which he lives. In the history of ideas, for instance, for the same set of facts there is always a considerable number of different interpretations, all of which can be coherent, non-contradictory, and capable of satisfactorily accounting for all the phenomena under examination. The historian of ideas also often attributes to past thinkers answers to questions which they surely never asked themselves but which he, from the perspective of his own age, considers important. There is nothing surprising in this; indeed, it is inevitable if we are to go on doing history. Given that the historian of ideas always devotes at least as much attention to understanding and interpreting known facts as he does to discovering unknown ones, and given, also, the variety of different interpretations that are tenable, the hope of arriving at an absolutely final and definitive interpretation is slim. Certainly there are technical criteria that can make us favor one interpretation over another. For instance, it is incontestable that the more facts an interpretation explains, the more it is, *ceteris paribus*, worth accepting. Some interpretations can survive a confrontation with all the facts (for example, all the texts of a given author) while others can account only for selected facts. Some use a methodology that has proved fruitful in other fields. Others can be suspected of being contradictory. And so forth. Even the most rigorous technical criteria, though they may eliminate interpretations that are flights of fancy or caricatures, cannot do away with the possibility of a whole range of different and incompatible interpretations of the same set of facts. And it is, of course, precisely because of this possibility that history can go on being done instead of coming to a stop in a permanently stunted form: the probability that unknown texts by Plato will come to light is fairly small, but there is no doubt that Plato's thought, as presented in existing texts, will never cease to be analyzed in different ways; it will be subject to the most varied interpretations, and no definitive, conclusive, invulnerable version will ever succeed in establishing itself for all time. This is true of all historical study where progress does not depend on the discovery of hitherto unknown data. And it is not surprising, considering that the questions we ask today, questions imposed on us by our own situation, are also the questions we ask of past thought, which never asked them and could not have asked them, for the concepts we use to study a problem have been formed in our own era and in a different way.

Clearly, when we ask questions like, "Is the Cartesian *cogito* an act of thinking about something outside the thinker or an act of pure self-knowledge?" or "Is Thomas More's utopia a Christian institution?," the method we use in trying to answer them is quite different from the one we use with questions like, "Was Siger de Brabant murdered by his opponents in the Church?" or "How long did Duns Scotus teach in Paris?" In the first instance, though we can always find data to support either reply, and though the questions are not entirely pointless, we realize that these writers themselves probably did not ask these questions, or at least did not formulate them in the same way. So here the historian does not so much discover answers as shape them from the material supplied by the authors. His conceptual apparatus is different, and so is the hierarchy of values he applies to problems. Thus the *découpage* he performs on the object of his studies is never "natural," in the sense that it does not accord with the *découpage* performed by the author he is studying; it is imposed by the conceptual tools he uses, and in that sense is artificial. This does not mean that it is necessarily false: an interpretation can be false only when it fails to observe the technical rules of research, of which the most important is the requirement that it coherently explain the greatest possible amount of data.

Thus the history of ideas is placed with regard to its material rather like the human species *vis-à-vis* the world: unable to create its object *ex nihilo*, it imposes its own system of cuts, slicing it up in a certain way, and, unconsciously applying its own hierarchy of values, selects the factors which seem most relevant and important from its point of view. (This is a simple statement of fact, not an expression of the belief that history *should be* seen as a projection of the present into the past. Such a prescription could lead to serious distortions; it would justify, to disastrous effect, the arbitrary selection of facts and the ignoring of facts that do not fit a theory.) This changeable system of cuts depends on conditions which are not determined at will by the historian – unlike, for example, a painter, who can never be accused of painting false pictures. We may say that the historian, like the painter, creates objects which do not exist in "nature," but the former is always bound by the principle of non-contradiction in his treatment of known data, while the latter is not, though he knows the material from which he ultimately produces his world. And there are limits to the similarity between the products of the historian's creative work and those which the human species as a whole creates out of its material "substance." The conditions that determine the structure of the conceptual apparatus a historian uses in his analyses change not only according to the historical era, but also according to the different views of the world that can exist in the same era in various environments, classes and social groups. Thus if countless different interpretations of the same set of facts can co-exist, all more or less conforming to the accepted technical rules of research, then the choice among them is determined by a more general choice: the choice of a certain view of the world. Such a choice is an integral part of historical interpretation. And since, inevitably, some factors in these different views of the world will always be unverifiable in the strict sense (which does not mean that all these views are irrational to the same degree), there will come a point in any analysis at which it will be difficult to see the next choice as a choice between "truth" and "falsehood": it will involve choosing a point of view, not a theory; it will be a practical choice, not a speculative one. It is in this sense that it is unreasonable to hope for the attainment of total and definitive "objectivity" in historical cognition. Which does not mean that we should renounce the attempt to enlarge as much as we can the role of rational factors in philosophical and historical enquiry, nor the hope of finding another adjective for statements that we cannot evaluate as "true" or "false" in the usual sense. In the cases under discussion, it is no longer a matter of choosing between two logical values, but simply between two values.

Value Cognition

This is the place for the second of the two remarks promised above. It is a truth rightly acknowledged and long demonstrated, particularly by thinkers of a positivist tendency, that value judgments cannot be validly deduced from descriptive statements, and that the former are never logically equivalent to the latter. The world of values and the world of things are distinguished in human cognition. But in the light of Marxist epistemology this statement alone does not suffice: it does not tell us the degree and nature of the difference between them or the range of possible applications of the criteria of truth and falsehood.

We can see from the above remarks that according to Marx, the choice between values (or rather – since we are not speaking of an intentional and voluntary choice – of preferences, which are determined by practical considerations) is an inevitable part of human cognition. In other words, the things our world is composed of are things that have been chosen, since they have been created (in the sense in which we have been using this word). So it would seem that every act of cognition inevitably entails the acceptance of certain values; and this in turn might lead us to suppose that the above distinction between two possible forms of intellectual assimilation is groundless. But this is not the case – as we can see when we consider that the judgments (or rather the practical attitudes) involved in human cognition not only need not be conscious in order to exert their influence, but have become a permanent *habitus*, peculiar to human nature, and as such historically immutable. Hence there is no need to remember their existence or take them into account in intellectual activity.

These attitudes, common to the whole human race, have made our external world what it is: enduring in the fundamental divisions into which we have sliced it up. The values and practical preferences we have introduced into it are hidden; we no longer see the mark we have stamped upon the world, or the permanent human factor at work in it. This mark is born and dies with man: there is no reason for him to be conscious of it as something separate. Our world can be considered as given, since no other exists and since everything we have added to it and shaped within it has, for us, become petrified into a sort of quasi-reality-in-itself. Not so in the case of those practical viewpoints and preferences which change with the course or human history, in ways we can clearly perceive. They determine how we divide our species by classes, nations, professions, sexes, generations, personalities, particular situations in life – in short, by everything that influences the sum of those values we each of us consider most important. Clearly, the world of values is not created automatically by the world of things that is common to us all and shaped by habits common to the whole species. And a description of it, or rather of the many worlds of values (i.e., value judgments), cannot be deduced from a description of the world of things (i.e., statements of fact). In this sense, the distinction made by the positivists is justified.

Putting aside the vast number of issues, debated for centuries and still contentious, that are connected with this famous distinction, we cannot help noticing that the reasons which make us dissatisfied with simply making it, noting that these two worlds are epistemologically of different kinds, are the same as those we formulated with regard to historical cognition; they can be broadened to include cognition of the human world in general. In all cognition there will be some factors that are not reducible to statements of fact (or let us say, rather, to theoretical statements, for we are speaking now not of statements about individual things, to which the natural sciences are also not reducible, but of "speculative" cognition). In other words, cognition also involves, besides all that can be reflected upon and verified by the application of technical rules, elements imposed by a general view of the world, where practical preferences and attitudes must decide questions to which we cannot supply scientific answers – for we have no technical rules to judge viewpoints. In domains concerned with the human world – sociology, the history of ideas, cultural history, and so on – choices determined by values are unavoidable. (Which, again, need not mean that such choices are arbitrary, unconditioned or simply dependent upon the free will of the individual.) Our awareness of this does not allow us to raise value judgments to the status of theoretical statements, but it does make their logical status similar to that of an important field of knowledge, namely knowledge of the human world.

We therefore have grounds for suspecting that in confrontations and conflicts between different value systems we are not logically much worse off than in disputes about generalizations in many disciplines in the humanities, although in the latter we seldom explicitly invoke values in support of our positions. When we compare the extent to which practical risks and practical reasons determine conflicting choices in the humanities with the extent to which the same factors determine choices in the natural sciences (in matters concerning the substance of the reply to a problem, obviously, not the selection of an object of research), and consider the role of practical reason in our acceptance of some theory or some value, we are inclined to conclude that the distinction between these two realms of scientific knowledge goes deeper than that between value cognition and what we commonly call scientific cognition in general. Observation of common disputes in these fields seems to substantiate this belief. So we should not exclude the possibility of an epistemology in which value cognition will, thanks to more through analysis of the ideological factors which influence the human sciences, achieve a status closer to that of theoretical cognition.

*   *   *

This attempt to analyze what is in my view a fundamental principle of Marx's epistemology leads to a simple conclusion: that early Marxism formulated an embryonic theory of cognition which, as the current of thought that called itself Marxist developed, was replaced by the radically different theories of Engels, and especially Lenin. (I say "especially" because of the radical terms in which Lenin couched his theory of consciousness as a "reflection" of reality, a process of copying and imitating reality.) We need not try to analyze all the reasons that led to the turn taken by this evolution; there are certainly several. (In Engels's case the influence of positivist scientism, widespread in his day, must have played a role; in Lenin's, the influence of the tradition of Russian materialism. But these are only partial explanations.)

Marx's *Manuscripts* also clearly show the connections he himself established between his concept of cognition, his "de-naturalization" of the world, and the idea of abolishing human alienation through communist society. And although today nothing could be simpler than showing how utopian was Marx's belief that "communism as the positive abolition of private property"[10] is identical with the abolition of human alienation in general, this is not sufficient reason to conclude that his epistemological starting point was philosophically sterile. Many philosophers have come up with similar ideas – embedded in a variety of different contexts and therefore also endowed with a variety of different meanings – quite independently of the Marxist tradition.

It is likely, in any event, that a method of analyzing human cognition, in everyday perception as well as in art and science, could be worked out precisely from this fundamental idea of Marx's: that man as a cognizing being is only part of man as a whole; that this part is involved in a constant process of tending towards ever greater autonomy, but can be understood only as an element in a continuing dialogue between human needs and their objects; and that this dialogue, called labor, creates both the human species and the external world, which thus becomes accessible to man only in its humanized form. One might say that in all the universe man cannot find a well so deep that, leaning over it, he does not discover, at the bottom, his own face.[11]

Revised for the present edition by Agnieszka Kolakowska.

10 *Ibid.*, pp. 235–36.
11 When writing these remarks in 1958 I had only a very hazy idea of the interpretation given to Marx's epistemology by Antonio Gramsci. I later had occasion to discover, with some satisfaction, that it is roughly in line with what I have set out here. Reading Gramsci's remarks on the subject (in his critique of Bukharin), I realized that the interpretation of Marx I have outlined here is nothing new. It is worth adding that Gramsci's reflections on Marx make no reference at all to the *Manuscripts* of 1844 – for the good reason that by the time they were published, Gramsci was already in prison.

Althusser's Marx

Althusser enjoys the reputation of having proposed a new, "structural-ist" interpretation of Marx[1] opposed to the "historicist" and "humanist" one which had long been dominant and which was mainly based on Marx's early philosophical writings from 1843–45. Althusser himself maintains, without explaining the matter closely, that he does not hold to the "structuralist" ideology. It would be futile to discuss this question which seems unimportant and blurred by the ambiguity of the word "structuralism." What matters is whether or not Althusser's interpreta-tion provides another, better, understanding of Marx and in what respects it differs from other existing interpretations.

Althusser's main idea may be briefly summarized as follows: most of contemporary commentators tried to describe the contents of Marxian doctrine in categories which are specific to the philosophy of the early Marx and, in particular, interpreted *Capital* as a continuation or develop-ment of these early, humanist and historical tenets. In reality, a radical rupture ("epistemological break") occurring in the year 1845 (the year of the publication of *The German Ideology*) separates these early writings from the latter ones, especially from *Capital*. This turning point means the passage from "ideology" to "science," a break with Feuerbach's humanist and historicist philosophy and with the Feuerbachian method criticizing Hegel, in favor of a scientific, structural description of eco-nomic reality. The problematic itself is changed: the question, and not only the answers, typical of Hegelian philosophy are rejected. The con-tent of *Capital* cannot be clarified through the early writings since what is specific in *Capital* is precisely a radical denial of this early "ideologi-cal" philosophy. Proper Marxism, the Marxism of *Capital*, does not con-tain any theory of generic human nature and it does not imply at all that

1 Louis Althusser, *For Marx*, translated by Ben Brewster, London: Penguin Press, 1969. Louis Althusser and Etienne Balibar, *Reading Capital*, translated by Ben Brewster, New Left Books, 1969.

a theory of the historical process may be an empirical theory ultimately reducible to the description of "concrete human individuals" as the proper subjects of history. On the contrary, the object of *Capital* is a theoretically constructed object, a whole that is the product of thinking, where "real subjects" are absent and abstract categories, characteristic of Marx, appear in their place: relations of production, productive forces, exchange value, surplus value. What distinguishes the new scientific theory of history as outlined in *Capital* and other mature works from the Hegelian philosophy of history is not that the former simply introduces, as factors determining historical evolution, productive forces and relations of production in place of the Idea which, through successive self-alienations and self-negations, comes to a fuller and fuller expression of its own hidden truth. For Marxism does not simply imply that different domains of social life differently express the same "basic" reality: it presupposes that each of them also has principles of development of its own and that, for this reason, some unevenly developed ingredients of various spheres of social life intervene in any social situation. Every social situation has to be conceived as a global structure where the meaning and the importance of elements are defined by the whole, not as "expressing" the whole but as being submitted to "structural causality." However, there are always in the structure dominant elements and none of them exactly matches the other ones in their level of development.

I will argue that the whole of Althusser's theory is made up of the following elements: 1. common-sense banalities expressed with the help of unnecessarily complicated neologisms; 2. traditional Marxist concepts that are vague and ambiguous in Marx himself (or in Engels) and which remain, after Althusser's explanation, exactly as vague and ambiguous as they were before; 3. some striking historical inexactitudes. I will argue, further, that the rules of interpretation which he proposes are self-contradictory; and, finally, that the whole construction, in spite of the verbal claims to "scientificity" is a gratuitous ideological project intended to preserve a certain traditional model of Marxism typical of Stalinist Communism.

The main design of Althusser reveals an ideological or simply a religious way of thinking. He does not oppose the young Marx to the old one but the young Marx to *the* Marx, thus presupposing that in some phases of Marxian thought something may be found that is Marxism *par excellence*, genuine Marxism. The question "whether the Young Marx was already and wholly Marx (FM, p. 52) or the statement that at a certain moment "the young Marx *did* become Marx" (FM, p. 70) are typical of religious thinking and can only be meaningful on the assumption that some texts must, *a priori*, be a revealed source of truth. That Marx during his life changed in some respects and did not change in others we can be certain of in advance, of course, since that is exactly what happens to everybody. And, as in anybody else's case, we may ask what is the proper content of his thinking at a given moment or in a certain period. We may try to explain how Plato writing *Protagoras*, differs from Plato writing *Timaeus* and how these differences may be put into an evolutionary schema; but the question of which Plato – the author of *Protagoras* or the author of *Timaeus* – is the *true* Plato is devoid of any rational meaning. It has meaning only in a religious perspective: when theologians (mainly in the epoch of the Reformation and Counter-Reformation) ask about the relation of the Old to the New Testament in these terms (has the New Testament developed or fulfilled or explained the promise of the Old – or has it simply abolished it?), this made sense because it was certain *a priori* that the Revealed Word must be true; the question of which texts are properly the last Revealed Word was important. In historical thinking this question is not simply irrelevant but it obviously cannot be put in a meaningful way.

Now, the difference between "the Young Marx" and "the Marx" or Marx *par excellence* may be reduced in Althusser to the difference between a humanist and anti-historicist ideology on the one hand and anti-humanist and anti-historicist science on the other. One would expect all these terms to be explained in Althusser. But it is precisely here we are disappointed. He says about ideology (FM, p. 231) that it is a system of representations (images, ideas, myths, concepts) with a logic and a function of their own. This is an extremely obscure formula that may also be applied to the history of philosophy, the history of science, to paranoic delusions or to poetry. There is no reason why it should not be applied to Marx's economic theories. In the sense used by Marx and Engels, the concept of ideology was intended to mean forms of social consciousness which prevent people from realizing that their thinking about the world is determined by some conditions which do not depend on them and which are not themselves ingredients of consciousness. In ideological thinking, people imagine that the logic of thinking itself rules their consciousness and they are organically incapable of being aware of the social situations and of the interests which mold their mental work. This concept of ideology as false consciousness or as thinking that cannot be aware of its own sources may indeed be useful, and was applied by Mannheim and other sociologists of knowledge. The defect of the concept, however, is that we never have criteria for stating that a certain theory or doctrine does *not* fall under the concept, even as far as natural science is concerned; nor may we ever be certain that a criticism of ideology is not *itself* ideological. No conceivable means are available for stating that *Capital* is not an ideology in this sense. Certainly, Marx maintained (not only in his famous letter to Ruge, but in *The Poverty of*

Philosophy as well, i.e., after the alleged "break") that his own theoretical work was to express the real historical movement, i.e., that he was aware of the social sources of his own thinking and that he was in this sense himself free from ideology. However, there is no way of finding out beyond doubt that Marx or anybody else who conceives of his own thinking as an "expression" of a certain historical process is not deluding himself about the meaning of his own self-consciousness.

Althusser maintains, however, that Marx's liberation from ideology is not located in his self-awareness of the social sources of his own thinking but in his passage to *science*. As is well known, the criteria of "scientificity" as applied to the social sciences are extremely vague and no generally accepted set of such criteria exists; hence, one would expect that on this point Althusser would be especially careful to provide some reasonable criteria that would permit the distinction to be made between "scientific" products and "ideological" ones, the more so since his whole interpretation is based on this distinction. But what he says (RC, p. 67) is that "the validity of scientific proposition as knowledge was ensured in a determinate scientific practice by the action of particular *forms* which ensure the *presence* of scientificity in the production of knowledge, in other words, by specific forms that confer on a knowledge its character as a (*true*) knowledge.

In other words – science is science when it has the form of scientificity! This grotesque statement is the extent of what we can find in Althusser about how to distinguish scientific work from other kinds of work. He notices that Marx does not pose the traditional question about the "guarantee" of knowledge. This is certainly true, but it is not *a priori* obvious that this fact should be considered as a mark of his peculiar superiority. To be sure, Marx rejected, and not only neglected, the Cartesian epistemological problem because the question itself, according to the ("ideological," not "scientific") Manuscripts of 1844 arises from a false consciousness that cannot realize the conditions of its imaginary independence, the idea of this independence being implied by the question. The validity of such a solution may be arguable but it is not this solution which Althusser is referring to (probably because it would require him to look for support in an "ideological" text). He simply states that the question of criteria does not arise in the sciences because "theoretical practice is indeed its own criterion" (RC, p. 59). An example is mathematics which, in Althusser's view, produces its own criteria of validity without recourse to "external" guarantees. And so, as in many other cases, the crucial questions are eluded. Certainly, one cannot blame Althusser for being unaware of discussions in the mathematical sciences concerning their criteria or validity and for believing that the questions of the foundations of mathematics simply do not exist because everything is settled in "mathematical practice." But even if this simple-minded idea was not erroneous in mathematics, what relevance does this have for the social sciences? Are we to understand that their validity is simply assured by their "practice." And on what basis is this validity attributed to *Capital* and denied to *The Holy Family*? On what basis can Althusser deny the scientific validity of the theology that has certainly produced "in theological practice" the criteria for legitimating its proposals? No answer. The whole question, which is crucial not only in validating but in giving a meaning to Althusser's interpretation is settled in this sloppy way.[2]

Let us see, however, what constitutes, as Althusser puts it, "Marx's immense theoretical revolution"" (RC, p. 182) or the fantastically innovatory character" (RC, p. 75) of his discovery or the "total theoretical revolution" which his theory brought about. Marx, according to Althusser, changed the object of political economy itself. In his chapter devoted to this question, Althusser criticizes the definition of political economy given in Laland's *Dictionary*, arguing that bourgeois economists reduced economic phenomena to human needs and thus produced an anthropological ideology, which was also characteristic of Marx's early writings. For Althusser, it is not needs which define economic phenomena and it is not human beings who are the object of political economy. The relations of production are not reducible to inter-subjective relationships; on the contrary, they define the social functions of individuals. Nor are human beings the subject of economic processes but the distribution of roles and functions in production (RC, pp. 160–80). This is perhaps what connects Althusser with structuralism insofar as this theory, according to an often-quoted, not very clear formula, states that meaning is given in the relations, while the terms of the relations from the point of view of

---

2   It should be added that Althusser uses the word "practice" indiscriminately for all kinds of human activity ("theoretical practice," "ideological practice," "political practice," etc.), without explaining what "practice" in general means. All he suggests is that it means simply anything that people are doing in whatever domain. One can understand his attempt to explain to the leaders of the French Communist Party that they are wrong to compel its ideologists to participate in "political practice," i.e., to distribute leaflets rather than writing, since, he says, to write theoretical works is a kind of "practice" too. But it seems that it could be explained in another way, without depriving the word "practice" of its specific meaning. The traditional Marxist distinction and the opposition of "practice" and "theory" becomes obviously pointless if "practice" means simply an activity. I do not maintain that this distinction cannot be criticized; perhaps it is wrongly conceived. But Althusser does not even try to show that there is something wrong with it. He simply does not seem to realize that this distinction has never existed in the Marxist tradition.

meaning are indifferent or "conventional"). This explanation is astonishing for two reasons. It is well known that Marx in *Capital* deals with "anonymous" productive processes and that he announces that he will consider human beings only as carriers or embodiments of some economic tendencies functioning independently of the will and individual intentions. This is not a rule preceding the analysis of capitalism, but only the repetition, in another form, of the same idea which occurs repeatedly in Marx's thinking, beginning with the Manuscripts of 1844. Namely, in capitalist society, human individuals are *in fact* dissolved in anonymous laws of the market, society itself forces them into a particular place in the productive process and deprives them of individuality. This process, described as a form of "reification," is for Marx simply a real phenomenon of capitalist production and the rule in *Capital* on this point is an exact reproduction of the idea found in the Manuscripts of 1844. Similarly, we find in *Capital* the original idea of socialism as a return to the individuality of which people – workers and capitalists alike – have been deprived in a society dominated by exchange value. This is why Marx in *Capital* opposes socialist *individual property* to capitalist private property (*Capital*, Vol. I, ch. 24, para. 7); this is why he repeats many times his old remarks about the dehumanization of the worker transformed into a commodity; and why he refers to the inevitable alienation of the producers from their product. therefore, if the "fantastic innovative" discovery consists in the idea that in a capitalist economy human individuals do not appear as individuals but as incarnations of abstract categories this discovery was made in 1843. If, however, Althusser is referring to a *universal rule* which allows us to put aside human beings in *any enquiry*, then such a rule does not exist in Marx. If it existed, it would only testify to a stronger dependence on Hegel than we usually assume (But Althusser precisely tries to show that this dependence is totally absent in Marx's "mature" works.)

The criticism that "anthropological" political economy reduces economic processes to human needs is one of many examples of those vague formulas which Althusser uses to knock down a non-existent adversary. If the theory means that the knowledge of some universal needs is a *sufficient* basis out of which economic laws for all epochs could be deduced, it would be amazingly absurd, to be sure. If it means, on the other hand, that human needs are simply the necessary condition of any economic process, then it is a trivial truth which Marx, incidentally, repeats in *Capital* by saying that the use value of any product is the necessary (but by no means sufficient) condition of its exchange value.

Althusser explains the "scientific revolution" in another way. Referring to Engels's Preface to the second volume of *Capital* and to some remarks of Marx himself, he tries to show that Marx, while constructing the concept of surplus value that was known to Ricardo only in particular forms without being generalized into one notion, made a discovery comparable to those of Lavoisier or Galileo. For, not unlike Priestly who discovered oxygen but was unable to conceptualize his discovery because he was trapped in the Phlogiston theory, classical economics discovered surplus value, but lacked the concept required to give to this discovery its theoretical meaning and to grasp its importance. Therefore, Marx is to Smith and Ricardo as Lavoisier is to Priestly, since, owing to the generalized conceptualization of their partial discoveries, he revolutionized the whole science of political economy.

So far Engels and Althusser. The comparison with Galileo and Lavoisier, however, seems very clumsy. By contrast to the Marxian theory of value, the passage from Phlogiston theory to Lavoisier's chemistry, not unlike the passage from Aristotelian physics to the mechanics of Galileo, meant in both cases the passage from speculative and purely qualitative categories to *measurable* and *empirically* verifiable ones. None of these merits are to be found in the concept of exchange value. No doubt, Althusser knows Conrad Schmidt's objection that exchange value is a category which cannot be subjected to measurement (He does not seem to know the more exact forms of this objection repeatedly put by theorists of economics, from Sombart to Joan Robinson.) But this is precisely where he sees, oddly enough, the proof of the scientific worth of Marxist theory: exchange value is not measurable because it is not a real thing but the concept of a certain economic relation, and concepts cannot be measured. It might seem that in this explanation any comparison with Galileo and Lavoisier is pointless, but Althusser does not appear to notice this. He is not interested in questioning the epistemological status of the statement that the exchange value of a commodity is determined by socially necessary labor time: is it an arbitrary definition (which certainly was not Marx's intention), or an empirical statement, and if so, how can we avoid it? It is enough to raise these questions to realize that, without answering them, general assertions that the theory of value has created a "new structure" or the "absolute beginning" of a new science are worthless. This does not mean that Marxian theory is worthless, only that those who want to reveal its value must use some other arguments than pointless comparisons with Galileo and the endless repetition of the word "structure."[3]

3   Marx's method may indeed be compared with that of Galileo in another respect. Galileo (especially in the *Mathematical Discourses*) realized that physics cannot simply be a description of experiments actually made but that it requires some idealized situation (geometrical models) impossible to be experimentally reproduced (when he, e.g., analyzes ballistic curves while neglecting the resistance of air, or when he describes the movement of the pendulum while neglecting the friction at the point of suspension). Certainly,

It is clear that the theory of value is an ideological construction and that it is a new version of the theory of alienation outlined in the 1844 Manuscripts. The whole chronology of Marx's evolution in Althusser's presentation is based on ignorance (1840–44 early "ideological" writings; 1845 "epistemological break"; 1845–57 transitory period; 1857–83 mature works). It has been pointed out by other critics of Althusser and it need only be repeated here, that, unbelievable as it may appear, Althusser cannot have read, while writing his books, Marx's *Grundrisse* (except the Introduction). To be sure, this text, of which the second, easily accessible German edition came out in 1953, was not translated into French until 1968 (except for the Introduction), but this should not be an insurmountable obstacle for an author who does not fail to remind us (perfectly rightly) that one should read Marx in German and not only in translations, and who is very careful to give us, with Marxist quotations, the German equivalent for the most common words. For anybody who knows the text of the *Grundrisse* to claim that Marx from 1845 onwards stopped thinking about society in the old "ideological" categories of "alienation," "negation," generic human nature," etc. is so obviously wrong that one wonders how to discuss it seriously. Indeed, the whole theory of man who objectifies but also alienates himself in products that afterwards govern over him as foreign powers, is repeated in the *Grundrisse* alongside the idea of the future return to man's generic nature and free universality. The *Grundrisse* confirms clearly what may be known from *Capital* itself – that the concept of exchange value is a new elaboration of the concept of the alienated product, or rather the integration of the latter into economic theory. Exchange value is nothing other than the "living labor" of man transformed into an alien force submitted on the market to the anonymous laws of exchange. It is man himself in his objectified and alienated form taking the shape of an autonomous anti-human power. Exchange value is not quantifiable because the meaning of this category is not to explain the movement of prices (prices depend on value but also on several other factors, and the

it is only thanks to these idealized models, involving some limit-conditions which cannot occur in reality – that modern mechanics could arise. Marx is partially reproducing this way of thinking when he analyzes certain imaginary situations and only later introduces successively other "disturbing" factors. He presupposes first a non-existent society consisting of capitalists and workers only; then he analyzes the production process taking no account of circulation; then circulation is considered without taking account of the influence of supply and demand relations, etc. Again, the comparison with Galileo is limited since the idealized geometrical models served as a starting point for the description of real movements in the sense that one could compare (quantitatively) the latter to the model and measure their deviation from the idealized situation. The same cannot be done with Marx's models.

relative influence of value – in the Marxian sense – in shaping them is unmeasurable) but to unmask the anti-human character of capitalist production. It is an "ideological" concept in any conceivable meaning of this word.[4]

"The total theoretical revolution" has, however, some other aspects. In particular, there are a few concepts which Althusser give as insight into the content of that revolution – "ideological" concepts of humanism, historicism and empiricism and the "scientific" concept of over-determination.

Althusser does not explain what precise meaning the word "humanism" carries for him but he indicates that he is thinking of the Feuerbachian theory of human nature that is to be restored to man. However, Marx criticized this theory in 1844, at least insofar as it implied a kind of universal inherent in particular every human being. But he never renounced the idea of the "social nature of man" (outlined in the *Critique of the Hegelian Philosophy of Law*), a nature of which people are deprived as a result of the capitalist organization of labor and of the atomization of society, this being a counterpart to the apparent socialization of life in the form of autonomous economic laws. This last idea is present and repeated many times in *Capital*. In the article "Humanism and Marxism" (FM, pp. 221ff, where we do not find any explanation of the concept of "humanism"), Althusser states that now, when the dictatorship of the proletariat in the Soviet Union has come to an end, a new epoch of socialist humanism certainly requires a new organization of life but not the return to the old discredited philosophical anthropology. Needless to say, Althusser does not reflect upon what, in general, "the dictatorship of the proletariat" in the Soviet system means, or on what basis the system could claim such a label, or what constitutes the new

4 One of the qualities which often used to be enumerated in distinguishing the sciences (nomothetic, of course) from "ideological" constructs is the predictive force of the former. We must note, alas, that in this respect the history of Marxism does not confirm well its scientific claims. To be sure, Althusser tells us that Marxist theory allows us "to understand that the Revolution as the 'task of the day' could only break out here, in Russia, in China, in Cuba, in 1917, in 1949, in 1958, and not elsewhere and not in another 'situation'" (FM, p. 207). Indeed, in "predicting" the past, i.e., stating that what has already happened had to happen where it did and when it did, with irresistible necessity, some Marxists are as strong as followers of any other determinist philosophy of history. Unfortunately, they are as weak as others in predicting what has not yet happened. I do not claim that there exist other reliable theories enabling us really to predict the results of the "historical rhythm" on a global scale. What matters is not the inevitable predictive incapacity of the Marxist philosophy of history, but the pious naïvete of its followers.

epoch without dictatorship. He naively accepts the declarations of the Congress of the Soviet Communist Party as valuable theoretical formulations and appears completely satisfied with them. From other passages, one would presume that "humanism" means for Althusser a statement that men, i.e., concrete individuals, are the proper subjects of the historical process. This statement, in such a form, is, however, too vague to be discussed. If it means that historical processes are going on in conformity with the individual intentions of their actors, it is obviously absurd. Nor can this be attributed to Marx in any phase of his thought, even the most "ideological," can this be attributed to him. If it means, on the other hand, that individual acts which, ultimately constitute all of social life consists, are submitted to regularities over which people have no power, then it is certainly as true for Marx writing *Capital* as it was for Marx writing the 1844 Manuscripts. Incidentally, the famous remark that men make their own history but not in freely chosen circumstances, dates from 1852, i.e., after the "epistemological break."

As far as the concept of "historicism" is concerned, we are not in a much better position (RC, pp. 119ff). Moreover, nor does Althusser define the concept itself, but we can approximately guess what it is intended to mean from some arguments of Gramsci which Althusser quotes as negative examples of historicist pseudo-Marxism. The point is that Gramsci considers all forms of culture, including science and including Marxist theory itself as ingredients or as articulations of existing social practice, and thus dissolves them into the current historical process and deprives them of autonomy. In reality, Althusser says, different domains of culture do not simply express a given epoch – in contrast to Hegelian philosophy – since each of them has a "logic" of development of its own. *Science*, in particular is not conceived in Marxism as an element of the super-structure, nor may Marxism itself, as a scientific theory, be so conceived. Marxism is not the ideology of the proletariat, but a science, which is why, in opposition to doctrines of "spontaneity" and in conformity with the well-known ideas of Kautsky and Lenin, it could not arise as a spontaneous product of the class consciousness of the proletariat but had to be imported from outside by intellectuals into the workers' movement.

This question is directly tied to the concept of "overdetermination" to which Althusser attaches particular importance (FM, pp. 89ff). He seems to believe that this concept is a discovery of a fundamental truth in Marxism, entirely overlooked until now by Marx's followers and his critics alike. he applies this concept above all to the question of the "revolutionary situation," but it has universal applicability. The point is that the general contradiction of capitalism (productive forces – relations of production) does not itself lead to revolution; there must be an accumulation of circumstances of various kinds which converge at a certain moment in an explosive unity. This may be explained by the fact that various domains of social life do not develop parallel to each other. Each of them has a rhythm of development of its own, the principle being always valid that "in the last instance" the social whole is determined by economic conditions. This Marxist theory runs counter to Hegel's concept, since in Hegel any historical "totality" express itself through all the spheres of life; the "spirit of the time" or the spiritual principle (essence) organizing the historical moment is articulated in all domains of culture as its "phenomena." However, from the Marxist point of view, the relation of various parts of the superstructure to the conditions of production is not a relation between "phenomena" and "essence," precisely because the superstructure enjoys relative autonomy and produces many "contradictions" within itself. Now, Mao Tse-Tung wrote that nothing in the world develops absolutely evenly. This phrase, which Althusser calls "the law of uneven development," and a few pages later "the great law of uneven development" explains that contradictions which accumulate in the historical process and explode in revolutions are not simply manifestations of one basic contradiction but come from "relatively autonomous" parts of the superstructure.

This theory, expressed in Althusser's works in extremely pretentious language, is nothing more than a repetition of Engels's principle of the "relative autonomy" of the superstructure in respect to economic conditions and is just as unclear as that principle. "The great law of uneven development," if it means anything, means that comparable units (e.g., individuals or industrial or tribal societies or trees or galaxies) do not change exactly in the same way since their environment is never exactly the same. This is of course a common sense platitude that may perhaps have a certain philosophical meaning, as we find, for example, in the writings of Herbert Spencer. To present it is as a dazzling achievement of Marxist thought and to call it "the great law" proves nothing. The same is true of "overdetermination." That important historical events, such as revolutions, result from the coincidence of many circumstances is a commonplace and one could hardly find anybody foolish enough to maintain that any detail of the historical process may be deduced from the general principle of "contradiction" between productive forces and relations of production. Neither is this commonplace specifically Marxist in any sense. What is specifically Marxist is Engels's famous phrase about the determinant forces of economic conditions "in the last instance." This is a vague statement, and that is not improved by Althusser's repetition of it without any further explanation. It is certainly true that Marx never tried to replace historical inquiry by general statements about "contradictions," nor did he hope that the course of history might be described by deductions from this statement. But this is precisely what makes the whole meaning of historical materialism unclear unless it is reduced again to the commonplace idea that many factors are at work in any historical event and that economic conditions are one of them. This is why some Marxists of the Second International were reluctant to admit Engels's well-known explanations in his letter to Schmidt, Bloch or Mehring. They believed, perhaps not without reason, that the idea of "Many factors" enjoying "relative autonomy" deprives Marxism of its specificity, and makes of historical materialism a banal commonplace, since the additional vague statement about the "determination in the last resort" has no meaning whatsoever in historical explanation as long as we are not able to define what are the limits of this "ultimate determination" and, similarly, the limits of the "relative autonomy" granted to other domains of social life, especially to various spheres of the so-called superstructure.

Again, the whole theory of "overdetermination" is nothing but the repetition of traditional banalities which remain exactly on the same level of vagueness as before. If we say, e.g., that the state of science, or philosophy, or of legal institutions, does not depend only, in a given moment, on the actual economic conditions, but also on the past history of science, of philosophy or of legal institutions, we will certainly have difficulty in finding anybody to contradict us. And Althusser's burst of indignation in attacking his non-existent enemies on this point seems rather exaggerated. Moreover, he contradicts himself directly, as far as ideology is concerned. After quoting with approval Marx's statement from *The German Ideology* that philosophy and religion, in a number of ideological forms, have no history of their own but that their apparent history is only the "real" history of the relations of production (FM, p. 83), he goes on to explain in the second book (RC, pp. 99ff) that, on the contrary, every domain of the "superstructure," including philosophy and art, *does* have its own specific history. This does not mean, as Althusser explains, that they are independent of the social "totality," but that their degree of independence is determined by their degree of dependence. This last remark is either a tautology or a vague statement to the effect that the state of philosophy, or art, or legal institutions, is partially dependent on the actual economic "totality" – a statement which belongs to common sense but is useless as long as we are unable to define the limits of this partial dependence.

Nor is Althusser able to explain the meaning of the idea that different domains of culture do not develop at the same rhythm when compared with each other. On what basis can we state that a certain change in science or in religion corresponds to a change in political or economic history (and we must know this in order to give meaning to the statement that the "corresponding" changes do not occur simultaneously)? And why should we expect that "revolutions" in all domains of culture should appear at the same time? What conceptual tools do we have for comparing changes in painting and in the movement of prices, or "revolutions" in physics or in political institutions in order to point out their parallelism or lack of parallelism? No answer.

However, all these confused generalities (the superstructure is "on the one hand" a tool of the "base," but "on the other hand" it has a relative autonomy, etc.) have always had and still have in the history of Marxism a well defined ideological role – especially in Stalinist Marxism which exploited them and benefited from their ambiguity and vagueness. Kautsky's statement, later appropriated by Lenin, that Marxism, being a scientific theory, could not be a spontaneous product of the working class but had to be imported from outside, by intellectuals equipped with scientific knowledge, became peculiar ideological instrument to justify a new idea of the party – the party of manipulators. Since the working class is incapable of articulating theoretically its consciousness, it should be incarnated in a political organism that could consider itself the carrier of this consciousness regardless of what the "empirical" working class thought about it, the "empirical" consciousness of this class is irrelevant in defining who in a given moment represents its interests. This is why the theory of a class consciousness instilled from outside and the whole idea of scientific socialism so conceived served to justify the fact that in all kinds of political activity and later in the exercise of political power, the working class may be and must be replaced by the political apparatus which is the vehicle of its consciousness at the highest level. The whole Leninist and then Stalinist principle of dictatorship which the proletariat exercises through the intermediary of its self-appointed representatives, is only a development of the idea of "scientific socialism" so conceived. In addition, the "great law of uneven development" offers another service to dictatorial power. Althusser says that "overdetermination" may explain, for instance, such phenomena as the survival of past ideologies in new social conditions since an ideology, having a logic of its own, may live beyond its proper historical context. This concept of "ideological survival" was a convenient political devise in the Stalinist dictatorship: "We have new, socialist relations of production" – the ideologists and the political rulers used to explain – "but the consciousness of the people does not keep up with the social development or 'lags behind' the economic structure," and this makes people hold on to their religious beliefs or steal state property or fail to love their leaders as they should. In other words, political rulers *know* what the consciousness of the society *should* be to match the relations of production: they are able to *deduce* from these relations the *proper* content of social consciousness, a level that empirical consciousness does not reach because of the "great law of uneven development." This fantastic pre-supposition that we can deduce from economic conditions, the content of consciousness as it *should be* must be admitted if the concept of "ideological survivals" is to be explicable. Needless to say, this concept is extremely convenient in political rule. Whatever repression is used against carriers of an "improper" consciousness, it is "historically justified" since its aim is only to bring a backward consciousness remaining from past society into line with the new conditions. The persecution of churches and every kind of repression against people who do not think exactly according to the actual wishes of rulers are always justified in the theory of "uneven development." Except for this political service, the concept of "ideological survivals" cannot possibly have any rational meaning since to imagine that one may deduce from a gratuitous historical schema the "correct" content of social consciousness appropriate to given economic conditions is an empty fantasy.

It is true nevertheless that the Marxian concept of determination does not consist simply in replacing the Hegelian all-embracing spiritual principle by another "material factor." Althusser points out, perfectly correctly, that Hegel's dialectical method could not simply be extracted from his system as an independent methodology, and that in Hegel himself "the method" is not indifferent to its object – although he should perhaps have mentioned that this point was stressed and developed with much better justification by Lukács fifty years ago. (Actually, the idea that there is "a contradiction" between Hegel's method and his system and that the former may be extracted and used in another, opposite, philosophical construction, was invented by young Hegelians, taken over verbatim by Engels and then repeated by Lenin and Stalin; otherwise, it is hardly to be found among Hegelian scholars.) Althusser insists that for this reason one may not speak of the "inversion" of Hegelianism in Marxian thinking and that Marx himself, while using this or similar expressions, was not fully aware of how his method differed from the Hegelian one. He insists that Marx, at a certain moment ("the epistemological break") stopped answering Hegelian questions and that we always ought to analyze the "problematic," i.e., the set of questions, in order to understand the real changes in philosophical development. This last remark is certainly justified. Although this would appear to be a commonplace among historians of ideas, Althusser considers it to be an important discovery. It is a rather well-known and commonly applied principle among historians that important changes in intellectual history occur when people do not simply give new answers to old questions but abandon the old questions as implying false or meaningless presuppositions. They know perfectly well, e.g., that the importance of early

Renaissance philosophy did not consist in giving new answers to Scholastic problems but in rejecting the problems themselves. The same may be said about the passage from the Renaissance philosophy of nature to Galilean mechanics, etc. These are, however, well-known generalities that manifest their meaning only in real historical investigations and to repeat them, as does Althusser, without saying concretely which Hegelian questions were rejected by Marx and which new ones were posed, does not help us much in understanding either the spiritual principle of time (as in Hegelian doctrine), particular elements of the social whole are conceived in Marxism as being determined by ("overdetermined") the structure of the whole and this "structure," which determines its elements, seems to him as especially innovatory methodological devise. In fact, the concept of a "whole" which is not determined by the qualities of its elements and which, on the contrary, has qualities and "laws" of its own, determining in turn the qualities of these elements, goes back at least to Aristotle. It was especially developed in *Gestalt* psychology and *Gestalt* theory which was able to endow it with empirical meaning. Thanks to many experiments intended to give the concept of "Gestalt" an empirical content, we may have a clear idea of its meaning. (To give a simple example: hens are conditioned to look for food in the darker of two surfaces placed before them; when the lighter surface is removed and a new, still darker surface is placed next to the second one, hens instinctively run to the new surface and not to the other one, which they have been conditioned to look for food. In other words, they react to the "structure" as opposed to "agglomerates.") To repeat now – as Althusser does – generalities about "structural determination" and the "irreducibility" of the whole of its elements (RC, pp. 183 ff) does not lead us beyond common sense platitudes.

Moreover, Althusser seems to believe that this concept of "Structure" is especially important in the struggle against what he calls "empiricist ideology." Empiricism means, according to him (RC, pp. 35 ff), a certain theory of knowledge which claims that knowing consists in extracting from the real object a pre-existing "essence" included in and blurred by external appearances. The sole example of this "empiricism" which Althusser cites is the famous comment by Michaelangelo on a statue which is hidden but ready inside the stone. But he believes that such empiricism constitutes the proper content of the epistemology of Locke and Condillac. The reader with an elementary knowledge of the history of philosophy will notice at once that what Althusser means by "empiricism" could well be understood as the Aristotelian or Thomist theory of abstraction, but that modern empiricism means exactly the opposite. Empiricism in the only sense in which it has been used in the history of philosophy precisely denies the idea that abstraction consists in extracting a *"universale in re"* or a "formal essence lodged within the object itself," and to attribute this Aristotelian theory to Locke and to contemporary "empiricists" (without saying who falls under this category) proves only yet again the author's historical sloppiness.[5] No wonder that after creating once again a non-existent enemy, Althusser has no difficulty in attacking him. He insists, moreover, that knowledge – in defiance of "empiricist" ideology – has nothing to do with pure, immediate, singular objects, but always with abstractions which are already elaborated and conceptualized (FM, pp. 183 ff). He fails to recall that this discovery was made long ago and that the criticism of the seventeenth century theory of abstraction (which views concepts as generalization of an immediate given, raw and unprejudged perception) has been made so many times that it has become a commonplace in contemporary philosophy of science. Not to speak of contemporary philosophers such as Karl Popper, who have devoted a good deal of their analysis to this problem, this denial of a "raw perception" as a starting point for scientific theories was not simply stated generally, but seriously justified in analyses of scientific procedures – by many "positivist" philosophers and scientists from the end of the nineteenth to the beginning of the twentieth century, among them well-known French authors such as Poincaré and Duhem. To propose, in general terms, this discovery as an "immense revolution" sounds naïve. In Marx himself, the idea of the object, which is not in its original immediacy to perception but is always constituted within the "socialized" cognitive assimilation of the world, is expressed precisely in the Manuscript of 1844 without waiting for the "epistemological break." To invent a new pretentious name for this traditional tenet ("the ever pre-givenness of a structured unity" – FM, p. 199) does not enhance our understanding.

5   There are other examples of historical ignorance in the work. For example, Althusser says (RC, p. 40) that "Spinoza warned us that the *object* of knowledge or essence was in itself absolutely distinct from the real object . . . the *idea* of the circle, which is the *object* of knowledge must not be confused with the circle which is the real *object*." In fact, one of the fundamental assumptions of Spinoza's philosophy is that "the idea" is not simply an object of knowledge but is exactly as "real" as the body and that both have the same ontological validity. Elsewhere (FM, p. 78), Althusser explains that there is in Spinoza a radical discontinuity between the first and the second kind of knowledge, whereby "although the second kind makes possible the understanding of the first, it is not truth." Now the first (unreliable) kind of knowledge in Spinoza (according to the *Ethics*: there is another classification in the *Treatise on the Improvement of the Intellect*) is enumerative induction, the second is deductive reasoning for which Euclid provided the model. To say that deductive reasoning "makes possible the understanding" of the *empiria* is void of meaning in Spinoza's philosophy.

The universally applicable and nowhere explained concept of structure has in Althusser another advantage in dealing with the question of how to investigate the relation between young Marx and *the* Marx of *Capital*. The issue is: are we allowed to look into the early writings for some tenets which can help us to understand mature Marxian theory? In *For Marx*, Althusser's answer is unequivocally negative (FM, pp. 51 ff). Against those who claim that everything, "the whole Marx," is already contained in the writings of 1843–45 (in fact there is nobody who maintains this) we *must not* look for "germs" of the true Marx in his early work. The reason is simply that "the system" cannot be reduced to its elements and that we should consider the ideology (or science) as a global unity, i.e., to explain it by its structure and not by its genesis. Otherwise, we fall into "empiricism," "ideological illusions" and theology. Again, while discussing Marx's Introduction of 1857 (RC, p. 64), Althusser quotes the famous remark that "the anatomy of man is the key to the anatomy of the ape" in order to state that while we need to know the contemporary structure of society if we want to understand its past, the inverse is not true, i.e., it is not true that we may be helped to understand contemporary society by analyzing its past. This principle is apparently applied to studies of Marx: we may benefit from the analysis of the Manuscripts of 1844 in the light of *Capital* (viz., as the result of the radical break with the "ideological" concepts of the early writings) but we are not permitted to read *Capital* as a development of some ideas included in the Manuscripts of 1844. Why not? Not simply because a "radical rupture" occurred in between, but because this is forbidden in principle, because the "structure" cannot be understood through its origins.

An astonishing interdiction! Marx's statement about the anatomy of the ape (apparently not accurate from the strictly anatomical point of view) is precisely the principle of the teleological understanding of history. If we can understand past forms through their future results, we look at them as they promise. The genetic explanation does not require this finalist concept; it is satisfied with stating how a certain structure somehow tended towards its contemporary form. Moreover, while the genetic explanation does not involve the teleological one, the teleological one, in its turn, involves the genetic. If we are allowed to understand past forms in the light of later ones, we are also allowed to seek in the past the "germs" of the present. In reality, the question of whether or not the knowledge of genesis is indispensable for understanding the "structure" is wrongly put. It simply depends on what we are asking. There are many questions which we can try to answer without genetic enquiry and many others which require a genetic explanation. In trying to understand how the contemporary combustion engine works, knowledge of its historical development is irrelevant. Similarly we can understand the functioning of banks without necessarily knowing the history of credit since the Middle Ages. But we cannot really understand contemporary painting without knowing anything about the history of painting and we cannot explain why England is a monarchy while France is not simply by comparing their contemporary "structure" if we are utterly ignorant about their respective histories. This seems so trivial that the whole discussion, in general terms, about the value of the "structural explanation" as opposed to the "genetic" one is void of meaning.

I am far from being a follower of Anglo-Saxon analytical philosophy. However, while reading some dialectical philosophers (Althusser is an example) I do find myself regretting their lack of any training in this philosophy and consequently of any logical discipline. Such a training would help them to understand the simple difference between "saying" something and "proving" it (Althusser often formulates a general statement and then quotes it later and then refers to it as saying "we showed" or "it was proved"), between a necessary and a sufficient condition, between a law and a statement of fact, etc. It would enable them, too, to understand what the analysis of concepts means. These two books by Althusser provide a disagreeable example of empty verbosity which, as I tried to show above, can be reduced either to common sense trivialities in new verbal guise, to traditional Marxist tenets repeated with no additional explanation, or to wrong historical judgments. They add nothing to our understanding Marx, or Hegel, or political economy, or the methods of social science, only pretentious language. They teach us only about Althusser and may be of use only to someone interested in this subject.

[1971]

A Comment on Heidegger's Comment on Nietzsche's Alleged Comment on Hegel's Comment on the Power of Negativity

This is no more that a footnote to one sub-chapter of the first volume of Heidegger's lectures on Nietzsche.[1] The footnote, however, deals with an issue of some importance to the understanding of both Heidegger and Nietzsche.

In the Interview published in *Der Spiegel* just after his death, Heidegger asserted that whoever had ears to hear knew that he had criticized the Nazi regime in his Nietzsche lectures.[2] It probably takes an ear subtler than mine to hear this criticism, even if it is true (as Alexander Schwan points out in the second edition of his excellent book *Politische Philosophie im Denken Heideggers*, 1989) that Heidegger was reluctant to interpret or to voice his nationalistic feelings in biological terms, as the official Nazi ideology normally did. My intention is to suggest, on one small point, that Heidegger employed his peculiar reading of Nietzsche to express – obliquely but clearly – his political commitment to German imperialism.

The object of Heidegger's reflection is the "essence of power" in Nietzsche's sense. (*Die Macht*, as we know, has no precise equivalent in English; depending on the context it could be translated variously as power, might, domination, strength, authority; "power" admittedly comes closest to the original meaning, and is used in the English trans-

1 See Martin Heidegger, *Nietzsche*, 2 vols. (Pfullingen: Neske, 1961), par. 11.
2 See "Nur Noch ein Gott kann uns retten," *Der Spiegel*, No. 23 (1976), pp. 193–219.

lation of the famous posthumous collection of Nietzsche's aphorisms; the actual order of the sentence given is unimportant.) Heidegger argues (rightly, it seems) that according to Nietzsche's meaning, the word "power" in the expression "will to power" adds nothing to the notion of "will"; it just helps to explain it. This is because every act of will, every act of willing, is nothing but a will to power: that is to say, a will "to be more," "to grow, to lift oneself up, to rise" ("Im Willen als Mehr-sein-wollen, im Willen als Wille zur Macht liegt wesentlich die Steigerung, die Erhöhung.") This is explained by the fact – though Nietzsche does not say so in so many words – that to remain permanently at the same level of power is bound to result in exhaustion; therefore the will, if it is not to collapse, must strive unceasingly toward an ever higher achievement. It can never be satisfied with the range of domination it has already acquired; it must – by its very nature – want more power.

The will to power is the will to have more and more power, to be stronger and stronger. Every will consists precisely in that: to gain more strength. This is the very principle of life, nay, the principle of Being, its inherent nature. Life's purpose is not merely to preserve itself – as Darwinism would have it – but to assert itself; self-assertion amounts to the will to be at the top of or at the head of ("Selbstbehauptung, d.h. Im Haupt, d.h. oben bleiben wollen," as Heidegger says is the never-ending return to the "essence," to the source; the will to grow and to expend is no less than existence itself, the essence of what *is*.

The will to power is creative, but the point of the creation is not just to make or produce something but to lift something higher to transform its essence (not das *Hervorbringen* but das *Hinaufbringen und Verwandeln*). Consequently, destruction, the power of negativity, belongs to the essence of creation, hence to the will, hence to Being itself.

That Being itself – or the very act of being – includes negativity is an idea that belongs to the heritage of German Idealism, Heidegger says. He supports it by quoting the famous passage fragment on the power of negativity from the preface to Hegel's *Phenomenology of Mind*.

> The tremendous power of the negative; it is the energy of thought, of the pure "I." Death, if that is what we want to call this non-actuality, is of all things the most dreadful, and to hold fast what is dead requires the greatest strength. Lacking strength, Beauty hates the Understanding for asking of her what it cannot do. But the life of Spirit is not the life that shrinks from death and keeps itself untouched by devastation, but rather the life that endures it and maintains itself in it. It wins its truth only when, in utter dismemberment, it finds itself. It is this power, not something positive which

closes its eyes to the negative, as when we say of something
that it is nothing or is false, and then, having done with it,
turn away and pass on to something else; on the contrary,
Spirit is this power only by looking the negative in the face,
and tarrying with it.[3]

Thus, Heidegger goes on, German idealism had the courage to attribute
Evil to the very nature of Being. Nietzsche himself had noticed that in
German pantheism, in particular in Hegel, "evil, error and suffering are
not perceived as an argument against divinity," whereas Schopenhauer's
moralism resulted ultimately in his denial of the world. Schopenhauer's
popularity in the second half of the nineteenth century, according to
Heidegger, was not a testimony to his victory over German idealism; it
resulted from the fact that the Germans were not "any more" up to the
level of this idealism; it is only now, by a circuitous route, that the
German spirit is extricating itself from this mode of decline.

The will to expand and to dominate (*Über-sich-hinaus-Herrsein*)
always and inevitably includes destruction. Being is the will to power.
By proclaiming this idea, Nietzsche revived, perhaps unknowingly, the
genuine Aristotelian insight obscured by the Scholastic theory of *actus*
and *potentia*. This Aristotelian-Nietzschean notion of Being belongs to
the very foundation of Western thinking and therefore is capable of providing an essential impulse to the spiritual challenge of the twentieth
century.

So far Heidegger. It can hardly be doubted that his analysis of
Nietzsche's thought was *not* intended as a purely historical interpretation. (Heidegger neither was, nor pretended to be, a historian, only a
philosopher of "historicity.") His endeavor was to shape an ideological
appeal, to find in the tradition of German thought a powerful source that
would legitimate the effort to meet the challenge of modernity.
Nietzsche, he supposed, revealed himself as a font of strong energy from
whose source the German spirit, hence German self-affirmation in the
will to power, could be resurrected.

Here, then, is the comment on Heidegger's comment:

First of all, it is quite clear that the quotation from Hegel supports
neither the Nietzschean nor the Heideggerian theory of the "will to
power"; in fcat, it has nothing to do with that theory. It was exploited by
Heidegger for a philosophical or ideological purpose quite out of keeping with its original meaning. Real substance, or the subject – says Hegel,
somewhat earlier in the same text – "is in truth actual only insofar as it
is the movement of positing itself. This substance is, as Subject, pure,

3   G.W.F. Hegel, *Hegel Phenomenology of Spirit*, trans. A. V. Miller (Oxford:
     Oxford University Press, 1977), p. 19.

simple negativity, and is for this very reason the bifurcation of the simple; it is the doubling which sets up opposition, and then again the negation of this indifferent diversity and of its antithesis, [the immediate simplicity]."[4]

The sentences quoted by Heidegger continue along the same line of thought. Spirit, by its very nature, has to reach and discover itself afresh, time and again, in the "absolute spirit": that is to say, it is bound to produce its own negation unceasingly, and is capable of persisting in this self-denial. What is meant here is neither death, in the sense of total annihilation, nor evil or error. Nor is there reason to suppose that Nietzsche, in praising German pantheism, had in mind the fragment of the *Phenomenology of Mind* under scrutiny here. Moreover, there is nothing specifically Hegelian or pantheist in the belief that evil, error, and suffering are not to be construed as an argument against divinity: they have never been thus construed in the entire history of Christian philosophy (St. Augustine included). On this point, therefore, Nietzsche is wrong, and Heidegger is twice wrong: first, in repeating Nietzsche's mistake; second, in suggesting that when Hegel originally featured "the power of negativity ," he had in mind the same creative (hence, destructive) "will to power" that Heidegger conceived as the principle of Being.

True, according to the Hegelian account, Spirit proves its "truth" historically by being victorious. This sounds sinister and suggests that in every struggle the winners are right by definition, right by the mere fact of having won. One must remember that Hegel is addressing himself to the phases of cultural history. His thesis is not meant to signify that any victory, no matter how unimportant or accidental, confirms the "rightness" of the victor. For example, it is certainly not the case that any boxer who happens to knock his opponent out thereby proves that he is the bearer of the "truth of Spirit." These questions are meant to be distinct. Still, we can hardly find (in Hegel) clear criteria by which to separate this historically significant victories from the merely trifling accidents. It is for this reason, of course, that Hegel's philosophy could be so easily used (or misused) to glorify the rightness, as such, of every victor.

Apart from that, however, the Hegelian speculation neither implies nor in any way endorses or suggests any (universal) metaphysics of the "will to power." That doctrine, taken in the Nietzschean sense, simply assumes that there is nothing in the world except the centers of will, each of which attempts endlessly to expand at the expense of others, to command as much room for itself as it can, and to enfeeble or destroy as many other centers of power as possible. Although Hegel believes that –

---

4   *Ibid.*, p. 10.

on the largest historical scale – Spirit proves or displays its truth by victory (which inevitably also anticipates a subsequent intrinsic split within itself), he by no means assumes that the whole of reality is anything more than an irrational collection of discrete centers of will, each of which strives blindly and separately to expend its power. For Hegel, no expansion of power could be "right" unless it was embedded in an all-encompassing historical plan, so that the meaning of particular events would depend upon the absolute meaning of the universal "becoming" of which they were a part. "Right" obtains only as a component of the grandiose march of the World-Spirit toward self-reconciliation through a series of self-denials and "meditations." Consequently, even though Spirit dispenses with moral criteria in the process of growth, its energy comes from the universal goal that it aims at. All this is utterly alien to the Nietzschean world-view, in which there is no room for goal, or progress.

Moreover. although he mentions Hegel, Nietzsche as the author of a theodicy (or a historiocidy) does not affirm his own metaphysics of the will to power (he does not call it a "metaphysics," but what else is it?) to be a Hegelian provenance, and we should not assume that it is. On this score, Heidegger commits three further blunders. First, in wrongly associating the Hegelian "negativity" with the Nietzschean will to power, Heidegger imputes (no less wrongly) the same blunder to Nietzsche.

Second, he suggests that the evil, error, and suffering of which Nietzsche speaks in the Hegelian context, is both the Hegelian "negativity" and a sign or expression of the Nietzschean will to power. But for Nietzsche, the natural expansion of the centers of will cannot be equated with evil, error, or suffering. The very idea of evil proves meaningless in Nietzsche, especially in the last collection of aphorism prepared for publication by his sister (prepared, as Schlechta proved, with an ulterior ideological purpose in mind).[5] The will (for Nietzsche) is what it is, and to measure it by moral rules would be futile; such rules never arise from an unprejudiced perception of the world; they arise only from human weakness; the universe produces neither good nor evil.

Third, Heidegger falls victim to a self-contradiction. On the one hand, he associates negativity with evil, error, and suffering; on the other, he seems to perceive in the expanding will to power not – like Nietzsche – the very nature of reality but rather a mark of a special dignity, a particular splendor, an eminent value, which the German spirit is manifestly called on to embody.

Moreover – and this is directly relevant to his political ideology –

5   See "Philosophischer Nachtbericht," in *Friedrich Nietzsche Werke*, ed. Karl Schlechta (Munich: Carl Hansen Verlag, 1972), 5:35–84.

when he praises the will to power and declares that it is the task of the German spirit to awaken it, Heidegger seems to make of Nietzsche the herald *par excellence* of just that historical mission. Is his reading of Nietzsche valid? Well, of course, the question is part of that more general time-honored question: What *was* the relationship between Nietzsche's philosophy and Nazi ideology? Was the Nazi assimilation of Nietzsche legitimate and credible? I shall venture no more than a brief remark on the issue.

Schopenhauer voices a quasi-Buddhist intuition: the world is horrible. There seems to be something pathological in the very particularization of existence; the individual is, so to say, a sickness of Being. But the principle human virtue remains compassion. Nietzsche heaps scorn on such moralizing: the virtue of compassion, he holds, is hostile to life; and the law of life consists in expansion as an end in itself. Is there, then, any practical conclusion to be drawn from his metaphysics of power? Apparently there is at least this: *fight on and fight on!* For what? For power, for the sake of further power. Whatever there is either asserts itself through expansion or destroys itself with its own sting like the mythical scorpion.

It is a widely held and well-grounded opinion – supported by Schlechta's analyses – that Nietzsche was neither a German nationalist nor an anti-Semite (one finds in his writings some nasty comments about the Jews, but there are even nastier ones about the Germans). It is quite unreasonable therefore to suppose that the Nazi ideology, of which those two components – German jingoism and anti-Semitism – were obviously the main pillars, was either potentially or explicitly in accord with Nietzsche's philosophy or could have been extrapolated from his intellectual message without severe distortion.

On the other hand, the Nietzschean *Weltanschauung* assumed a kind of universal imperialism, embracing all aspects of reality and explaining virtually everything: the basic law of Being is expansion, and Being knows neither good nor evil. In other words, whatever expands, destroying or absorbing the environment, not only cannot be judged by mere moral rules – by the norms of civilization or custom, by the principles of decency or of human rights or of similar pathetic figments of human imagination – but, through expansion, reveals only its vitality: it is real, and it is therefore valid and legitimate.

I was once asked by students, during a seminar, the following classic question: "What do you think Nietzsche would have said if he had had the opportunity to see the Nazi regime in action?" I repeat here my answer roughly as I phrased it then: "Granted the inevitable uncertainty of counterfactuals, expressed in the *modus irrealis* of the past tense, I think we can give a reasonable answer. (It would make no sense, of course, to ask 'what would Aristotle have said?' but in Nietzsche's case the temporal distance is not too great; we still share the same cultural reality; his sister after all lived long enough to become a Nazi). My guess is that had he survived until World War II, Nietzsche would have utterly despised the Nazis – but for wrong reasons. In terms of his won philosophy, there cannot be anything intrinsically wrong or reprehensible in genocide (including, presumably, the gas chambers), in the extermination of other nations, in imperialist expansion, in the search for *Lebensraum*, in martial cruelty. the point is not that, in these regards, the *Germans* would have been entitled to special rights and privileges or that the Jews and the Slavs would deserve to be destroyed. The point is rather that Germany's expansion and the extermination of foreign tribes would not be qualitatively different from a shark's swallowing smaller fish. In both cases, we are faced with the law of life, to condemn which would be as silly as to condemn Being itself. I think Nietzsche would have looked at the Nazi with utter contempt; in his eyes they would have been a rabble without dignity, miserable parvenus lacking altogether the aristocratic virtues he loved and praised so effusively, not just a bellicose tribe but a gang of sadists."

It is quite incredible that the Nazi ideology could have sprung fully armored from Nietzsche's head. Nevertheless, the Nazi assimilation of his work or as a merely insolent distortion of its meaning. Nazi ideals were well settled in this tradition of the master race: by efficiently enslaving and destroying other peoples, it proves that it *is* the master race. The Nazis enriched that doctrine with some supplementary ideas of their own, in particular with the bogus biological definition of superior and inferior races. For, to gain practical application, the idea of an all-embracing ontological imperialism had to be suitably incarnated in a politically specific, well-defined imperialism.

Let us return to Heidegger, then. Heidegger's attempt to harness the Hegelian philosophy to the chariot of German spirit is, as we have seen, full of errors and confusion. Nonetheless, he did absorb the Nietzschean metaphysics in its original meaning and supplement it with the notion of a particular mission of German culture. Certainly, there was nothing new in this idea. But *in* the historical context within which it was uttered, its message (never of course spelled out in so many words in the text under scrutiny) was unmistakably clear: encouragement and praise for German imperialism then and there.

It is worth nothing that apart from jumbling together three different ideas of negativity – the Hegelian (negativity as an internal split of Spirit in progress), the Nietzschean (the expansive energy of any particular being), and the traditional (evil, error, suffering) – Heidegger adds to the confusion by introducing a fourth sense of negativity: he insists that creation – always and unavoidably – is destruction. In the latter sense, however, negativity becomes an empty tautology: whatever happens, whatever changes, one condition is replaced by another. When I move my finger, for instance, one arrangement of the molecules of the air is disturbed and supplemented by another. What is created entails the "destruction" of what it replaces. Once this barren meaning is added, without further differentiation, to the other three, the glory of German imperialism begins to seem indisputably self-evident.

It is not my intention to claim on the basis of this fragmentary criticism, however, that Heidegger's philosophy was entirely propelled, as it were, by the ideologically focused will to strengthen national Socialism, or that that had been its intended meaning from the very beginning. Nevertheless, certain of its essential, hardly secondary, themes did turn out to be remarkably well-adapted to that particular task. This does not imply, of course, that the entire philosophy is to be condemned, or held to be a product only of a sick mind. Heidegger was beyond doubt a *Bahnbrecher*, as the Germans like to say. He opened new avenues to our eternally uncertain exploration of the meaning of what it is "to be," and he was not the only thinker whose work could have been employed for evil purposes without distortion, while at the same time it actually advanced in a seminal way the work of our civilization.

The Epistemology of Striptease

I. On the Wisdom of the Bible

To imagine that the attractions of striptease need no explaining is an achievement of which none but the truly innocent are capable. The true naïf likes to conceal his innocence under a paper hat of cynicism; he lives in the hope that he will be taken for a sophisticated connoisseur of life, and his innocence for wisdom, if he can label all human motivations with the aid of just three or four words – words like "greed," "lust for power" and "sex drive." But in doing so he only reveals the full extent of his infantile naiveté, and a boundless magnanimity which testifies to his blissful ignorance of the presence of evil in the world. For to explain the rich, complex world of our experience in terms of these simple, basic drives, scarcely concealed nowadays and perfectly evident to direct empirical observation in our pre-reflexive life, is to reduce it to something far too primitive and naive. This is not only because we know, as a matter of common sense, that every one of our actions involves such a hopelessly tangled web of different motives – some ambivalent, some stronger and some weaker than others – that asking about the "primacy" of any one of them is absurd. More detailed studies of the matter (greeted with popular derision) have long been able to reveal that the simple and familiar can often, at heart, be complex and mysterious, and that human motives, at first glance almost palpably evident, are in fact a thick, treacly morass, harboring within its depths the strangest and most unsuspected things. The psychoanalysts, metaphysicians and religious scholars who venture into it are forced, in attempting to clear a way through, to go back to the murky beginnings of humanity, of all organic life, of existence itself.

Those tempted to mock the invocation of metaphysical depths to explain the sight of a naked stomach would do well to restrain their facile wit and return to their childhood Bibles, to ponder lessons learnt at a tender age, when they were unaware of the gravity of the matter.

For according to the account bequeathed us by the Book of Genesis, the first knowledge our forefathers acquired after eating of the forbidden fruit was the awareness of their own nakedness. At first, the Book of Genesis tells us, they were naked and unashamed. But when they had tasted the fruit of the tree of knowledge, they discovered that they were naked. Whereupon they felt ashamed – not of their crime, but of their nakedness – and hid themselves from the Lord's gaze in some bushes. Seeing their shame, God knew that they had broken His law, and expelled them from Paradise. It was after this expulsion that Adam and Eve lay together and knew each other carnally for the first time.

This account is worth reflecting upon, for hidden within its depths, beneath the glorious mythology constructed by the ancient Hebrews, lie the entire foundations of the theory of nakedness which has been so important in our culture.

The principles of this theory are as follows.

First, our (ostensibly) natural nakedness is not perceptible as naked-ness – i.e., as a separate fact – without special knowledge: we do not become conscious of nakedness "in itself," but only in opposition to "being clothed." In other words, nakedness is a cultural phenomenon, not a natural one.

Second, the same may be said of our shame of nakedness. To depart briefly from the Bible: shame is an attitude we have towards ourselves as objects of another's gaze. More precisely, it is the inferiority we feel at the sight of ourselves-seen-by-others in a humiliating situation. The rules whereby we define a situation as humiliating are not, of course, "natu-ral." Shame is the result of a split self-consciousness: we see ourselves through the eyes of others, as objects of their perception, while still retaining our sense of identity as experiencing subjects[1]. And this split in

---

1   Sartre considers this question in some detail in *L'être et le néant*, where he ana-lyzes the case of someone caught spying through a keyhole. Max Scheler, in his *Über Scham und Schamgefühl* (Schr. aus dem Nachlass, Bd. I), says that shame, along with the libido, is an autonomous element of the sex drive, and points out that shame is what allows us to leave the auto-erotic stage, for by distancing us from our bodies it creates the need for a sexual partner. But what he means by "shame" here is more a feeling of modesty than the con-sciousness of being ashamed – a disposition rather than an emotion. Nevertheless, it is clear that this disposition cannot be defined just in terms of distance towards one's own body; we need a specific idea of what that dis-tance consists in – namely, our readiness to experience our own bodies as a humiliating aspect of ourselves.

turn produces that secondary phenomenon which we call "being ashamed of ourselves" – the feeling of shame we have in front of ourselves, without an audience.

To return to the Bible:

Third, our knowledge of nakedness is neither empirical nor based on convention. That nakedness is a thing of which we ought to be ashamed – i.e., that such a thing as nakedness exists – is something we learn neither from our own experience nor through observation. The idea of nakedness must have been present in the universal mind: only from there could it have penetrated into that malevolent fruit and through its agency brought enlightenment to the sinning couple after their offence. Adam and Eve did not *invent* nakedness and establish it by convention; they *discovered* it as a "given," already in the world. And knowledge, once acquired, cannot be given back – renounced, erased or changed by convention; it is irreversible. This also explains how we can feel shame without an audience: it is that permanent audience, the all-seeing eye, which makes our shame possible.

Fourth, the idea of nakedness was, after the information received from God about the forbidden fruit, the first item in the sum of human knowledge. In forbidding the fruit of the tree of knowledge, God appeared to Adam and Eve as an abstract law-giver; but in their experience of shame (shame not before each other but before God) He appeared for the first time as a person: this was their first existential contact with God. God's announcement about the constitution of Paradise – thin on content but extremely clear – was the first interpersonal contact in history (as the second chapter of Genesis relates); the second came after the discovery of nakedness, and thus the discovery of shame. Thus the first anthropological doctrine was based on the opposition of two situations: naked vs clothed. This classification, together with the consciousness that God created man naked and that nakedness is shameful, inevitably leads to the following conclusion: nakedness is both natural and shameful; therefore the natural state, or being in a natural state, is shameful.

Fifth, since it was only after their expulsion from the Garden of Eden that the first couple had carnal knowledge of each other, we may conclude that the recognition of nakedness as nakedness was a condition of all procreational activity. It follows not only that (as Kierkegaard observed) original sin is the cause and necessary condition of man's propagation, but also that every act of carnal love is inseparably associated with the consciousness of shame – that shame of nakedness which is an irreversible fact. Thus carnal love becomes a return to the natural state, which we know to be a shameful one. But it is an illusory return, for innocence cannot be regained: we cannot return to a state of pre-knowledge. We can only recreate the visible circumstances in which the original act took place; it is through our feeling of guilt that they are revealed to our understanding.

The Biblical myth of original sin perfectly codifies a number of the fundamental beliefs of Mediterranean culture. They can be listed as follows:

Nakedness is shameful;

the fact that nakedness is shameful is not deducible from anything; it has no explanation. Nor is it the result of convention. It is a given, a transcendental law;

our knowledge of the fact that nakedness is shameful is not natural, but must be acquired; and its acquiring is man's first act of denaturalization. This act of denaturalization – the recognition of the distinction between being naked and being clothed – is the foundation of culture (as opposed to nature);

we live in the permanent, ubiquitous presence of an all-seeing eye which penetrates our clothing and presents us to ourselves as naked – i.e., natural – i.e., in a state of shame.

Each of these premises is logically independent of the others, and must be accepted separately. Together they form a logically coherent whole which may be expressed by the statement: *man's truth is his shame.* Man's true state is his natural state, and the natural state is a state of shame. In the natural state that shame is unconscious, because natural man is not aware that he is shameful; but his shame is a fact – a given, decreed by divine law. When man becomes aware of his shame, he hides it; that is the point at which he leaves the natural state and becomes cultured. But his shame, although hidden, can never be erased: it is kept alive by the omniscient all-seeing eye, ubiquitous and ever-vigilant. A double relation has been established: between truth and nakedness on the one hand, and between truth and shame on the other. The former is evident in such expressions as "the naked truth," "the bare facts," etc., but also in the etymology of the Greek word for "truth," to which Heidegger devoted so much attention: *aletheia* – that which is not hidden by appearances. The latter is revealed in the way we talk about "appearance" and "reality": for example, when we say of someone that he has "revealed his true nature." We assume that appearances are beautiful and reality ugly.

Thus we have arrived at the conclusion (faintly absurd-sounding when put this way, but nevertheless expressive of something deeply rooted in our thought) that *true* man is naked, and clothes *hide* the truth about him. The return to truth is also a return to shame – no longer unconscious, but irreversibly known. So we are condemned to oscillate forever between shame and deception. (In heaven will we be naked or clothed? Surely one of the Doctors of the Church must have addressed this question when pondering the details of our resurrection?)

II. An Appeal to the Authority of Husserl

Before we go further, a parenthetical remark: what are the origins of our conviction that nakedness is shameful and that clothing is concealment? We have no reliable information on the matter; no facts on the basis of which to pursue the question. But this need not be an obstacle: doing history without any facts at one's disposal became a respectable occupation when Descartes, in his *Principia*, Pufendorf in his *De Officio* and Husserl in his *Origins of Geometry* showed us how to go about it. Ever since they, by their own example, established that most peculiar of disciplines, transcendental history, this risky field has been open to anyone who, in a situation distinguished by the complete absence of facts, would like to plunge in and have a go. The legitimacy they conferred upon this new field has been beneficial and important, especially since the general acceptance of the belief – clearly formulated in the field of ethnology by Malinowski[2] – that the word "original," when used in an absolute sense (as in "original knowledge," "original language," "original state of man," etc), has no scientific meaning, and is merely a left-over from evolutionist metaphysics. And indeed, a rigorous scientific study cannot ask questions about the absolute beginnings of any human institution, for such questions have no scientifically meaningful answers: no scientific hypothesis could be constructed from them, since we have no data which could establish its truth or falsity. Scientific inquiry in the sociological and anthropological realm has freed itself from the need for absolute beginnings. We no longer interpret the customs and beliefs of so-called archaic peoples by measuring them against our own standards and the current state of our knowledge (like Frazer) or morality (like Morgan). Durkheim led the way in discrediting the practice; after him came Malinowski, and finally Levi-Strauss. Questions about absolute origins were abandoned together with the idea of an ultimate (i.e., valid for us) criterion of judgment; consequently, both the origin and the final result of the phenomenon under investigation were excluded from the field of inquiry once and for all – an outcome which, if we want to be able to distinguish between metaphysics and reconstructive hypotheses, was as beneficial as it was inevitable.

2   Bronislaw Malinowski, *The Sexual Life of Savages*, London, 1932; Introduction to the third edition, p. xxiii.

In philosophy (whose laws are different but no less harsh: it is just that their severity reveals itself gradually, over a much longer period of time), the natural consequence of this exclusion was a new ebb of questions about absolute beginnings. This in turn, unsurprisingly, strengthened rather than weakened the discipline of transcendental history mentioned above. Unsurprisingly because transcendental history is not concerned with facts: it does not aspire to reconstruct unknown facts on the basis of those we know. Its aim, rather, is to *explain* cultural processes, and arrive at a rational understanding of the way they work. Such an understanding involves reconstructing the origins of the given process, and the task of transcendental history is to do this in conditions where no facts are available, and thus where such a reconstruction cannot be achieved by ordinary historical means. In other words, transcendental history reconstructs origins in order to *make sense* of the facts, not to add to them; its reconstructions make no claim to being factual. End of parenthesis.

We may suppose, then, that in our reconstructed model of (rather than hypothesis about) the original state, clothing of a rudimentary kind was man's most distinctive feature: the feature which most palpably distinguished him from the rest of the living world. I say "most palpably" because while other distinctive and clearly visible features of our species, including, of course, morphological ones, amply suffice to distinguish the human species from the animal kingdom, they do not express the *degree* of man's distinctness. For the primitive eye and the embryonic self-consciousness they are basis enough for instant recognition: enough for primitive man to identify, unmistakably and at a glance, every example of his own species. But clothing alone shows him more: not just that he belongs to a certain species which can be distinguished from others, but that the way in which he differs from those others is crucial, and sets him apart from the animal kingdom. For it is one thing to be able to identify one's own species – something even the most primitive of creatures do in their behavior – and quite another to attain, even if dimly at first, that essentially human consciousness of being different from the rest of the organic world. And it is equally clear that the features which since the ancient world we have identified as the essential and defining characteristics of what it is to be human ("*animal risibile*," "*animal rationale*," etc), those uniquely human features which we see as marking out a new stage of evolution, are not the same as those by which primitive man recognized his own species as being outside the animal kingdom.

Of all the features which marked out the beginning of that new evolutionary stage, clothing is the most striking – more striking, by the quality of its uniqueness, than certain features of movement and build (such as two-leggedness, for example); more striking even than the use of tools. So it would be perfectly reasonable to assume that the use of clothing was contemporaneous with that first gleam of self-knowledge which was man's consciousness of his uniqueness; that it was, for the primitive mind, the basic recognition signal of the species; and that it was here that the opposition between human and animal was rooted, and from here that it developed. But it follows, too, that in that borderline world between human and animal, clothing must have been more than just symbolic; for those who were conscious of having crossed the border, it must also have been the central point of the world on the other side – the point in which the new reality was crystallized. Hence, too, conversely: all the manifold respects in which man belongs to the animal world came to be concentrated in nakedness. Nakedness was the view from the other side of the border man had crossed. Naked man was an animal; his nakedness was a sign that, in spite of everything, he still belonged to the animal world.

Thus nakedness became a shameful stigma, and clothing a way of hiding the animal in us – a way of hiding the shameful truth about man. And thus, too, may have arisen the intuition contained in the Biblical myth: that man's truth is his shame. We are animals; we can hide the fact with the aid of clothes, and forget about it to the extent that we can forget about our nakedness under them; but our native truth-seeking instincts soon remind us that clothes are a mask – a disguise, a way of hiding from ourselves the unpleasant truth about ourselves.

Gradually this intuition develops and articulates itself more clearly. The all-seeing God is born, and is a constant witness of our shame – our animal side, our natural state. The natural state is a sinful state; naturalness bears a stigma. By the same token, even the search for truth is suspect: the natural truth-seeking instincts of the inquiring mind are tainted by an aura of sin. The whiff of sin which clings to them is faint, obscure and never explicitly formulated, but it is there. *Libido sciendi* is the fruit of an evil impulse; it is the work of the Devil.

Naked man may be the true man, but for all that he is worth less than the man who is clothed. Whoever has conversed naked with someone who is clothed knows for certain that in such a conversation the naked man can never be right. The naked man may be the true man, but he has no dignity; he is more animal than man, and cannot win against the man who is clothed.

III. Nature Split in Two
Thus we are faced with two stereotypes of nakedness, mutually contradictory and representing the two sides of our image of man – that divid-

ed image which words like "culture" and "nature" preserve in our minds. In the first stereotype, we are animals, and our clothing a disguise. This stereotype assumes that nakedness is man's natural state and clothing a deception. In the second, it is culture, not our animal side, that defines what it means to be human. This stereotype assumes that clothing is an essential part of that definition – no less essential than such human characteristics as two-leggedness, language, laughter and the ability to use tools. Here human nature *is* culture, and nakedness a state of pre-culture. Nakedness can thus be seen either as form of clothing (by definition, since our nature is defined as culture, and clothing is part of that nature) or simply as a state of pre-humanness, i.e., the absence of humanness.

This second stereotype is not a theory concocted by anthropologists but a spontaneous product of rudimentary culture. We use the word "nature" both in opposition to the word "culture" and as its synonym, but this duality is not the result of verbal confusion or the sloppiness of ordinary language (which, on the contrary, is endowed with a keen intelligence, and reveals many truths); it expresses our incurable ambivalence towards our own bodies. Our image of the human body is shaped and dominated by culture; it is a cultural "given," presented to us in a form which is already civilized. At the same time, we perceive the body as anti-culture or pre-culture – as something animal. The nudist who wants to "return to nature" and the outraged preacher who condemns nudism as unnatural and dissolute are both right; but although each is right from his side of the image, those two points of view cannot be joined together into a coherent whole. The ideological juggling with the word "nature" and its equivalents that has gone on for centuries has not been groundless or pointless; historians who toil at classifying the innumerable meanings of the word would reveal lamentable naivety if they tried to pin the blame for this semantic confusion on philosophers, deploring their incompetence in matters of definition. The notorious eighteenth-century worship of nature (and of the naked savage), the equally notorious nineteenth-century disdain for it as primitive and immoral, the twentieth-century rehabilitation of something which was no longer nature, but nature rediscovered as a form of culture within a framework of universal relativism – all these are not only successive periods of greater or lesser ideological detachment towards one's own civilization, but also changing approaches to the stereotype of nature, with an emphasis now on one, now on the other of its two contradictory facets.

There is an analogous duality in our attitude to human sexual behavior, to the extent that we are able see it as a distinct domain. We learnt long ago that human sexuality cannot conceivably be regarded as a simple "given," a fixed element of the pre-civilized world, the result of the body's natural hormonal mechanisms and no more; we have learnt that it is tightly bound to the cultural context. Anthropologists have long been at pains to convince us that the very idea of two sexes is, in human societies, a social and cultural phenomenon: as if it was our underwear which determined the structures our bodies, and not the other way around. I will not dispute this view here. I certainly concede that the words "man" and "woman," "male" and "female," etc., derive their meaning not from their referents but from the structure of the whole system of signs used in any given society. I also agree that the distinction these terms convey is not an anatomical one, or more than an anatomical one: they distinguish between two kinds of creatures not by their naturally given anatomical features, but rather by their various social functions. I would only point out that both the total "culturization" of nature (the reduction of nature to cultural conditions) and, at the other extreme, the "naturalization" of culture (the reduction of culture to fixed and pre-existing biological conditions), are equally attempts to free human nature from its duality, and as such equally fail to capture the dissonance inherent in our common conception of nature.

One might say that Malinowski, when he called his savages "modest" because they took care to cover up their genitals in public, unwittingly revealed a vestigial Morganism – the habit of judging other civilizations by the standards of our own. The disciples of Levi-Strauss, well schooled in strict relativism, have learnt not to make this mistake. But if anything can be said to be the supreme product of a well-defined cultural formation, it is precisely relativism – that strict, culturally indifferent relativism which is equally detached towards all cultures, including its own. This is not surprising: we know that the less developed a civilization, the more sluggish and apt to stagnate, the more rigidly it immobilizes us within our own folklore, binding us tightly to the standards of our own set of cultural beliefs; we regard our own values as absolute, and are less and less able to step outside them and judge them with an objective eye. That effort of objectivity, culminating in the ability to consider all cultures, including one's own, as equal, is possible only in our sophisticated western-European civilization; no other could have produced it. Thus it is only in a very restricted sense that it can be viewed as an emancipation from that civilization's cognitive norms. Moreover, universalism and openness towards other cultures are themselves cultural characteristics. This does not mean that they are necessarily illusory or unsuccessful; it does mean, however, that they cannot be disinterested. They *always* have an ideological underpinning, and since that underpinning is culturally determined, they cannot be said to be entirely free and presuppositionless epistemological points of departure.

This underpinning can be of two kinds: *either* it is the belief that there exists a model of human nature[3] which every culture realizes (or perverts) in its own particular way, *or* it is an absolute historicism, i.e., the rejection of all values – a kind of skeptical nihilism which permits only detached observation from a neutral, value-free standpoint. All forms of universalism and relativism and all claims of total, unlimited objectivity reveal themselves, when scratched, to be based on one or the other of these two ideological positions. One is utopian and the other skeptical, but both these varieties of universalism are attempts to get around that latent contradiction inherent in our spontaneous conception of human nature. And both fail. The utopian-paradigmatic approach to human nature fails because it wants to but cannot take account of and encompass those features or tendencies of human nature which are mutually contradictory and nevertheless essential parts of that nature. It is paralyzed by them, as it were, and cannot function. And the skeptical-neutral approach fails because the detached observing mind, if it is elevated to the status of unique arbiter and given a total monopoly over our cognitive efforts, cannot even admit questions about primary or "original" human characteristics: it will reject them as meaningless, seeing them as some vestigial form of conceptual realism, or something even worse. Thus universalism, whether its underlying ideology is one of hope or of resignation, will always have trouble reconstructing human nature if it attempts to capture that nature's fundamental lack of coherence.

This state of affairs affects the way we think about nakedness. Here, too, there is a duality. We see nakedness either as part of a lost ideal of innocence, a regretted part of man's original nature; or as a cultural phenomenon, one of many, as indifferent as any other. There is nakedness as our "true," animal side, concealed by clothing; and nakedness as a particular instance of clothing, a kind of zero clothing which can exist only within a given civilization (for outside civilization there is no such thing as humanness). In order to express our experience of nakedness fully, to encompass both aspects of it and capture the contradiction between them, we would have to perform an almost impossible feat: we would have to identify with our own culture while at the same time maintaining an objective detachment towards it. We need to identify with it to preserve the purely cultural meaning of nakedness; we need the detachment to be able to see man clothed (or "attired," to use an old-fashioned term) as an animal disguised, and man naked as that animal unmasked.

3   A great deal has been written about how natural stereotypes are culturally determined. See A. Gehlen, *Anthropologische Forschung*, 1963, p.78ff. For other interpretations, see Bronislaw Baczko, *Rousseau: Samotnosc i wspólnota [Solitude and Community]*, Warsaw, 1964, chapter II.

This schizophrenic attitude may be difficult to express clearly, but it is what makes up our ordinary, unarticulated experience of nakedness, and it alone can explain the essential aspects of the phenomenon of striptease.

IV. The Dialectical Structure of Perception during Striptease

Let us return to the beginning. It would be naive at best, and grossly simplistic, to say that people who watch striptease are after sexual thrills and leave it at that. This is not a sufficient explanation of their motives. There is no "natural" connection between nakedness and sexual arousal; the connection is created by culture, and it is created anew every time. Nor does this connection explain anything; on the contrary, it raises more questions than it answers. (In Victorian times every inch of a woman's exposed skin was considered erotic; to reply that "fashions change" is, again, only to raise further questions.) One of the things it notably fails to explain is the large number of female spectators at strip shows; unless we are prepared to embrace the unlikely conclusion that these are all lesbians, we must look elsewhere for an explanation.

Two elements are always involved in the pleasure of watching striptease. The first, shared by all theatre audiences, is identification with the performer. It is the classical element of catharsis, in this case provided by the projection of one's own exhibitionist urges. The second is, on the contrary, a sense of the performer's otherness: the intensely experienced feeling that she – the observed – is distinct and different from oneself – the observer. The feeling of distance or inequality between performer and audience is further heightened by the feeling that the performer is in some sense being forced to exhibit herself.

Let us consider the first of these elements. Exhibitionist tendencies – the ability to derive pleasure from exposing oneself in front of others – need not in themselves be considered pathological. Margaret Mead relates the story of a New England villager who one day had a divine revelation: he believed God had told him that everyone should do absolutely whatever he liked. When they heard this, the other villagers immediately tore off their clothes and began running around like animals, emitting grunts and howls. None of them, it seems, could think of anything better to do.[4] The exhibitionist tendencies that lie dormant in us, sublimated in art (where psychologists have taught us to recognize the signs of their presence), can be interpreted as symptoms of a longing for the impossible: a longing to return to the animal state which we consider to be our "true" state – the state in which we are "truly" ourselves.

4   Margaret Mead, *Male and Female*, 1956. p. 52.

They reveal that we subconsciously think of ourselves as animals in disguise, and feel ill at ease in the garb civilization has imposed on us; they arise from our sense that culture is something alien. We feel that we, or at least some part of ourselves, *ought* to return to the animal world, for that is where we "truly" belong. Exhibitionism is a manifestation of that feeling, and of our urge to break the taboo which forbids us to reveal ourselves as the animals we are. Watching striptease is a projection of that urge: a way of vicariously throwing off the disguise. It is a vicarious return to one's "real self," a way of affirming one's "true" identity.[5] At the same time, it provides the thrill of the forbidden, for we sense that affirming this identity is a betrayal – the betrayal of a secret. We feel that our animal side is and should remain mysterious, and we know that the ascetic discipline which culture imposes is there precisely in order to prevent us from unveiling that mystery.

Let us now go on to the second of these elements. Here, too, there are two aspects. Deriving pleasure from watching another person (in this case the performer) expose her shame can be interpreted as a form of sadism – sadism in the neutral, purely sexual sense of the word, understood as "sexual sadism" (which Freud saw as a combination of two genetically unconnected tendencies), as opposed to "infantile sadism" (which he considered a different phenomenon, not necessarily linked to the sexual act – at least, he did not argue for the existence of such links). It is a pleasure which feeds on another person's shame. And just as the first aspect of our pleasure (the process of identification with the performer) is connected with betrayal, so this second aspect (the process of alienation from her) is connected with exposure. When we project our desire to "return to our true self," we want to betray a secret; here, when we distance ourselves from the performer, we want to uncover one. We are, in other words, guided by a form of curiosity.

While curiosity may be the result of a natural reflex (the so-called

5 Exhibitionism would indeed be incomprehensible if (as H. Schelsky claims in *Soziologie der Sexualität*, 1963, pp. 70–71) it were no more than the provider of vicarious gratification through a partial sexual relationship, resorted to either from fear of a real one and a preference for anonimity and lack of commitment, or *faute de mieux*: from the lack of a sexual partner. Such an interpretation presupposes that exhibitionism is the a manifestation of another, more basic or primary phenomenon. However, this phenomenon manifests itself in different kinds of behavior: it lies behind voyeurism, for example, and in particular behind the preference for the services of prostitutes – and we do not treat these as perversions or individual anomalies. Such an interpretation therefore provides no basis for treating exhibitionism as something separate and distinct. The element of shame – or shamelessness – in exhibitionism cannot be ignored; and it is precisely this element that is also connected with our specific awareness of nakedness as a distinct phenomenon.

"orientation reflex"), it is not reducible to purely biological instincts of self-preservation. It is a kind of expansion drive, used by our organism not only for the purpose of self-preservation – to identify and ward off danger – but also to further its own development: by exploring those aspects of its surroundings which pose no threat to its survival, the organism expands its vital powers. In human beings this drive has attained an extraordinary level of autonomy: it has developed into the disinterested need to find out about our surroundings, without any considerations of utility or practical gain. Whether we call it curiosity, inquisitiveness, or a desire for truth, it has become an independent faculty, needing no justification.

Curiosity and sadism are indeed related. The pleasure we derive from an exciting intellectual discovery is similar to the perverse satisfaction derived from an act of violence. In the same way, any creative effort which exposes some unique aspect of ourselves, some hidden trait of our personality, inevitably betrays a tinge of exhibitionist excess. In both cases the affinity can be ignored; nevertheless, in the emotion we experience when watching striptease sadism and intellectual curiosity are intertwined. The curiosity is similar to that which a child displays when it rips apart a doll to see what is inside; if there is an element of sadism in such games, as Freudians have claimed, it is indistinguishable in practice from intellectual satisfaction. Since we experience nakedness both as man's shameful secret and as his hidden truth, exposing it is, for the observer, not only a sadistic game but also a form of intellectual exploration – like an expedition to some exotic place.

Let us now consider both elements together. Our consciousness of ourselves as human is divided: we are conscious of belonging to two opposing orders, defined and understood by their opposition to one another: nature and culture – twins born together in man's act of self-creation. Nakedness became a symbol of the first; it represents the truth about man, his animal side. Clothing became a symbol of the second; it represents that secondary truth, or meta-truth, which hides the first but at the same time – because it is a disguise, and because we know it to be a disguise – reveals it. We recognize ourselves in both orders, aware (more or less consciously) of the dissonance between them. Our identification with the first order, nature, expresses itself in the exhibitionist urge and its cognitive correlate, which is the urge to reveal our secret truth. This urge, in both its aspects, is accompanied by the consciousness that it violates a taboo of nature. Our identification with the second order, culture, expresses itself in the sadistic urge: the desire to watch, from a superior (clothed) position, as another's shame (nakedness) is exposed. We see the other as belonging to nature, and the contrast allows us to experience and affirm our belonging to a higher order – culture. This urge, too, has its, cognitive correlate, which is the expansion drive, manifesting itself in us as a disinterested curiosity.

In a strip show, as these two urges oscillate within us and we swing from one opposing form of identification to the other – from projection to alienation, from exhibitionism to sadism, from nature to culture – they blend together into one indivisible emotion. Striptease is an attempt (inevitably a failed attempt, although a certain distraction and lack of attention may make it seem successful) to synthesize the two opposing orders which together define what it means to be human. It may not be a very important element of our culture (there are other attempts at this synthesis, all equally unsuccessful), but it is a useful illustration.

V. Reply to Objections
I shall now try to reply to three possible objections. The first is fairly primitive, but it may well be raised. It goes like this:

What, then, is man? Are we to say that he is nothing but a beast in a hat rammed on to its head against its will? A bucking boar trying to shake off the proddings of the spear?

To which I reply: the boar does not carve his own spear, nor does he prod himself with it. But we do. The restrictions culture imposes on nature are a human invention, no less than "nature" itself, and no less than "culture," its supposed persecutor – those twinned, inseparable opposites each of which exists only by virtue of the other, and is understandable only in terms of the other. It is we who have created both. A system of sexual restrictions is an essential condition of all human cultures – a claim few anthropologists would dispute. If all these constraints were suddenly to melt away from our collective consciousness, if our super-egos lost their sway over us on a universal scale, all human civilization would be reduced to a heap of rubble within two generations. It is worth reminding ourselves that the difference between puritan and liberal sexual codes is negligible when compared to the abyss which separates us from that hypothetical natural state of total freedom – a fact easily missed, for many of the vast number of constraints and taboos which hem us in seem so obvious that they are seldom formulated, and thus pass unnoticed. Nevertheless, constraints, however loose, are still constraints, and these particular constraints are one of the ways in which culture imposes its rigors on us. For this reason I take a skeptical view of philosophies of harmony which – like the Thomists – see culture, or the "human spirit," as a sort of superstructure, ennobling but undemanding, gracefully draped over an animal body. Scheler seems closer to the truth in seeing culture as an act of ascetic negation on our part – the rejection of our own bodies.[6]

The second objection concerns striptease itself, and goes like this:

Every spectator at a strip show knows perfectly well that he is there for sexual thrills; it is absurd to attempt to demonstrate that this basic drive, primitive but ubiquitous and familiar, is not one of his motivations.

To which I reply: yes, I am aware of the fact, and have no wish to gloss over it. I am not guided by a compulsion to deny the obvious or a fondness of paradoxes. I do maintain, however, that the sexual drive by itself is not sufficient to explain our behavior, even when we are conscious of being motivated by it. It is not clear-cut and all-explanatory; it, too, requires explanation. Ever since our culture established rules which permitted certain forms of manifesting sexual hunger and brought it out of the shadows and into the light of day, we have been less resistant to accepting that sexual motives underlie our behavior; we understand and recognize them. But they are not explanation enough. Sexual behavior is never, at any stage, just sexual behavior pure and simple: it is always influenced by culturally acquired patterns. This is why it is always legitimate to ask how and why it is that certain phenomena or conditions, such as nakedness, have become sexually significant – part of the sexual domain – and are perceived as belonging to a pattern of behavior associated with sexual activity. Furthermore, the belief that sexuality itself needs no explaining – that it is a given, simply "found" in nature – is a questionable one, and has been much criticized, most notably by Jungians. So it is also legitimate to ask to what extent sexual behavior is a particular case of something else: a manifestation (or a disguising) of a different, even more basic drive. The assumption that, in a sophisticated system of disguise and self-deception, the bottom line is always sexual – that the sex drive explains everything and lies at the root of everything – is a left-over of puritan (and, in the realm of theory, Freudian) thinking. The same puritan/Freudian prejudice is responsible for the belief that if we are conscious of our sexual motives, they must be "real," and cannot be concealing instincts or drives of another kind – deeper and even more basic. In bringing the sexual drive out into the light of (partial) respectability, modern civilization has fashioned it into a possible disguise for other things – a way of concealing other motives and drives.

The third and last hypothetical objection deserves to be addressed

6   Max Scheler, *Die Stellung des Menschen im Kosmos*, 1928.

because it touches on a question that concerns the way we think about culture in general. It is this:

Assuming that the interpretation advanced above is defensible, it still seems patently artificial, and in bad taste, to appeal to the fundamental structure of humanness in order to explain a phenomenon as trivial and frivolous as striptease, which is, after all, no more than a form of entertainment, with little or no cultural role.

To this I reply: the fundamental structures of human life can manifest themselves in the small and trivial as well as the great and momentous; they are present not just in the things which draw the attention of anthropologists and philosophers because of their obvious importance and impact – things like war, religion, racial hatred, sexual life as a whole, political conflicts, the family, culture and art – but also in mundane customs, everyday gestures, seemingly insignificant habits. Uncovering the powerful springs of human behavior by tracing the course of minor tributaries, following the branches of our lives that lie on the periphery of culture, is not only legitimate but useful: it fulfils a function of its own. For it is precisely through the minor and the trivial that the omnipresent power of those fundamental structures is most visible.

For example: our culture teems with vestiges – absurd, truncated relics – of past religious experience. It is considered legitimate to study the general anthropological background of the use of stimulants, for example; but it is also legitimate to look for links between the role of drugs and alcohol in modern culture and the role of stimulants in religious rites of the past. It might seem absurd to discern echoes of metaphysical depths in the belchings of a vomiting drunk at a railway station buffet and ludicrous to compare the role of modern drinking to that of religious ecstasy; but those to whom this seems ludicrous and absurd should rather be laughing at themselves, for they are missing something fundamental. The fact that certain important elements of collective life – institutions, beliefs, myths, powerful experiences – are sometimes preserved in vestigial and distorted form, as misshapen caricatures of their source, is a blessing for anthropological research, and vital to it. *Si magna parvis . . .* Mircea Eliade, for instance, has remarked that the custom of turning off the lights at midnight at the New Year is a remnant of the great old mythological structures in which the course of the world proceeded through alternating cycles of growth and decay[7], each rebirth of the world taking place in a period of total chaos and confusion. There were certain rituals to celebrate the world's entry into the chaos which

---

7 Mircea Eliade, *Traité d'histoire des religions*, 1959, pp. 340–41.

heralded its rebirth; our custom of turning off the lights at the year's end is, unbeknown to us, a continuation of one of those rituals. Levi-Strauss wrote an excellent anthropological analysis of how we name our horses and dogs.[8] The examples are many, and prove abundantly that this type of anthropological enquiry, far from being a suitable object of derision, is a rich and important source of knowledge. To understand culture as a whole, we need to understand the origins of its particular manifestations, even the most insignificant-seeming. The trivial gestures of our lives contain within them misty reminders of the origins of human culture, just as our bodies reveal traces of our remote ancestors – the lemur, the fish, the starfish. Each of us, in all our activities – whether we are daydreaming, waging war, making love, writing scientific treatises, babbling drunkenly or watching a strip show – is both an individual and a member of a species; whatever we do, we remain the same individual and the same species, defined by our biological (as a species) and cultural (as individuals) origins. It is only when we understand our behavior structurally and genetically, as a whole, that we can understand what makes us human; understanding *this* is simply what understanding our humanness *means* – what it comes down to. Arriving at such an understanding is therefore the proper goal of philosophical anthropology. The many layers of our psychological structure move and shift in different ways and at different speeds, like the layers of the ocean; but the motion of the waves visible on the surface is ultimately determined by the totality of the layers beneath. The movements at the surface may appear random, dictated by the whims of chance, but they are not.

Translated by Agnieszka Kolakowska

8   Lévi-Strauss, *La pensée sauvage*, 1962.

The Priest and the Jester
Reflections on the Theological Heritage of Contemporary Thought

The main questions which have puzzled theologians for centuries have lost none of their relevance. They have survived to puzzle us, and though we may phrase them differently, we have done all we can to ensure their survival. Philosophy has never freed itself from its theological heritage; its questions have always been no more than clumsy formulations of those eternal enigmas which confound us still.

But are they, in fact, enigmas? Not always; we sometimes see riddles where there are none because we cannot bring ourselves to accept the facts, even when these are obvious and undeniable.

For example, nothing is more deeply rooted than our belief in moral entropy: we have a profound conviction that the second law of thermodynamics applies also to the moral sphere. We believe that our world will ultimately reach a state where merits are rewarded and crimes punished, wrongs avenged and good deeds recompensed; that all moral accounts will be settled and human values realized in a final reckoning. This belief allows us to rejoice whatever befalls us, for we shall be amply rewarded in heaven.

Accordingly, the first question philosophy took over from theology was the question of whether eschatology is possible at all. Our way of putting it is slightly different and ostensibly non-theological: we ask whether the human values which we accept can ever be fully realized: whether history tends in a particular direction, and if so whether it tends towards some ultimate reckoning where universal justice will be done.

It is no wonder that we ask such questions. The principal cause of philosophical reflection about history is discontent with it; its principal hope is that man's essence will one day be fully reconciled with his existence, and the immutable aspirations of his nature at last fulfilled. In other words, that he will be deified. And since such a state would put an end to the discontent which gives rise to the philosophy of history, one might say that the principal hope of the philosophy of history is a situation which will lead to its own extinction. Whatever optimism is to be found in it derives from its incurable suicidal tendency.

This secular eschatology presupposes, of course, that man's "essence" is a value, and consequently that its realization is a good thing, which history, in its wisdom, will bring about. Secular eschatology trusts in history's final judgment – the day of reckoning. We are hardly in a position to sneer, for which of us has not, at some time or other, succumbed to this belief? Each time we think that history will avenge the suffering of the dead, or that age-old accounts of wrongs will one day be settled, we express our faith in the last judgment. Each time we assume that the aspirations of "human nature" will be fulfilled, we demonstrate our belief in eschatology – and thus in the finiteness of man's existence.

The question of eschatology – whether it is possible, and whether belief in it is justified – is one of the main questions preoccupying the modern philosopher of history, and therefore also an important element defining the modern view of the world. It emerged with a new force in the eighteenth century in Europe – the moment when "History" and "Progress" deposed Jehovah and usurped his throne, and made it clear that they were perfectly capable of replacing him in His main functions. At that moment historical eschatology revealed its possibilities. When History and Progress proved acceptable substitutes for God, ready to assume his burden and lull his wretched subjects into contentment by visions of a happy end to their strivings and sufferings, the history of humanity became a compelling argument for atheism.

But belief in historical progress need not presuppose a belief in eschatology; endowing historical facts with value does not by itself entail chiliastic visions. For these an additional assumption is needed, namely the assumption that the course of history tends towards a certain permanent and well-defined end, and that this end, when reached, will definitively resolve all conflict. It makes no difference whether we call this result the end of history or its beginning; in every eschatology the end of history on earth is both an end and a beginning: the end of human suffering and the beginning of a blessed new existence, a state of which we know nothing except that it will be one of eternal happiness and joy.

The question of whether eschatology is possible, whether answered in the negative or in the affirmative, has become a central question in philosophical anthropology – a discipline which touches upon most of the vital issues of philosophy. But theology was never more than a projection of anthropology onto the domain of the non-human. Philosophical anthropology continues to seek solutions to the conflicts of human nature – the conflicts which arise between natural human aspirations and the external forces which influence our fate. It can seek them (as Christian existentialists like Jaspers or Marcel have done) in transcendence; or (as Marxists do) in history; or (as Freud once did) it can pronounce the conflict unresolvable. This last view is also embraced by atheist existentialists, although they state it somewhat differently. But whatever the arguments, and whatever the technical language in which they are expressed, the question itself is common currency: almost everyone will have an answer ready, shaped by personal experience and the influence of tradition (which may conflict with experience or confirm it). These popular versions of answers need not be argued theses; they may not be explicitly formulated, and sometimes are not even consciously expressed. Most often they emerge in practice, implied by our general attitude to life: whether we see it as no more than a collection of successive facts or events, each existing and having meaning only as long as it lasts, or whether we believe that each of these facts or events is something more than the content of its time span – an expectation, a hope of facts as yet unrealized, an unveiled sliver of some ultimate prospect of fulfillment. The answer determines how we approach the facts and events of our everyday lives: as the absolute and final reality, to be taken at its direct, empirical face value, or as sections of a broader path at the end of which lie peace and consolation: pennies in a piggy-bank, saved up towards our (or mankind's) eternal retirement. In the latter case we run the risk of dismissing present facts and present values as insignificant; in the former, of dismissing those that go beyond the present and require, for their fulfillment, a certain amount of effort and preparation on our part. The choice is a common and familiar one, almost banal: either (at one extreme) we fritter away our lives by disregarding present values in favor of some imagined ultimate values (which may turn out to be illusory); or (at the other) we impoverish them by shutting our eyes to the possibility of greater values, refusing to recognize facts that go beyond the present and demand a transcendental interpretation – one that endows them with meaning by virtue of their relation to something greater that lies beyond them. These are the two poles between which everyday life oscillates. The extent to which we are drawn to one rather than the other depends on why we ask the question in the first place: from a need for consolation, to help us bear the suffering of our lives, or from a fear that we might waste our life on illusions – a fear that increases with each disillusionment we experience. The magnetic force exerted by each depends on the relative importance of these two factors.

The choice, when put this way, may indeed be banal, but it is part of a larger issue which, inherited from theology, has preoccupied philosophy for centuries. Another issue directly connected with it, and also inherited from theology, is that of theodicy. In its modern version the question of theodicy translates into a question about the rationality of history: whether the course of history is guided by some universal, purposive force, some Reason which can justify and give meaning to individual suffering and unhappiness. Traditional theodicy teaches that God's infallible justice shines through the wretchedness of the damned and that human misery proclaims the glory of His supreme goodness. The question theodicy deals with is not quite the same as that which is dealt with by eschatology: eschatology tries to make sense of *all* facts by relating them to the prospect of an end, an ultimate resolution; theodicy tries to justify the existence of evil – each particular instance of it – by the idea of a universal order, a rationality or a divine reason which governs the world, regardless of whether this justification is part of that end.

Ideologies based on theodicy need not be conservative (although in general they tend to be, and most of them have been). They are conservative if they try to justify *all* evil, regardless of its cause and the role played in it by human decisions; they are not necessarily conservative if they limit their justification to evil which results from freely made human choices. Theodicies of the first type are simply ideologies of human powerlessness in the face of the external conditions which influence our lives: they tell us that we must resign ourselves to the fact that we cannot change the world, but claim to compensate for this resignation by endowing it with value. Theodicies of the second type can boil down to ideologies which sanction the risks of participating actively in human conflicts, whether on the side of good or of evil.

Theodicy is not limited to abstract theories or restricted to the history of philosophy. Like eschatology, it is also part of popular philosophy – the philosophy of everyday life. Our acceptance or rejection of it is evident in our attitudes and behavior; it is a practical philosophy, one of which we may be only dimly aware but which we apply in our daily lives. On this level it can express itself in a number of ways. Some may find consolation in the thought that their suffering and misfortunes are God's will, brought about by His unerring hand in order to do good elsewhere in the world, according to His unfathomable plan. Others may find it in the more general belief that nothing happens in vain: that suffering is never wasted, but scrupulously totted up and inscribed in the ledgers of some bank of history, accruing interest which future generations will be able to draw. Those who truly believe such things can draw genuine solace from them, and there would be no reason to deprive them of this source of consolation if they resorted to it only when the misfortune was irreparable and the evil unavoidable, instead of relying on it even in those cases where the misfortune could be reversed or the evil opposed, and doing nothing.

242

But most often it is in just such cases that theodicy is resorted to, and in practice its effects are notorious. The conviction that nothing in human life happens in vain, that all things have a purpose dictated by History or willed by God, is a powerful inducement to sloth, and reinforces our inborn conservatism and inertia; it encourages our instinct to resign ourselves passively to our fate and shields us from guilt and rational criticism. How easy and tempting to say to ourselves: "Our fate is only a tiny fragment of the fate of the world; all individual suffering serves the common good, everything influences everything else, and through it all a permanent order is maintained. All evil, everything bad that happens, is a sacrifice on the altar of the whole, and sacrifice is never in vain." Nothing bears out this optimism: there is no evidence that the fates of individuals are ever "balanced out," on *any* historical scale. Clear-eyed observation shows that while in some cases suffering might serve some purpose, in others it serves none: it is just that and no more – bare suffering. It shows that much effort and sacrifice, and many lives, are wasted every day, to no purpose whatsoever. In short, the holistic and equalizing vision of the world has no basis in our observation of reality. Yet it endures, apparently resistant to argument: our longing for the consolations it provides seems to be stronger than the evidence of our senses, and this vision of the world remains one of the most deeply rooted human superstitions. Let me repeat that there would be no need to condemn it or belabor its irrationality if it were only a way of reconciling ourselves to what is past and irreversible: a false but harmless rationalization of things we can do nothing about. But it is not harmless, for it also functions as a way of rationalizing things present: it is an excuse for accepting situations of whose irreversibility and inevitability there is no evidence.

Theodicy, in other words, is a way of *turning facts into values*. It endows facts with a significance that goes beyond the empirical appearances, seeing them as components of a teleological order, an interconnected whole in which each part has a specific role to play. The tendency to discern value in facts derives from a way of thinking much older than any speculative theology: it is a legacy of an ancient, magical view of the world, where events were thought to have invisible properties which gave them damning or sanctifying powers. The belief that our real, present suffering will be compensated for by future blessings, bestowed upon us or upon posterity, presupposes a similar belief: that events, and in particular the misfortunes which befall us, have invisible properties linking them to a rational order of the world, and by virtue of this link are endowed with value. This belief is of exactly the same type as any belief in magic forces. For the moment, however, we are not concerned with criticizing the belief in magic, but with identifying the points at which modern thought, even secular philosophical thought, is forced to address questions whose roots lie in theological and even pre-theological – i.e., magical – traditions. *All* belief or disbelief in a teleologically ordered world where History or the Godless universe endows events with *value*, a property independent of our perception, is belief or disbelief in theodicy. This does not mean that questions about an immanent order in the world are not real questions; we tacitly confirm that they are real every time we agree to answer one, even if our reply is negative. We also confirm that the question about theodicy is a real and meaningful question, and thus that the idea of theodicy itself is not an absurd one – for in deeming a question answerable we presuppose that the field of knowledge with which it is concerned has some claim to existence. Thus theodicy is part of modern philosophy, whether we call it the metaphysics of values or reflections about man's place in the universe or about historical progress: in all these areas, each one a part of the estate of contemporary non-religious philosophy, theodicy, and thus magic, is an important and far from obsolete element.

Both the belief in eschatology and the belief in theodicy are attempts to find meaning and justification for our lives in something that lies beyond them, some absolute reality which endows all other reality with meaning while itself requiring no interpretation by reference to anything outside it. Absolutes tend to be adopted as a moral foundation because they are a metaphysical foundation: when the world is seen as a metaphysical construction, all its elements become manifestations or particular instances of its metaphysics, and it is only as such that they can be understood. But there are other issues where the idea of the absolute plays a more direct role – issues once important in theology but no less pertinent in their modern form, and still of vital interest not only to philosophers but to all those who want to discover the reasons behind their behavior.

Chief among these is the question of nature and grace. It was central to the conflicts which marked the history of Christianity (Pelagianism, the Reformation, Jansenism), together with the question of theodicy (the Manicheans, the Cathars) and of redemption (the Monophysites, the Arians, the Socinians), but it clearly remains as urgent and complex today as it was at the time of the Council of Trent, for it is a question about determinism and responsibility. In its most general form it concerns the relation between individual responsibility and all the external factors which determine individual behavior: in what sense and to what extent the human individual "can" or "cannot" resist the influence of independent forces which shape his behavior; in what sense he can be said, in view of these influences, to be morally responsible for his actions; to what extent that responsibility lies with forces over which he has no control. There are many versions of this question – biological, sociological, historiosophical, metaphysical. Some of these variants have become empirical and empirically solvable problems and have lost their purely philosophical character; others have remained within the realm of philosophy of history or metaphysical speculation. But in every case the sources of our enduring interest in the question are the same as they have always been: what we want to know is to what extent factors (biological or historical) independent of us can justify our actions *post factum*, and to what extent such factors can provide reliable guidelines for future decisions. Historical determinism is an area in which a particularly complex tangle of questions has sprung up – questions that remain among the most vital of contemporary philosophical concerns.

"We do not have the freedom to achieve any particular thing; we only have the freedom to do what is necessary or to do nothing. Historical necessity carries out its task, with the individual or against him." This attitude concisely summarizes the idea of historical predestination: it tells us that all attempts to resist are doomed from the start, and thereby also justifies our actions, which, since they are dictated by historical inevitability, could not have been otherwise. The words quoted come from the end of Spengler's *Decline of the West*, but they encapsulate a much more general line of thought. All constructions which include the idea of natural cycles of civilization – like Toynbee's, for example – are variations of one model: the vision of the world in *De Civitate Dei*. In this sense opponents of historical determinism, like Karl Popper or Isaiah Berlin, can be said to be continuing the Pelagian tradition of the idea of salvation. Marxist literature on the subject is varied, but mostly concerned with some version of the decisions of the Council of Trent. These were as follows: actions which accord with the intentions of the historical absolute are ultimately determined by that absolute. Nonetheless, there is no irresistible grace; the absolute extends to all the possibility of cooperating with it, and each individual is responsible for his decision to accept or reject that offer. Since (it is assumed) not all will take up the offer of redemption, the world is divided into the chosen and the rejected. This division and all its consequences is predetermined, and an irrevocable part of the absolute's plans, but each individual freely chooses the category into which he will fall.

I mention all this not in order to ridicule a concern which is still vital in contemporary philosophy, but rather to bring into relief the hidden rational side of a theological problem which is no longer vital in its original form, but endures in another. There is nothing surprising in this: the central problems of any world view often persist long after our way of expressing that world view has changed, as a result of cultural transformations and conceptual shifts (which also define our lexical resources).

If the above analogies are directed against anything, it is at most against that haughty disdain which characterizes Enlightenment and free-thinkers' attitudes towards problems considered vital in the past – as if today we were not busy trying to solve the exactly the same problems, with the aid of different technology. Ridiculing them is no less absurd than ridiculing people in the Middle Ages for going about on horseback instead of in jet planes. Just as planes are a more efficient means than horses of achieving a certain end, so modern philosophy of history is a more effective means of dealing with problems once approached through disputes about the Trinity and irresistible Grace.

Nor is it surprising that we should want to understand how and to what extent independent forces can influence our behavior, or that sometimes we want to go even deeper, beyond the forces which are merely direct transmitters of energy, and uncover the elementary and autonomous forces which lie behind them – in other words, to get a glimpse of the absolute. If the historical process is such an absolute, then secular philosophy of history has simply taken over the old task of theology, reformulating the same problem in modern terms.

Reflection on the problem of nature and grace can spring from a variety of needs and serve a number of purposes. We may want to find some principle in which we can put our complete trust – a principle that would resolve all conflicts and relieve us of the burden of responsibility. Or we may want to find that highest tribunal on whose justice and mercy we can rely, safe in the knowledge that it will protect us from harm if we follow its precepts and reward us liberally for our obedience. Or, again, we may simply be seeking assurance that we have chosen the right side in life and that everything we do in its name is therefore just. Some solutions to the problem of nature and grace serve to absolve us of responsibility, for all responsibility is assumed by the absolute; this is the Calvinist solution. Others preserve our responsibility, but only in cases where clearly formulated rules exist which, if followed, will infallibly lead us to the right action; this is the Catholic solution. Others still leave us with total and unconditional responsibility, fully answerable to the absolute for every one of our actions, but with some uncertainty as to the intentions of the lawgiver; this is the Jansenist solution. All assume that the power of the absolute is both legislative and judicial; the area of subtle dispute concerns the extent to which it is also executive. Another area of dispute concerns our knowledge of the absolute's laws: whether they can be clearly known and how we can come to know them; whether we can fulfill them if they are known; and whether, if they are not adequately known, ignorance of the law is an acceptable excuse for transgressing them. It is around such questions that all the theological controversies of the sixteenth and seventeenth centuries turned: questions about nature and grace, about predestination and salvation through faith or works. But the existence of a principle that is at once the source of all duty and the tribunal which judges our actions, assessing how well we have fulfilled that duty, was not itself a matter of dispute; those who today deny the existence of such a principle deny a proposition theology once deemed so obviously true that it was rarely even formulated, let alone questioned.

If we disregard all the social conflicts which influence the debate about nature and grace and look at it from the point of view of individual motives, we can see that it is a conflict between two opposing currents. On the one hand there is the need to ground one's existence in something outside oneself – a need which seems to spring from a fear of the idea that we are isolated entities responsible for our own decisions; we want to leave ourselves behind, as it were, escape our selfhood, shed our individuality. And on the other hand there is the fear that our actions and decisions are somehow not real: that some alien force resides in us which is not only the effective executor of our intentions but also the will which decides what those intentions are. This conflict – between the drive to affirm the self and the drive to destroy it, or rather between fear of losing one's self and fear of one's self – is the most general way of describing the content of philosophical thought. To put it another way, the history of philosophy testifies to this conflict's existence.

It is worth noting that the problem of original sin, closely connected to that of nature and grace, also persists in a modified contemporary guise. For it is a problem which deals with the satanic element in man and thus, more generally, with revolt against absolute power. In its modern version it has, accordingly, become a problem about utopia, understood as an attempt to overcome the historical absolute – that power against which all revolt is supposedly doomed to failure. The question of redemption and incarnation, too, has its secular modern form: it has become a question about the role of the individual in history, and concerns that mechanism by which the historical absolute is incarnated in certain exceptional people. It is also a question about what such people represent: are they individuals who are able to draw energy from some transcendental source, or entirely spontaneous and autonomous "creative principles" in history?

All these issues concern a problem which the philosophy of history inherited from theology: the relation between man and the absolute. But there are also important problems in areas outside the philosophy of history, most notably in the theory of knowledge, which spring from the same source. The most vital of these today is the problem of revelation.

A capricious deity will never reveal all its secrets, but it does sometimes grant mortals a dimmed reflection of its wisdom, in accordance with the capacity of their owlish eyes, so that they may gaze upon it without being blinded. Revelation is simply the absolute on the cognitive level: a collection of unconditionally valid and unquestionable data. It is our way of communicating with the absolute. We need revelation not in order to know for certain what the world is really like, but in order to be able to evaluate, without hesitation or doubt, every opinion about the world that we encounter. Thus revelation, from the point of view of its purpose, is a sort of inquisitor's handbook. It is a granite throne from which we may pronounce verdicts with no possibility of error; and we need its support, for our rickety skeletons alone are not strong enough to hold us up. Supported by revelation we can do more than move the earth: we can stop it in its tracks.

Revelation is the constant hope of philosophy. We can see that this is so when we look at philosophical "systems" which claim to establish certainty: in accordance with some almost instinctively accepted order, they invariably *start* by establishing certain knowledge, the absolute beginning of all thought; certainty is their point of departure, not their conclusion. They assume that once the absolute is given as the beginning, the end is also given; that once we are on solid ground, moving about on it is no longer interesting, for if we already have something certain and unshakeable, our thought continues on its way by itself, smoothly and efficiently, like a marble rolling across ice. Revelation would seem to be that first push which thought needs to set it rolling; after that the ball rolls on by its own momentum, automatically. But it doesn't. It doesn't because automatic thought is not really thought: it is the antithesis of thought. Thought, in the strict sense in which we are using the word here, means creative thought – precisely that activity which no automatic mechanism can replace. Philosophy is a constant effort of questioning: a questioning of everything that seems obvious, and thus also of existing revelations. But a revelation of one's own is a tempting thing, and the temptation is an eternal trap for critics: when a philosophy that aspires to the name of "system" questions the revelations of others, it is invariably in order to present its own in their stead.

Indeed, there are few methods of thinking which do not tacitly espouse the Thomist principle that the aim of every movement is rest: "*Impossibile est igitur quod natura intendat motum propter seipsum. Intendit igitur quietam per motum...*" This principle presupposes that the essence of movement is its opposite, namely rest: that movement realizes itself by annihilating itself and becoming the absence of movement. In other words, it presupposes that all movement is a kind of imperfection – a defect or lack in the thing that moves, for in moving it is striving towards something (namely rest); its striving reveals a need, which must be satisfied in order for that thing to realize its nature. In philosophy this principle appears in the form of the belief that human thought is expressive of an imperfection: we think only in order to attain ultimate certainty, i.e., the perfection of our thought, and therefore rest. Thought, like any other movement, attains its goal and fulfils itself only once it has ceased to be movement and come to a stop – in other words, when it has ceased to exist. But the craving for absolutes, for ultimate certainty and revelation is one of the simplest needs to satisfy: seekers after revelation generally find it almost as soon as they become conscious of their need to seek it. And when the revelation has been found, and thought has attained its long-awaited fulfillment, philosophy begins (it thinks) building a "system." But in fact it has reached an end, not a beginning: the roof of the construction is already up when we think we have only just laid the cornerstone. All philosophical absolutes and certainties are substitutes for revelation – the theologian's alleged point of departure but in fact all that he needs for his conclusion. Theology, too, starts from the belief that the truth is there, given to us; the intellectual effort it involves consists not in wrestling with reality to break down its resistance, but in assimilating the true content of something that is already there in its entirety, waiting for us.

The crucial, historically fundamental expression of secular revelation was Descartes's *cogito*: the attempt to question all that seemed obvious, all that was traditionally assumed as certain. It was constructed in such a way that the very act of questioning, the act of destruction, was complete only when the new certainty – the consciousness of one's own mental processes – was established. Descartes knew that questioning must have an end, in both senses of the word; it would have been meaningless for him if it did not reach a stopping-point – a point where questioning was no longer possible; a point literally beyond question. He knew that if we decide to abandon shifting sands, it is in order to stand upon firm ground. The aim of questioning, for him, was to destroy questioning and bring it to a stop, just as the aim of movement was to reach a point where movement stops – a point of rest. The aim of uncovering the weak points of successive revelations was to reach a revelation without any weak points – a revelation that could not be questioned.

Philosophy after Descartes was largely a series of attempts to imitate this procedure. Philosophers took up the question in the form in which Descartes had posed it (which entailed assuming half of his answer as well), and their persistent attempts to modify and reformulate the *cogito* lasted until well into this century. The course of European idealism in particular brings into relief a feature of the Cartesian revelation which it shares with all others, namely the fact that its starting-point is also its conclusion. For since the consciousness of one's thought processes is the ultimate cognitive given, we cannot get at any reality that lies beyond those thought-processes; their reality is the only reality. Or, as Gilson put it, since an immanent world is what we start with, an immanent world is also what we end up with. Which is hardly surprising: the nature of the reality we perceive will obviously depend on the nature of the data at our disposal – those ultimate data from which we go about trying to reconstruct it – and to privilege certain kinds of data by declaring them ultimate is to deny reality to anything that cannot in some way be reduced to them. Thus if the immanent world is our cognitive absolute, it is also the only world accessible to our cognition – just as Spinoza's *causa sui*, being the starting-point of thought, is also, inevitably, its conclusion, for it is the only world whose reality can be defended. Similarly, those who consider the material objects of everyday life as the absolute givens are forced to conclude that these are the only possible data, and the reality constructed from them the only possible reality; while those for whom sensory perception constitutes the only absolute given will construct their reality exclusively from their perceptions. The absolute given which forms the starting point of the philosophical thought process predetermines all the rest: once we stand upon an absolute, that is where we stay; we cannot progress beyond it. All further movement is an illusion: we can only run in place, like a squirrel on a treadmill.

And yet there remains, at the heart of philosophy, an incurable nostalgia for revelation, a constant, ever-present longing for the ultimate and unquestionable. Taine's positivism sought it in an "ultimate law" of reality which reveals the unity of the world; an "eternal axiom" to which all our knowledge can ultimately be reduced. Phenomenology aspired above all to get at the reality which is "given" in the final and ultimate sense; and any reality "given" in this absolute sense could only be an immanent reality. In this light, the idealism of Husserl's later works seems a natural consequence of the internal logic of a doctrine originally intended to provide, chief among other things, a way out of subjectivism. Husserl's case clearly illustrates the contradiction inherent in any analogous quest for revelation. If we say that the ultimate data of reality can only be immanent and want to suspend judgment about transcendent reality, giving it what Husserl called a "cognitive zero index," we need a coherent concept of transcendence in order to constitute those data; but the concept of transcendence can only come from that natural, pre-critical cognitive stance whose results we want to ignore, or "put into parentheses." The initial principle – the principle whereby pure phenomena were endowed with ultimate status – cannot even be formulated without the aid of a concept drawn from outside the realm of pure phenomena; in other words, its formulation requires data from the realm of natural knowledge. Thus Husserl's cognitive absolute turned out to be weighed down by the same required ballast of non-absolute knowledge as the Cartesian *cogito* – an assumption made by an imaginary mind that is no more than distilled intellectual substance, entirely independent of all content that experience and acquired knowledge may have deposited in it. The act of questioning presupposed the object questioned, and the formulation of the principle contradicted the principle: the very thought act wherein transcendent reality is relegated to the Husserlian "parentheses" presupposes that transcendent reality *is* a cognitive given, however many "*distinguo*"s we attach to the word "datum." Thus an absolute which cannot be defined without a simultaneous definition of its opposite reveals itself as an imaginary absolute – a fiction.

Modern positivism also succumbed, at least initially, to the temptation to pursue the cognitive absolute. Moritz Schlick's conferral of absolute status on empirical statements was just another variant of an operation performed in countless doctrines before him, in the hope that it would provide a secular substitute for revelation.

The problem of revelation is a problem about the existence of ultimate data, but it is also a problem about the extent to which conceptual thought is able to formulate and understand such data. It involves, in other words, the problem of mystery; and this, too, like the problem of revelation, is a problem that modern philosophy inherited from theology. In its modern form, the problem of mystery is a problem about the limits of rationalism: about whether and to what extent certain basic components of cognition, or of reality itself, are discursive. Questions raised by personalist doctrines about the non-communicable nature of personality are the same questions, carried over into the human sphere, that theology asked about divinity; far from attacking theology, personalism in its metaphysical guise – the monadology of the human – appropriated theology's problems. But here, again, it does not necessarily follow that these problems were illusory: the question of the discursiveness of that indivisible whole which is the human personality is a real question. The word "persona" itself, in its ancient sense of "mask," presented a very real difficulty, one with which philosophers are still grappling. It is most often resolved by the simple expedient of saying that personality is inexpressible; this, however, even if it is true, is no more helpful than saying that God is a mystery unfathomable to the minds of mortals.

The problem of the relation between reason and faith also has its modern formulations. We come up against it whenever think about the extent to which experience and rational reflection can contribute simultaneously to the resolution of cognitive conflicts, or about the extent to which unverifiable beliefs contribute to our vision of the world. We return to it whenever we reflect about how to deal with facts that conflict with our accepted system of beliefs about the world – that coherent body of general assumptions which underlies our understanding of the totality of our past experience: may we ignore them, and if so to what extent? or should we try to fit them, or force them, into our system of beliefs, even if this involves imposing an artificial interpretation on them? We dispute about it whenever we dispute about the unverifiable assumptions made by the empirical sciences, or about the existence of privileged criteria for deciding between conflicting sets of experiences. All these problems contain a large theological heritage; they are they daily bread of scientific thinking, yet they have much in common with the problems which arose when revelation was the skeleton around which the totality of our knowledge was organized into a coherent "system." And at their root lies a familiar conflict: a conflict between the same two opposing tendencies which have emerged in almost all the problems we have discussed here. On the one hand there is the monist or integrationist tendency, which aspires (in its extreme form) to encompass the universe in a single formula, or at least discover one leading principle which would explain all of reality; on the other there is the pluralist tendency, which is not overly concerned with the coherence of our knowledge and harbors no ambitions to build a forest out of the individual trees, but prefers to accept each separate fact as an absolute, even if some of those facts conflict with one another. William James was the most radical exponent of the latter view, maintaining that we should accept facts one by one, as they come, without getting into a panic if they appear to conflict, and seeing no reason for despair in our inability to find a general principle or law that would encompass them all. We have, he said, no grounds for supposing *a priori* that some fundamental iron law governs every nook and cranny of the universe and all that takes place in it; we are perfectly entitled to observe that different things happen in different ways, and to proceed from this observation to the view that any attempt to reduce their plurality to a unity would be vain and artificial. We should accept each fact as its own explanation; our store of general knowledge about the world should adapt flexibly to every new fact and circumstance. And if successive experiences cause the world to crumble before our eyes like a disintegrating jumble of ill-fitting, unconnected fragments hastily thrown together, it is the world that is to blame, for that is simply what the world is like: random, lawless and disorganized, full of chaos and chance, more like a junk heap than a library where everything has its place, indexed and catalogued and fitted into the whole scheme of things.

And yet the monist obsession – the insistent attempt to order the world according to a single principle, the pursuit of that one magic formula which would explain reality and make it transparent, the quest for the philosopher's stone – has proved more enduring than all the vicissitudes of our intellectual development. This is in some measure because philosophy itself naturally favors such monarchist leanings: it likes to believe that successive eras of great scientific discovery bring us ever closer to an ordered world, gradually unveiling principles of increasing generality – subsuming principles of which those known to us are merely individual instances. Ever since it began to aspire to the name of a scientific discipline, philosophy has looked to science to bear witness to its claims. When it attempts to shake off its monist aspirations, it turns around and becomes science's accuser, denouncing its pretensions and claiming that a scientific ordering of the world is not a reflection of how the world really is, but merely of how our own brains are organized.

All the above examples – which are just that: examples merely, proferred in an attempt to justify theology not by a systematic analysis of its structure but rather through illustration – are drawn from the concerns of speculative scholastic theology. But the riches of mystical theology, too, have been preserved in modern thought, in all their splendor. They are particularly apparent in four areas of modern philosophy: the practical interpretation of knowledge; dialectics; integral theories of the world; and theories dealing with the substantial nature of ultimate reality.

The first of these areas is the most notable, for mystics were pioneers in the pragmatic approach to cognition. Since (they reasoned) the properties of the absolute elude linguistic capture, the human language being geared to describing finite things, our knowledge of God can only be practical. It does not, strictly speaking, tell us anything about what He is really like; it tells us only how best to worship Him and how we may approach His greatness through self-renunciation. But this knowledge is not merely a list of instructions we must memorize before carrying them out: it is both the command and its fulfillment. Reason does not precede the will, but contains it: the act of will is also an act of understanding. Thus our knowledge of God is exactly as great as the amount of love we give Him.

The practical interpretation of knowledge, hardly dated since it was taken up by the first pragmatists, can be seen as a sort of general summing-up of the mystical program: let us put aside questions about the world "in itself" and treat scientific theories as practical guidelines for our behavior in particular circumstances. Pragmatism stands in opposition to realistic epistemologies just as mystical theology stood in opposition to speculative theology; it rejects pointless questions about how things really are and prefers to ask how we should act.

The second heir and guardian of mystical theology's estate is dialectics. The mystics, seeing that all attempts to capture the absolute with the aid of the ordinary concepts at our disposal led to contradictions, became masters of an intellectual strategy that proceeds by thesis and antithesis: to say that no categories of human language can apply to God is to say that they *all* apply to Him, each time we speak about Him. Consequently, God simultaneously both is and is not; He is both everything and nothing, maximum and minimum, affirmation and negation. But mystical texts also prefigure, and often contain fully formed, the idea of alienation and of its overcoming, and of the evolution of the world as a negation which entails its own contradiction. Eriugena's vision of the world contains almost the full skeleton of dialectical logic: the world, as an emanation of God, is alienated from its source and by its finiteness negates it, but at the same time strives to return to it and identify with it by overcoming itself. Moreover, in mystical theology, as in Hegel's logic, the concept of alienation need not be entirely negative: the absolute sends out its theophanies because such is its essential nature, and then re-absorbs them, and is somehow enriched by this process. Similarly, original sin and man's fall may be seen as a necessary stage on way to future happiness, made certain by the sacrifice of the Redeemer. *"O felix culpa quae talem ac tantum meruit habere redemptorem,"* says the medieval song: O blessed sin which has merited such a Savior. When writings in the philosophy of history talk of progress fulfilling itself through its "negative side," or of alienation as something we are subjected to in order that we might be enriched by overcoming it, it is echoing the same ideas.

Third on the list of the contributions of mystical theology to modern thought are integral theories of existence. Gestalt theory exists well-nigh fully fledged in mystical texts (although in a much more general form, closer, in terms of its modern equivalent, to the Bergsonian approach than to the methodology of Gestalt theorists): only the absolute enjoys a truly independent existence, and all differences between individual things are either manifestations of a sort of pathological estrangement, which will disappear when the world returns to the bosom of the absolute, or the products of our distorting imagination, which wants to impose on an indivisible unity a principle of multiplicity and differentiation that is alien to it.

Lastly there is the issue of the substantiality of the absolute: the problem of whether and how the concept of substance can be applied to it. This, too, was problem of mystical theology which blossomed afresh in the twentieth century. Does ultimate reality – the primary "stuff" of existence – have substance? Or is its substantiality an epiphenomenon, given to and possibly even shaped by our cognitive faculties, while metaphysical primacy lies elsewhere – in events, relations or acts? These questions have an obvious theological heritage. In the twentieth century, a number of otherwise quite dissimilar doctrines, radically different in origins, aims and assumptions, rejected substance as metaphysically primary in favor of various principles traditionally considered as attributes of substance. Giovanni Gentile's actualism, Russell and Whitehead's theory of events and Natorp's theory of relations, to name just three, all meet at this one point – a point very distant from the genealogy of each, and moreover one of which all three may well have been entirely unconscious, and would have considered quite alien to their thought. But then we all have spiritual ancestors whose portraits we would not care to hang in the family dining room, and whose existence we reluctantly recall only when forced to do so by the malicious gossip of neighbors.

So far this list has been no more than a loose collection of examples with a common purpose: to show that many of the issues which are alive and important in philosophy today, in both its "technical" and its popular forms (the concerns of the latter always echoing those of the former) and across a wide and varied spectrum of philosophical doctrines, are continuations of old theological controversies, or rather new (and somewhat more sophisticated) versions of problems familiar from the history of theology. It would be useful, however, to be able to give a systematic description of the conflicting views of the world described here; to this end, guided by that same instinct which lies at the root of the human mind's monist longings and gives birth to monist interpretations of reality, I will try to subsume them under an ordering principle.

Most of the above examples have revealed themselves as springing from a single basic opposition within philosophy; each is a specific variant or manifestation of it. Thus they have illustrated attitudes for or against eschatology – i.e., for or against ordering the events of our daily lives by reference to an absolute which will in time be realized; for or against theodicy – i.e., for or against looking to the absolute for a justification for every instance of evil in the world; for or against interpreting man in terms of grace (rather than in terms of nature) – i.e., for or against attributing to the absolute the responsibility for our actions; for or against revelation – i.e., for or against seeking an ultimate, unquestionable cognitive principle as an infallible foundation of knowledge; for or against a monist theory of cognition – i.e., for or against aspiring to intellectual control over reality through a set of ultimate, fundamental laws that explain everything; for or against a totalistic interpretation of the world – i.e., for or against a view of the world where everything acquires meaning by reference to the absolute, of which it is a manifestation, a part or an instance. In short, for or against the hope that there is a cognitive or metaphysical absolute; for or against seeking absolute foundations.

I have tried to capture the nature of this conflict by presenting it as a clash of two fundamental tendencies which philosophy seeks to express in discursive form. The thought that the human individual is entirely responsible for himself, "indefinable" and irreducible, can inspire fear, and give rise to a need to break through one's isolation and seek firm moorings in absolute reality: to annihilate one's individual self by defining and explaining it through something beyond it. The opposing tendency is to affirm the irreducibility of the individual and reject all arguments which try to justify individual existence through something else: to deny that immobility is the true nature of something which is mobile, and refuse the prospect of an absolute, ultimate reality.

To what peculiarities of human nature (to resort to this much-abused phrase) are we to attribute the attraction of the ultimate? Why do we have this irresistible yearning for the absolute, the hope of finding some supreme principle which will explain the world and assume responsibility for our existence, our behavior and our thought?

A number of different theories have been advanced to explain our yearning for self-definition – or perhaps simply our yearning for non-existence – through an absolute that lies beyond us. Theologians have tried to convince us that our Creator instilled in us a natural propensity to gravitate towards Him, and that this propensity governs human thought; they call it our natural religious feeling. This is a case of trying to justify a doctrine through an appeal to facts which can be accepted only if we first accept the doctrine they are meant to support. Moreover, it is hard to see what grounds there could be for confining within the label of "religious feeling" a phenomenon that can just as easily occur in areas quite unconnected with the realm of what we are wont, both in science and in everyday life, to call religion. Before we set about defining *homo religiosus*, we would do well to define religion; otherwise we risk committing the (common enough) error of defining religion in terms of religious feeling and religious feeling in terms which presuppose a definition of religion. But it is simpler to treat religion, in all its historical forms, as a particular instance of a much wider phenomenon.

The theological explanation disposed of, there are still plenty of others to choose from. Unfortunately, they are all various ways of expressing the same idea; furthermore, all are so dubious that they can hardly be called explanatory in any strict sense. Let us look at four such attempts.

The first, formulated by Freud but abandoned by most Freudians, is the theory of the death-wish. This says that all living things suffer from a nostalgia for a return to a non-organic state; there is a natural instinct to reduce tensions and ultimately to eliminate them altogether, which entails the end of all organic processes. The death-wish is thus opposed to the libido, and may also lie at the root of the efforts of the human mind to find principles which would reduce individual existence to some impersonal form of being.

The second such theory is familiar in a number of versions: methodological (Ockham), theological (Malebranche) and physical (De Maupertuis); Avenarius and the empirio-critics went on to develop it in detail as a principle of economy. In its broadest, metaphysical form, it says that everything in nature, including the processes of human thought and the behavior of all organisms, operates according to a principle of least effort and simplest means. Freud's death-wish theory may be seen as a specific instance of this principle, applied to the organic world; and seen as a law according to which everything naturally tends towards reducing tensions and differences, the principle of economy also accounts for the instinct to seek monist interpretations of reality, and for that propensity of the human mind to reduce individuals to an undifferentiated absolute.

Third comes the principle of simplification as formulated by Gestalt theory. According to this principle, all Gestalt systems or entities have an innate tendency to assume the simplest possible form: the most regular, the most symmetrical and the least differentiated. This, too, is a variation on the principle of economy, and can serve similar purposes.

The fourth and last example is Sartre's principle that "being-for-itself," i.e., human existence – defined as pure negativity in relation to the rest of the world, and thus as a form of freedom, but only a negative freedom, understood as privation – suffers from a constant and contradictory longing to become "being-in-itself": it wants to free itself from the nothingness which plagues it, but cannot, for nothingness, or freedom, is also what defines it. Thus the desire to annihilate nothingness and become part of the world "in-itself" is a desire to annihilate oneself as an individual existence, and hence to cease to exist.

We can see that each of these four theories is merely a translation of the same idea into a different language. All four involve a variety of difficulties and elicit numerous doubts. Strictly speaking, they are all attempts to formulate a philosophical generalization of the principle of increasing entropy (Wlodzimierz Szewczuk, in his penetrating analysis of Gestalt psychology[1], remarks on the similarities between the principle of increasing entropy and the "pregnancy principle" formulated by Wertheimer and Köhler). Both the theory of the death-wish and the principle of economy are, like the other two variations discussed, attempts to raise (or some might prefer to say to lower) the principle of increasing entropy to the dignified status of a universal metaphysical law, applicable not only to all forms of energy, both known and hypothetical, but

---

1   Szewczuk, *Wlodzimierz, Teoria postaci i psychologia postaci* (*Gestalt Theory and Gestalt Psychology*), Kraków, 1951.

also to human behavior, emotions and reasoning. If we adopted such a principle, if we recognized the supreme rule of a universal tendency to reduce tensions, asymmetries and differences, the whole history of philosophy could be interpreted through it; all those expressions of nostalgia for an absolute which have filled the life of philosophy over the centuries would be no more than instances of this principle in operation. The content of philosophical enquiry would be entirely deducible from this one feature which the human mind shares with all other forms of energy; every metaphysical doctrine would be explained and accounted for by the metabolic processes of the human brain, and the persistent bond between conservatism as a philosophical attitude and conservatism as a feature of the world – that inertia of collective life which we call reaction – would also be just another manifestation of the workings of this principle.

But if such a principle really did govern our thinking, then that eternal conflict which lies at the heart of philosophy – the conflict between the quest for the absolute and the flight from it, between the fear of one's individual self and the fear of losing it in the very principle in which we place our hopes of a foundation – could not have arisen. It would not exist. And yet not only does it exist, but the whole history of philosophy can be arranged around it. The history of our entire intellectual culture could be described in terms of this fundamental conflict between two currents in human thought: the conservative current, which expresses the process of increasing entropy, and the current which expresses the process of increasing tension. It is present in all areas of human culture – in art, in philosophy, in custom; in every sphere of intellectual life it is this conflict that gives birth to the new, for new ideas arise from the constant need to question existing absolutes. And even though every new current of thought which tries to break free from accepted absolutes ends up by establishing its own, and each revolution ultimately becomes a conservative state, yet in time it always gives way to the next, and itself becomes an absolute to be questioned.

Can any intellectual method, even the most radical, escape this fate, resist the pull of inertia? History indicates that this is unlikely. The very hope of formulating such a method would be incoherent, for it would be tantamount to a hope of finding the ultimate, absolute method – and thus a method which would contradict its own assumptions. The history of ancient skepticism is instructive in this regard: the approach whose premise was to question all dogmas and accepted truths, an approach which rejected even the name of "doctrine," was itself transformed into a dogma, rigid and barren, as immobile as the principles it wanted to question. No principle of universal questioning can escape the paradox of the liar.

Thus there are no known absolute, infinitely flexible methods impervious to the threat of petrification by history. Some methods, however, have shown themselves to be more enduring and less vulnerable to this threat than others. This is because they have managed, in spite of whatever dogmatic assumptions and beliefs in absolutes they may initially have contained, to develop tools of self-criticism. There are probably several methods which have succeeded, over time, in developing such tools; in the twentieth century alone, Marxism, phenomenology and psychoanalysis have all demonstrated this ability. To concede this is not, of course, to accept all the particular and mutually contradictory claims which these methods make; it is only to recognize their ability to overcome their own absolutes and seek out the hidden premises of their radicalism. That is what allows them to endure, not only as the temples of their believers but also as intellectual organisms capable of change. And although each of these doctrines contains a current of orthodoxy which is incapable of variation, and can only repeat its original claims in their original form, each has also spawned progeny that is capable of evolution and independent life. Other "great doctrines" of the twentieth century, like Bergson's philosophy, have never been able to go beyond their first stage; they remain in history as closed systems, finished and unalterable. They may have their worshippers, but they have no descendants.

The conflict between philosophies which want to question absolutes and philosophies which want to perpetuate them seems irresolvable, as ineradicable as the existence of the conservative and the radical current in all spheres of human life. It may be called the conflict between the priest and the jester. The philosophy of the priest and the philosophy of the jester have expressed the two basic currents of thought in almost every historical era. The priest is the guardian of the absolute; he sustains the cult of truths accepted by tradition as ultimate and unquestionable. The jester is the impertinent upstart who questions everything we accept as self-evident. He moves in good society but is not of it; he is an outsider. If he belonged to good society, he could at best be merely a purveyor of dinner-party scandal. In order to point out the unobviousness of its obviousnesses and the non-ultimacy of its ultimacies, he must be outside it, observing it from a distance; but if he is to be impertinent to it, and find out what it holds sacred, he must also frequent it. Georges Sorel considered philosophy's role as the jester when he was writing about the Encyclopedists, but here the word was used in a pejorative sense: the jester was merely the plaything of aristocrats. Philosophers have indeed played jester to monarchs, but their jesting contributed to earthquakes – precisely in its role as the play of jesters.

Priests and jesters cannot be reconciled; each would have to be trans-formed into the other. (Which does sometimes happen, although most often it is the jester who is transformed into the priest, as Socrates was transformed into Plato, rather than the other way around.) The jester's philosophy always has the same role: it reveals the shakiness of the seemingly unshakeable and casts doubt on the seemingly certain; it exposes the contradictions of the seemingly obvious, the self-evident, the incontrovertible; it ridicules accepted common sense and discovers truths in absurdities. In short, it assumes all the jester's daily chores, and with them the unavoidable risk of ridicule. The thoughts of the jester range over all conceivable extremes, according to time and circumstance; for yesterday's paradoxes are today's sacred truths, and absolutes on the equator can be blasphemies in the polar regions. The attitude of the jester is a constant effort of reflection on the possible truth content of opposing ideas. It is thus dialectical by nature: it wants to overcome what is there simply because it is there. It flows not from contrariness but rather from a mistrust of all that is established. In a world where it seems that every-thing has already happened, the jester represents the movement of the imagination. Thus he is defined partly by the resistance he must over-come: as Fichte observed, thought cannot proceed without obstacles to overcome, just as a car cannot start on ice or an airplane take off in a vac-uum.

For the same reason, philosophy cannot consist in pure reflection about itself or take place in the closed world of a monad; the subject and object of reflection cannot be identical, for no cognition could then take place. An act of cognition in which subject and object were identical would be a contradiction in terms: an act of immobility. Thus if philoso-phy undermines absolutes, if it denies that all of reality can be reduced to a single principle and affirms the pluralism of things and their non-reducibility, and hence also human individuality, it does not do so because it is a monadology and conceives of the individual as a self-suf-ficient atom. It does so because individuality can be affirmed only in opposition to the rest of the world and through its relations to it – rela-tions of dependence, responsibility and resistance.

A philosophy which rejects absolutes and prospects of finality is nec-essarily incomplete. It cannot be a homogeneous, closed and perfectly consistent whole, for it lacks foundations and does not want a roof; its aim is not to become a complete structure, but to undermine existing foundations and rip off the roofs of existing structures. It is the intellec-tual equivalent of a person who is by nature indiscreet and disrespectful, and it possesses all the faults and virtues typical of such people. For this reason the conflict between the philosophy of the jester and that of the priest at times resembles a clash between the insufferable symptoms of adolescence and the insufferable symptoms of senile dementia – with the difference that only the first of these are curable.

The argument up to this point, attempting as it does to explain a wealth of facts by a single ordering principle, may easily be suspected of succumbing to the monist temptation which it is at such pains to criticize. But the attempt to order facts is not itself necessarily inconsistent with an anti-absolutist philosophy: order may be the slogan both of the police and of revolution. It is only a particular kind of ordering that is inconsistent with anti-absolutism: one that wants to subsume the totality of existing and possible worlds under one unifying principle, and draws its satisfaction from the consciousness of being ultimate, exhaustive and all-encompassing. The police ideal is the order of an exhaustive card-catalogue; the philosophical ideal is the order of an active imagination.

Both priest and jester commit violence upon the mind, the one by the confining collar of his catechism, the other by his stabbing pricks of ridicule. There are more priests than jesters at a king's court, just as there are more policemen than artists in his realm. This is probably as it must be; it seems natural and inevitable that exponents of mythologies should outweigh the critics of mythologies. Such a distribution of power reflects the strength of the idea of one world of things, greater than that of the idea of a multiplicity of possible worlds. This, too, is natural: it is easier to sink than to soar upwards. All this is evident when we observe the astonishing speed with which new mythologies rush in to replace those which have faded away. In the intellectual life of societies in which the mechanisms that had sustained traditional beliefs have rusted over, fresh myths proliferate like mushrooms. Often they flow from technological progress and scientific discoveries. Thousands of people seem to imagine that some kindly inhabitants of other planets will resolve the difficulties the human race has not been able to cope with; others place their hopes for the resolution of all social conflicts in the word "cybernetics." A hail of gods rains down at the funeral of the one surviving god; the godless have their saints and blasphemers build temples. Perhaps the longing for absolutes and the need to reduce tensions must be as strong as it is – incomparably more widespread than the urge to increase tensions – if the whole structure is not to be blown sky high. If so, then the priests have their *raison d'être*. But that is no reason to want to join their company.

*   *   *

The priesthood is not merely a cult of the past seen from today's perspective. It is also the past itself, enduring in unchanged form: a way in which the past continues beyond itself. Thus it is not only a certain intellectual attitude towards the world, but also a form of existence: the persistence of a reality which is no longer there. The attitude of the jester is the opposite: here it is not the past but the possible – the potential future – that is realized before it comes into existence. For our reflections about existence also exist: they are part of the world, no less than anything else that exists in it.

*　　*　　*

This author declares himself in favor of the jester's philosophy: the attitude of skepticism and suspicion towards absolutes of any kind. This choice is not arrived at by a consideration of arguments for and against; choices in such matters tend to be value-laden. It rests on the belief that the attitude of the jester, while not without its dangers and absurdities, contains the possibility of expressing values which are not purely intellectual ones. To adopt this attitude is to adopt a view of the world which holds out a hopeful but difficult prospect: that of a gradual and laborious process of working out, in our interactions, how to reconcile those elements of human thought and behavior which are hardest to reconcile: how to achieve goodness without universal indulgence, courage without fanaticism, intelligence without disenchantment and hope without blindness. All other fruits of philosophical thinking are of little worth.

Translated by Agnieszka Kolakowska

Heresy[1]

1. *The Original and the New Testament Sense of Heresy.* The Greek word
haireo means "to take"; in med. *haireomai* – "to take for oneself" or " to
choose." The word *hairesis* means a choice, an act of choosing or an object
of choice. The New Testament speaks on various occasions of "heresy,"
meaning a sect or a faction; and it mentions the "heresies" of the
Sadducees, the Pharisees, and the Nazarenes (*Acts*, 5:17; 24:5; 26:5). That
the word even then was not neutral and had a pejorative meaning we
may gather from the fact that St. Paul, in his apology before the authorities, speaks of his way which "they call" heresy (*Acts*, 24:14; cf. *Acts*,
28:22), and in *1 Cor.*, 11:19, he mentions " heresies" – meaning sects or
splits – among his followers (cf. *Gal.*, 5:20). Still, what the word refers to
is a particular religious group, rather than an erroneous doctrine, even
though St. Peter speaks of false prophets and false teachers who bring
heresies among the people (*2 Pet.*, 2:1); this may mean both " splits" and,
closer to the modern sense, doctrinal errors.

2. *The Roman Church's Definition.* It should be noted that references
both to the original and to the New Testament senses ("choice" and
"sect") have never been entirely forgotten in Christian teaching, and are
preserved in part in the theological background of the modern concept.
Even in everyday speech we often speak of "heresy," meaning not necessarily the condemnable doctrine itself, but a sectarian movement professing this doctrine. As to the etymological sense of the word "heresy,"
it is far from irrelevant to the use of the word in Christian theology. To
use one's own will alone – and thus make a choice of one's own, without
being guided by God and the Church – amounts to choosing evil, both
in moral and in doctrinal matters. If I make a choice, I am claiming the

---

1 "Heresy," written in English, published in Italian as "Eresia," in: *Enciclopedia*,
   Vol. 5, Giulio Einaudi editore, Torino 1978.

superiority of my personal judgment; I choose my will against God's will. Considering the corruption of our will, purely human choice in matters of faith is an option chosen in error and not an act of selecting which could be right or wrong, depending on the circumstances. From this standpoint it seems theologically valid that an act of human choice in the realm of faith inevitably results in heresy, and that heresy is a doctrine chosen or affirmed by the human will (*humano sensu electa*). This was pointed out by St. Jerome, St. Augustine, and many later writers. So far, the etymology has not died out in the modern use of the word "heresy."

The official definition of heresy in the *Codex Iuris Canonici* (1325, par. 2) was, significantly, the definition of a heretic, not of a heretical statement. It involved the denial of, or doubt about, any truth of the divine faith provided 1) that the person who denies or doubts is baptized; 2) that he claims to be a Christian, and 3) that he persists in his error. (*Post receptum baptismum si quis, nomen retinens christianum, pertinaciter aliquam ex veritatibus fide divina et catholica credendis denegat aut de ea dubitat, haereticus; si a fide christiana totaliter recedit, apostata; si denique subesse renuit Summo Pontifici aut cum membris Ecclesiae ei subiectis communicare recusat, schismaticus est*).

The third point is important because it indicates that not everybody who has uttered a heretical statement is to be automatically considered a heretic. A person who is potentially a heretic should be obstinate and defend the wrong idea, authoritative definitions and prohibitions notwithstanding. It is repeatedly stressed in the Catholic literature that heretics *resistunt contumaciter, emendare nolent, defensere persistent*, etc. A person might have uttered a heretical statement in ignorance, but if he retracts it immediately upon being admonished, he is not stigmatized as a heretic. He might have been induced by other people without his own *hubris* being involved (people who *non sua audacia sed aliena seducuntur in errorem* are not heretics). Thus Fénélon's book, *Explications des Maximes des Saints*, was condemned in Innocent XII's *Breve cum Ailos ad Apostolatus* (1699). However, since the author immediately bowed to the Papal verdict and did not try to stick to his doctrine, he was not condemned personally. Meister Eckhart is not usually spoken of as a heretic, but in John XXII's constitution, *In argo dominico* (1329), a number of his statements were explicitly described as heretical (this happened after the author's death).

As to points 1 and 2 above, it is important to the definition of a heretic that he wants to remain within the creed (and quite often within the Church community as well) in regard to which he was condemned as a heretic. A heretic, both in the historian's eyes and in Christian teaching, is someone who appeals to the same canon as the orthodoxy, but interprets this canon in a different manner; more often than not, he does not want to be an innovator, but to restore the original divine message, and thus he frequently accuses the orthodox of heresy. If he is labeled a heretic, rather than his adversaries, it is because he has been defeated, or is in the minority, or else because the orthodox have succeeded in keeping the continuity of the religious body intact. Those who either have never accepted the original canon or reject it altogether – unlike those who claim that they know better how to interpret it – are pagans, atheists, or apostates, but not heretics. This distinction is historically important because the way the Church deals with enemies "from within" is different from how it copes with its external foes. In fact, heretics have always been a much greater danger to the Church than Jews, pagans, apostates or libertines and, consequently, they have been dealt with more severely. Apostasies reduce the numerical strength of the religious body, whereas heresies threaten its unity. In this respect, all ideological organisms, both Churches and political movements, show the same instinctive and easily understood pattern of reaction.

3. *Heresy and Schism.* Heresy is to be distinguished from schism, which is a deliberate separation from the organism of the true Church (i.e., from any Church claiming to be the only successor of the Apostolic Church, and the only bearer of truth). A heretic need not want a schism; indeed, in most cases he wants to improve or to reform the existing body by restoring it to its original purity. Conversely, the act of separation may involve no departure from orthodox doctrine; it may be based on disagreements about non-dogmatic issues. Thus it may be argued that the Donatists in the 4th century were schismatics rather than heretics when they rejected the validity of the sacraments conferred by those priests who had surrendered to the pagan authorities under Diocletian; still less did the break with Rome by Henry VIII of England involve any doctrinal separation. On the other hand, it is difficult to imagine how a schism in the Catholic Church could not be, at least in modern times, a heresy as well, granted that it has to defy, even if only implicitly, the indisputable and supreme authority of the Pope – such an authority having been established as a part of the official doctrine. And conversely, whoever is branded a heretic by the Church authorities is separated from the unity of the body and, on the assumption that this separation resulted from his evil will (and not from the verdict of the Church), the act of accepting and defending a heresy becomes *eo ipso* an act of schism ("apostasy," meaning the open rejection of Christian teaching; the word is used mostly for acts of individual defection from the Church, while "schism" denotes, rather, a collective split). Although the sin of disobedience, in

Catholic terms, has to be distinguished from the sin of professing a false doctrine, the latter involves the former (if the heretic is obstinate, *pertinax* – but this is included in the definition of a heretic), and the former implies the denial of orthodox teaching, at least on the point concerning Papal authority.

4. *The Historian's Definition.* A historian cannot accept the definition of heresy accepted in the Roman (or any other) Church, otherwise he would be assuming the viewpoint of a particular body, and the teaching of this body would be decisive in identifying historical facts. This is a crucial point in answering the question of how far the historian's own beliefs are relevant to his tasks as a historian. If he is willing to admit, for instance, that the five statements attributed to Jansenius, and condemned as heretical by Innocent X in 1653 in the bull *Cum Occasione*, are indeed heretical, in the sense that they contradict Scripture, he is using the Catholic interpretation of the Bible and has to admit it as valid in identifying and classifying historical events. But if he wants to set aside from historical inquiry his personal beliefs or disbeliefs, his definition of heresy would be: heresy (or a heretic) is what (or who) was defined as such by the Church authorities. This is the only operative definition, and it implies that the historian accepts as binding all the decisions of all the ecclesiastical bodies. The historian assumes that heresy does not originate in a departure from orthodox teaching, but is established by its having been condemned. To a historian, heresy is not only a doctrinal, but also an institutional fact.

The same consideration is valid in defining who is a heretic. In the history of the Roman Church, it is always particular people in specific situations that are condemned, rather than doctrinal statements alone. Among many hundreds of heretical statements officially condemned throughout the history of the Church, many can be found, even though not phrased exactly the same, in the writings of one or another of the great teachers of Christianity. This is, for instance, the case with propositions concerning divine grace and the mystical union. Thus the statements and recommendations concerning the total passivity of the human soul in moments of mystical union were condemned in several ways in Innocent XI's bull *Coelestis Pastors*. They were formulated, in this case, by Miguel de Molinos. The same idea of total passivity can be found in the writings of St. John of the Cross. St. John may be suspected of heresy on one more point as well: he denied that human natural knowledge could reach God, or that a cognitive way from creatures to God is possible. The Church, in the first Vatican Council (among others), repeatedly condemned such a denial. In such cases the chronology does not matter from the Church's standpoint since a certain statement is supposed to be heretical by its content alone (confronted with Holy Scripture), and thus it has always been heretical, even though it might not have been explicitly condemned as such in official documents earlier on. To the Church, not surprisingly, a statement does not become heretical as a result of a condemnation – its heretical character is intrinsic, not historical. Indeed, the opposite view, implying an evolution or changes in dogma, was itself condemned as a modernist heresy. This may have produced embarrassing situations. For example, we know that St. Albert, St. Bonaventure, and St. Thomas, among others, clearly denied the theory of the Immaculate Conception of the Virgin Mary. This was confirmed in the Council of Trent and in Pius IX's bull *Ineffabilis Deus* of 1854. Of course, neither for the Church nor for historians may such cases justify the label "heretic" applying to St. Thomas or to St. John of the Cross if we remember the above mentioned restrictions imposed on the definition of heretic.

5. *Orthodoxy and Heresy: The Great Saint and the Great Heretic.* One more difference between the standpoint of a historian and that of a believer needs stressing. For both, heresy is a function of orthodoxy, and has to be defined as relative to it. However, to a historian, the converse relation is valid too. Historically, orthodoxy is formed as a function of heresy. Orthodoxy – the accepted truth – is established and articulated against a background of heresy. Paradoxically, more often than not dogmas are crystallized in the struggle against their rejection. The symmetry is not perfect, though. Once a dogma has been clearly defined, to deny it openly is, of course, to incur the stigma of heresy. When Luther explicitly defended some of John Huss's views that had been condemned by the Council of Constance, he challenged a well-established orthodox position. Yet, ever since the early Christological controversies, successive dogmas took shape as a result of theological struggles, and thus they appeared as responses to anti-dogmas – orthodoxy and heresy emerged together. Thus, for example, the radical wing of the Franciscan order in the 13th and 14th centuries, the so-called Spirituals or, later, the Fraticelli, maintained total poverty as a necessary condition of the perfect life, on the model, they claimed, of Christ and the Apostles. After this claim had been condemned under Clement V and John XXII (the Franciscan ideal of total poverty having been previously satisfied by a clever decision of Pope Nicholas III, who declared all the order's possessions to be the property of the Church), it became in fact heretical, and the orthodox view emerged out of this heresy. The periods of great struggles against heresies were, at the same time, the periods when major elements of the

Catholic teaching were effectively formed. Thus the orthodox doctrine of the Holy Trinity emerged in the 4-5th centuries in the battles against Arians, Monophysites, Nestorians, Sabellians, etc. The Catholic doctrine of grace and justification took its definitive shape (so far) under the pressure of the Reformation and its various offshoots. The history of dogmas and the history of heresies are aspects of one and the same process where the question of priority is usually blurred or insoluble.

This is why to a historian (at least to a historian who rejects determinist metaphysics) there is nothing *a priori* obvious in the fact that a certain idea became heretical, or that certain Christian reformers were destined to be condemned. Acts of condemnation or beatification depended largely on contingent historical circumstances. It might have been the case that God's hand was guiding this process, but the historian is not in a position to prove it. Conversely, in the biographies of many great saints and doctors, we find moments of suspension or hesitation in history: we suspect that they could have become great heretics rather than great teachers of orthodoxy, and that some insignificant (in our eyes) factors pushed them in one direction rather than the opposite. Again, the contingencies of history seem to have been at work in both results: it is fair to say that if some great heretics were indeed reformers who failed, so some great saints were fairly near to heretics. This could have happened with St. Francis, St. Ignatius of Loyola, or St. John of the Cross. This is quite understandable: many of the great saints were reformers, innovators, critics, and people of extraordinary moral and intellectual strength and courage. They defied their religious milieu and very often had to cope with strong resistance from the conservative elements in the Church. They could have failed, as could all people, but they did not, and Christianity owes its survival to the courage and obstinacy of such titanic figures within its history. There is between great heretics and great saints a category of cases that are still dubious, existing in permanent suspension or doctrinal limbo, and sharing some properties of both. Origen, John Scotus Eriugena, Meister Eckhart, Savonarola, Erasmus of Rotterdam – all belong to this category for different reasons: actual condemnations of some of their statements, condemnations of their persons, books on the Index, their doctrine being placed under suspicion, etc. It is not clear how we ought to treat such a great teacher as Tertullian who later in his life joined the Montanist sect. Recently, Teillhard de Chardin seems to have achieved this very sort of ambiguous position.

6. *The Roman Church as the Privileged Case in the Study of Heresies.* That the concept of heresy is naturally associated, in the historian's mind, with the history of the Roman Church, is accounted for by the very content of this concept as defined above. The history of all the great religions

(and of many small sects as well) abounds in doctrinal quarrels, splits, and mutual condemnations of squabbling factions. However, the Roman Church is indeed a privileged case. Once we accept, for the purposes of historical inquiry, that a heresy was a doctrine defined as heresy by the religious authorities, we immediately see that the more institutionalized a religious body, the better codified the procedure of condemning, and the better established the condemning tribunal, the more easily a doctrine or movement can be identified as heretical. Nowhere is the situation so clear, in this respect, as in the Roman Church, with its hierarchical structure and with the indisputable supreme authority that issues doctrinal verdicts. Protestant bodies are less structured and, consequently, usually lack a single authority to pinpoint and excommunicate dissidents.

This is likewise the case with Judaism and Islam. Was the messianic movement initiated by Sabbatai Tsvi in the 17th century a heresy within Judaism? We would probably say yes, because it was rejected and persecuted by rabbinical authorities. This is, however, an exceptionally uncontroversial case. In other cases the question is difficult to answer because of the status of rabbis, who are interpreters of law rather than guardians of dogma. If some of them enjoy any special authority, this is a result of custom, or of their personal merits, and not inherent in the institutional position. This is why it seems pointless to ask which, if any, of the contemporary trends in Judaism is heretical or orthodox (one might ask this question about various tendencies in Catholicism, at least now, but here we may expect that an authoritative judgment will be issued). Besides, the infrequency of heresy and of splits within Judaism may be explained in part by the fact that for centuries it has been a minority religion with clearly distinct cultural characteristics, so that the rebels or potential heretics could always express their opposition by joining one or another group in Christian society. Perhaps there is only one unquestionable and authenticated case of Jewish heresy – Christianity.

Certainly, among prominent Protestant writers, in the 16th and 17th centuries in particular, accusations of heresy addressed both to Catholics and to various radical sects are fairly frequent. Historians, however, feel naturally reluctant to identify on their own account some persons or ideas as heretical within a Protestant body. The lack of a single dogmatic authority makes it difficult or impossible, except for some extreme cases. Those radicals of the Reformation who openly and unambiguously rejected the very idea of the visible Church as both incompatible with Christ's message and harmful to salvation (like Sebastian Franck, Johannes Denck, Obbe Philips, Jacob Acontius, Dirk Coornhert) can probably be counted as heretics within the Protestant world. So may those who openly espoused the Unitarian (or Arian) view and rejected the divinity of Christ altogether (like most of the Polish Socinians and many Dutch liberal Christians).

We find sometimes, to be sure, small sects that tried to imitate the Roman order and to vie with or to surpass the Catholics in doctrinal and organizational rigidity. These were, however, insignificant, marginal groups, which as a rule barely survived their founders (as an example, we may cite the sect of the Labadists, which lasted for a few decades at the end of the 17th century). In the Roman Church we have few doubts about which idea is heretical. It should be mentioned nevertheless that the Church formally rejected many propositions without calling them heretical. In papal bulls and other official documents we find various adjectives, and these distinctions ought to be observed. A statement might be insolent, offensive to pious ears, false, impious, pernicious, scandalous, seditious, blasphemous, etc., without being plainly heretical.

7. *Suppressing a Heresy; Domesticating a Heresy.* There is no single way of dealing with a heresy. This depends on the danger it poses to the unity of the Church, on its real or potential strength, and on the authorities' strategic skills. Neither can any general rules be formulated as to the most efficient method of destroying heresy. A straight, head-on destructive response might be successful, yet it certainly is not always. The Cathars in the 12th and 13th centuries were practically annihilated by persecutions; the Hussites were not. The enormous effort employed by the Church in the first decade of the 20th century, under the pontificate of Pius X, to eradicate the Modernist movement ended with an apparent victory: heretical ideas seemed to have been uprooted within Catholic religiosity, their advocates silenced or rejected. It turns out, however, that this was a spurious success: the Modernist heresy was too strongly rooted among the educated classes to be stifled. It looked for various ways of expression, avoiding any direct defense of the condemned statements, but smuggling them in in somewhat altered forms. The Church sustained great losses as a result of its inability to tame it or to find for it a safe and controlled outlet. The victory turned into defeat. The Church, satisfied with its immutability, was gradually losing its intellectual influence. It turned the educated elites against itself and widened the gap between Christian tradition and modern civilization, instead of trying to reconcile them.

Jansenism was another example of a heresy that, for ecclesiastical and political reasons, was fought against with utmost bitterness and was to all appearances crushed, but in fact won. After all the intrigues, condemnations, and bulls, after the demolition of the Port Royal, etc., the followers of Jansenism were indeed intimidated into silence. Yet what may be called the Jansenist consciousness among the French intelligentsia and the lower clergy was by no means eradicated; it persisted in a strong religious subculture and played an important role in the French Revolution. The anti-Jansenist battle, seen from the contemporary perspective, was lost, as was the anti-modernist campaign.

Both cases – Jansenism in the 17th century and Modernism at the beginning of the 20th – are models of the Church's inability to use the weapons of domestication against heretics. In both cases the Church, instead of narrowing down the definition of heresy, destroying the most intransigent core and displaying charitableness towards the mass of the faithful, broadened the concept of the heretical trend (thus also broadening the battlefront) and included in it many people who were willing to remain faithful and obedient. Thus it enfeebled itself considerably by multiplying its enemies, and gave the heretics a broader field of maneuverability. In 1713, one became a Jansenist, and thus a heretic, by believing, for instance, that " there is no God and no religion where there is no charity" (statement 58 from the bull *Unigenitus* of Clement XI, condemning the errors of Pasquier Quensel). In 1907, one became a Modernist by saying that the sacrament of matrimony arose from the theological explanation of the doctrine of grace and sacraments (Decree *Lamentabili*, nr. 51), or by holding certain very specific views about the chronology of the New Testament texts.

It is worth adding that in the anti-Jansenist campaign it was the Jesuits who were urging the most severe measures, while in the anti-Modernist battle, the Jesuits' strategy was more cautious than that actually adopted by the Pope.

It is true nevertheless that if the strategy of an outright, intransigent attack against heresy risks reinforcing the opposition by extending the concept of the heresy under attack, the strategy of domestication generates dangers of its own.

The Church can domesticate a heresy by assimilating some of its elements and limiting their power so that they can be digested and made harmless. Needless to say, whether a given heresy can be domesticated at all depends not only on the Church's skill, but also on the nature of the movement and the persons involved. The natural inclinations of potential heretics might be of importance: some were simply ready to obey, some were rebellious. The ideal of poverty, which in some forms organized popular discontent and became the ideological slogan of a number of anti-Church movements in the Middle Ages, was successfully domesticated in the Franciscan movement (whose extremist faction was destroyed). Yet the founders of the order were obedient while Valdes was not. The Church assimilated and neutralized the ideal of poverty by approving the mendicant orders that were symbolically to incarnate, within Christianity, this aspect of the Evangelical legacy. By the intermediary of these orders, the Church took over the weapons of its critics, so to speak, and prevented them from being turned against it. The convulsions of the Reformation period produced many attempts within the Roman Church to halt the progression of schisms and heresies by assimilating some of the values, slogans and techniques of the adversary. Indeed, a good deal of the Counter-Reformation consisted precisely in attempts at an internal reform of Catholicism. Various spontaneous initiatives appeared, some more successful, some less so. These attempts, however, themselves gave rise to phenomena which (especially in later phases) often went beyond the limits of safety, generated in their turn heretical or half-heretical movements and provoked a destructive response from the the Church - just as a disease can be caused by the antibodies which the organism produces to combat it, or by too strong a dose (and in some social phenomena the right dose can never be precisely calculated) of the vaccination that was supposed to prevent it. However precise or imprecise such medical metaphors might be, cases where domestication reproduced the very heresy it had tried to eliminate were frequent both in the Roman Church and in the great Protestant churches, which had to cope with heresies of their own.

One example is the heterodox mysticism known in Spain as the Alumbrados movement. While it focused the whole of religious life on direct experience of God and, consequently, treated with scorn its "external," i.e., liturgical and sacramental side, it exposed the Church to the danger of uncontrolled mysticism, a form of religiosity where the "visible" Church as a whole appeared unimportant or even useless, if not harmful. The spontaneous Catholic response to this religiosity was Spanish (and later French as well) orthodox mysticism, which took up some of the important values of this heresy and limited them in such a way as to neutralize its corrosive impact. It decreed mystical contemplation to be a special form of religiosity reserved for the spiritual elite of closed monasteries. It rejected the inadmissible formulae of the illuminists, but preserved their main idea, which seemed to be the ideological force of the heretics – the idea that human natural powers not only cannot further salvation, but also are as many obstacles to be removed. Nothing can help except for God's operations in the depths of the soul, and these are gratuitous gifts and cannot be deserved or earned.

Orthodox mystical religiosity flourished for several decades and it gave Christianity some outstanding writers and teachers. At a certain point it went beyond the admissible limits and tried to become – in the form of Italian, Spanish and French Quietism – a movement of laymen, who used it as a pretext to disregard any religious and moral discipline. The Quietists (of whom Molinos and Madame Guyon were the most famous specimens) revealed once more the destructive force of a religiosity whose function was, among others, to combat a heresy with the heresy's own weapon.

Another example of an attempt to domesticate heresy was the Jansenist movement in France. Without (except in their formative years, in the teaching of St. Cyran) a mystical tendency, with its unavoidable longing for perfect passivity, and thus for the utter dissolution of individuality in mystical union, the Jansenists concentrated religious values on the idea of original sin and of corrupted human nature. What the specific Jansenist religiosity shared with the Protestant value system was the refusal to admit that our corrupt nature could lead us to God – whether in the moral or in the cognitive sense. Hence its general anti-Scholastic orientation (natural reason is incapable of grasping divine reality with its own powers); hence the belief that the power of grace has to violate our natural inclinations in order to make us just in God's eyes; hence moral education based on the profound awareness of one's own sinfulness, a tendency to dismiss base motivations (fear and shame) as invalid and of no use in religious life, and scorn for "facile devotion." Jansenism tried, more or less consciously, to adopt the values which made the austere Calvinist religiosity attractive to the educated upper middle classes of French society. It developed a moral rigidity that admitted almost no gradations, and no alleviating circumstances for the sinner. The Jansenists proposed a religiosity for a spiritual elite and claimed it was the only genuine Christian way of salvation. Having never been a movement of regular clergy, Jansenism could not be confined to the monasteries. And its principles were indeed unacceptable as universal rules of Catholic life unless the Church wanted to be transformed into an isolated sect of saints, with no room for the maneuvers which are inescapable in practical mass-education. Thus the attempt to domesticate a heresy became a source of heresy.

Jesuit religiosity (in the form it developed in the 17th century) was an attempt to assimilate within Christianity some of the values and ideas of secular pagan humanism. In striking contrast to Jansenism it made use of everything that in the Christian tradition could serve the rehabilitation of nature and of human natural abilities and dispositions, both of the will and of reason. Jesuit literature elaborated a well-codified technique of conversion, implying that all natural inclinations and desires are basically good and may be used for good purposes if properly guided. Thus Jesuit morality went dangerously far in negotiating with nature, and a long list of "scandalous and pernicious" statements of Jesuit "laxists" was condemned in successive pronouncements of the *Sacrum Officium* under Alexander VII and Innocent XI (in 1665, 1666, and 1679). Again, the assimilation of heterodoxy went beyond the safe limits of orthodoxy.

Are we not witnessing, today, similar attempts within Catholic culture to undo decades of stubborn resistance to modern civilization and to accommodate Christianity within its values? Should we not shortly expect a reaction against what is clearly a far-reaching appeasement of the secular spirit in various segments of the Church?

8. *The Social and Religious Meaning of Heresy.* Virtually all students of heresy look for social discontents and grievances which heretical movements and ideas are supposed to "express." Among Marxist historians, it is commonplace to assume that heresies are nothing but class interests organized in "religious forms," and that their religious ideas can always be explained as elaborate disguises of particular class aspirations. To answer the question of how far these assumptions are valid we need, it seems, some further distinctions.

It is certainly the case that European medieval culture was almost entirely enclosed in the Christian code: Christianity monopolistically supplied all the domains of social life with specific forms, and thus all "secular" claims and interests used Christian symbols to express themselves. Thus it is true that when particular class interests employed Christian symbols, they often appeared as heretical movements. This does not necessarily entail that the inverse is true, i.e., that all heresies have to be interpreted in class terms, or that all heretical ideas are nothing but symptoms or "distorted" expressions of class causes; such an assumption is historically groundless. It derives, rather, from a certain philosophy of history that implies that all "real" human interests can be described in class terms and that people have always been wrong (or have deluded themselves) when they believed that they were fighting for religious, national, or political values and considered them values in themselves. This assumption seems arbitrary – in any case, it is no less arbitrary than its opposite: that all "real" values are ultimately religious and all other values are just a distorted expression of them. In fact, throughout the Middle Ages, and still in the 16th and 17th centuries, heresies were quite often protests against the contamination of the Church by the "worldly" spirit. They called for the restitution of religious life and Christian norms precisely as religious. In conditions where secular and ecclesiastical authorities vied with each other for power, where heresy was a crime punishable by state law, heresies expressed not only secular interests, but very often the desire for a genuine, independent religious life as well. Great heresies, more often than not, were explosions of great religious revival, attempts to regenerate the genuinely Christian spirit and to free Christianity from its mundane involvements.

There is no recognizable meaning in the assertion that Luther, in his theory of grace, simply wanted to express the discontent of the German bourgeoisie with its exploitation by the Church, and that he was not aware that this was what he wanted; neither is such an assertion verifiable, even though it might be perfectly true that Luther's reform gained enormous support in Germany because people expected that its implementation would converge with their material interests.

To scholars, heresies differ from each other, both in the extent to which their popularity may be interpreted in terms of particular social grievances and in the degree of correspondence that can be found between these interests and specific religious content. In many cases this correspondence seems easy to establish. The slogan of evangelical poverty and humility, one of the most powerful elements of various medieval heretical movements, was certainly closely related to protests against the wealth of the Church and against secular power. It frequently attracted people from poor classes, peasants and craftsmen. It is plausible to argue that the heresy of the Bulgarian Bogomils, which had been spreading in the Balkans since the 10th century, "expressed" the social discontent of underprivileged layers. It was based on a popular variety of the dualist world-view. It is likely that dualist philosophy, in a version which included total scorn for physical reality as the work of the devil, or at least as incurably corrupted by evil forces, favored an ascetic morality and that one could easily infer from it the refusal to enjoy earthly goods. The metaphysical dualism which penetrated the Christian world, mostly by the intermediary of the Manichaean heresy (though we know little about the effective role of Manichaeism in shaping the Bogomil or Cathar movement) had in some cases well-attested connections with the attacks of poor classes on the Church's wealth and on social inequalities. This is, however, far from being a one-to-one correspondence. There are no reasons to maintain that the meaning of dualist Christianity lay in its suggestion that terrestrial wealth should be condemned and that it could be used as an ideological weapon in peasants' attacks on the upper classes. There is no necessary connection – logical or historical – between the specific interests of the lower classes and religious asceticism, which included abstention from sex, wine, meat, the use of swords, etc. (in fact, in some cases the moral rules of popular heresies were the opposite of asceticism). Neither did the slogans of poverty necessarily imply a dualist world-view; we find no such dualism either among Waldenses or in the Franciscan movement; St Francis seemed, on the contrary, to follow traditions which stressed the essential goodness of the world, as expressed in the biblical "*cuncta valde bona.*" Those who advocated the ideal of poverty were not necessarily motivated by aspirations specific to the lower classes. Like most heretics, they were deeply religious people, moved primarily by religious considerations. Peter Valdes, who at the end of the 12th century initiated the movement of the "poor men of

Lyons," was himself a rich merchant; he gave away his possessions for the sake of evangelical poverty and he preached against Cathars, not only against the corrupted clergy.

We should thus be wary of surrendering to this "reductionist" temptation, even in apparently easy cases, of which another example was the so-called Utraquism in the Hussite movement at the beginning of the 15th century. It was the demand that all Christian people, both laymen and clergy, should take Holy Communion *sub utraque specie,* i.e., including both bread and wine – wine being reserved in the Church for the priests. That this demand originated in the desire of equality of believers in the Church, is certain. So is the meaning of the popular support given to the Hussite program. However, that the Hussite heresy was "nothing more" than a demand for social equality, and that the latter can be reduced to particular class interest, is not credible.

The case of Luther is instructive in analyzing complicated connections between psychological, theological and social aspects of heretical movements. The beginning of his heretical career, not conceived of in such terms by himself, to be sure, was a personal experience which taught him that man could not rely on his own natural forces in combating sin and corruption, but that he ought to accept his inevitable status as a sinner and to surrender to God's mercy: only God can liberate us from the clutches of the demon and give us the gift of faith which will justify us in spite of our iniquities. Theologically, this experience was articulated as a summons to go back to the original, genuine concept of faith as it was elaborated in St. Paul's Epistles (total spiritual regeneration, not just belief) and to understand that it is faith only which can justify us (*sola fide impius iustificatur*). The consequence of this theology was a new approach to moral and religious practice: our "works" have no intrinsic value and are irrelevant to salvation; they are good or bad depending on whether or not they are rooted in faith, and faith is a supernatural gift we cannot possibly deserve. Consequently, it is vain to try to accumulate personal merit in the hope that it will weigh in the verdict which awaits us on the day of judgment; all the "works" the Church encourages us in are irrelevant, even harmful, if they are done in the delusion that they would be of help to us in God's eyes. What was meant by "works" was, of course, all the material support given to the Church by its members and all the "external," liturgical or customary duties the Church imposed. As a result, freedom from "works" meant, among other things, freedom from tithes, from fasting, from private masses. It meant, in effect, a cheap church. That large numbers of people welcomed this theology, in particular in Germany (which felt strongly exploited by the Church), is not astonishing. And so the powerful echo of Luther's challenge to Rome is easy to explain in terms of material interests. This is, however, far from being proof that the Lutheran revolution was nothing more than a "disguised" expression of the needs of the German middle class in their conflict with the papacy. People may support a heresy because it favors, in some respects, their immediate claims, yet it is not credible either that such claims could explain the origin of heretical ideals, or that religious motivations – obviously dominant in the mind of all the great heretics – can be accounted for by a strange self-delusion. Heresy remains basically a religious phenomenon, no matter how much its social influence can be interpreted in terms of the particular interests of conflicting segments or classes of society. People who want a religion that does not compel them to accept this or that form of oppression still want a religion. The theory according to which they fall victim to a delusion, and are unable to understand clearly their "real" interests and "real" motivations, is itself a historico-philosophical one. The historical material can never validate it; on the contrary, it has to precede historical empirical knowledge in order to have any meaning. This is the case with Marxist, psychoanalytic, or ethnic doctrines which attempt to detect the "genuine" interests allegedly always concealed behind the religious "form."

If the connection between the specific dogmatic content of a heresy and its social function is clear in some cases, it is more difficult to detect in many others, even if we are able to discern social, political, national, or other "secular" factors which contributed to the spread of a given heretical movement. The connection can be traced with reasonably good evidence in the aforementioned cases of Luther's theology of grace or the Hussite Utraquism. It is, however, difficult to determine how some heretical views on the Holy Trinity and Christ's divinity in early christological debates were related to specific non-religious claims involved in sectarian movements. The difference between the Sabellianists, who denied the real distinction of persons in the Holy Trinity, and the Photinians, who refused to accept the pre-existence of Christ, could hardly be explained in terms of particular social aspirations. In the great schism that ultimately led to the separation of the Eastern Church from Rome in the 11th century, the main theological issue was the so-called *filioque*. The Western Church insisted that the Holy Ghost issued from both the Father and the Son ("filioque" – an expression absent from the Nicene Creed), which the Eastern Church rejected. Whatever political issues were at work here it is difficult to connect them with the theological content of the controversy. It may be that dogmatic differences between churches and sects are sometimes due to chance, in the sense that a theological standpoint adopted as the distinctive mark of a heresy or sect may have been clear enough to establish an identity of its own and become a shibboleth, yet have had no recognizable content linking it with the "secular" causes that might have been responsible for the function of the heretical movement. This is the case even with many modern heresies, with well known and documented histories. It is not clear how conflicting views on the Eucharist and Transubstantiation among 16th century heretics and reformers could relate to the social background and grievances of their followers. If, according to Calvin, the power of Christ's blood and body was really conveyed in the act of Holy Communion without any change occurring in the substance of bread and wine, while according to Zwingli, the Eucharist served simply to remember Christ's sacrifice, it is difficult to relate the theological content of this difference to the different social and political interests which were behind the support given to both reformers, no matter how clearly these different interests can be identified. The same may be said of many small sects, more or less ephemeral, which emerged and multiplied in the 16th and 17th centuries, and which are often impossible to relate to any specific social groups. It seems that there is a strong element of chance in how heresies create their dogmatic identity, and that sometimes having a distinctive theological shape matters more than the content of dogmas.

9. *Political, Intellectual, and Popular Heresies.* We may divide heresies into several categories according to their social meaning. First, there are heresies which originate in a schism "from above"; in these, political considerations are patently overwhelming and dogmatic differences are non-existent or unimportant, or come only later as a result of a break in the Church's unity. This is the case of the Eastern schism and of the separation of the Church in England from Rome under Henry VIII (the new dogmatic codifications came only afterwards). It was so in most cases when the Protestant or Calvinist creed was adopted as a state religion.

Secondly, there are heresies of a clearly "scholarly" nature: theological or philosophical ideas developed by one thinker which either remained his private views or gained only small circles of followers, without becoming a real heretical movement. Most rationalist heresies, and many heresies of a mystical tendency, have been of this type; the latter sometimes appear in the form of small conventicles of devotees.

Early Christian heresies more often than not were limited to the educated classes, to people able to grasp the distinctions, sometimes extremely subtle, between different views on the two natures of Christ or on the relations among the persons of the Holy Trinity. Still, some of them went on to become, for various social reasons, an ideological basis for larger communities. Thus, Monophysitism (the denial of the reality of human nature in Christ) became in the 6th-7th centuries, in slightly modified form, the dominant variant of Christianity in Egypt, Armenia, Nubia and Ethiopia – primarily as a form of opposition against the Byzantine rule. And Nestorianism (which separated man and God in Christ in such a way as to come close to the two personalities theory and refused the Virgin Mary the title of Mother of God) was the main vehicle of Christianization in the Persian Empire, and later in Central Asia and in China. Arianism (which attributed the dignity of the true God to the Father only and saw Jesus as a created being) became the religion of the Visigoths, Ostrogoths, and Vandals. In such cases, however, the theological content of the heresy seemed to have little to do with its adoption by some tribes or states.

Many characteristically scholarly heresies can be cited: Origen, who taught the eternity of creation and believed in the ultimate salvation of all souls (he died in 254, and his teaching was condemned repeatedly in the 5th and 6th centuries; the definitive condemnation occurred at the Second Council of Constantinople in 553); Gottschalk, who in the 9th century defended the idea of double predestination; Eriugena, who advocated a pantheist concept of God-world relations; Abelard, who, in the first half of the 12th century, denied the transmission of original sin and preached a markedly rationalist doctrine; Latin Averroists in the 13th century, who preached the eternity of matter, denied universal Providence and insisted on the unity of the human intellect, which alone is immortal (individual souls are not); Michael Servetus, who attacked the dogma of the Trinity and was burnt in 1553 in Calvin's Geneva; Michael Baius, who advocated the extreme version of the Augustinian theory of grace and was condemned by Pius V in 1557 in the bull *ex omnibus afflictionibus* (he denied, among other things, any contribution of human will to salvation and he also denied the distinction between venial and mortal sins); Frohschammer and Rosmini, condemned respectively in 1862 and 1887.

Sometimes a heresy becomes a real movement within the Church (or a sect), yet its influence is limited to educated people. This was the case of various Gnostic sects in the 2nd – 3rd centuries; of the Quietist devotion in Italy in the 17th century; of the Jansenist movement in France; of the Modernist heresy at the beginning of the 20th century.

Thirdly, there are genuine popular heresies. Whether or not they develop from theological ideas advanced by one prominent thinker (like John Huss or Martin Luther), they have two features in common: they affect large segments of the uneducated population, peasant or urban, and there is a clearly identifiable link between their dogmas and their social meaning. Most medieval heresies up to, and including, the Great

Reformation of the 16th century were of this character: Bogomils, Cathars, Waldenses; so were the Anabaptists in the 16th, many English sects in the 17th, and Methodists in the 18th century.

Medieval popular heresies had a number of common themes. They attacked the corruption of the clergy, the wealth of the Church and its collusion with oppressive secular powers, simony, and the hierarchical ecclesiastical order. They called for a return to the purity and simplicity of apostolic times, insisted on the literal meaning of the evangelical ideals of poverty, love and equality, and sometimes preached the communion of goods. They wanted to abolish or reduce the complicated liturgical system and do away with indulgences, pilgrimages, the cult of images, etc., in some cases going so far as to reject the "visible" Church. The slogan of universal priesthood, and thus of the abolition of the separate status of the clergy, appeared frequently; so did the demand for the universal accessibility of the Holy Scripture in the vernacular, and the insistence on the Bible as the unique and complete norm, both in dogmatic and in moral issues, which denied the validity of the Church's decrees and rules. Practically all of the major elements of Protestant religiosity, elaborated through four centuries of heretical ferment, were ready by the moment of Luther's attack in 1517.

10. *Persistent Patterns in Heresies.* When we set aside the social and political meaning of heretical movements and try to isolate their dogmatic content, we notice some enduring patterns of mentality which give rise to recurrent forms of heretical religiosity. Christianity developed out of the concepts of Incarnation and Redemption; these included the belief that divine grace stepped down to earth in Jesus Christ's historical and physical existence, and that Incarnation was necessary to liberate the human race from the fetters of sin, which people could not throw off by themselves. The idea that God, or God's word, took material shape and became flesh strongly suggested that the whole of the physical world and of our bodily life could not be evil, otherwise one might be forced to admit that the supreme goodness was mixed with evil. The same idea was suggested by the Old Testament conception of creation. On the other hand, Jesus's message and St. Paul's Epistles contained strong hints to the effect that human bodily life not only is unimportant and does not deserve our concern, but also inevitably produces evil and remains under the sway of the devil. The "natural" world included not only our bodies, but human reason, will, and desires as well. Thus the question of the relations between the corruptible realm of nature and the eternal values was a permanent source of anxiety, and reflections on this relation made up, in one form or another, the whole of Christian thought, orthodox and heretical.

One of the great currents in the history of heresy was precisely the refusal to accept that the world of nature could produce any positive values or, in a radical version, simply the belief that the material world as a whole is the work of an evil force. This radical version seems to have been widespread in the first centuries of Christianity among the Gnostics. Gnosticism emerged before Christ, but later on some of its currents assimilated elements of Christianity to produce various sects, which may be considered Christian heresies. Gnostics tended to believe that the physical world was created by a malignant demiurge and that human souls, of which heaven is the true home, are imprisoned in bodies. Jesus Christ, having no share in evil, could not have had a real physical body or have really been resurrected. The spiritual liberation of men requires both an ascetic life, which runs against all our natural desires, and progress in esoteric knowledge, which the Gnostics claimed to possess, and which was accessible only to a few.

It should be noted that this utter contempt for the body could lead, and did in fact lead, in two opposite directions: either to extreme asceticism or to extreme license (since the body cannot be saved and whatever happens to it does not matter, no restrictions in this area are needed). This latter, a convenient anarchist interpretation of dualist cosmology, can be found in various sects and circles both in Antiquity and in modern ages.

The Gnostic equation of the visible world with evil was reinforced in Christianity, after Gnosticism proper had vanished, by the influence of Neoplatonist philosophers among Christian thinkers, and by the impact of Manichaeism, which carried into Christianity similar ideas taken from Iranian mythology. There is no evidence of a real link between Manichaean theology and the 12th century Cathar movement in Southern France and Northern Italy; yet the similarity of ideas is striking. The Cathars maintained that an evil power was responsible for the creation of matter and the union of souls with bodies. Thus they dismissed the bodily existence of Jesus as an illusion and abandoned the worship of the cross (to them Jesus was not God but a great spirit-redeemer). They preached and practiced rigorous rules concerning sexual life (entirely forbidden to the class of "the perfect"), property, fasts, a vegetarian diet, and abstention from war. The Cathars fell victim to repeated crusades in the first decades of the 13th century, and disappeared as a result of what may be called a genocide sponsored jointly by the Papacy and the French Crown.

The opposite tendency, stressing the essential goodness of the created world as a manifestation of God, can be found among pantheist Christian teachers, and it is sometimes linked with mystical doctrines.

From Eriugena onwards, this pantheist trend in Christianity lasted almost uninterruptedly, even though it often went so far beyond the Christian tradition that it could not properly be called a heresy, as in the case of Giordano Bruno. Although in orthodox teaching evil had no positive, ontological reality (otherwise one would have made God the author of evil), and was defined as pure negativity or absence of good (*carentia*, *privatio*), this did not imply the hope of universal salvation. This idea strongly tempted Christian philosophers with a pantheist bias, up to Teilhard de Chardin. These thinkers seemed unable to accept that evil could be everlasting; they wanted to expect the ultimate salvation of everything in the final divine unity.

One of the aspects of the same controversy about the relations between God and the world was the question of Jesus's divinity. Here two opposite trends appeared in early Christianity. There were, on the one hand, those who denied the reality of human nature in Christ (without denying his physical existence). In the 4th century, Appolinarius, a Syrian bishop, argued that Christ was a divine spirit in human flesh and that he could not possibly have had a human soul. In the 5th century, Eutyches, and other followers of Monophysitism (one-nature theory), maintained that Christ shared the same substance with the Father, yet not with men, and thus he could not have had a human nature in the same sense as he had a divine one. From the orthodox point of view, denying Christ's full humanity amounted to denying the redemption, because this last concept implied that Christ saved the human race as a result of having fully shared its lot. Monophysitism (along with its varieties like Monotheletism, or one-will theory, and Monoenergism, or one-activity theory) was repeatedly condemned in the Church and, although it survived in a few separated Christian churches in the Near East and Africa, it was never revived in the Catholic world.

The opposite heresy, Arianism, proved to be much more resistant. Arius, a priest of Alexandria, advocated in the first two decades of the 4th century the heretical doctrine that Jesus was God's noblest creature, yet not God himself. He was not coeternal with the Father and had been given the title of God's son for his merits as foreseen by God. The Arian doctrine provoked within the Church a long-lasting and complicated struggle, and it was by no means *a priori* obvious that the "homoousia" theory (the identity of substance in the Father and Son) would finally emerge as the orthodox view and that Arius would be defeated. Several compromise formulae were proposed, which led to a number of other heresies. Arius's chief opponent, Athanasius, was temporarily defeated, and had to go into exile from Alexandria four times before his view ultimately prevailed and was accepted as orthodox at the Second Ecumenical Council at Constantinople in 381. In the 16th and 17th centuries, the label "Arianism" came back and was largely used to stigma-tize all adversaries of the Trinitarian creed, including the radical Unitarians, who maintained that Jesus Christ was nothing more than a man of extraordinary moral qualities.

The question of whether, and how far, the created world might be a place where positive values are generated was most directly tackled in the controversy about the respective roles of divine grace and the human will in salvation. The New Testament, and in particular St. Paul's *Epistle to the Hebrews*, suggested that the legal order of the Old Covenant between God and His people had been entirely done away with after Jesus's coming. Instead of being a contract in which God had promised the people a reward for obedience to His laws, the Christian religion was based on the bond of love, which by definition is given freely, and not for merit. The concept of original sin, which had deeply corrupted human will, supported this view, and implied that our merits could never earn us eternal bliss. Thus if we are saved, it is only thanks to divine mercy and not because our deeds made us worthy of salvation. This view, while stressing the need for humility and the omnipotence of divine love, easily lent itself to a nihilist interpretation (since I cannot contribute anything to my salvation, my conduct does not matter). Moreover, it could lead to the belief that God is not interested in our moral standards, and if He saves some people while condemning others to hell, He does so on an incomprehensible whim, which would make Him, in terms of human justice, a capricious tyrant rather than a loving Father.

The principle of pure love, the inevitable disposition of the human will to evil, and the idea of grace as the only cause of salvation, were all strongly emphasized by St. Augustine. The heresy which vindicated the role of human free will in salvation is known as Pelagianism. Pelagius, said to be a Briton and a monk of exemplary virtue, taught in Rome in the last years of the 4th century and gained great popularity, especially in aristocratic circles. He argued that men were able to achieve moral perfection by their will alone, and that many in fact had proved it. God's assistance is important, he claimed, but not a necessary condition. We must not devolve the responsibility for our sins upon the lack of grace. Salvation or condemnation follow naturally from our good or bad actions, and our actions result from our free will. The transmission of original sin was denied altogether by Pelagius's successors, if not by himself.

In spite of numerous works written by St. Augustine against the Pelagians, and in spite of condemnation by Emperors, Popes and sever-al councils (in particular the Council of Orange in 529), the heresy kept reappearing in different forms throughout the history of the Church.

It was nourished by the very existence of the institutional body which, to carry on its educational work, had to codify the system of obligations and rewards for its members, to distribute the gifts of grace according to a legal order, and thus to limit the idea of free grace. There was an inherent tension in the very fact of the visible, organized Church proclaiming the religion of love and the abolition of law. This tension, however, makes up the substance of Christianity, and it was bound to keep on generating opposing heresies, which tried to make Christianity perfectly consistent in either of two directions. Yet perfect consistency time and again proved extremely dangerous. To claim that salvation is a reward for merits and that merits result from human free choice amounted to making the whole of Jesus's passion, and thus the whole of Christianity, empty and useless. To claim that gratuitous grace, distributed according to rules which are incomprehensible to us, does not merely help us but actually enables us to do good at all seemed to make all moral codes meaningless in terms of salvation and, indeed, made the very existence of the visible Church devoid of purpose.

The 16th century Reformation started by attacking precisely this point. The first target was "merits" as institutionalized in the system of indulgences that were sold for money. The return to the Augustinian, and thus Pauline, concept of faith and grace was meant to be a moral renewal of Christianity, corrupted by the false Pelagian theory of free choice and of salvation which could be earned by the virtuous by the proper use of their will. On the other hand, a religion based entirely on faith, i.e., on trust in God's mercy, and implying that all human acts are sinful because they are human, made moral education pointless. This was not, of course, what Luther or Calvin meant. Luther believed that good works followed naturally from faith but had no value of their own: good works are works of a good man and a good man is such because God wants him to be; virtue is a by-product of grace and not the cause of salvation. Luther wanted to reform the Christian conscience, not the world, which by definition is in the hands of the devil. It is arguable that if he had been consistent he would have proclaimed that only the invisible Church, the gathering of all the elected, is the Church proper and that the visible body does not need reform and cannot be reformed. His failure to go that far was what his radical critics objected to. They argued that he stopped half way when he tried to improve the Church instead of abandoning the idea of the Church altogether, as their radical dichotomy between Christianity and the world suggested.

Calvin's theology was in this respect less ambiguous. He clearly believed that predestination works independently of people's actual or predicted merits – all our merits being in any case God's merits – and that God's reasons are unfathomable; whoever is not elected has no means to alter his destiny, whoever is elected cannot resist grace (the crucial point). Still, God is not the author of evil; sinners are responsible and justly condemned for their sins while the virtuous are such thanks to God's charity. This does not mean that the visible Church is unnecessary. Each Christian is in duty bound to belong to the visible Church and to abide by strict rules of conduct. The purpose of the Church and of moral discipline, however, is not to contribute to people's salvation (which is entirely in God's hands), but only to diminish the number of acts which offend the Lord. The point is that God's glory is the supreme goal of our life, a value-in-itself, and not an instrument of the salvation of individuals. This theocentric approach made the existence of the Church and of moral rules consistent with the theory of double predestination.

The Catholic theory of grace and merits was finally established in response to Protestant challenge at the Council of Trent (1545-1563). It implies that God is the only cause of our salvation, but this does not mean that men have no share in it, since they are free to reject grace. After all, the main difference on this point between the great Reformation and Roman orthodoxy is that the latter denies the irresistible nature of divine grace. It would be fair to say that this definitive version of the doctrine of justification is much further from the Pelagian tradition than from the Lutheran or Calvinist creed.

It was the theory of irresistible grace attributed to Jansenius that was the main item in his later condemnation. The Jansenists, on their part, accused their Jesuit adversaries (not without reason) of Pelagianism. It needs stressing, however, that the condemnation of many statements made by Jesuit writers did not directly involve the Molinist (so called after Molina, famous Jesuit controversialist) theory of grace, only practical moral advice.

The Reformation, by liberating a general spirit of criticism, contributed to the proliferation of sects and heresies which quite often had nothing in common with the intentions of the great reformers or with the content of their teaching. Among them are obviously Pelagian doctrines (such as Arminianism, i.e., the theology of Arminius and of his followers in the Remonstrant movement in the Dutch Reformed Church), several varieties of anti-trinitarianism (Socinians, Polish Brethren) and various mystical and chiliastic groups. Many of them were branded as heretical by Protestants.

It was in this period that the very concept of heresy came under attack from liberal Christian writers who stood up for universal religious tolerance. In the 16th century among the most notable advocates of tolerance were Sebastian Castellio (a Sabaudian), Dirk Coorhnert (a

Dutchman), Andrzej Modrzewski (a Pole). They argued against persecutions of heretics, but in fact they questioned the very notion of heresy, since according to their idea of Christianity all the controversies about the details of the formulation of Christian dogmas were either meaningless or unimportant. They all were strongly influenced by Erasmus of Rotterdam and they all rejected the Calvinist theory of grace and of predestination; to all of them it was important that free human will was capable of choosing between good and evil. It is noteworthy that the doctrine of double predestination and all forms of fatalism usually favored intolerance toward dissidents. This correlation is not absolute, but it is very significant.

A special case in the history of heresies is the idea that the temporal order can and will be entirely transformed into the divine kingdom. Starting with the Montanist sect in the 2nd century, Christianity repeatedly produced Millenarist or Adventist sects which either expected the imminent Second Coming of Jesus and the establishment of His direct rule on earth (suggestions to this effect are not lacking in the New Testament) or even tried to build the perfect kingdom of God with human forces (an undertaking clearly contrary to the inherited doctrine). Among the latter the most notable examples may be found in the history of revolutionary Anabaptism in the 16th century (the label "Anabaptism" being misleading, yet widely used). In theological terms, chiliastic expectations were strongly influenced by the writings of Joachim of Fiore, a 12th century Cistersian who predicted the advent of a new epoch of the Holy Ghost, when all the institutional forms of life, all authorities and laws would be done away with and replaced by the direct communion of people with God. Joachim's teaching concerning the Holy Trinity was condemned at the 4th Lateran Council in 1215 without his chiliastic prophecies being directly involved in this condemnation.

Chiliastic ideas are still alive in various contemporary sects (Jehovah's Witnesses, Adventists). They are connected to a longing, shared by many believers, for a Christianity that has retained its primordial charismatic character.

11. *No More Heresies?* Since the end of the 17th century the Roman Church has been less and less concerned with heresies proper. As a result of the increasing secularization of many domains of social and cultural life, Christianity had to face enemies who could no longer be defined as heretics. The famous *Syllabus* of Pius IX (1864) condemned 80 errors of rationalists, pantheists, liberals, socialists, agnostics, etc., of which hardly any deserved the name of heresy. These were ideas of people who did not pretend to be Catholics or, in many cases, even Christians. The last of the statements condemned said that the Pope should reconcile himself to

progress, liberalism and modern civilization. The last important battle with what may be called heresy was the anti-modernist campaign. Modernists entirely deprived the Church and its dogmas of supernatural values and reduced them to purely historical dimensions, while relegating religious life to the communion of individuals with God; this approach was obviously incompatible with any claims to Christian orthodoxy, however loosely interpreted.

It is possible, nevertheless, that the reluctance of today's Church to condemn heresies has other causes, not only the fact that the secular spirit seems to be more threatening. For the first decades of the 20th century, the Church was still very concerned with rigorously defining its creed and for this purpose it condemned many doctrines, movements and people – they were not heretical, yet they were enemies: communists, Nazis, atheists, freemasons, spiritualists. Since the beginning of the pontificate of John XXIII (1958-1963) the Church has condemned virtually nobody; and it was in this period and as a result of the 2nd Vatican Council that there emerged among Christians various movements which seem to deserve the name of heresies. Many people, including priests, who call themselves Christians and remain within the Church body, either reduce the entire meaning of Christianity to political activity or make it clear that they accept traditional dogmas only in a vaguely symbolic way and do not consider them "true" in any recognizable sense. They are not condemned, though, and this is probably not because of the general ecumenical mood prevailing in the Roman Church but because of an overwhelming feeling of insecurity; and because of the inability of the Church to define its place in the contemporary world. A certain reaction against this dogmatic and institutional "laxism" has been observable recently, yet it would be too risky to make prophecies about the outcome and the future development of this ambiguous situation.

The concept of heresy is widely used outside the proper Christian or religious context to denote similar phenomena in ideological political bodies. The analogies are striking. Political movements with a strongly built-in need to remain faithful to an inherited creed and with a hierarchical structure, especially movements that appeal to Marxist ideology, inevitably generate the same phenomena we have observed in the history of the Church. This is clear in movements that have an identifiable authority with the power to pronounce verdicts about the truth and to condemn dissidents, and thus in all the varieties of communism, which anathematize each other. The most common term used, which is exactly analogous to "heresy," is "revisionism"; it corresponds to what heresy was supposed to be in Christianity: a departure from the established canon as defined and interpreted by the authorities in power at a given time. It is true, however, that communism has never achieved remotely the precision that was characteristic of the Roman Church in defining its dogmas and its canonical scriptures; still, all the analogous phenomena appear in its history (Holy Writ, perfectly orthodox fathers, less perfectly orthodox fathers, heretics, popes and anti-popes, councils and anti-councils, schisms, apostasies, apostolic succession, not to speak of the Inquisition). There are analogies in the structure – not only in the content – of the ideology as well. This, in the eyes of orthodox Catholics, confirms the traditional Christian saying that the devil is an ape of God.

It is likely that all movements and bodies which are, or are supposed to be, based on an all-embracing ideology or on a world-view, are bound to generate heresies and all the related phenomena. This seems to follow from an almost permanent contradiction in culture: such bodies have to see their ideology as truth in a non-historical sense of the word, and in philosophical and religious matters truth has to be re-defined according to the vicissitudes of human civilization.

Bibliography (general works only): Gottfried Arnold, *Unparteiische Kirchen-und Ketzer-Historie*, 1699-1700; C. W. F. Walch, *Entwurf einer vollstandigen Historie der Ketzereien, Spaltungen und Religionsstreitigkeiten bis auf die Zeiten d. Reformation*, 1762-1785; J. Brosch, *Das Wesen der Häresie*, 1936; J. H. Blunt, *Dictionary of Sects, Heresies, etc.*, 1874; J. Linderboom, *Stiefkinderen van het Christendom*, 1929; I. Döllinger, *Beiträge zur Sektengeschichte des Mittelalters*, 1890; H. Belloc, *The Great Heresies*, 1938; W. L. Wakefield and A. P. Evans, *Heresies of the High Middle Ages*, 1969; G. Welter, *Histoire des sectes chrétiennes*, 1950; A. De Stefano, *Riformatori e ereti Medioevo*, 1938; D. Cantimori, *Appunti sulle eresie dei secoli XI-XIII*, 1945; G. Leff, *Heresy in the Later Middle Ages*, 1967; Emile G. Leonard, *L'histoire générale du protestantisme*, 3 vol., 1961-68 (copious bibliography); N. Cohn, *The Pursuit of the Millennium*, 1957; R. A. Knox, *Enthusiasm*, 1957; R. M. Jones, *Spiritual Reformers in the 16th and 17th centuries*, 1959; T. Manteuffel, *Narodziny herezji*, 1963; C. B. Hylkema, *Reformateurs*, 2 vol., 1900-02; E. M. Wilbur, *A History of Unitarianism, Socinianism and its Antecedents,*–1946; G. H. Williams, *The Radical Reformation*, 1962; L. Kolakowski, *Chrétiens sans Eglise*, 1968; *Hérésie et société*, ed. by J. Le Goff, 1968 (includes a rich bibliography compiled by H. Grundmann); D. Christie-Murray, *A History of Heresy*, 1976.

The Libertine

1. Moral and Philosophical Libertinism

The libertine is essentially a figure of the 17th and 18th centuries. To be sure, the word was used both earlier and later, but in the 17th and 18th centuries, particularly in France, libertinism was a powerful trend in ideas and customs, which left a profound impact on European history.

In the 16th century the term "libertine" was occasionally used to designate, or rather to denigrate, Antinomianist religious groups – like the sect of David Joris in the Netherlands. These seem to have preached a kind of moral anarchism, based either on Saint Paul's idea of the New Covenant, which abolished the Law in favor of grace and love, or else on the pantheist concept of the world, which implies that everything is of divine origin and thus that nothing "natural" can be evil. The accusations that these sects actually preached and practiced sexual permissiveness and promiscuity on this foundation may have been well justified in some cases and less so in others.

Yet by the 17th century this use of the word "libertine" was almost obsolete. The target of anti-libertine attacks was not religiously motivated moral anarchism but rather growing godlessness coupled with moral dissoluteness. The word did not have a derogatory sense: at least some people applied it to themselves. The cognate word was *esprit fort* and La Bruyère (in *Les caractères*) thought it useful to explain that its meaning was derisory, something not all *esprits forts* were aware of.

Roughly, the term " libertine" referred, in the language of the times and in philosophical or theological disputes, to one of three figures: a *debauché*, an unbelieving worldly dilettante, or a philosophical skeptic. These categories were by no means mutually exclusive, either in reality or in the critic's view. On the contrary, orthodox Christian writers repeatedly stressed that moral licentiousness and unbelief in religious matters – and still more outright atheism – inevitably went hand in hand and that doubts about, or a disparaging attitude to, the teaching of the Church was bound to be coupled with moral depravity. This connection was certainly real in many cases and it was not very hard to find numerous examples of it in court life; but the accusation failed when applied to most of the outstanding figures in the intellectual movement known as "libertinage érudit," even though it may have been true in the case of a few minor figures.

Yet the connection between moral and philosophical libertinism was probably different from what Catholic and Protestant writers wanted to prove. Their point was that the decline in moral standards, as they conceived of them, in particular in sexual manners, was causally linked to loss of religious faith. In fact, sexual permissiveness could be, and indeed was, legalized, on various grounds – an amazing variety of philosophical and religious doctrines were exploited quite efficiently for the purpose. Some people doubtless looked for justification in a sort of metaphysical naturalism: because Nature is good and benevolent, there cannot be anything wrong with following the innate drives with which it endowed us. At the same time, similar conclusions – as Catholic critics did not fail to point out – could be easily drawn from the rigid Calvinist doctrine of double predestination: my salvation or damnation, far from being a reward for my good conduct, depends entirely on God's arbitrary decrees which have nothing to do with my merits (which are in any case inexistent); consequently it does not really matter, in terms of my eternal life, how I behave in temporal affairs. It is known that even the austere Jansenist theory of grace, suspected as it was of coming close to the Calvinist theory, was occasionally interpreted in the same sense. However, the exactly opposite theological doctrine of the Jesuits could produce similar moral leniency – conformably to the schema of "easy devotion" as depicted and derided in Pascal's *Provinciales*. Nor were some mystical doctrines immune to this kind of moral interpretation. This can be attested to, for instance, by the history of Italian Quietism. Provided that the evidence presented in Miguel de Molinos's trial and his secret doctrine, condemned by the Sacrum Officium in 1682, were authentic (and there are no reasons why they should not be), the reasoning was simple and apparently convincing: because our body is hopelessly in the clutches of the devil, spiritual liberation consists in complete separation of the soul from carnal reality. Once this is achieved, it does not matter much what my body does, particularly in sexual conduct; whatever happens, the body's actions cannot spoil the soul, devoted to permanent contemplation.

It needs stressing, however, that in all these cases – including the coupling of philosophical and moral libertinism – the convenient practical conclusions or prescriptions were by no means logically implied by the philosophical premises referred to, let alone intended by those who had formulated them. The relationships between metaphysical or theological ideas on the one hand and moral rules on the other being notoriously ambiguous, one may be certain in advance that any religious or philosophical doctrine enjoying fairly large influence will be exploited, however implausibly, to justify various moral principles, including, in particular, sexual liberty, and that this fact can be used by the adversaries of any doctrine to discredit it on moral grounds. This is amply documented in the religious polemics of the Reformation and Counter-Reformation period and even in today's ideological controversies. The accusation that a certain world-view led inexorably to moral depravity and implied the abolishment of restrictions in sexual matters has appeared very frequently throughout the history of religious and ideological battles, and can usually be supported by pointing to cases of people who do make such use of their philosophy. Briefly, it is not logical relations that connect metaphysics with sexual customs.

That such connections were frequently established in 17th century libertinism is certainly the case. Sexual freedom was often praised and presented as an application of the general rule "follow Nature," i.e. one's own desires, and this rule was derived from the concept of man as belonging entirely to the realm of matter and having no eschatological responsibilities. There was a widespread sort of simplistic *Weltanschauung* combining religious indifference with moral nihilism; its popular version was epitomized in the epigram of a second rate French poet, Claude de Blot l'Église:

> 'Ce monde icy n'est qu'une misère,
> Et l'autre n'est qu'une chimère.
> Bienheureux qui f . . . et qui boit!
> J'y vivray tousjours de la sorte,
> Priant le bon Dieu qu'ainsi soit
> Jusqu'à ce qu'un Diable m'emporte'

("This world is nothing but misery, and the other world just a chimera. Happy is he who f... and drinks! This is how I will always live, praying to the good Lord that it will be so until the Devil carries me away.")

2. Popular Skepticism
Popular libertinism, fairly common among both nobility and bourgeoisie in France (Mersenne famously remarked that there were fifty thousand atheists in Paris alone; but it is not known how he arrived at this figure), was usually not aggressively anti-religious; more often it was indifferent. This is confirmed even by the violent Catholic critic Père F. Garasse, the

Jesuit author of *La Doctrine Curieuse des Beaux Esprits de ce Temps* . . . (1623). Skeptical or indifferent attitudes toward the Christian tradition were obviously reinforced both by the growth of science and by the horrors of the religious wars and the fanaticism they had displayed. Political motives were often mixed with philosophical ones: libertines naturally opposed the attempts of Rome to influence the French crown and to limit the sovereignty of the monarch; this may have been why they were not severely persecuted. There were criminal laws to punish blasphemy and atheism, but they were seldom and inconsistently enforced; the cruel execution of Giulio Cesare Vanini for godlessness on the order of the parliament of Toulouse (1619) was not a representative event and Vanini himself, with his rebellious and violent temper, was not a typical example of the libertine spirit, the latter being an attitude of ironical and mild doubt, rather than of intransigent and accusatory rebellion. There are, to be sure, a number of overtly atheistic texts from this period, but they were usually anonymous pamphlets or manuscript treatises (one of them was the *Theophrastus redivivus,* a large and clearly atheistic Latin work by an unknown author). The widely circulating libertine literature offered rather a secular humanism, philosophically shallow, appealing to common sense, praising the pleasant life, little interested in science and still less in theology and indeed doubtful about the value of knowledge in general. Occasionally, yet characteristically, libertine writers made general declarations of their religious loyalty while stressing their fideistic approach; religious questions, they said, belong entirely to the domain of faith and there is no point trying to penetrate divine mysteries with the poor resources of human Reason. In the first generation of libertines Francois de La Mothe le Vayer (the author of the widely read *Dialogues d'Orasius Tubero,* 1630) and in the second Charles de Saint-Évremond may be cited as typical representatives of this attitude.

Taken in isolation, the general idea that religious truth cannot be proven or even supported by feeble "natural Reason" was by no means anti-Christian, of course; it appeared frequently in the history of Christian culture, among mystically oriented medieval theologians, and throughout the history of the Reformation, often taking the form of violent attacks on corrupt Reason and miserable "human logic." It appeared sometimes, though not very often, among French Catholic writers of the 17th century, occasionally in the form of religious skepticism. The most prominent example of the latter was Pierre Daniel Huet, bishop of Avranches, who lavishly employed all the arguments of ancient and modern skeptics to demonstrate that man had no reliable criteria of truth and that the only certitude accessible to us was to be found in Revelation. This did not make him a libertine, though. The libertine, for all his well sounding fideistic statements, was simply not interested in religious values, in God, in the immortality of soul, in the truth of the Bible or in the Divine promises. This was the figure Pascal had in mind when writing the *Pensées*: he seemed unable to understand how a reasonable creature could dismiss the question of eternal life and of salvation or consider it futile.

At the same time many libertines obviously accepted human mortality and made melancholy comments on the subject; to quote a few typical expressions from the sonnets of Jacques Vallée des Barreaux: "Tout n'est plein icy-bas que de vaine apparence" (everything here is full only of vain appearances); "Le diray-je, Mortels, qu'est-ce que cette vie? C'est un songe qui dure un peu plus qu'une nuit" (Should I tell you, mortals, what this life is? It is a dream that lasts a little more than one night); "Mais je compte pour rien d'avoir perdu la vie" (But it is nothing to me to have wasted my life).

It would be certainly unfair to say that the libertines' fideistic declarations were in all cases nothing but a defensive device to protect themselves from accusations and persecution. Their attitudes to religious traditions were by no means identical. There were among them convinced atheists like Vanini or Cyrano de Bergerac and there were those who believed in God and eternal life, even though they were not interested in theological disputes and more or less indifferent (scornful would be a better word) to confessional disputes about the Holy Trinity, the mystery of the Eucharist or the problem of grace. This was the attitude of Naudé, Le Vayer and Gassendi. In later generations there was Pierre Bayle, who would gain a well-deserved reputation of skeptic *par excellence*; indeed in this capacity he exerted an enormous influence on the philosophy of the Enlightenment. Among both his critics and his followers his fideistic pronouncements were usually ignored or dismissed as a mask, but we now have good reasons to take them quite seriously; it appears that he was really a sincere believer who, under the impact of the rationalist critique, escaped into a 'religion of the heart' as many did in this period. If he was not given credence, it was not because such a solution was unusual but because he concentrated on collecting and endorsing various skeptical arguments undermining or destroying the rational justifications of established Christianity, and since affirming one's own faith with occasional phrases was a typical libertine tactic, not surprisingly, readers tended to shrug off such professions even when they were meant seriously. As a result, Bayle, a believing Christian at heart and also in his role in the history of ideas, became an exponent of anti-Christian skepticism. One of his contributions was the clear separation of moral libertinism from philosophical doubt: he repeatedly stressed that an atheist

(Spinoza was the chief example, and next to him Vanini) can achieve the highest standards in moral life and therefore personal morality does not necessarily depend on religious beliefs.

The typical pattern of such arguments was the following: "Since the immortality of the soul cannot be supported by any experience or by natural reasoning, we should be particularly grateful to our religion for having given us certainty in this matter, based on Revelation." It is to be found in many sources from the 16th to the 18th century – starting with Pomponazzi's famous treatise *De Immortalitate animae* and ending with David Hume's essay on the same subject. In both these cases the statement was probably not meant seriously, but in many others it was. Sometimes the degree of seriousness is difficult to assess.

It is true, however, that, as far as the meaning of the word "libertine" was concerned, the Christian apologists eventually won the semantic battle: the "libertine" was increasingly identified with a debauchee and in the 18th century this moral sense of the word was practically established; hardly anyone now applied the term to himself.

3. Main Tenets of Libertine Philosophy

As to philosophical libertinism, it may be defined in the most general way as a continuation of Renaissance humanism and of Italian naturalism in the period of the Counter-Reformation and the Catholic revival. Its main tendencies can be summed up as follows:

an empiricist, anti-scholastic attitude in the interpretation of human knowledge;

an anti-Aristotelian, skeptical approach to metaphysics;

an anti-Cartesian, atomistic physics;

the separation of secular knowledge from theology; and

the separation of ethics from faith; a morality of pleasure and moderation as opposed to a morality based on fear and rigid rules.

These should be seen as tendencies rather than as a strictly definable set of statements, as philosophical libertinism was a state of mind and not a school in a narrow sense; different people expressed its ideas with various degrees of radicalism.

Erudite libertinism (of which the most comprehensive analysis is still to be found in the classic book of 1943 by René Pintard), though mistrustful of dogmatic, all-embracing philosophical systems as well as of all claims to cognitive certitude, was animated by a spirit of curiosity and its main proponents were highly learned people interested in the historical and (less frequently) natural sciences. Unlike worldly dilettantes who, when they repeated skeptical slogans, often expressed their lack of interest in serious studies, the philosophers of libertinism displayed in their 'Pyrrhonian' critique and in their anti-metaphysical approach not only their independence from authority but also the cautiousness of modern scientists.

Their attitude to religion, as in the case of less educated libertines, ranges from an almost unconcealed godlessness to fideistic piety. Yet even those who can hardly be taken seriously when professing their Christian loyalty were convinced that peace and order in society cannot be assured without basic religious beliefs being kept intact in the minds of the populace: the common people need the old prejudices for moral reasons. According to Gabriel Naudé, one of the leading writers of the libertine movement, his great teacher, Cesare Cremonini, used to say in private that he believed neither in God nor in the devil, nor in eternal life, but he wanted his butler to be a good Catholic, otherwise he might one day cut his throat (the same Cremonini is said to have ordered that his grave bear the inscription, *Hic iacet totus Cremonius*). This was apparently quite a frequent approach. Godlessness or skepticism was considered acceptable for the intellectual elite, but when spread among the uneducated it could bring nothing but harm. This is why many libertines were far from being spokesmen of religious tolerance. Their contempt for dogmatic quarrels and sterile confessional struggles went hand in hand with the idea that some kind of state religion, binding for all and protected from attacks, is a necessary condition of social order; and the main virtue of this official religion would be not that it is true in a literal sense but that it is the only one, which would free society from the fruitless and dangerous squabbles of sects and prophets. Thus, curiously enough, they preached intolerance not because of their religious zeal, but, on the contrary, because of their indifference. Politically they tended to support absolutism, in particular after the experience of the Fronde. Similar views on the need for a state religion, obligatory in public life but leaving everyone his internal freedom, were not uncommon among European philosophers in periods when sects were mushrooming, each with its infallible interpretation of the Scriptures. Such views were shared by some of those who entirely reduced religious beliefs to political functions (Hobbes, and to a certain degree, Spinoza). Libertines were of the opinion that there was nothing wrong with changing one's religious affiliation when one changed countries (some did it several times). On the assumption that organized religion is a part of the political structure, rather than a collection of dogmas, it seemed natural to see belonging to a church as just a citizen's duty, like paying taxes.

The target of libertine criticism, not restricted by political considerations, was hermetic science, astrology, occultism, ancient oracles and various popular superstitions (there were frequent discussions of ghosts, comets as ominous signs, etc.) On this point the libertines seemed to be allies of the Catholic Church; however, this was a doubtful blessing for the cause of Christianity. Their critique, often scornful of pagan miracles and oracles, focused too often on cases that strikingly resembled some popular Christian legends. These latter were sometimes directly attacked as well. The critics did not make general declarations denying miracles; only particular miracles, not miracles in general, were their targets. But one would look in vain in their writing for examples of genuine miracles.

4. Gassendi as a Philosopher of Libertinism

The most outstanding scholar and philosopher in the libertine milieu was beyond doubt Pierre Gassendi (1592–1655). He was a priest for all of his adult life, scrupulous in performing his pious duties. Nobody ever accused him of libertinism in the moral sense and his Catholic orthodoxy was not questioned either; in the Church he was never suspected of heresy or lack of faith and, unlike Descartes, he enjoyed a good reputation among the Jesuits. He started his philosophical career with a trenchant attack on Aristotle and his followers from the skeptical standpoint (*Exercitationes paradoxicae adversus Aristoteleos,* 1624). But the critique went beyond Aristotle. He made it clear that the target was metaphysical inquiry as a whole. Human knowledge, in Gassendi's view, is incurably uncertain; no absolute criteria of truth can ever be found. Gassendi's astronomical and physical works display a similar mistrust of speculation about the "nature of things," the same skeptical phenomenalist, empiricist approach. Along with Mersenne, Gassendi was one of the most active popularizers of Galilean physics. However, in the opinion of Alexandre Koyré, the outstanding historian of science, he never properly assimilated the mathematical approach of Galileo; he seemed to demand that physics be a record of experiments as they actually had been carried out – a 16th century attitude which Galileo had to overcome before the new mechanics could emerge. It was his failure to adopt Galileo's mathematical spirit that was the reason, according to Koyré, why Gassendi, in spite of his great knowledge and scientific meticulousness, did not gain an eminent place in the history of science.

The philosophical fame of Gassendi and his importance in the 17th century development of ideas was chiefly due to his reconstruction and ardent defense of Epicurean philosophy, both in physics and in moral issues. And although in later works his "Pyrrhonism" would be somewhat restricted, the fundamental rules of his empiricist and nominalist philosophy would not be altered. They may be summed up briefly: all our natural knowledge comes from sense data and all perceptions are singular; we have no real abstract perceptions. There are no innate ideas and the knowledge we are capable of attaining can never encompass the metaphysical reality of 'substance'. We know how things appear, not what they 'really' are. No truth of revealed religion – in particular God's existence and the immortality of the soul – can be conclusively proven within the limits of experience. Human beliefs, in metaphysical as well as in moral matters, change with the age, the ethnic group, the climate; there is no *consensus omnium* and if there were, it could not be relied upon as a criterion of truth.

Gassendi in fact expounded and systematized, before Locke, the phenomenalist program of science which invalidated the distinction, within human knowledge, between phenomena and essence, between form and matter. This program was anti-scholastic, of course, yet by no means anti-Christian. We find the same combination of, on the one hand, phenomenalistically and pragmatically conceived science and, on the other, genuine religious faith grounded in authority and revelation, in the philosophy of Gassendi's friend Mersenne, who cannot be counted among the libertines – indeed, he employed his pen to combat them. This attitude can be traced back to the late mediaeval nominalists.

This was one, though not the only, reason for Gassendi's and other libertines' anti-Cartesianism. Its best exposition may be found in Gassendi's critique of Descartes's *Meditations*. The very concept of substance, the theory of innate ideas, the belief in an unmediated self-cognition, the notion of infinity and, last but not least, Descartes's arguments for the existence of God and of an immaterial soul, were unacceptable within the libertine world-view. Since all our ideas originate in sense perceptions, both innate knowledge and direct insight into one's own soul are obviously impossible; we know ourselves only through the intermediary of external perceptions. Thus there can be no primordial act of *cogito* that would enable us to establish the credibility of other cognitive acts. Infinity is not a positive concept on which the ideas of finite things could be logically or psychologically dependent; it is, on the contrary, the vague and doubtful result of the mental act of negation (Hobbes's criticism of the concept of infinity was exactly the same). Nor do we have reliable, still less infallible, intellectual intuition, as opposed to a purely subjective and uncertain feeling of 'obviousness'; this Cartesian distinction is empirically unfeasible. The idea that we were created in God's image is credible only thanks to Christian faith, otherwise it would imply an idea of God endowed with human attributes or would be unintelligible.

It is true that while Gassendi's earlier writings seemed positively to exclude any possibility of valid proofs of God's existence, in his later texts he appears to admit that the work of Providence can be seen in the finality of the world order; but this concession does not affect Gassendi's phenomenalism within "natural" knowledge. He was a philosopher and he was Christian, certainly, yet he was not a Christian philosopher: these two areas of thought co-existed separately in his mind, scarcely interfering with each other.

The empiricist interpretation of cognitive processes is supplemented with an anti-Cartesian, atomist, Epicurean physics. Both versions of natural philosophy – Cartesian and Epicurean – may be called mechanistic; in both all events in the material world are entirely reducible to 'local movement'. In other words, whatever occurs is the displacement of bodies according to the laws of mechanics; the only real properties of bodies are "geometric," and their 'secondary' qualities are nothing but our subjective ways of perceiving movement. The atomistic theory seemed closer to common sense than the Cartesian identification of matter with pure extension or space. Atoms, according to this theory, are primordial indivisible elements of the material world, indivisibility rather than our inability to split them up being their inherent property; their movements are strictly determined (Gassendi rejects the Epicurean *clinamen*) and their shape, speed and size suffice to explain the entire variety of things as we perceive them. As to the emergence of living organisms, it is plausible to assume that God from the very beginning gave atoms a potential ability to feel and to procreate so that the principle of life is, as it were, a universal characteristic of matter. This "hylozoistic" hypothesis appeared frequently among 16th and 17th century philosophers; it was shared by Paracelsus, Cardan, Bruno, and van Helmont, among others. To Gassendi it was sufficient to explain, within the mechanistic outlook, the apparent specificity of the living world and it did away with the Cartesian theory of the "bête-machine." In fact, many libertine writers, including Gassendi, not only rejected the latter theory as paradoxical, but attributed some intellectual abilities to animals, thus blurring the sharp distinction between the human race and lower species.

Gassendi admits, nonetheless, the existence of an immaterial and immortal human soul alongside, and above, the animal one; this sublime soul or *mens* appears as an article of faith and Descartes's arguments to give it a rational foundation turn out to be invalid. The idea of a double soul in man is more strongly emphasized in his later writings and there is no reason to assume that he did not take it seriously, i.e., that he did not believe in immortality; still, he failed to show how the theory of the higher soul is compatible with his radical sensualism. The natural logic of his philosophy seemed to leave no legitimate place for this theory, which he otherwise accepted as a part of his Christian faith.

Epicurus was for Gassendi the main source of wisdom not only in the philosophy of nature but also in the much more sensitive field of ethics. His remarks on the subject touch on a number of common topics in libertine literature:

Human moral opinions and customs are changeable and depend on historical and geographical circumstances; the only constant element is the universal human search for happiness, meaning pleasure. In contrast to the Stoics, who praised virtue as a value and a goal in itself, Gassendi accepted Epicurean hedonism, which implied that the virtues are good insofar as they produce or increase happiness. Pleasure – again, in keeping with Epicurus's concept of it – consists chiefly in spiritual harmony, peace, moderation, and freedom from violent passions. It is a flexible, tolerant, common sense morality, scarcely affected by specifically Christian ideas such as divine grace, original sin, disinterested love, or awe in the face of the Last Judgment.

5. The Influence and the Relevance of Libertinism

The libertine philosophy, given its content, could not spread in the form of a "system"; suspicion of closed, all-explanatory and universal systems was one of its important components. Consequently, the limits of this philosophy cannot be clearly delineated, as they can in the case of Cartesianism and other doctrines with a clear shape. Its influence was primarily negative. It popularized an anti-metaphysical spirit, pointed out the uselessness and emptiness of most of the traditional ontological and scientific categories, sneered at the self-confidence and arrogance of warring philosophical factions, and exposed the degree to which all human opinions are fragile and dependent on transient fashions and customs. The libertine erudites read and praised many ancient and Renaissance scholars and writers; they used arguments they found in Lucretius, Sextus Empiricus, Cicero and Seneca, as well as in Montaigne, Charron, Lipsius, Scaliger, Cardan, Pomponazzi; they had no masters whom they accepted as infallible, though their sometimes aggressive anti-Aristotelianism was perhaps mitigated by centuries of domination by Aristotle's unshakable authority in science.

Among the prominent French writers who contributed to the popularity of the libertine world-view, La Fontaine and Molière take pride of place. Molière, according to his first biographer Grimarest, was Gassendi's pupil. This information may be uncertain, but Molière's libertinism is not. Some of the targets of his mockery in his comedies are characteristic in this respect: speculative science, Jansenism, Cartesianism, popular superstitions. Tartuffe's figure seems to combine a Jesuit, a Jansenist, and a mystical spiritual advisor.

Libertinism not only played a tremendous role in the gradual destruction of scholasticism (which was already under attack from many directions) and in spreading religious indifferentism. Over the following generations, in the second half of the 17th century and later, it also undermined the influence of Cartesianism, or rather, it erased from the Cartesian legacy all the elements which, rightly or wrongly, seemed to offend common sense: the theory of innate ideas, the concept of animal automatism, the identification of matter with extension, the psychological argument for God's existence. Even though full-fledged orthodox Cartesianism had existed for a time, the syncretic, Gassendo-Cartesian philosophy (perhaps initiated by Cyrano de Bergerac) gained more and more ground. Fontennelle praised Descartes, but mainly for his attempt to explain natural phenomena in terms of natural causes and for having demolished the speculative conceptual apparatus of Aristotelianism. However, Fontennelle accepted very few specifically Cartesian tenets.

Libertinism as a philosophical current was a transitory phenomenon: it conveyed the legacy of the 16th century secular and skeptical spirit to the free-thought of the Enlightenment; through it the shock-wave of the Renaissance kept its momentum in the period of the Counter-Reformation.

The French libertine milieu produced no great philosophers. But its ideas were in their essential points similar to those which, in the following century, would characterize the radical phenomenalism associated with the development of modern positivism and scientism.

Is the libertine a living figure today? This depends upon which aspect and which variant of the libertine movement is taken into account. The problems raised by philosophical skepticism remain as topical in contemporary philosophy as they were in the 17th century or, for that matter, in the time of the Greek sophists. But libertinism contributed little to the enrichment of the arguments and concepts of the skeptical theory of knowledge; it was not radical enough. The libertines had no clearly-shaped skeptical doctrine; they attacked dogmatism, fanaticism and metaphysical prejudices without trying (apart from Gassendi) to build a systematic epistemology. Contemporary skeptical arguments do not owe much to this particular tradition.

As for aggressively anti-religious libertines, their legacy seems to be of little importance today; their heirs are radical freethinkers, but their place in the contemporary struggle of ideas is insignificant. This version of libertinism was important as long as the aspiration of churches to wield power over secular life, to control social institutions and science, were strong and successful. Since then, anti-religious zeal has lost some of its grounds. As for radical political atheism, it has nothing to do with the libertine tradition.

What used to be called libertinism in the moral sense – with particular emphasis on sexual licentiousness – has lost its grounds for other reasons in the age of general permissiveness, at least in the Western world. People who want to avail themselves of sexual liberty do not need any special philosophy for the purpose and in availing themselves of it they are not exposing themselves to the danger of the stake.

But there is one crucial point in moderate libertine thought which remains relevant to our time, and is by no means obsolete: the separation of religious faith from scientific discourse and rational argument. To be sure, the libertines – those who made their declarations in good faith, not atheists protecting themselves from persecution – were not the first to establish this separation. In fact, attempts to codify the rules of noninterference between faith and knowledge go back to the High Middle Ages. The emergence of a strong urban class and the struggle of intellectuals for emancipation from theology were clearly connected, and we know the various ways in which this independence of secular knowledge was asserted. The nominalist tendency, for example, was to draw the dividing line in such a way that no common area of questions would remain (separation by subject-matter), while some Latin Averroists proposed the somewhat schizophrenic idea of double truth, which implied that the same person may accept two statements directly contradicting each other provided that he accepts one of them (e.g., that the world was created in time or with time) on God's authority within the order of Revelation and the other (e.g., that the world is eternal) according to the verdicts of secular Reason. The libertines, as we have seen, advanced various more or less radical proposals to establish this separation. In our day similar attempts are increasingly being made, but their cultural meaning seems to be different from, or even opposite to, the old one. The main purpose then had been to guarantee secular science freedom from external control, from theology, from the Church and from dogmas, even though the advocates of this division often stressed, some no doubt sincerely, that this was in the best interests of religion, which would thereby be protected from the indecent curiosity of worldly intellectuals. The intentions behind such statements varied. To some scholars and scientists, this was the simplest way of getting rid of religious problems without abandoning the religious beliefs they very often continued to profess, though only in general, not specific denominational forms: the belief in God, in Providence, in immortality. Other, profoundly religious minds, expressed in such a separation their acceptance, sometimes tragic, of the irreversible results of rationalism: they had to redefine their faith in avowedly irrational terms and thus made it immune, as it were, to the assault of secular logic. This was essentially Pascal's attitude, and later Bayle's. At the beginning of the 20th century we find the same approach in Catholic Modernism. Today the purpose of the separation is obviously not to protect science from the control of theologians, who abandoned such claims long ago. The purpose is, on the contrary, to avoid confusing faith and knowledge and to show how the cognitive and moral functions of faith have a legitimacy of their own and do not need to be validated 'scientifically': faith is an expression of man's participation in another dimension of reality, not a lower kind of science. Variously phrased, such proposals often closely resemble arguments familiar from the libertine tradition. Paradoxically, it is the rebellion of Faith against the monopoly of secular Reason, and not the rebellion of science against theology, that seems to be the main form in which the legacy of libertinism remains alive.

A comprehensive survey of the phenomenon of libertinism and copious bibliographical information are to be found in: René Pintard: *Le libertinage érudit dans la première moitié du XVII siècle*, Paris, 1943, and: J. P. Spink, *French Free-Thought from Gassendi to Voltaire*, London, 1960.

Bibliographical Notes

1. "The Two Eyes of Spinoza." Written in Polish ("Dwoje oczu Spinozy"), published in *Antynomie Wolnosci. Z Dziejow filozofii wolnosci. Warsaw*: Ksiazka i Wiedza, 1966.

2. "Spinoza: A Metaphysics of Suicide or of Survival?" Written in German ("Spinoza: Selbstmord oder Selbsterhaltungsmetaphysik?"), delivered at the conference Entretiens in Jerusalem, 6–9 September 1977, published in *Spinoza, His Thought and Work*, Nathan Rotenstreich and Norma Schneider, eds. Jerusalem: The Israel Academy of Sciences and Humanities, 1983.

3. "Pierre Bayle and the Critique of Spinoza's Metaphysics of Substance." Written in French ("Pierre Bayle. Critique de la métaphysique spinoziste de la substance"), published in *Pierre Bayle, Le Philosophe de Rotterdam*. Études et documents publiés sous la direction de Paul Dibon, avec la collaboration de Richard H. Popkin. Amsterdam: Elsevier, 1959.

4. "Dutch 17th-century Nondenominationalism and Rational Religion: The Mennonites, the Collegiants and the Spinozan Connection. I" Written in Polish ("Antykonfesjonalny nurt mennonicki wobec *religio rationalis*"), originally published in *Archiwum Historii Filozofii i Mysli Spolecznej*, vol. 9, 1963, included as chapter III in *Swiadomosc religijna i wiez koscielna. Studia nad chrzescijanstwem bezwyznaniowym XVII wieku* (*Religious Consciousness and Church Allegiances. Studies in Seventeenth-Century Non-denominational Christianity*), Warsaw: Panstwowe Wydawnictwo Naukowe, 1965.

5. "Dutch 17th century Nondenominationalism and Rational Religion: The Mennonites, the Collegiants and the Spinozan Connection. II." See note 4 above.

6. "The Mystical Heresy and the Rationalist Heresy in Dutch Calvinism at the End of the Seventeenth Century." Written in French ("L'hérésie mystique et l'hérésie rationaliste dans le Calvinisme néerlandais de la fin du 17e siècle"), published in: *Débats du Colloque de Royaumont: "Hérésie et societé dans l'Europe pré-industrielle 11e–18e siècles,"* Jacques Le Goff ed. Paris – La Haye: Mouton & Co., 1968.

7. "The Tragic Career of Uriel da Costa." Written in Polish ("Kleska i kariera Uriela da Costy"), published as Preface to *Uriel da Costa: Wizerunek wlasny zywota.* Warsaw: Panstwowy Instytut Wydawniczy, 1960.

8. "Pierre Gassendi – Christian, Materialist, Skeptic." Written in Polish ("Piotr Gassendi – chrzescijanin, materialista, sceptyk"), published as Preface to *Pierre Gassendi: Logika.* Warsaw: Panstwowe Wydawnictwo Naukowe, 1964.

9. "The Philosophical Role of the Reformation: Martin Luther and the Origins of Subjectivity." Written in Polish ("Filozoficzna rola Reformacji"), published in *Archiwum Historii Filozofii i Mysli Spolecznej.* vol. 15, 1969.

10. "Richard Avenarius and the Apparent Suicide of Philosophy." Written in French ("Richard Avenarius et le suicide apparent de la philosophie") for the *Festschrift für Jan Patocka. Die Welt des Menschen, Die Welt des Philosophie.* Hrsg. von Walter Biemel und dem Husserl-Archiv zu Löwen Publisher Haag. The Hague: Martinus Nijhoff, 1976.

11. "Karl Marx and the Classical Definition of Truth." Written in German and delivered as a lecture at the Univeristy of Tübingen in December 1958, published in Polish ("Karol Marks i klasyczna definicja prawdy") in *Studia Filozoficzne*, Nr. 2, 1959.

12. "Althusser's Marx." Written in English, published in *The Socialist Register*, 1971.

13. "A Comment on Heidegger's Comment on Nietzsche's Alleged Comment on Hegel's Comment on the Power of Negativity." Written in English, published in *The Heidegger Case on Philosophy and Politics*, Tom Rockmore and Joseph Margolis eds. Philadelphia: Temple University Press, 1992.

14. "The Epistemology of Striptease." Written in Polish ("Epistemologia strip-tease'u"), published in *Tworczosc* 4, 1966, Warsaw.

15. "The Priest and the Jester: Reflections on the Theological Heritage of Contemporary Thought." Written in Polish ("Kaplan i blazen. Rozwazania o teologicznym dziedzictwie wspolczesnego myslenia"), published in *Tworczosc* 10, 1959.

16. "On Our Relative Relativism." Written in English, published in *Debating the State of Philosophy: Habermas, Rorty, and Kolakowski,* With Contributions by Ernest Gellner and Others, Jozef Niznik and John T. Sanders eds. Westport, Conn.: Praeger, 1996.

Bibliography of
Leszek Kolakowski's Writings[1]

I. Editions and Translations

1. *Spinoza's* Ethics, edited by L. Kolakowski, 1954; contains an introductory essay "Spinoza i tradycje humanizmu nowozytnego" ("Spinoza and the Traditions of Modern Humanism").

2. Leibniz, Gottfried Wilhelm, *Nowe rozwazania dotyczace rozumu ludzkiego* (*New Essays Concerning Human Understanding*), edited by Izydora Dambska,1955; contains an introductory essay by L. Kolakowski, "Racjonalne i irracjonalne elementy filozofii Leibniza" ("The Rational and the Irrational Elements in Leibniz's Philosophy").

3. Z *Dziejow polskiej mysli filozoficznej i spolecznej* (*The History of Polish Philosophical and Social Thought*), ed. by L. Kolakowski, Warsaw, 1956, vol. I; contains an article by Kolakowski "Problematyka historii polskiej filozofii i mysli spolecznej XV–XVII wieku ("Problems of the History of Polish Philosophy and Social Thought in the XV–XVIIth Centuries").

4. *Filozofia XVIIgo wieku. Wybrane teksty z historii filozofii: Francja, Holandia, Niemcy* (*17th Century Philosophy: France, Holland, Germany*), selected and edited by L. Kolakowski, 1959; contains an introductory essay by L. Kolakowski: "Swiatopoglad 17go stulecia" ("The Seventeenth-century Worldview"), and his translation of fragments from the writings of Spinoza, Guelinx, Louis-Paul du Vaucel, Martin Becan, Johannes Coccejus, Martin de Barcos, Henricus Regius, Peter Balling, Henry de Boullainvilliers, Hieremias Drexelius, Puffendorf.

---

1 An extensive bibliography of his writings which also includes articles (published in, or translated into, various languages), up to 1971, was prepared by George Kline in a special edition of TriQuartrly, Fall 1971, entitled *A Leszek Kolakowski Reader*.

5. *Listy mezow uczonych do Benedykta de Spinozy, oraz Odpowiedzi autora, wielce pomocne dla wyjasnienia jego dziel* (*Spinoza's Letters*), 1961, translated and edited by L. Kolakowski, 1961; contains Kolakowski's introductory essay "Spinoza wsród przyjaciol i wrogow" ("Spinoza Among Friends and Foes").

6. *Filozofia Egzystencjalna. Wybrane teksty z historii filozofii* (*Existentialist Philosophy. Selected Texts*), edited and prefaced by L. Kolakowski and K. Pomian, 1965; contains an introductory essay by L. Kolakowski, "Filozofia egzystencji i porazka egzystencji" ("Philosophy of Existence and Failure of Existence").

7. *Spinoza. Pisma Wczesne* (*Spinoza's Early Writings*), edited by L. Kolakowski, 1968; contains Kolakowski's translation of Spinoza's *Short Treatise, On the Improvement of Human Understanding* and *The Theologico-Political Treatise*).

8. *The Socialist Idea. A Reappraisal*, edited by Leszek Kolakowski and Stuart Hampshire, 1974; also in Spanish as *El mito de la autoidentitdad humana: La unidad de la sociedad civil y la sociedad política*, 1976.

II. Books

1. *Szkice z filozofii katolickiej* (*Essays on Catholic Philosophy*; Polish only), 1955.

2. *Wyklady z filozofii sredniowiecznej* (*Lectures on Medieval Philosophy*; Polish only), 1956.

3. *Swiatopoglad i zycie codzienne* (*World-view and everyday life*), 1957; also in Serbo-Croatian (1964).

4. *Jednostka i nieskonczonosc. Wolnosc i antynomie wolnosci w filozofii Spinozy* (*Freedom and the Antinomies of Fredom in the Philosophy of Spinoza*; Polish only), 1958.

5. *Der Mensch ohne Alternative. Von der Möglichkeit und Unmöglichkeit, Marxist zu sein*,1960; also in Hebrew (1964), Swedish (1964), Finnish (1966), Norwegian (1966), Danish (1967), Japanese (1967), English (1968, 1986, 1971), Dutch (1968), Spanish (1970), and Russian (Florence, 1974).

6. *Notatki o wspolczesnej kontreformacji* (*Notes on Contemporary Counter-Reformation*; Polish only), 1962.

7. *Trzynascie bajek z krolestwa Lailonii dla duzych i malych* (*Tales from the Kingdom of Lailonia for Big and Small*), 1963; also in German (1965), Dutch (1968), Spanish (1969), and English included in *Tales from the Kingdom of Lailonia and the Key to Heaven* (1989).

8. *Klucz niebieski albo Opowiesci budujace z historii swietej zebrane ku pouczeniu i przestrodze* (*The Key to Heaven*), 1964; also in German (1964),

Dutch (1968), Spanish (1969), Czech (1969), Italian (1968), and English translation included in *The Key to Heaven, and Conversations with the Devil* (1972), reprinted in *Tales from the Kingdom of Lailonia and the Key to Heaven* (Chicago: The University of Chicago Press, 1989).

9. *Rozmowy z Diablem* (*Conversations with the Devil*), 1965; also in German (1968), Dutch (1969), Czech (1969), Spanish (1977), Italian (1978), and English (1972) included in *The Key to Heaven: Edifying Tales From Holy Scripture to Serve as Teaching and Warning* and *Conversations with the Devil*.

10. *Swiadomosc religijna i wiez koscielna. Studia nad chrzescijanstwem bezwyznaniowym siedemnastego wieku 1965*; also in French as *Chrétiens sans église. La conscience religieuse et le lien confesionnel au XVIIe siècle* (1969), and Spanish (1982).

11. *Filozofia pozytywistyczna. Od Huma do Kola Wiedenskiego* (*Positivist Philosophy. From Hume to the Vienna Circle*), 1966; also in German (1972), Serbo-Croation (1972), Italian (1974), French (1976), and English published as *The Alienation of Reason. A History of Positivist Thought* (1968).

12. *Kultura i Fetysze. Zbior Rozpraw.* (*Culture and Fetishes. A Collection of Essays*), 1967; also in Spanish (1971) and English as *Marxism and Beyond. On Historical Understanding and Individual Responsibility* (English edition, 1968; American edition appeared under the title *Toward a Marxist Humanism: Essyas on the Left Today*, 1968).

13. *Traktat ueber die Sterblichkeit der Vernunft. Philosophische Essays* (1967).

14. *A Leszek Kolakowski Reader*. A collection of essays published in a special issue of *TriQuarterly*, Fall 1971.

15. *Geist und Ungeist Christlischer Traditionen*, 1971; also in Italian as *Senso e non-senso della tradizione cristiana*, 1975.

16. *Obecnosc Mitu* (*The Presence of Myth*; published by the Polish emigré publishing house KULTURA, Paris), 1972; also in Hebrew (1971), German (1973), Spanish (1975), Portuguese (1981), English (1989), and Italian (1992).

17. *Der revolutionäre Geist*, 1972; also in French translation as *L'Esprit révolutionaire; suivi de Marxisme-utopie et anti-utopie* (1978).

18. *Husserl and the Search for Certitude*, 1975; also in German (1977), French (1985), and Polish (1989).

19. *Glowne Nurty Marksizmu* (*Main Currents of Marxism*), 1976–79; also in German (1976), English (1997), and French (1987; the third volume has never never appeared in French).

20. *Leben Trotz Geschichte*, 1977.

21. *Toleranz und Absolutheitsansprüche*: Leszek Kolakowski, Bernhard Welte, und Johann Maier (1980).

22. *Religion: If There Is no God...* 1982; also in French (1985), Spanish (1985), Dutch (1987), Polish (1989), Bulgarian (1996), and Italian (1997).

23. *Gespräche mit Manès Sperber und Leszek Kolakowski* (1982).

24. *Czy Diabel moze byc zbawiony i 27 innych kazan* (*Can the Devil be Saved and 27 other Sermons*; a collection of essays) (1984).

25. *Bergson*, 1984; also in French (1985), Hebrew (1988), and Polish (1997).

26. *Le village introuvable*, 1986 (a collection of essays).

27. *Intelectuales contra el intelecto*, 1986.

28. *Metaphysical Horror*, 1988 (corrected edition, Penguin, 2001); also in French (1989), Italian (1990), and Bulgarian (1996).

29. *Pochwala niekonsekwencji. Pisma rozproszone z lat 1955–1968* (*In Priase of Inconsistency. Collected Essays Written Between 1955–1968*; in Polish only), 3 vols., 1989 (contains complete bibliography of Kolakowski's articles written between 1955–1968).

30. *Modernity on Endless Trial* (1990); also in Polish (1989), and Bulgarian (1994).

31. *God Owes Us Nothing: A Brief Remark on Pascal's Religion and the Spirit of Jansenism* 1995; also in Polish (1994), Spanish (1996), and French (1997).

32. *Debating the State of Philosophy: Habermas, Rorty, Kolakowski, and Others*, 1996; also in Polish (1996) and Spanish (2000).

33. *Mini Wyklady o Maxi-Sprawach* (a collection of mini-lectures delivered for the Polish Television; 1996, 1998, 2000); also in German (1997), in English as *Freedom, Fame, Lying and Betrayal* (1999), and French as *Petite philosophie de la vie quotidienne*, 2000.

Leszek Kolakowski

Leszek Kolakowski was born in 1927 in Radom, Poland. He studied at Lodz University and at Warsaw University. He received his Ph. D. in 1953 for his dissertation *Jednostka i Nieskonczonosc. Wolnosc i Antynomie wolnosci w filozofii Spinozy* (*Freedom and the Antinomies of Freedom in the Philosophy of Spinoza*). From 1953 to 1968 he was Professor of the History of Philosophy at Warsaw University. During this period he also worked at the Institute of Philosophy of the Polish Academy of Sciences. Between 1957 and 1959 he was editor-in-chief of *Studia Filozoficzne* (*Philosophical Studies*), the main philosophical journal in Poland, until he was removed upon the request of the Soviet authorities.

In 1945 Kolakowski joined the Communist Party; however, already in 1954 he was accused of "straying from Marxist-Leninist ideology." Soon after the "October thaw" Kolakowski was attacked by Wladyslaw Gomulka, the First Secretary of the Polish Communist Party, and branded the "main ideologue of the so-called revisionist movement." In 1966, after delivering his famous speech on the 10th anniversary of the Polish October, Kolakowski was expelled from the Party. On May 25th, 1966, he became the object of malicious attacks in the press and was removed from his university chair for "forming the views of the youth in a manner contrary to the official tendency of the country." In 1968 Kolakowski left Poland. Between 1968 and 1981 he was on the Index of forbidden authors; his publications could not be cited or referred to.

Kolakowski was visiting Professor in the Department of Philosophy at McGill University, Montreal, in 1968–69; at the University of California at Berkeley in 1969–70; and at Yale University in 1975. From 1981 to 1994 he was Professor in the Committee on Social Thought and the Department of Philosophy at the University of Chicago. He is a fellow of All Souls College, Oxford, where he was Senior Research Fellow from 1970 until his retirement in 1995.

Kolakowski is a fellow of the British Academy; the Académie Universelle des Cultures; the Academia Europea and the Bayerische Academie der Künste; a Foreign Fellow of the American Academy of Arts and Sciences; a member of the International Institute of Philosophy; the Pen Club, the Polish Academy of Sciences, and philosophical associations in Britain and Poland.

He is the recipient of numerous awards: the Jurzykowski Prize (1969), the Friedenspreis des Deutschen Buchhandels (1977), the Prix Européen de l'Essai (1981), the Praemium Erasmianum (1982), the MacArthur Fellowship (1983), the Jefferson Award (1986), the Prize of the Polish Pen Club (1988); the Lang Award (1992) awarded by the University of Chicago Press for the best book of the year (*Modernity on Endless Trial*), the Prix Tocqueville (1993), the Premio Nonino (1997), and most recently the Kluge Prize of the Library of Congress (2003).